AMERICAN MANHOOD

American Manhood

Transformations
in Masculinity from
the Revolution to
the Modern Era

E. ANTHONY ROTUNDO

BasicBooks
A Division of HarperCollinsPublishers

Portions of chapter 2 appeared in Mark C. Carnes and Clyde Griffen, eds., *Meanings for Manhood: Constructions of Masculinity in Victorian America*, Chicago, The University of Chicago Press. © 1990 by The University of Chicago. All rights reserved. Portions of chapter 4 appeared as "Romantic Friendship: Male Intimacy and Middle-Class Youth in the Northern United States, 1800–1900," in *Journal of Social History*, 23(1), Fall 1989, 1–25.

Designed by Ellen Levine

Library of Congress Cataloging-in-Publication Data

Rotundo, E. Anthony
   American manhood: transformations in masculinity from the Revolution to the modern era / E. Anthony Rotundo.
    p. cm.
    Includes bibliographical references and index.
    ISBN 0–465–01409–7 (cloth)
    ISBN 0–465–00169–6 (paper)
    1. Men—United States—History—19th century.   2. Masculinity (Psychology)—United States—History—19th century.   I. Title.
HQ1090.3.R69   1993
305.32'0973—dc20   92–53247
                                                CIP

94 95 96 97 ♦/RRD 9 8 7 6 5 4 3 2 1

To my mother, Barbara Rotundo,
and to the memory of
my father, Joseph Rotundo

CONTENTS

PREFACE

THIS book began fourteen years ago. Fascinated by what I learned from reading the new women's history, I wondered what would happen if I tried to study men's past in the same way. I was eager to study men as people, not public actors; to learn about men out of the historical spotlight as well as in it; to understand men as men, as one sex in contrast to the other.

My curiosity turned into a research project. I decided to study manhood among the most influential group of Americans in the nineteenth century: white, middle-class, Yankee Northerners (I explain this choice more fully in the appendix). In the first stage of the project, I sought to understand manhood through the letters and diaries of men and their families. This private writing took me as close to the feelings, attitudes, and daily experiences of men as I could get, and the insights I gained form the core of this book. As my work evolved, however, I realized that I needed an understanding of many elements in men's lives that were not addressed in letters or diaries, vital elements such as boyhood experience, sexuality, and life in the workplace. For this I turned to many other sources, including autobiographies, printed advice to men, and research by early social scientists.

As I have pursued this research and then turned to writing, my thinking about manhood has been influenced by certain ideas about gender that I would like to share with the reader. These principles, which were really hypotheses that I learned from historians of women, were supported time and time again by my explorations of manhood. I have learned that gender ranks with race, region, class, and ethnic background as one of the great cleavages that divide society, and that the values, behavior, and life opportunities of people on one side of this cleavage are distinctly different from those of people on the other side. I have also been reminded of important facts that I took for granted: that gender is the basis for a system of personal relationships that order the lives of most human beings and promise emotional sustenance; and that gender is the basis for contrasting images, labeled *male* and *female*, which guide our behavior and shape our view of the world. My work and the work of others has also confronted me with the fact that gender provides the foundation for a system of power relations, a series of political and economic distinctions based on sex.

Yet, while this is a book about gender as a cultural, social, and political force, it is also a book about individual people and about the way particular men created their manhood within the limits of their time and place. As I have tried to understand the kinds of decisions that middle-class men made in the nineteenth century, I often found myself thinking of an image from the mythology of my own family. It is an image from my early boyhood in which I am setting off hand in hand with two of my uncles for a walk downtown. On one side of me is my Uncle Min, a politician and a hunchback who never grew to a full five feet. On the other side of me is my Uncle Tick, a fireman and a former athlete, tall and strong. Both Min and Tick were respected as men by the people who knew them, but they had very different tasks in adapting to the complex codes of manhood that governed their lives. I hope that this book, which by its very nature is full of broad statements about manhood, respects men's varied needs and possibilities.

The image of my uncles and me has also provided me with another sort of reminder. Those two men who held my hands both influenced the man I grew up to be. Different as they were, they were just two models among many in my life. There is, in fact, a profusion of ideals, values, and role models that make up my own manhood. Some of these elements cohere nicely, but some are discordant. As I have written this book, I have been more aware of my inner discord on issues of manhood than of my inner coherence. To the extent that manhood in our time is about achievement, reason, and inner strength, I'm comfortable trying to be a man. But to the extent that I've internalized manly ideals of antagonism, personal isolation, and the suffocation of tenderness, I find myself at war with the ideals I've learned. I want to live in a world where more uncles take the hands of their nephews (or nieces) for a walk downtown—and where they feel manly for doing it. In the end, I'm sure that my nagging disputes with manhood in our own time had a lot to do with my desire to write this book.

Anyone who works on a book for fourteen years is bound to accumulate many debts—financial, intellectual, and personal. I am happy to make here a public acknowledgment of mine.

Grants from the National Endowment for the Humanities and the Rockefeller Institute's Gender Roles Grant program gave me invaluable time to write. Phillips Academy's generous sabbatical program provided me with a year to work on my book. I also benefitted from a summer study grant from the William R. Kenan, Jr., Charitable Trust Program and from a Crown Supplemental Grant to do research while I was a graduate student. Indeed, the Crown Fellowship Program supported my whole education as a historian at Brandeis University. A visiting fellowship from the Transformation of Philadelphia Project (at the Philadelphia Center for Early American Studies) was a stimulus at a turning point in this book's development.

I am indebted to many people who provided me with vital services in the writing of this book. The staffs at dozens of historical societies whose names are listed in the notes helped me in countless ways. I am grateful to the librarians at the Goldfarb Library at Brandeis for their help, and to my friends who work at the Oliver Wendell Holmes Library at Phillips Academy for their warm and efficient support. I owe great thanks to Jan Lisiak and her staff at Phillips's Computer Literacy Center for their patient and timely help with computer problems of all sorts. And Judy Saladini, Kathryn Wright, and Alma Beck were efficient and uncomplaining in typing my eccentric handwriting onto disk.

I owe a great deal personally to friends who have offered me hospitality, diversion, and warm companionship on many, many occasions—Ethan Berry, Ted Byers, Austin and Christina Campriello, Betsy Eaton, Pete Eaton, Mike Fosburg, Robert and Jorinda Gershon, Pat Skibbee, Peter and Lisa Smith, and Judy Taylor. Doug and Terry Kuhlmann and Vic Hennigsen deserve special mention for bailing me out in a number of last-minute emergencies. At Phillips Academy, Thomas T. Lyons helped create a congenial work environment by arranging for my wife and me to share one job, and many administrators in the ten years since have continued to treat our changing needs supportively. Cathy Royal and K. Kelly Wise were especially kind in adjusting pieces of my workload at key moments.

I am indebted as well to a number of scholars whose aid has made this a better book than it would otherwise have been. Michael Kimmel and Joseph Pleck have been energetic in keeping me connected to inter-disciplinary scholarship on men. Peter Filene, Linda Kerber, Jan Lewis, Regina Morantz-Sanchez, Steven Stowe, Lisa Wilson, and Michael Zuckerman have all made useful responses to pieces of this book. Nancy Cott and Philip Greven, Jr., read the whole book in its earlier life as a dissertation, and their comments helped to shape its final form. Ellen Rothman was a great research companion, a discerning critic, and a major influence on the book in its early stages. Steve Fraser, my editor at Basic Books, has been perceptive, patient, and persistent in just the right ways. David Hackett Fischer's infectious enthusiasm made him an in-spiring teacher, and his bold and convincing vision of American history lies at the foundation of this book. Above all, I am grateful to my mentor, John Demos. The way I think as a historian is as close to John's way as I can make it. He has been a wise teacher, a sage counselor, and a pene-trating critic. Even better, he has been a warm and loyal friend.

Finally, I owe a deep debt of gratitude to my family. Ruth Ann Whit-ney, Peggy Rotundo, Danny Danforth, Rose Rotundo, Ralph and Jane Bristol, Bill and Faye Dalton, and Newell and Dalli Bacon have given me shelter, support, financial help, and lots of love. My mother, Barbara Rotundo, contributed her editing and child-care skills and a quiet place to work, but more than that she taught me to care about people and about the past. My father, Joseph Rotundo, died before I grew to man-hood, but his impact on me as a boy and the example he left for me as a man are as fine a legacy as a father could leave to a son. I thank my daughter, Barbara, and my son, Peter, for all their love, their eagerness to help, and their many delightful distractions. Above all, I am grateful to my wife, Kathleen Dalton. While it has often helped me to be mar-ried to a biographer of Theodore Roosevelt, it has been even more im-portant that Kathy has been my yokemate, my computer maven, my in-tellectual partner, and, most of all, my beloved best friend. I could not have written this book without her.

AMERICAN MANHOOD

Introduction

TOWARD A HISTORY OF AMERICAN MANHOOD

I N our time, many people are searching for the true essence of manhood. Who is a "real man"? What is "naturally" male? How does a "manly man" act? We sift the evidence of human behavior, from modern customs to ancient tales, hoping for clues to the fundamental nature of manhood.

The response of this book to the quest for true manhood is that manliness is a human invention. Starting with a handful of biological differences, people in all places and times have invented elaborate stories about what it means to be male and female. In other words, each culture constructs its own version of what men and women are—and ought to be.[1]

Scholars talk about this process by distinguishing between *sex* and *gender*. In their language, *sex* refers to the division of animal forms into *male* and *female* according to basic differences of anatomy. *Gender* refers to the meanings that people attach to a person's sex. In other words, sex is a matter of biology and gender is a matter of culture. This book is about gender and the cultural invention called *manhood*.[2]

Like any human creation, manhood can be shaped and reshaped by the human imagination; that is, manhood has a history.[3] The pages that follow describe an important piece of that history. Specifically, they tell the story of a transformation in the meaning of manhood for Americans. This is a story with special resonance for us in an era with an organized men's movement. Thousands of men are engaging today in the rituals and encounters of that movement, while countless other men (and women) have read the key texts of that movement, such as Robert Bly's *Iron John* and Sam Keen's *Fire in the Belly*. Like the concept of manhood itself, this search to recover a lost essence of manliness has a history. Exactly a century ago, thousands of American men were questing to reconnect with primitive roots of their maleness through ritual and writing. To understand that quest—and the current one—we need to understand the larger flow of the history of manhood.[4]

The vehicle for this larger story is the experience of the Northern middle class, a small proportion of the American population who used their vast economic and cultural power to imprint their values on the nation. As this class developed and extended its influence, its own ideas of male and female changed dramatically. These notions of manhood have gone through three different phases, each of which included its own images and expectations of men.

The first of these phases, *communal manhood*, developed in the densely woven social world of colonial New England.[5] There, a man's identity was inseparable from the duties he owed to his community. He fulfilled himself through public usefulness more than his economic success, and the social status of the family into which he was born gave him his place in the community more than his individual achievements did. Through his role as the head of the household, a man expressed his value to his community and provided his wife and children with their social identity.

William Bentley, a minister in Salem, Massachusetts, described men of this communal world in his diary. His descriptions of daily life show how manhood was closely entwined with the needs and expectations of a man's neighbors. One of Bentley's countless anecdotes tells of Retire Becket, a man who had followed many generations of Beckets into the shipbuilding trade. Though Becket had the reputation of "an honest dealer," he was forced to declare himself bankrupt. Bentley describes the results: "His debts are numerous, and they tend to hurt many honest men. To his forest men, to his carpenters, to his employers, to his mechanics he is everywhere in debt." In this world where creditors were neighbors and kinsmen were clients, a man's failure at work was never a private concern. It sent ripples through the entire community, injuring neighbors and directing embarrassment and shame back at the man who failed.

In the same vein, a man's failures in his family were a matter of deep concern to those beyond his household. William Bentley relates the painful experience of a Salem merchant named Goodale who could not control his son. According to Bentley, Goodale was "a Gentleman of liberal education, and pleasing manners," but he "led his oldest son to an indolent and vitious life" by "gratifying foolish extravagancies." The young man's high living put a strain on his father's health and finances. More than that, the son's conduct was "the occasion of . . . most severe public censures" against his father. Young Goodale became such a personal worry and a public shame that the elder merchant had to send him away to the Carolinas. The shortcomings of a youth were charged directly to the father who brought him forth into the community. The line between public and private barely existed in eighteenth-century towns and villages, and that social fact had a profound influence on the way people conceived of manhood.[6]

People understood manhood not only in terms of its social setting but also in terms of its contrast with womanhood. The fundamental belief about men and women before 1800 was that men were superior. In particular, men were seen as the more virtuous sex. They were credited with greater reason, which enabled them to moderate passions like ambition, defiance, and envy more effectively than women could. This belief in male superiority provided the foundation for other forms of inequality before the law and in the household.

This communal form of manhood lingered on through the first decades of the nineteenth century, but it was eclipsed by a *self-made manhood* which had begun to grow in the late eighteenth century. The new manhood emerged as part of a broader series of changes: the birth of republican government, the spread of a market economy, the concomitant growth of the middle class itself. At the root of these changes was an economic and a political life based on the free play of individual interests. In this new world, a man took his identity and his social status from his own achievements, not from the accident of his birth. Thus, a man's work role, not his place at the head of the household, formed the essence of his identity. And men fulfilled themselves through personal success in business and the professions, while the notion of public service declined.

"Male" passions were now given freer rein. Ambition, rivalry, and aggression drove the new system of individual interests, and a man defined his manhood not by his ability to moderate the passions but by his ability to channel them effectively. Reason, still viewed as a male trait, played a vital role in the process of governing passion, but important new virtues were attributed to men. In the new era of individualism, the old male passion of defiance was transformed into the modern virtue of independence. Now, a man was expected to be jealous of his autonomy and free from reliance on external authority. In this world where a man was supposed to prove his superiority, the urge for dominance was seen as a virtue.

These male passions provided the driving force in the lives of nineteenth-century men like Henry Varnum Poor. Poor was born in 1812 in the frontier town of Andover, Maine, and he grew up to be a leading business writer and railroad expert. His success came from his ferocious energy and his mighty determination as much as it came from his talents. He compared himself in strength and will to an elephant, an ox, or a lion. Poor boasted that he was constantly "on the go," and his wife marveled at his tendency to "shoot around like a rocket." As Poor put it, "there is nothing like work to . . . give [a man] self-respect." Poor's work gave him an outlet for his manly passions at the same time that it built his self-regard as a man. Moreover, his career offered a way to use those aggressive passions to mold his own social identity. Poor was born into the elite of a backwoods village; his vigorous efforts placed him among the elite of the nation.[7]

As the selfish passions of men like Poor were sanctioned and set loose in the nineteenth century, people began to fear that civilization would be replaced by chaos. They worried that the pursuit of self-interest would tear apart the social fabric. Some people believed that men, through rituals of reason and debate, could civilize themselves. But others feared that, with the male tradition of public usefulness fading, men would no longer protect the bonds of society. Thus it was that women became guardians of civilization and the common good in the new order of individualism. Woman's nature was sharply redefined; she was now viewed as the source of virtue. Since woman's moral sense was considered stronger than man's, females took on the tasks of controlling male passion and educating men in the arts of self-denial. Given their "inherent" virtue, women were not seen as inferior to men so much as different from them. In this era of individual choice, personal preference governed the marriage decision. The marital bond was now a union of love, based on the attraction of opposites. In hard, worldly terms, however, women still took their social identities from those of their husbands, even though they were expected to help shape male character. Women could not participate in all the privileges of individualism, as men did.

Henry Poor summarized a common belief about the sexes when he said that "the chief end of women is to make others happy." His wife, Mary, shared in that belief. She devoted her life to the care of her husband and six children. Although Mary was a friend of the pioneering woman physician Elizabeth Blackwell, she wrote that she "would rather my daughters would love and marry . . . than to turn out quite so strong minded [as Blackwell]." In her pursuit of the conventional woman's role, Mary Poor sought not only to make others happy but also to make them good. As the chief companion and regular disciplinarian of her children, she taught her children to focus on constructive activity and steer their energies away from vice and folly.[8]

The successes (and failures) of her efforts are evident in the life of her son, Will. In his early teens, Will wrote an essay on his philosophy of life that combined his mother's virtuous self-restraint with his father's strenuous determination. "The successful ones," he noted, "are those who lay before themselves a life of work, self-denial, and usefulness." A man who wished to succeed, said Will, must "devote all his time to the completion of . . . one thing," and, most of all, he must never let himself "be discouraged by any adverse circumstances." Will put his creed into action when he grew up. In business and as an investor, he became a wealthy man, the friend of presidents and tycoons. And when a financial panic late in his life forced him to sell much of what he owned, Will plunged back into business with the same vigorous intensity that had marked his youthful rise to success.[9]

Yet there were other themes in Will Poor's life that separated his values from those of his parents—and that pointed to new definitions of manhood. Will lived out the code of civilized self-denial in a fashion different from that of the men of his parents' generation. As hard as he worked, he also allowed himself a range of enjoyments that made him look self-indulgent in comparison to his parents. He had an active social life, and set aside more time than his father had for play with his children. He took pains to keep his body fit and strong, and he loved to hunt. Will was also an avid consumer, and his extensive book collection even contained a number of erotic titles. When Will Poor spoke of self-denial, he clearly did not have his parents' ascetic code in mind. And yet, faced with financial disaster, he did not hesitate to sell most of what he owned and devote himself to business with single-minded vigor. Will Poor was, in fact, a transitional figure. Raised on the assumptions of self-made manhood, which his father had embodied, he also participated in a newer form of manhood that was more indulgent of passion.[10]

Arising in the late nineteenth century, this new *passionate manhood* was in some respects an elaboration of existing beliefs about self-made manhood, but it stretched those beliefs in directions that would have shocked the old individualists of the early 1800s. The most dramatic change was in the positive value put on male passions. In the closing years of the century, ambition and combativeness became virtues for men; competitiveness and aggression were exalted as ends in themselves. Toughness was now admired, while tenderness was a cause for scorn. Even sexual desire, an especially worrisome male passion in the nineteenth century, slowly gathered legitimacy. Indeed, the body itself became a vital component of manhood: strength, appearance, and athletic skill mattered more than in previous centuries.

A new emphasis on the self was essential to these changes. In middle-class culture, "the self" came to mean that unique core of personal identity that lay beneath all the layers of social convention. A person's passions were vital components of the self. Where nineteenth-century views had regarded the self and its passions suspiciously as objects of manipulation (self-control, self-denial), twentieth-century opinion exalted them as the source of identity and personal worth (self-expression, self-enjoyment). Play and leisured entertainment—once considered marks of effeminacy—became approved activities for men as the nineteenth century ended, and consumer choice became a form of male self-expression. A man defined his identity not just in the workplace but through modes of enjoyment and self-fulfillment outside of it. In a world where the passions formed a vital part of the self, older forms of virtue—self-restraint, self-denial—became suspect.

The contrast between men and women—sharp in the 1800s—blurred from "opposite" to merely "different," and the goal of marriage began to change from a union of opposites to a union of unique selves. With the passing of the twentieth century, even the sense of difference between the sexes has been replaced in some circles by a new emphasis on their underlying similarity. Under these circumstances, the subordination of a woman's identity to that of her husband has grown more difficult to justify.

In our own era, the prevailing forms of manhood have begun to face hard critical scrutiny. Different critics have aimed at different problems. Some charge that modern concepts of manhood have alienated men from each other, while others emphasize the alienation of men from women. Certain critics focus on the damage done to men who have lost touch with their own senses of tenderness and care, and other detractors stress the damage done to women by the unfair distribution of power between the sexes. Still others have identified ways in which concepts of manhood have swayed public policy and political choice in the twentieth century.[11] This book will evaluate these charges in the context of history, while also identifying positive effects of the same concepts.

Our beliefs about manhood have played a powerful role in determining the kind of life and the kind of society we have. These notions of manliness have left their imprint, for instance, on political language, with its profusion of sports metaphors and its preoccupation with toughness. They have framed our definition of the male homosexual as a man bereft of manhood. And they have nurtured our cultural romance with competition as a solution to all problems, from economic productivity to a fair divorce settlement. How our concepts of manhood have developed—and affected the world we have inherited—are the chief concerns of this book.

Manhood is not a social edict determined on high and enforced by law. As a human invention, manhood is learned, used, reinforced, and reshaped by individuals in the course of life. In order to understand the transformation of middle-class manhood, we need to explore this personal process as it operated in the crucial century of change—the nineteenth. In the early 1800s, self-made manhood became the dominant cultural form, and it was later in the same century that passionate manhood evolved. By studying the lifelong process by which men learned and reshaped manhood during that era, we can know more intimately the way in which a great cultural transformation took place, and we can better understand the people who built the forms of manhood we have inherited.

Middle-class men who lived in the nineteenth century experienced a life that, though resembling our own in some ways, was utterly separate in others. As small boys, they were dressed in the clothing and hairstyles of girls. In youth, they struggled along a path to manhood that was less clearly marked than today. There was little system to the passage of a boy through his years of education, and there was even less system in the process that gave him credentials for a life in commerce or the professions. Being engaged to marry was a status that often lasted two years and sometimes stretched to eight. In that era, the conceptual distinction between boyhood and manhood was much sharper than it is now; the man was expected to be a distinguished figure—sober and purposeful—while the boy possessed a sense of play that was utterly unacceptable in a man. The pattern of men's personal relationships was different as well. In young manhood, romantic—even passionate—friendships between males were socially accepted. Throughout manhood, men's physical and cultural world was separated from women's much more than it is today.

Middle-class men of the 1800s also experienced certain kinds of gender conflict in their own feelings. These conflicts were a response to the fact that middle-class culture seemed to place gender labels everywhere.

A man's aggressions were male; his conscience, female; his desire to conquer, male; his urge to nurture, female; his need for work and worldly achievement, male; his wish to stay home and enjoy quiet leisure, female. More than that, a man learned his lessons about gender from both men and women, and the lessons he learned were not the same. For instance, individualism might look like selfishness to his mother, while it showed assertive, manly autonomy to male peers. Men often found their own emotions clashing. In *Ivanhoe*, a favorite novel of American men in this era, one of the heroes died in battle not from "the lance of his enemy" but as "a victim of his own contending passions." The notion of contending passions resonated deeply with *Ivanhoe*'s legion of male readers.[12]

Contending passions had another meaning as well for these men. In this era, men were subject to new expectations about the way they managed feelings of rivalry. These competitive impulses, which had been targets of condemnation in early America, gained a measure of respect in the nineteenth century. Still, they remained a preoccupation for men and for middle-class culture in general. The history of this preoccupation is an important part of the story of Northern manhood in the 1800s.

As we observe how men learned manhood, reshaped it, and coped with its inner conflicts, we will follow their public lives as well. Nineteenth-century men and their concepts of manhood helped to define the character of many important American institutions. Modern legal education, for instance, is based on the nineteenth-century model of the case method, in which students engage in "Socratic" classroom struggles over specific cases with their professors. As one of its early practitioners noted, the case method replaced an older method, based on lectures, which had not been "a virile system." Many of the customs and folkways of the United States Congress have their origins in the early nineteenth century, when not only the federal government but the capital city itself were virtually all-male settings; continued years of male dominance in Congress have only elaborated the masculine culture established in the early 1800s.

The modern forms of the medical profession were also established in the nineteenth century. As the scientific physician became the dominant model and women were swept to the margins of the profession at the end of the 1800s, a network of medical schools, hospitals, and medical associations emerged to dominate the health-care field. With this new set of institutions and ideals came a growing emphasis on "male" reason and authority in the practice of medicine and a shrinking focus on "female" nurture. Clearly, men of the last century incorporated their own customs and beliefs into the institutions they built. Since we still inhabit these professional and public institutions, nineteenth-century manhood of the Northern middle-class variety is still impinging on us daily.[13]

This is an important historical moment in which to emphasize such findings. In the current political climate, gender is often dismissed as a tool of understanding. The study of gender has been derided as a woman's obsession, an intellectual plaything of feminists that would drop from consideration if not for their political pressure. I hope that this book will help to correct this dismissive attitude. So many of our institutions have men's needs and values built into their foundations, so many of our habits of thought were formed by male views at specific points in historical time, that we must understand gender in its historical dimension to understand our ideas and institutions.

Since men have held the great predominance of power over the last two centuries, one inevitably studies male domination in studying recent gender history. And since humans tend not to behave at their best when left with a predominance of power, the picture of middle-class men in relation to women over the last two centuries is bound to have its unattractive side. Men have often acted thoughtlessly, sometimes viciously, and nearly always for their own advantage, in dealing with women *as a sex*. Thus, it is easy to study issues of sex and gender and portray men as faceless oppressors.

Such a simple portrait, however, would not help us to understand how gender operates as a cultural and political force. Besides, such a picture does not do justice to the varieties of male behavior or the complexities of inner motive. Few men would recognize themselves in such a generic portrait. In this book, I have tried to describe the rich mixture of feeling, intention, and conduct that flows through social customs and political structures to emerge as individual behavior. The forms of power and belief in times past will matter in the pages that follow, and so will the diversity of male experience.

Chapter I

COMMUNITY TO INDIVIDUAL

The Transformation of Manhood at the Turn of the Nineteenth Century

ANYONE who tries to learn about manhood before 1800 encounters a world of meaning far different from that of the twentieth century. Early New Englanders rarely used words like *manhood* and *masculinity*. In fact, the significance of gender was not a topic of constant discussion, as it would be in later years. Still, the lack of an obsession with gender before 1800 did not mean an absence of ideas on the subject. People recorded their ideas of what it meant to be a good man, and they were influenced by their own religious texts and by new ideas pouring in from abroad. In their laws and in the enforcement of discipline, they revealed many assumptions about the meaning of manhood. Distinctions between men and women helped to order society in colonial New England, and played a notable part in the systems of belief that flourished before 1800.

Communal Manhood

If there was one position in society that expressed the essence of manhood for early New Englanders, it was man's role as head of the household. Every person—young or old, male or female—had to find a place within a family, but the family head could only be a male. In time, most men could head a household, and colonial New Englanders learned to associate males with authority through their constant contact with men in that role. The two other institutions at the heart of the society—church and state—were also governed solely by men, but those figures of authority might be distant. It was the man at the head of the family who embodied God's authority in the daily life of each person.[1]

Why did men hold this position? Why, in other words, was authority male and not female? The Puritans who shaped New England's institutions and customs built their society on their religious beliefs. Their God was a man, and, when He created humankind, He made a man first and then made woman as a helpmeet. Puritans read in their scriptures that God said to Eve, "Thy desire shall be to thy husband, and he shall rule over thee."[2] And they knew as well that woman, not man, had started the fall from grace. Thus, the Puritans, who believed that God arranged all living things in rank order, placed man above woman and second only to God.[3]

When the men of early New England explained their superiority in earthly terms, they spoke of their greater strength of body and mind. In a world where all but a few people lived by the work of their hands, men's physical strength seemed to qualify them better than women to support the household. And since men were also credited with greater strength of mind, they seemed more fit than women to make wise decisions in governing a family.[4]

Eighteenth-century New Englanders elaborated these distinctions between the sexes. They divided human passions into those that were typically male and those that were quintessentially female. Ambition, assertiveness, and a lust for power and fame were thought to be "manly" passions. A taste for luxury, submissiveness, and a love of idle pleasures were considered "effeminate" passions. But whether a man was struggling with manly or effeminate passions, he was assumed to have greater reason than woman—and it was reason that helped a person to govern the passions. To New Englanders of the seventeenth and eighteenth centuries, men's powers of mind suited them better than women to head a household.[5] Because most males eventually occupied this role and few females ever could, governing a family meant participation in a division of power by gender. To head a household, for all intents and purposes, was to be a man.

To understand why this social trust—this male prerogative—was so important, one must understand the nature of the family in New England before 1800. The family, to start with, was the primary unit of production. Farms, shops, and great mercantile firms were all family enterprises. The family also served as the fundamental unit of society. Early Americans—and men in particular—reckoned their status in great measure by the family in which they were born. Even as a man's family helped to locate him within the ordered ranks of society, it placed him in historical time as well, for his family linked him to generations of ancestors and descendants.[6]

In the view of the community, the head of the household was the embodiment of all its members. The basic unit of the political system was the family, and the head of the family was its link to community governance. He was the household's voting representative in public councils, and public officers held him responsible for the behavior and welfare of those in his care. In addition, the family was viewed as "a little commonwealth," which meant not only that it was the government writ small but that the government was the family writ large. The head of the household set the standard of firmness and vigilant concern by which public rulers were measured.[7] He was also responsible for the godliness of his family, leading them in daily worship. To head a household, in sum, was to anchor the status system, preserve the political order, provide a model of government, sustain piety, ensure productive activity, and maintain the economic support of one's dependents.

Even with so much authority vested in one person, the household was not governed by tyranny. It was a patriarchy, the rule of a family by a father figure. Ideally, a father loved each member of his household, but even where such love did not exist, the head of the Puritan household was constrained in his actions by the duties he owed to each person in his charge. In particular, a man's wife—though not his equal—was his partner, and some of his power was readily delegated to her. But to all members—sons and daughters, servants, boarders, and aged kin—the head of the family owed benevolent rule, and he could expect to answer to his community if he failed badly in this or any other duty.[8]

Indeed, *duty* was a crucial word for manhood, as it was for New England society itself. Every social relationship was organized as a conjunction of roles (father-son, husband-wife, neighbor-neighbor, for example), and each role was governed by a set of duties owed to others. The importance of these obligations showed through in everyday language. Even grown men signed letters to their parents, "Your dutiful son," and people wrote constantly of their "Duty, to God and Man."[9]

Sociologists tell us that any society is organized by roles, but some societies balance the importance of social roles by paying great attention to the distinctive qualities of each individual in ordering human relationships. Colonial New England was not such a place. There, people thought of their world as "an organic social order in which rights and responsibilities were reciprocal and in which terms like *individuality* or *self-reliance* had little place."[10] A person's identity was bound up in the performance of social roles, not in the expression of self.

Every colonial New Englander, regardless of sex, put a high premium on the fulfillment of duty; but in a place and time where men wielded the social authority, they especially were judged by their contribution to the larger community. Before 1800, New Englanders saw a close link between manhood and "social usefulness." A mother could boast that her little son's growing integrity and honor were "good foundations upon which one may reasonably build hopes of future usefulness." Likewise, a study of heroes in magazine articles of the late eighteenth century has shown that a man's "publick usefulness" was a crucial measure of his worth. Men who carried out their duties to family and community were men to admire.[11]

The performance of social obligation often required a man to act against his own will. To carry out such obligations, a man had to learn submission to superiors, to fate, to duty itself. The Christian faith of New Englanders was a stern, effective teacher of submission. It enabled acquiescence in the will of God and resignation to the "pleasure of the Sovereign of the Universe."[12] Submission was more than a Christian virtue, though. It was also a habit of thought well suited to life in a society of rank order. So young people deferred to old, sons yielded to fathers, women submitted to men, and men of all ages acquiesced in their social responsibilities. Moreover, society was arranged by class as well as age and gender. People of the upper orders expected their inferiors to defer to them, so a man bowed to his superiors just as he submitted to God's will.[13]

But no man, however well placed, could deal cruelly with his inferiors. Every man was expected to treat dependents with kindness and restraint. Life in a New England community involved delicate balances, maintained at an intimate distance. People placed a high value on personal qualities that kept social relations smooth. A man was admired if he was gentle and amiable. This quality demanded self-restraint and placed a tremendous emotional burden on the details of social behavior, but the effort was considered worthy. If a man could cultivate a high regard among his fellows while minimizing conflict, he became a valuable asset in a close-knit society.[14]

The ideal man, then, was pleasant, mild-mannered, and devoted to the good of the community. He performed his duties faithfully, governed his passions rationally, submitted to his fate and to his place in society, and treated his dependents with firm but affectionate wisdom. Pious, dutiful, restrained—such a man seems almost too good to survive on this earth.

In fact, it is not clear that the men who conjured up his image expected him to exist in pure form. He was, after all, a composite of ideal traits, a collection of virtues that men yearned to bring to life. And, when one reads the descriptions of his character, one senses the lurking fear of a wholly different set of male traits. When the minister William Bentley sketched his vision of "the good man," he filled it with statements about what this paragon did *not* do; he was "without dissimulation," "pure from guile," "easily dissuaded from revenge." A physician named Alexander Anderson, reading a biography of Gustavus Vase, explained his deep respect for the man in this way: "I admire his resignation—a very useful virtue—I speak from the want of it myself."[15]

Behind the admiration for the virtuous, socially useful man, then, lay the fear of a different kind of person—a man who was contentious and willful, who stood up and fought for his own interests. This defiant behavior frightened men who wanted to believe in a corporate ideal. They were alarmed when selfish impulses were set loose around them, and they were even more alarmed to know that those same impulses were at work inside themselves.

From the earliest days of Puritan settlement, self-assertion played a crucial part in the daily life of New England. The very duties that demanded submission to some people and some social expectations required action against others. Whether the head of a household was laying claim to a scarce resource on behalf of his family or chastising a child for idleness, self-assertion was needed for the performance of a man's social duties. Moreover, a new society on a different continent presented men with endless opportunities for personal gain. The man who was willing to vent his "manly passions"—ambition, avarice, assertiveness— had the best chance of exploiting those opportunities. Some historians have described the operation of individual initiative from the moment of Puritan settlement. There were many acceptable outlets for this sort of initiative in the seventeenth century. The constant creation of new towns on the New England frontier—while in part a response to overcrowding in older settlements—could also represent an assertion of economic ambition or even a set of ideas at odds with the orthodoxies of earlier communities. Meanwhile, personal wealth was admitted, along with age, sex, and birth, as a determinant of social rank in the Puritan colonies. The development of a small but visible merchant class in coastal towns also testified to a certain tolerance for individual ambition. And the near-constant state of warfare with the native peoples of the region enabled men to express their manly passions to the fullest—and often bloodi-est—extent with the enthusiastic support of their society.[16]

It is worth noting that this tolerance of certain forms of self-assertion was extended to men more than to women. To be sure, women per-formed certain male duties as needed, they carried on their own infor-mal networks of trade, and they were honored for moments of bravery in frontier warfare.[17] But these exceptions to the rule were far more limited in scope than those allowed to men. And the most dramatic acts of sup-pression in Puritan New England (the prosecutions of Anne Hutchinson and of numerous "witches") were directed against assertive women, not assertive men. In theory, any acts of individual ambition threatened so-cial unity. In practice, a woman who refused to be submissive challenged a patriarchal society more profoundly than did a defiant man.

For men, the flexibility of the social code created an area of compro-mise between communal ideal and individual desire. Much economic ambition could be rationalized as a man's way of adding to the common wealth, and political self-advancement could always be explained as a desire to serve the community in some greater cause.

Most historians of early New England agree that assertive individual-ism was contained without being suppressed until the early 1700s. Throughout the eighteenth century, however, the manly passions were an increasingly divisive social force. In 1704, a Massachusetts minister named John Danforth denounced "The Vile Profanations of Prosperity," announcing with dread that "This Sheba, SELF, has blown the Trumpet of Rebellion." The rebellious claims of the self were most evident in sea-ports where merchant families lived in growing luxury and where arti-sans found the best opportunities for self-advancement. Meanwhile, the steady westward migration created many new towns in each generation and slowly weakened communal values. At the same time, new modes of thought supported individual action. In the second quarter of the eigh-teenth century, the Great Awakening advanced the idea of personal in-dependence and undermined hierarchy as a social principle. By midcen-tury, a new stream of ideas was flowing from England to North America. Critical of a static social order and patriarchal authority, these revolu-tionary ideas gained adherents quickly.[18]

By the 1770s, then, Americans had learned to feel more comfortable with the notion of self-assertion. By throwing off their belief in the virtue of submission, they prepared themselves for revolution. In turn, the uprising against British authority raised the idea of the independent self to a new level of reverence. The war for independence—and the change in attitudes toward individual initiative that came with it—were often framed in the language of manliness. The Declaration of Independence itself used the word *manly* to mean resolute courage in resisting tyranny: "[The King] has dissolved Representative Houses repeatedly, for opposing with manly firmness his invasions on the rights of the people." And when Royall Tyler wrote the first successful American comedy, *The Contrast,* in 1787, he created a character to embody American virtues and named him Colonel Manly. What were these Manly American virtues? The Colonel was brave, frank, independent in thought and feeling, and free from submission and luxury. The use of the language of manhood to suggest virtue continued throughout the period. Benjamin Goodhue, a staunch opponent of the French Revolution, wrote of relations with that country in 1798: "We shall be compelled shortly to either manfully oppose the injuries We endure . . . , or submissively submit to the degrading terms those haughty Despots choose to impose."[19]

During the revolutionary crisis and the early decades of the new republic, the language of manliness was used more and more for positive social purposes. To some extent, this positive new usage represented an addition to old concepts of manhood. Benjamin Goodhue's pointed contrast of *manfully* with *submissively* indicates the changed meaning of manliness. A man was one who resisted arbitrary authority, who refused submission. This new addition to the old definition of manhood had subversive implications, for a social order based on rank could only exist where men were encouraged to submit.

In the late eighteenth century, as men were using *manliness* with new meanings, they were also creating a new society based on the free expression of the traditional manly passions—assertiveness, ambition, avarice, lust for power. These male drives would provide the motive force for political and economic systems of a novel sort. The new federal constitution, instead of suppressing self-interest, assumed its existence and built a system of government on the play of competing interests. Unfettered individualism was not yet honored in public discourse, but the individual citizen—with all his rights and interests—was now the source of power in the American republic. Likewise, a more dynamic form of commercial life was in the making. National leaders like Alexander Hamilton saw compelling reasons to turn loose the forces of individual enterprise. And the modern systems of banking and finance, which are fueled by personal profit and individual interest, have their roots in this era.[20]

The late eighteenth century, then, was a time of nascent individualism. The forces of community and tradition faltered in their struggle to contain personal ambition, and the claims of the individual self appeared in all realms of a man's life with growing legitimacy.

Since the settlement of New England, the aggressive passions that threatened social order had been associated with manhood and with selfish interest. When John Danforth had railed against "this Sheba, SELF," he was lamenting the presence of "manly" vices such as greed and assertiveness. Throughout the eighteenth century, the connection between male passion and individual interest had persisted. Thus, when influential thinkers of the late eighteenth century pondered the growing claims of the self, they thought only of the *male* self. From the start, individualism was a gendered issue.[21]

To gain full consideration as individuals, women had to follow a path very different from that of men. The first positive recognition of the female self—unique, separate from others, and transcendently important—came not in the public realm, but through romance. Though romantic love was not enshrined as a cultural ideal until the nineteenth century, it grew steadily in importance during the second half of the eighteenth. At that time, romantic love disentangled itself from family considerations in choosing a spouse. A couple, when "struck with love," experienced a reaction between unique selves. Romance was a profoundly individual experience. Although American men and women had certainly fallen in love before the late eighteenth century, their experience had not as a rule been glorified. As romantic love moved to a cultural position of honor and fascination, it brought the distinctive traits of the individual woman (and the individual man) into a favorable light.[22]

While romance exalted the unique female self in the private realm, the recognition of woman as an individual in the public arena never happened in the eighteenth century. In this dimension, individualism touched men and women differently. As American men erected a new political system in which power flowed upward from the individual man, however, women's attempts to create some legitimate political role for themselves helped to lay the basis for the new gender arrangements that would flourish in the nineteenth century.[23]

Women of the new republic, like the females of the colonies, could not vote or hold public office.[24] In constructing a place for themselves in politics, women turned to two common articles of social faith: that a woman's proper place was in the home; and that a republic could only last if its citizens—that is, its male participants—had a strong sense of public virtue. Men would have to learn this virtue somewhere, and where better than the home? Republican mothers would instill incorruptible honesty and a love of liberty in their boys.[25]

By creating this new role for themselves, women were filling a gap created by the nascent individualism of men. In the past, men had held the moral responsibility for the good of the community. Under the new constitution, political self-interest was assumed, and men began to create "an aggressive, egalitarian democracy of a modern sort."[26] With male self-assertion emerging as legitimate political behavior, women took men's place as the custodians of communal virtue.

This new role did not place male and female on equal footing; in fact, women were providing a service to men and society. By preserving the sense of common social virtue, women were freeing men to pursue self-interest. As historian Linda Kerber has written, "The learned woman, who might very well wish to make choices as well as to influence attitudes, was a visible threat to this arrangement."[27]

Viewed in one way, women's new political mission simply re-created the supportive, subordinate role women had always played in the colonies: the new, moral womanhood made the new, individualistic manhood possible. On the other hand, republican motherhood laid the foundation for a different and more effectual women's role in the nineteenth century. It gave women a clearly defined political function, something they had never had before. Republican motherhood, moreover, elevated the status of domesticity by giving it relevance and importance in relation to the public domain. And woman's new function as the custodian of virtue exalted her to a higher moral plane. No longer viewed primarily as the sinful daughter of Eve, she was now thought to exert an uplifting moral influence on men.[28]

These changes laid the basis for a new relationship between the sexes in the nineteenth century. Though still subordinate to men, women were increasingly seen as separate, too. Their high moral status made the domestic world a base of influence as well as a confinement. As the age of individualism began, the redefinitions of manhood and womanhood were part of the same process.

Self-made Manhood

In 1802, an ambitious young man named Daniel Webster was setting out in the world to seek his fortune. Like so many other men of his era,

Webster saw before him a wide-open, changing society that was full of risk and possibility. In a metaphor of movement, he described what he saw:

> The world is nothing but a contra-dance, and everyone *volens, nolens*, has a part in it. Some are sinking, others rising, others balancing, some gradually ascending towards the top, others flamingly leading down. Some cast off from Fame and Fortune, and some again in a comfortable allemande with both.[29]

Webster joined eagerly in this dance of social fortunes.

Nor was he alone. At the dawn of the nineteenth century, young men of the North faced a world of immense opportunity. The settlement of vast new areas inspired visions of great wealth. The Revolution had introduced a more dynamic view of the social order, and the new American governments had removed some of the old legal barriers to social advancement. Most of all, the spread of the market economy created new opportunities.[30]

As obstacles fell and opportunities grew, the reassessment of self-interest and individual initiative, which had begun in the late eighteenth century, gained momentum and spawned new ideas. One of these ideas gripped the popular imagination with special force in the early nineteenth century: the notion that free competition would reward the best man. People believed that a man could now advance as far as his own work and talents would take him. This belief in a free and open contest for success shared a common assumption with another new attitude that emerged at the turn of the nineteenth century: that the individual, not the community, was the fundamental unit of society.

This shift in thinking from community to person had profound implications for notions of manhood. Men rejected the idea that they had a fixed place in any hierarchy, be it cosmic or social. They no longer thought of themselves as part of an organic community from which they drew personal identity. And they ceased to see themselves as segments in an unbroken family line. The metaphors by which men had defined themselves were losing their power in the new century.

In their stead, a new image developed. Society was a collection of atoms—unranked humans without assigned positions of any sort—and each found his proper place in the world through his own efforts. This new man—this atom—was free of the cord of generations that had given his forefathers a place in historical time. The past did not weigh him down in his struggle to make himself whatever he dreamed of being.

The individual was now the measure of things and men were engrossed with themselves as *selves*. The dominant concerns were the concerns of the self—self-improvement, self-control, self-interest, self-advancement. Passions like personal ambition and aggression—though not seen as virtues—were allowed free passage in society. And the important bonds between people were now fastened by *individual* preference more than birth or social duty.[31]

With assertiveness, greed, and rivalry set free in the marketplace and in the public councils, old dilemmas arose in new forms. The Puritans had viewed those passions as a threat to social order and had tried to control them through a code of communal beliefs and rules. That older system could not work in a society based on the individual. How, then, could the new order be saved from destruction by the very engines of male passion that drove it? How could the individual man be civilized?[32]

Of course, manhood was more than an abstract idea. It was also a standard of behavior for individual men. In this era of competition and self-advancement, men had to vent their aggressive, "manly" passions, but they needed to learn how to do it without being socially destructive. Two different strategies emerged to prevent liberated self-interest from laying waste to the social order. These tactical methods contradicted each other, and the conflict between them did much to define bourgeois manhood in the nineteenth century.

To understand the two main strategies that men used to control their aggressions, it helps to look at the ways of defining manhood by naming its opposite. If a man is not a man, then what is he? One answer is obvious in the context of this book about gender: If a man is not a man, he must be like a woman. But nineteenth-century men had a second answer: If a man is not a man, he must be like a boy.

What was the difference between a boy and a man? The "stigma of boyishness," as one man called it, had to do with frivolous behavior, the lack of worthy aims, and the want of self-control. Any action that was likened to "the play of boys" was contemptible, and a man was "juvenile" if he indulged in boys' sports. In James Fenimore Cooper's *Last of the Mohicans*, Natty Bumppo chides himself for using up his ammunition impulsively by shaking his head "at his own momentary weakness, . . . [and] uttering his self-disapprobation aloud. . . . 'Twas the act of a boy!' he said." In the same novel, the Mohican, Magua, vowed on the eve of battle that he and his warriors should "undertake our work like men," not like "eager boys." Boys had enthusiasm, not judgment, and aggression without control.

A sense of carefully guided passion marked the difference between boyhood and manhood. Henry David Thoreau revealed this assumption in *Walden* when he described the difference between oral and written language. The spoken word he associated with boyhood, "transitory, . . . a dialect merely, almost brutish, and we learn it unconsciously like the brutes from our mothers." However, the written word "is the maturity and experience of that [spoken language]; if that is our mother tongue, this is our father tongue, a reserved and select expression, . . . which we must be born again in order to hear." Thoreau scornfully heaps mother and son together, connecting the woman and the boy to what is unconscious, spontaneous, "almost brutish." Manhood, by contrast, is a "reserved and select expression," mature, consciously learned, under the careful control of reason.[33]

What lies beneath this contrast between boyhood and manhood is a set of assumptions about how to control the aggressive passions that were considered a male birthright. As the thinking went, a boy was driven by his passions, by his eager, impulsive, "almost brutish" nature. Yet he needed to become a purposeful man. How would he make this transition? To suppress his aggressions—or even to moderate them—would deprive him of the assertive energies that he needed to make his place in the competitive arena of middle-class work in the nineteenth century. But without a clear focus, those energies would be wasted. They might even become destructive.

With little conscious articulation, men devised experiences that helped transform the impulsive passions of the boy into the purposeful energies of the man. Academies, colleges, and apprenticeships in commerce and the professions served some of these purposes. Probably more effective were the ubiquitous debating clubs, literary societies, and young men's associations that sprang up inside and outside the formal institutions of learning. True to their era of individualism, these groups did not rely on elder authorities to shape their manhood. Rather, their youthful members socialized each other.[34] In the absence of women and older men, they trained each other in the harnessing of passions and the habits of self-command. Aside from these self-created institutions, some young men turned to demanding life experiences—as sailors, cowboys, boatmen, forty-niners, wandering laborers, and (most dramatically) Civil War soldiers—to teach them the self-discipline needed for the active life of the marketplace.

The training in manhood that these schools of experience provided was not based on a conscious philosophy, nor did it grow from articulated plans or procedures. Men happened upon these arrangements and they did not describe—or prescribe—them in any systematic fashion. In an era of voluntary associations and ungoverned competition, this informal system of turning boys into men (which will be described more fully in chapter 3) made a kind of spontaneous sense.

But this was a haphazard way to channel energies and limit impulse. In fact, this system looked dangerous to men and women raised in an earlier society where passion was governed by deep-seated ideals of order and the eager vigilance of the community. To many, this new system looked like no system at all. Individual desire threatened social ties, unchecked competition raised the specter of destructive personal conflict, and self-assertion without social control posed a real possibility of anarchy. As the public world of the individual emerged, a new set of social arrangements arose alongside of it to provide moral order. In the process, a second system for governing manly passion was born.

Through most of the nineteenth century, manhood was a matter of age *and* gender. Many of the traits that marked a man were found wanting in both women and boys. Reason and emotional control played little part in womanhood or boyhood, according to conventional wisdom.

But the contrasts based on age and gender differed in crucial ways. Boys shared a common male nature with men. They did need help in cultivating qualities like self-control and reason (which were regarded as "potential" in males, requiring development), but boys were "inherently" like men. Women, on the other hand, diverged sharply from men in their "intrinsic" nature. And, unlike boys, women were scorned if they cultivated manly qualities. The definition of manhood based on gender difference was a bit more sharply etched than the one based on age.

In fact, the assumed differences between women and men provided a foundation for the doctrine of separate spheres. This elaborate cultural construction evolved in the early nineteenth century. It was a system of symbols that middle-class men and women used to order their social world and understand their mutual relations. Historians have recently come to appreciate the profound impact of the idea of separate spheres on politics, personal relationships, and American culture at large. According to this view, the social realm was divided into two spheres— home and the world. Home was the woman's domain, so it was filled with the piety and purity that were "natural" to the female sex. This atmosphere of virtue made home the logical place to raise children, and woman the fit and proper person to do the job. The female sex extended its moral influence over men as well. In the good and godly environment of the home, women supplied the other sex with moral nurture and spiritual renewal.[35]

Men needed to be strengthened in conscience and spirit because they spent so much time in "the world." The world, according to this moral geography, was the realm of business and public life. It was the emerging marketplace of competitive trade and democratic politics, the arena of individualism. And, just as women's domesticity fitted them for the duties of the home, so men's presumed aggression suited them for this rough public life. Indeed, the world was viewed as the locus of sin and evil. It demanded greed and selfishness of a man, tempted him with power and sensual enjoyment, and set him against other men.[36] An article that appeared in an 1830 issue of *Ladies Magazine* described the world by way of contrast with the values of home:

> We go forth into the world, amidst the scenes of business and pleasure . . . and the heart is sensible to a desolation of feeling: we behold every principle of justice and of honor, and even the dictates of common honesty disregarded, and the delicacy of our moral sense is wounded; we see the general good sacrificed to the advancement of personal interest.

Still, virtue had its own sphere, "the sanctuary of the home," where a man could fortify himself against the evil influences of the world: "There sympathy, honor, virtue, are assembled; there the eye may kindle with intelligence, and receive an answering glance; there disinterested love, is ready to sacrifice everything at the altar of affection."[37] From this point of view, the social fabric was torn every day in the world and mended every night at home. Men's sphere depleted virtue, women's sphere renewed it.

This view of the social world had its own historical roots. It built upon the idea of republican motherhood and tapped the growing cultural belief that women were the virtuous sex. As many Northern communities were shaken by evangelical tremors at the start of the nineteenth century, the doctrine of the spheres drew upon the evangelical perception of the world as a sinful place.[38]

Most of all, this new ideology was a response to emerging changes in the workplace. As commercial markets spread at a growing pace, the tempo of middle-class work quickened, and men in business, law, and finance needed increasingly to spend time in each other's presence, both in the office and out. In the second quarter of the nineteenth century, the commercial and professional offices themselves were moved out of homes and into specialized districts. Thus, men were working longer hours and spending more of those hours farther from home. First by time and then by space, men's work limited their presence at home. As many middle-class women were freed by their husbands' prosperity from the necessity of paid labor, they focused more than ever on their domestic duties. Increasingly, women seemed creatures of the home; increasingly, men did not.[39]

The doctrine of separate spheres responded to changes in the workplace, and it may also have affected those changes in their later stages. The changes themselves were physical, however, and the ideology of the spheres gave them a different dimension by attributing a moral meaning to them. The ideology was at once a critique of the new commercial world and a blueprint for adapting to it. This elaborate metaphor identified the new world of individualism and self-interest as evil. Then, rather than question this evil, the doctrine of the spheres offered women as a mechanism to temper it.[40]

The idea of the separate spheres was the climax to some of the cultural changes that began in the eighteenth century. While men of the colonial era had struggled to reconcile ideals of public virtue and personal interest, those ideals realigned themselves along a male-female axis in the nineteenth century.[41] In other words, the doctrine of separate spheres entrusted women with the care and nurture of communal values—of personal morality, social bonds, and, ultimately, the level of virtue in the community. Men were left free to pursue their own interests, to clash and compete, to behave—from an eighteenth-century point of view—selfishly. Women now stood for traditional social values, men for dynamic individualism.

Because bourgeois women were expected to sustain the morality of the men, they acquired the basis for a female political role. Building on the concepts of republican motherhood and the republican wife, the doctrine of separate spheres further empowered nineteenth-century women to cultivate virtue in their sons and husbands. This gave them an indirect means to change behavior in the public arena, but they soon seized more direct forms of influence. After all, it would be difficult to take responsibility for a man's personal virtue and ignore his behavior in public. And it would be hard to watch over personal morality and social bonds without tending social morality as well. When the line between private and public virtue was so hard to draw, woman's role as the custodian of moral goodness inevitably pulled her into the public arena. The metaphor of separate spheres implied a political role for women, even if it denied one explicitly.[42]

The feminine custody of virtue had a second crucial implication: it put women at odds with expected male behavior. After all, if the doctrine of separate spheres was a critique of "the world" and the world was man's realm, then the doctrine was also a critique of manhood. Looked at in these gendered terms, the ideology of the spheres was a plan for the female government of male passions. It gave men the freedom to be aggressive, greedy, ambitious, competitive, and self-interested, then it left women with the duty of curbing this behavior.

Here, then, was a second idea of how to control male passion. While one concept of control assumed that male groups would focus assertive energies and diffuse their potential for social destruction, the second one directed women to bridle the aggressive drives—the engines of individualism—that were associated with men and their sphere. These two philosophies of control were more than merely that; they were really opposing conceptions of manhood. Although they shared basic assumptions about men's intrinsic nature and social purpose, the two conceptions made sharply different judgments of value about manliness and the male sphere. One trusted the unchecked operation of men's nature to be self-correcting and to create the greatest social good. The other envisioned ungoverned manhood as a socially destructive force.

These two strategies for the control of male passion balanced against each other neatly: one meant learning at home, the other meant learning in the world; one meant lessons from females, the other meant lessons from males. But the most obvious piece of symmetry was missing: one strategy involved mothers, while the other involved peers. Where were fathers? In the new society that developed early in the nineteenth century, fathers declined in their importance to sons, and their place was taken by mothers. This change had great significance for the lives of middle-class men and boys; it also had great significance for the way in which middle-class boys learned the strategies to control "male" passion.

Parents and Sons

When Francis J. Grund visited the United States in the 1830s, the Englishman noted that among Boston businessmen a man might "become the father of a large family and even die without finding out his mistake."[43] With allowance for hyperbole, this is still an astonishing change. Throughout the colonial period, the father had been the dominant figure in the family, yet by the 1830s he was secondary in the household. How had this happened so quickly?

In truth, the foundations of the patriarchal style had been eroding throughout the second half of the 1700s, as ideas and social conditions began to change. By the middle of the eighteenth century, a growing population in the old farming towns of New England had led to a decline in the amount of land available to each man. Thus, fathers could no longer control their sons by promising the gift of a farm later in life. The father lost power and authority.[44] This gradual change in the middle years of the 1700s paved the way for acceptance of a new concept of parenting, one that reached America from England in the 1760s and 1770s. In the emerging view, parents were no longer to act as stringent authorities, but were to increase their roles as moral teachers.[45] In this context, the new notion developed that woman was the embodiment of virtue.[46] Thus, the female sex was viewed as inherently suited to the new concept of parenthood, while males appeared less fit for a primary role. By the early nineteenth century, when the work of middle-class men began to pull fathers away from home, fathers readily yielded their traditional role in shaping the character of their sons.[47] Indeed, the change was probably underway in many families even before the father began spending his time elsewhere.

What was left for a father to do in the nineteenth century? The role he now played was reduced, yet still important. He remained as head of the household, which meant that decisions about the running of a bourgeois family were ultimately a man's.[48] Furthermore, it was his work that supported the household financially. He also served in roles that involved him more directly with his children, especially his sons.[49] One of these was his function as chief disciplinarian. Any major infraction of family rules meant that a boy would have to confront his father. Of course, the mother handled the moment-to-moment punishment, since the father was gone for so much of the day. This undoubtedly made the father's ultimate role in discipline more fearsome, and it must have served to underline his authority and his distance.[50]

A father did have other important duties that asserted his authority in less awesome fashion. He was expected to prepare his son in a practical sense for entry into the world. A father, for instance, was in charge of his son's education. In an era before age-graded universal schooling, this involved far more decision making than it does in the twentieth century. And the decisions about education led directly toward a most important choice—the choice of a calling.[51] Fathers were expected to advise their sons on this matter, and they used whatever influence they had to get their young men started.[52] In some cases, fathers themselves tried to select a son's career. Many of the most dramatic clashes between fathers and sons came over the issue of career choice.[53]

A bourgeois father prepared his son for the world in another way—he supplemented his wife's work in the teaching of virtue. Few moments of major discipline were complete without a lecture from the father; and, as the head of family religious devotions and the chief tutor to his sons, the father had many other opportunities to offer moral instruction. While much of this moral education simply reinforced his wife's teaching, a man held sway over certain areas of ethics. These were values governing work, achievement, and property. Fathers taught their sons the importance of perseverance and thrift, of diligence and punctuality, of industry and ambition. This more than any other was a task that fathers seemed to relish.[54]

Yet a man's obligations to his sons were not only instrumental and worldly; he was also encouraged to love and cherish them. Given the lofty formal expectations held up for a father, and given his growing absence from the household, this love was not always offered with great personal warmth or informal ease. But there are, scattered through the middle-class family documents of the nineteenth century, instances of tenderness or relaxed fun between father and son.[55] Once a son was grown and established in his own life, a warm, friendly relationship often emerged.[56]

As the nineteenth century passed, the trend toward absence of the father grew. Longer work hours and lengthy commutes from the new middle-class suburbs removed men even more from the presence of their sons.[57] Yet, in the final decades of the century, a quiet countertrend emerged. Some men were becoming more involved with their sons. They sought closer emotional ties, expressed affection with growing ease, enjoyed playful times with their boys.[58] In these relationships at the end of the century, there was a glimpse of a different sort of future and a new set of expectations for fathers and sons. At the time, though, this newer style remained a countertrend, quietly visible in relation to the dominant theme of formal authority and father absence.

Father-son relationships in the nineteenth century presented a complex picture. Fathers still had a place of emotional importance in the lives of their sons. A father was the first man a boy knew, was the ultimate source of material comforts, made decisions that controlled a boy's life, and was a boy's predominant role model as a man. Yet he was still a diminished figure, frequently absent from the house, and for most middle-class boys, not the primary parent.

The reduction of fathers' status had partly to do with changes inside the father's life and role. But the reduction was also due to a dramatic enlargement of the other parenting role. For the first time in American history, the mother had become the primary parent.

Of course, women had played a vital role in the lives of their sons and daughters throughout the colonial period. They had always been responsible for the physical care of the children, and they were expected to nurture their young ones emotionally during the early years of childhood. But there were new expectations of motherhood that emerged at the turn of the nineteenth century—expectations that helped to start a revolution in the relations between mothers and sons.[59]

We know that in the late eighteenth century, the cultural assessment of women's moral character shifted from negative to positive. This change brought another change in its wake: mothers were now expected to mold the character of their sons, a task that in previous generations had always belonged to fathers. Encouraged by ministers and social critics who told them that the fate of the republic hung in the balance, middle-class women tried to give their sons a sense of virtue that would suit them to face the new, impersonal world of commerce and competition.[60]

Closely related to this moral expectation was a more personal one: a mother was expected to build strong and lasting bonds with her son. This marked a dramatic change from earlier conceptions. Colonists had believed that a woman's love was uncritical and indulgent. That was fine for nurturing a small child, but unconditional love, the colonists thought, would ruin older children, especially boys.[61] Thus, after the age of five or six, most colonial boys passed to the influence—if not always the physical care—of their fathers.[62]

In the late eighteenth century, Americans reassessed the mother's role. With affection now viewed as a vital part of child-rearing, a woman's unstinting warmth and tenderness suddenly became an asset. It was, in itself, good for children, and it could help as well in the crucial task of character development.[63]

Circumstances conspired to encourage women in fulfilling this mission. With family size declining, a mother could devote more attention to each child.[64] Now that the father was gone from home most of the day, a woman could focus her energy more directly on her children. In addition, sons now remained at home for much longer. During the seventeenth and eighteenth centuries, they were often apprenticed or bound out as servants before their midteens; by the end of the nineteenth century, young men were sometimes staying with their families until their late twenties.[65]

Most mothers took on these new challenges of nurture and uplift with energy and a great sense of purpose. There was a sense not just of stewardship, but of companionship in women's relations with their sons. A New York City woman named Sarah Gilbert described life with her son as a series of shared activities: "He was my companion wherever I went, we ... [knelt] in prayer together, we ... went to the house of God together, in the pleasurable promenade was my companion[,] in a business walk he was with me." Henry Poor remembered a similar experience in the hardscrabble Maine frontier town where he grew up. His mother "was almost the only friend and companion of my boyhood and youth." He added: "I felt myself on such terms of familiarity and sympathy with her, that I could pour out my whole heart without reserve."[66]

Meanwhile, nineteenth-century mothers were devoting themselves faithfully to their other major task, the development of moral character. A woman could cultivate virtue through stories, conversation, shared prayer, or simple exhortation, and her intimate familiarity with her sons helped her to use these different techniques of moral instruction for the greatest effect.[67]

But a boy needed to do more than learn his mother's lessons. He needed to internalize them and carry them out into the world. In short, he needed to make them part of his conscience. This "tyrannical monitor"—as one youth called his conscience—was not easily developed, but many mothers found a method (unconsciously, it seems) for helping it along. By linking her own happiness to her son's good behavior, a woman could pull her child's deepest feelings into her moral world and keep them fastened there. As one mother wrote to her son: "O! think how it would break my heart if you were not a *Good boy*, if you are not even exemplary."[68]

Through this combination of love and moral suasion, many boys developed strong consciences. A letter written by John Kirk, a salesman and abolitionist, suggests the staying power of maternal efforts. Kirk was a grown man with children of his own when he wrote to his mother:

How often have I been admonished by your godly prayers and your pious exhortations, when far from home and friends, how often when none but God could see or hear [me, your] monitions followed me, and caused the tears of penitential sorrows and affection to flow from my weeping eyes.[69]

After a full life, Kirk still heard his mother's prayers: she had a power over him which transcended time and space. When the conscience of a nineteenth-century man spoke, it generally spoke in feminine tones.

The content of a mother's message of virtue was what one might expect. It was a warning against drink, gambling, and sex. But more persistently, it was an injunction against those vices that came easily in a world engulfed by commerce—selfishness, greed, envy.[70]

A woman's lessons to her sons contained worldly messages, too. A young man would not survive long in the world if he were not industrious, persevering, and wise in his use of time. But the fundamental lessons were lessons of self-restraint. Above all, a boy learned from his mother to hold back his aggressions and control his own "male" energies.[71]

It was in this new environment that middle-class boys of the nineteenth century were shaped for manhood. With the father no longer dominant and with the mother a powerful and effective tutor in virtue, a boy learned early in life to bridle "male" impulse and approach the world with wary caution. But before he reached the world of men, he entered the world of boys. There he learned another, very different idea of how to cope with his drives and ambitions.

Chapter 2

BOY CULTURE

IN 1853, a popular etiquette writer called Mrs. Manners launched an angry attack on the boys of America. "Why is it," she asked, "that there must be a period in the lives of boys when they should be spoken of as 'disagreeable cubs'? Why is a gentle, polite boy such a rarity?" She continued her assault in that tone of embattled hauteur so common to etiquette writers: "If your parents are willing for you to be the 'Goths and Vandals' of society, I shall protest against it. You have been outlaws long enough, and now I beg you will observe the rules."[1]

For all her wounded righteousness, Mrs. Manners expressed a widely shared view. Source after source described boys as "wild" and "careless," as "primitive savages" full of "animal spirits." They were commonly compared to Indians and African tribesmen. One writer even called them a race unto themselves—"the race of boys."[2] The literary critic Henry Seidel Canby—reflecting on his own boyhood in the 1880s and 1890s—emphasized the separation of boys' world from the world of adults: "There was plenty of room for our own life, and we took it, so that customs, codes, ideals, and prejudices were absorbed from our elders as by one free nation from another."[3]

This "free nation" of boys was a distinct cultural world with its own rituals and its own symbols and values. As a social sphere, it was separate both from the domestic world of women, girls, and small children, and from the public world of men and commerce. In this space of their own, boys were able to play outside the rules of the home and the marketplace. It was a heady and even liberating experience.

Technically, of course, boy culture was really a subculture—distinct, oppositional, but intimately related to the larger culture of which it was a part. Boys shuttled constantly in and out of this world of theirs, home and then back again. Their experiences with boy culture helped to prepare them in many ways for life in the adult spheres that surrounded them. Boy culture, then, was not the only world that a young male inhabited, nor was it the only one that left its mark on him. Still, within its carefully set boundaries, boy culture was surprisingly free of adult intervention—it gave a youngster his first exhilarating taste of independence and made a lasting imprint on his character.

To be sure, this was not the first time historically that Northern boys had been free from supervision. Perpetual supervision of *any* child is impossible. But the circumstances of boys' lives in the nineteenth century freed them from adult oversight for long periods of time in the company of other boys, and this was different from the colonial experience. In the villages of New England during the 1600s and 1700s, a boy past the age of six was given responsibility for the first time. He began to help his father with farm work, which put him in the company of another generation and not among his male peers. His father did give him independent chores to do, but they tended to be solitary activities like tending livestock or running errands to other farms. Of course, boys did gather and play in colonial New England, but circumstances made it hard for them to come together on a regular basis in the absence of adults. They lacked the independence and cohesion as a group that boys developed in the nineteenth century.[4]

These later generations of the 1800s spent more time in the peer world of schoolhouse and schoolyard. Middle-class boys were needed less to do the work of the family. They were increasingly isolated from males of the older generation. A growing proportion of them lived in large towns and cities, which brought them in contact with a denser mass of peers. And, in a world where autonomy had become a male virtue, there were positive reasons to give boys time and space of their own. In sum, the conditions were ripe in the nineteenth century for a coherent, independent boys' world.

Nineteenth-century boys lived a different sort of life in the years before boy culture opened up to them—a life so different from what came later that it bears special notice here. Until the age of six or so, boys were enmeshed in a domestic world of brothers, sisters, and cousins. They rarely strayed from the presence of watchful adults.[5] Mothers kept an especially keen eye on their children during these early years, for popular thinking held that this was the phase of life when the basis was laid for good character. Thus, for his first five to seven years, a boy's adult companions were female and his environment was one of tender affection and moral rigor.[6] By the time that boys reached the age of three or four, their mothers were beginning to complain about their rowdy, insolent ways.[7] But however much they rebelled, these little boys were still embedded in a feminine world.

The clothing that boys wore during their early years served as a vivid symbol of their feminization: they dressed in the same loose-fitting gowns that their sisters wore. One Ohio man described the small boys' outfit of his childhood as "a sort of Kate Greenaway costume, the upper part of the body covered by a loose blouse, belted in at the waist, allowing the skirt to hang half-way to the knees." Under these gowns, they wore "girllike panties" which "reached the ankles."[8] Such "girllike" clothing gave small boys the message that they were expected to behave like their sisters, and served also as a token of the feminine environment that clothed them socially at this point in life. More than that, boys' gowns and smocks inhibited the running, climbing, and other physical activities that so often made boys a disagreeable addition to the gentle domesticity of women's world. Whether they meekly accepted the way their parents dressed them or rebelled against its confinements, boys were put in a situation where they had to accept or reject a feminine identity in their earliest years.[9]

Finally, at about age six, Northern boys cut loose from these social and physical restraints.[10] Although they would continue to live for many years in the woman's world of the home, they were now inhabitants of an alternate world as well.[11] In the cities, middle-class boy culture flourished in backyards, streets, parks, playgrounds, and vacant lots, all of which composed "a series of city states to play in." For those who lived in small towns, the neighboring orchards, fields, and forests provided a natural habitat for boy culture.[12] By contrast, indoors was alien territory. A parlor, a dining room, almost any place with a nice carpet, repelled boy culture. Boys did sometimes carve out their own turf within the house—usually in the attic, where dirt, noise, and physical activity created fewer problems than in the clean, placid lower floors. And the house was not the only indoor space that was alien. Boy culture languished in the school and in the church, and it never even approached the offices and countinghouses where middle-class fathers worked.[13]

How did a small boy enter this new realm at first? One man remembered simply that he "was aware of a great change in [his] world. It was no longer contained within a house bounded by four walls . . . [but] had swelled and expanded into a street."[14] Perhaps the change came for most boys with a similar lack of fanfare. Certainly, the autobiographies and family correspondence of the time reveal no special rite of passage that marked the entry into boy culture. As they broke away from the constant restriction of home, boys also shed forever the gowns and petticoats of younger days. Suddenly, the differences between themselves and their sisters—so long discouraged by the rules and habits of the home— seemed to be encouraged and even underscored.[15] For their sisters were still enveloped by the moral and physical confinements of domesticity and by the gowns and petticoats that were its visible emblems. With great clarity a boy saw that female meant fettered and male meant free.[16]

Boys, of course, were not absolutely free any more than the girls were literally chained. Indeed, their worlds of play and sociability overlapped at many points. At play, girls shared the yard with their brothers, and on rainy days boys cohabited attics and odd rooms with their sisters. Girls and boys enjoyed many of the same games, such as hide-and-seek and tag, and they pursued some of the same outdoor activities, such as sledding and skating. But their social worlds and their peer cultures were distinct. Boys had a freedom to roam that girls lacked. Physical aggression drove boys' activity in a way that was not acceptable for girls. The activities of both sexes mixed competition with collaboration, but the boys placed a stronger emphasis on their rivalries and the girls stressed their cooperation more heavily. Most importantly, the social worlds of boys and girls had different relationships with the world of adults of the same sex. Boy culture was independent of men and often antagonistic toward them. Girls' common culture was interdependent with that of women and even shared much of the same physical space. There was continuity, if not always amity, between the worlds of female generations.[17] The same was not true for men and boys. The nineteenth-century emphasis on male autonomy encouraged a gap between generations of males.

Boy Culture: Games and Pastimes

Boys now enjoyed the liberty of trousers and the independence of the great outdoors. More than that, they were beyond the reach of adult supervision for hours at a time. Boys were suddenly free to pursue a range of activities that would have been difficult if not impossible in the domestic world. The physical activities that had been hindered in early boyhood now became particular passions. Hiking, exploring, swimming, rowing, and horseback riding took on special meaning for boys newly liberated from domestic confinement.[18]

Of course, the boys who grew up in small towns and on farms had the best opportunities to hike and swim, but those who lived in cities had their own chances. Through most of the nineteenth century, urban areas were dotted with patches of scrub woodland where boys could play and explore.[19] Even in the huge cities of the century's later years, rural life could be imported in the form of parks and swimming lessons or improvised in vacant lots and backyards.[20] City and country boys had more or less equal access to the best-loved winter activities of boy culture, such as sledding, skating, or throwing snowballs.

While boys pursued these pastimes for the simple pleasure of exercise, they engaged in many other activities that set them head to head in hostile combat. Friends fought or wrestled for the fun of it, while other boys goaded playmates unwillingly into fights with each other. The varieties of physical punishment that boys inflicted on each other were as numerous as the settings in which they gathered. At boarding schools in the late nineteenth century, new students were forced by older students to run between two lines of boys who tried to bruise them with clubs and well-shod feet; in another variant, new boys ran naked around the inside of a circle while veteran students hit their bare buttocks with paddles. In Hamilton, Ohio, where William Dean Howells spent much of his boyhood, youngsters threw stones at their friends purely for sport or even as a form of greeting. Beneath this violence lay curious veins of casual hostility and sociable sadism. One of the bonds that held boy culture together was the pain that youngsters inflicted on each other.[21]

If boys posed a danger to one another, they were downright lethal to small animals. Boys especially enjoyed hunting birds and squirrels, and they did a good deal of trapping as well. There were several reasons for hunting's great appeal. In the rural North of the nineteenth century, the gun and the rod were still emblems of the male duty to feed one's family. The hunt, in that way, was associated with the power and status of grown men.[22] Yet city boys—given the opportunity to hunt—took the same lusty pleasure in it that their country cousins did. They just liked the challenge of the kill. Another practice that links the hunting habit to the violent tendencies of boy culture is the extravagant sadism that youngsters sometimes showed when they killed their prey. Boys turned woodchuck trapping into woodchuck torture, and they often killed insects simply to inflict suffering. While the boyish interest in hunting and fishing reflected in some part a remnant of earlier manly duties, it was also related to the pleasure that boys took in fighting and even stoning one another.[23]

Not all of boys' play was so openly violent or so freeform. Popular boys' games such as marbles, tag, blindman's buff, leapfrog, and tug-of-war, demanded physical skill, and most involved exercise and competition as well. An informal, prehistoric form of football mixed elements of tag, rugby, soccer, and the modern gridiron game with a large dose of free-for-all mayhem. There were also a number of variants on the current sport of baseball. What united these varied pastimes in contrast to modern games was a lack of elaborate rules and complicated strategies. Spontaneous exercise and excitement were more important than elaborate expertise in boys' games of the nineteenth century.[24] Other pastimes were more personally expressive. Games that developed on the spur of the moment or that grew slowly within the context of a friendship or a gang revealed many of the preoccupations of boy culture. A favorite subject in these improvised games was warfare. Sometimes, the young combatants took on the roles of the knights they read about in books, while during the Civil War they played the soldiers of their own time.[25]

The most popular variant on these war games seemed to be the struggle between settlers and Indians. In this case, the boys were often inspired by the stories of people they knew or by the local folklore about ancestral generations.[26] One revealing aspect of these games involved the choosing of sides. By race and sometimes by ancestry, the boys were kin to the settlers. Yet there is no indication that any stigma attached to playing an Indian. Indeed, the boys relished the role of the Indian—assumed by them all to be more barbarous and aggressive—as much as they did the role of the settler.[27] These settler-and-Indian games allowed boys to enter and imagine roles that were played by real adult males. Such imitative play was a vital part of boy culture, and there were a number of other popular activities that allowed even closer copying of adult men. Some towns, for instance, had junior militia companies just like the ones for grown-ups, and they often staged mock battles. Boys were also enthusiastic spectators at the militia musters for adults, and joined in the action if they could.

There were other settings in which boys could imitate men and even participate in their tasks. During the antebellum era, political parties pressed boys into service for their rallies and parades. Youngsters carried signs and torches and lit victory bonfires; they also generated a certain amount of unassigned activity, such as fighting with young supporters of the other party and lighting victory bonfires even when the opposition won.[28] The boys who lived in antebellum cities followed another exciting man's activity by attaching themselves to volunteer fire companies. Historians have written about the role that these companies played in the cultural life of the artisan and laboring classes.[29] But the work of the volunteer fire units was too dramatic for even the most privileged boys to ignore. Every neighborhood had a fire company and, when the cry of "Fire!" rang out, each one dragged its engine through the city streets and then pumped as hard as it could to play a stream of water on the fire as quickly as possible. The work was hard but stirring, and the competition between companies was so fierce that it sometimes led to violence. In short, the work of the volunteer fire companies contained almost every element needed to seize the imagination of a nineteenth-century boy.

Most boys took particular interest in imitating—or taking part in—the work of a specially admired man: their father. Opportunities to do this differed considerably for city and country lads. Rural youngsters, after all, lived in closer proximity to their fathers' work, and there was much greater need of their help. Even the businessmen and professionals of the small towns kept farms or farm animals for domestic use, and they needed to rely on menial labor from their sons.[30] On the other hand, affluent city boys were lucky if they could imitate any of their fathers' work activities. Not only were urban boys separated from the work world of their fathers, but most of those middle-class men did work that was too abstract to interest a youngster. Buying, selling, and keeping accounts were not activities that caught a boy's fancy.[31] Beneath this difference, though, lay the essential similarity of urban and rural boy culture, both in values and in purposes. Boys from both settings were drawn to activities that offered excitement and physical exercise. Dirt and noise were often by-products of such pastimes. And certain boys' activities provided special opportunity to enter and imagine the roles of adult males.

Above all, the pastimes favored by Northern boys set their world in sharp contrast to the domestic, female world—the world from which they emerged as little boys and to which they returned every evening. Where women's sphere offered kindness, morality, nurture, and a gentle spirit, the boys' world countered with energy, self-assertion, noise, and a frequent resort to violence. The physical explosiveness and the willingness to inflict pain contrasted so sharply with the values of the home that they suggest a dialogue in actions between the values of the two spheres—as if a boy's aggressive impulses, so relentlessly opposed at home, sought extreme forms of release outside it; then, with stricken consciences, the boys came home for further lessons in self-restraint. The two worlds seemed almost to thrive on their opposition to each

other. Boys, though they valued both worlds deeply, often complained
about the confinement of home. The world that they created just beyond the reach of domesticity gave them a space for expressive play and
a sense of freedom from the women's world that had nurtured them
early in boyhood—and that welcomed them home every night.

Boy Culture: Bonds and Fissures

The contrast between boy culture and the domestic sphere extended to
the nature and strength of the bonds that cemented each of those two
social worlds. The nineteenth-century home was held intact by love and
also by adult authority. Its primary purpose was nurture, and this tended
to draw its members together in emotional support and in common
bonds of conscience and self-sacrifice. By contrast, the world of boy culture was held intact by less enduring ties. The expressive play that gave
boy culture its focus was conducive to self-assertion and conflict more
than to love or understanding, and this led boys to create a different sort
of bond than that which held together the domestic world.

Friendship was certainly the most important relation between boys,
and within their world it took on some distinctive qualities. One writer
has said that, in boys' world, "friendships formed . . . which [were] fervent if not enduring."[32] Evidently, these fond but shifting ties had as
much to do with availability as with deeper affinities. An autobiographer,
describing his younger days in Connecticut, said that "in boyhood . . .
friendships are determined not more perhaps by similarity of disposition
and common likes and dislikes than by propinquity and accidental association."[33] Boys' friendships tended to be superficial and sudden, however passionate they might be for the moment.

Given the ephemeral nature of these bonds, it is not surprising that
the strongest and most enduring friendships were forged at home between brothers and cousins. Alphonso Rockwell, who grew up in New
Canaan, Connecticut, during the 1820s and 1830s, described the close
friendship between himself and his cousin Steve: "We were the same
age, and from our sixth to our sixteenth years we were constantly together. Hardly a day passed without our seeing each other."[34] Kin friendships like this one rose on a foundation of love and familiarity that already existed. Of course, a strong friendship could develop across family
lines, too. Henry Dwight Sedgwick and Lawrence Godkin, who were
cross-street neighbors in New York City during the 1860s and 1870s, enjoyed common activities and shared a deep antipathy to the "muckers"

from down the block. They remained devoted friends for several years, but Lawrence is most notable in Henry's autobiography for his steadfast loyalty in times of peril.[35] Good companionship and unshakable fidelity were the keys to friendship between boys, not confiding intimacy. Indeed, the consideration of loyalty was so important in the competitive milieu of boy culture that these youthful relationships often took on the qualities of an alliance.[36]

Loyalty also laid the basis for one of the great passions of nineteenth-century boys—the formation of clubs. Meeting in attics and cellars, these clubs ranged from a small-town cabal that specialized in melon theft to a natural history "museum" established by Theodore Roosevelt. Two common purposes of these boys' clubs were nurture and athletics. Fellow members raided local orchards and gardens, then they cooked and ate their booty together. Boys formed athletic groups that organized extensive competitions among members. The two purposes of nurture and competition were not mutually exclusive, either. One such club in a small Indiana town met in the attic of a local business building to eat pilfered melons and corn together. When the secret meal was finished, the boys retreated to a nearby woods to pummel each other in fierce boxing matches which ended "frequently in bloody noses, blackened eyes, and bruised bodies."[37] This club represented a curious mixture: affection joined with combat; mutual nurture combined with assault and battery. Such mingling of friendship with combat was typical of boy culture.

In point of fact, boy culture was divided as surely as it was united. Club memberships were always limited, which guaranteed the exclusion of some boys. For example, when Theodore Roosevelt started his natural history museum as a boy, he invited two of his cousins to join but pointedly excluded his brother, Elliott. Secret words and codes further isolated outsiders, even as they united those who belonged. Rivalry, division, and conflict were vital elements in the structure of boy culture. Just as friendship between boys bloomed suddenly and with fervor, so, too, did enmity. While good friends often enjoyed combat with each other, hand-to-hand battles did not always take place in a friendly context. Instant hostility frequently arose between boys and was "taken out on the spot," for the youngsters preferred to settle "a personal grievance at once, even if the explanation is made with fists."[38] New boys in town often had to prove themselves by fighting, and older boys amused themselves by forcing the younger boys into combat with each other.[39]

The fiercest fights of all involved youngsters from rival turf. Indeed, such "enemy" groups played a powerful role in unifying local segments of boy culture, and many boys' gangs were really just neighborhood alliances designed to protect members and turf from other gangs. In the countryside, these divisions pitted village against village or the boys from one side of town against boys from the other. In cities, lines were drawn between the youngsters of different neighborhoods. In a large, densely packed metropolis like New York, the crucial rivalries could even develop between boys at opposite ends of the block.[40] Sometimes these geographic battle lines reflected nothing more than the simple accident of residence; but they often coincided with sharp differences of class and ethnicity, adding extra layers of meaning to boyish antagonisms. Reflecting on his own boyhood, Henry Seidel Canby recalled the fierce hostility between Protestant boys from the comfortable neighborhoods of Wilmington, Delaware, and the Irish Catholic boys from the nearby slums. To reach their private schools every day, the youngsters from the "better" families had to cross through enemy turf and pass the public and parochial schools the Irish boys attended. Canby wrote: "Each of us, by one of those tacit agreements made between enemies, had his particular mick, who either chased or was chased . . . on sight. . . . It was an awful joy to spot your own mick."[41]

Social differences much less dramatic and vivid could also form the basis for animosity. Henry Dwight Sedgwick described the rivalry between the boys at the Fifth and Sixth avenue ends of New York's Forty-eighth Street in the years around 1870. Henry and the others who lived near Fifth Avenue knew that their houses were larger than those at the other end of the block and that their down-street neighbors had open-topped garbage cans which sat out in plain sight instead of under the stoop. Sedgwick and his friends were also aware of a less visible difference: "Our fathers' offices and places of business might have interests in common with the offices and places of business of their fathers, but our drawing-rooms, no. Our women folk could not call upon their women folk." At most, the difference between the two groups of Forty-eighth Street boys was the difference between various rungs of the middle class, but this contrast—highlighted by geography—was enough to set them against each other.[42]

While these differences of class and neighborhood carved the boys' world up into large segments, there were finer gradations within boy culture that produced fewer dramatic confrontations but occupied much more of a boy's daily attention. In particular, differences of size and skill became major preoccupations in boy culture. The distinction between bigger and smaller boys expressed itself in a variety of ways. Throughout the century and across the Northeast, bigger boys bullied smaller ones. In Wilmington, Delaware, this custom was so common that Henry Seidel Canby wrote: "Every little boy had a big boy who bullied him."[43]

Meanwhile, college and boarding school students during all parts of the century were carrying on that ritualized form of bullying known as haz- ing.[44] Smaller boys became victims in various kinds of organized games as well. They played the deserters and spies who were shot in games of soldier, and they were the riders who were knocked off their big-boy "horses" in one version of settlers-and-Indians.[45] In some activities, the distinction between age and size blurred: "little" and "young" usually meant the same thing with boys.

Among boys who were close together in age and size, another division existed—a series of informal rankings based on skill. They rated each other by weight, height, "pluck," spirit, appearance, and all sorts of ath- letic skills from swimming to stone-throwing to ability at various orga- nized games. The frequent fights between boys established a vitally im- portant kind of pecking order. Those urban boys who spent much of their time in school ranked each other's scholastic abilities on a finely graded scale. Although youngsters determined some of these ratings by open contest, they established many others through unceasing observa- tion.[46] While this constant process of comparison did not divide boy cul- ture as deeply as class and geography did, it did provide a basis for elab- orate, cross-cutting hierarchies within the group and set the stage for many personal jealousies and conflicts.[47]

In fact, the boys' world was endlessly divided and subdivided. Clearly set apart from the worlds of men, of very small boys, and of the entire female sex, the realm of boyhood was split into groups by residence, eth- nicity, and social status. These chunks of boys' world were ordered inter- nally by a shifting series of competitive rankings. Personal animosity cre- ated further division. Linking boys across these many fissures were fam- ily ties and the loyalty of friendship. But friendships among boys were volatile affairs—intense, short-lived, and constantly shifting. To a great extent, then, boys' realm was—like the grown-up world of their fa- thers—based on the isolated individual. Although it was a little culture based on constant play and full of exuberance and high spirits, it was also a cruel, competitive, uncertain, and even violent world. How, then, did it hold together? It held together because boys adhered faithfully to a common set of values.

The Values of Boy Culture

Boy culture embraced two different sorts of values. First, there were ex- plicit values, those traits and behaviors that boys openly respected in one another. Then there were implicit values embedded in the structure of boy culture, values youngsters rarely expressed but which they honored constantly through their daily activities and experiences. Both of these layers of value added to the distinctiveness of boy culture, and both formed a part of the legacy of boy culture by leaving a permanent imprint on youngsters' characters.

Boys revealed many of their values in the activities they pursued. In a world that centered on physical play, bodily attributes and physical prowess loomed large. Traits such as size, strength, speed, and endurance earned a boy respect among his peers.[48] More subtle but just as highly valued was the gift of courage. One writer on boyhood called courage "the ethics for ideal conduct in emotional stress," and for most boys behavior under physical stress was just as important.[49] Moments of bravery fell into two different categories, stoicism and daring. Stoicism involved the suppression of "weak" or "tender" feelings that were readily exposed in the feminine world of home—grief, fear, pain. The boys' game of "soak-about" was a classic expression of the demand for stoicism. In this game, a group of boys tried to hit another boy with a hard ball in any vulnerable spot that was available.[50] The victim could not cry out if he was hit—and, just as important, the youngster had to face the possibility of such pain without flinching.

Boys valued the ability to suppress displays of fear as well as of pain. When young Alphonso Rockwell and his cousin Steve were surrounded by five menacing rivals, "it was unquestionably a fact that we were scared." Rockwell remembered that his reaction then was the same as it was many times during his service in the Civil War—"to seem not to fear when I was really very much afraid." Instead of showing fear, young Rockwell's soldierly response was to pick up a stick with one hand and clench the other into a fist. The rival group backed down.[51] This stoic courage, a feat of self-control, contrasted sharply with daring courage, which was an achievement of action.

Like stoicism, daring found ritual expression in boys' games. In the contest called "I Conquer," a boy performed a dangerous feat and as he did so shouted the name of the game to his comrades. The cry challenged the other boys to duplicate the feat or lose the game.[52] Lew Wallace remembered the boyhood compulsion to dare, noting that he and his friends were "given to [this] 'dare' habit; . . . the deeper the water, the thinner the ice, the longer the run, the hotter the blaze, [then] the more certain [was] the challenge."[53] These experiences with the courage of daring may have left a lasting imprint on the boys who underwent them. A number of historians and commentators have noted that the ideal of achievement which grown-ups taught to boys was really the cautious, abstemious ethic of the clerk, rather than the bold and daring code of the entrepreneur.[54] Young males did not learn to be venturesome from the adults who preached hard work and self-denial, but from boy culture with its constant pressure for daring courage. Boldness, like stoicism, was a form of courage that youngsters cultivated in boyhood.

Physical prowess and the various forms of courage were uppermost among the qualities that boys valued, but there were also others that they expected of each other. Boys demanded loyalty between friends and loyalty of the individual to the group. Their concept of the faithful friend closely resembled the code of fidelity that links comrades at arms. The true test of this loyalty came at moments when one boy was threatened and the other came to his aid. When an Ohio boy named Frank Beard was in his early teens, he rose to the defense of his cousin and took a thrashing from a much older youth who was larger and stronger than he. This was the ultimate act of loyalty to a friend.[55] Loyalty to the group expressed itself in dealings with outsiders. When boys banded together to defend their turf against rival groups from other towns or neighborhoods, they were performing a vital act of group loyalty.[56] The clubs that boys often formed were also based on loyalty to other members of the club and to its codes and secrets.[57]

There was another group of outsiders to whom boys responded with an exclusive sense of group loyalty—grown-ups. One of boy culture's basic taboos prohibited youngsters from appealing to any adult for help and even from revealing information that would compromise their independent activity. If a boy violated this sanction, his peers repaid him with scorn and abuse. To be labeled a "crybaby" was one of the worst fates for an inhabitant of boy culture.[58]

Together with courage and physical prowess, loyalty was one of the most valued of qualities among boys—and it was the one that they demanded most fiercely of each other. Beneath this layer of values that boys honored consciously, however, there was another layer that developed from the habits and activities of boy culture. The youngsters themselves rarely discussed these implicit values—it seems that they lay just outside of boys' consciousness—but the boys learned some of their most important childhood lessons by learning to practice these valued traits and habits.

Of these implied values, the one that was most pervasive in boy culture was mastery. For one thing, youngsters were constantly learning to master new skills. The boys' many games and pastimes helped them develop a great variety of physical abilities. They also learned a wide range of social skills from their intensive social contact with each other and from the negotiations that threaded in and out of their daily round of activity. Boys' experience in their separate world likewise taught them how to impose their will on other people and on nature itself. Their education in social mastery went on constantly while they were among their peers. Most of their popular pastimes forced boys to seek each other's defeat and thus prove individual mastery. At another level, boys strove for mastery by trying to set the agenda for their group of comrades ("dare" games like "I Conquer" were an extreme version of this impulse). Some boys practiced mastery through bullying.

Boys' attempts to master their environment were often directed at the physical rather than the social world. In a world where people no longer relied on hunting and fishing to feed themselves, the killing of animals taught boys the habit of dominion over their natural environment. Furthermore, there were city boys who hunted to enlarge their collection of stuffed and mounted animals. From this pastime, boys learned to subordinate nature to their own acquisitive impulses. When they named and classified the animals they killed, boys were learning to make nature serve the cause of scientific advance. Other forms of boyhood mastery fed on this same technological drive. The building of toy ships that would actually float, the construction of snow forts, the performance of crude scientific experiments—these common boyhood activities taught youngsters the skills (and the habit) of mastery over nature in the service of human needs and knowledge. The experience of boy culture encouraged a male child to become the master, the conqueror, the owner of what was outside him.

At the same time, boyhood experiences were teaching a youngster to master his inner world of emotions. Games like "soak-about" taught boys to control their fears and to carry on in the face of physical pain. Peer pressure also forced them to control those "weak" feelings, as the fear of being labeled a "crybaby" restrained the impulse to seek comfort in times of stress. As boys learned to master pain, fear, and the need for emotional comfort, they were encouraged to suppress other expressions of vulnerability, such as grief and tender affection. Boy culture, then, was teaching a selective form of impulse control—it was training boys to master those emotions that would make them vulnerable to predatory rivals.

Their activities not only put a premium on self-control, but also created an endless round of competitions. Even activities that were not inherently competitive—swimming, climbing, rock-throwing—yielded countless comparisons. Youngsters were learning to rank their peers, and at the same time they developed the habit of constantly struggling up the ladder of achievement. Moreover, as each boy asserted his will incessantly against the others, he grew accustomed to life as a never-ending series of individual combats.

This environment existed in part because boy culture sanctioned certain kinds of impulses. Even as it curbed the expression of tender, vulnerable emotions, boy culture stimulated aggression and encouraged youngsters to vent their physical energy. The prevailing ethos of boys' world not only supported the expression of impulses such as dominance and aggression (which had evident social uses), but also allowed the release of hostile, violent feelings (whose social uses were less evident). By allowing free passage to so many angry or destructive emotions, boy culture sanctioned a good deal of intentional cruelty, like the physical torture of animals and the emotional violence of bullying. Yet much of the cruelty in boys' world was spontaneous and impulsive: as boys' aggressions were given free rein, the sheer exuberance of exercise and the pure joy of play prevailed, and needless cruelty and unthinking meanness often followed. Boys loved to compare themselves to animals, and two animal similes seem apt here. If at times boys acted like a hostile pack of wolves that preyed on its own kind as well as other species, they behaved at other times like a litter of playful pups who enjoy romping, wrestling, and testing new skills. Such play is rarely free of cruelty or violence, and the same can be said of boy culture. Playful spontaneity bred friendly play and rough hostility in equal measure.

The violence that friends inflicted on each other often signified more than the playful assertion of dominance or the unbridled expression of hostility; ironically, some of boys' violence was an expression of their fondness for each other. Since boys worked to restrain their tender impulses in each other's presence, they lacked a direct outlet for the natural affection between friends. This warm feeling sometimes found expression in the bonds of the club and the gang and in the demanding codes of loyalty that bound young comrades together, but another avenue of release for these fond impulses came through constant physical exchanges. Samuel Crothers described boys' world as a place "where the heroes make friends with one another by indulging in everlasting assault and battery, and continually arise 'refreshed with the blows.'"[59] Seen in this light, the boys' stoning of arriving and departing friends in William Dean Howells's hometown becomes a perversely affectionate form of salute. This curious marriage of violence and affection also found ritual expression in the small-town club where the boys fed each other and then beat each other bloody in boxing matches.[60]

The fact that boys expressed affection through mayhem does not mean that violence was merely a channel for fond feeling. Boys held back their deepest reserves of cruelty when they scrapped with friends, saving their fiercest fury for enemies. In their cultural world, where gestures of tenderness were forbidden, physical combat allowed them moments of touch and bouts of intense embrace. By a certain "boy logic," it made sense to pay their affections in the coin of physical combat that served as the social currency of boys' world.

Self-assertion and conflict, in other words, were such dominant modes of expression within boy culture that they could even serve as vehicles for tender feelings. Yet even these were not the most important values of boy culture. There was one value that governed all conduct, that provided a common thread for boys' activities together, that served as boy culture's virtual reason for being. This ultimate value was independence. What made boy culture special in a youngster's experience was that it allowed him a kind of autonomy that he had not enjoyed in early childhood. It gave him an independence that he did not have in any other area of life.

The experience of boy culture did more than simply teach boys to value independence, though. It also taught them how to use it. Boy culture challenged a youngster to master an immense variety of skills; forced him to learn elaborate codes of behavior and complex, layered systems of value; encouraged him to form enjoyable relationships and useful alliances and to organize groups that could function effectively; and demanded that he deal with the vicissitudes of competition and the constant ranking and evaluation of peers. Most of all, the culture of his fellows required a boy to learn all of these tasks independently—without the help of caring adults, with limited assistance from other boys, and without any significant emotional support. At the heart of nineteenth-century boy culture, then, lay an imperative to independent action. Each boy sought his own good in a world of shifting alliances and fierce competition. He learned to assert himself and to stand emotionally alone while away from his family. For the part of each day that he lived among his peers, a boy received a strenuous education in autonomy.

Boy Culture and Adult Authority

One of boy culture's most striking features was its independence from close adult supervision. This autonomy existed, however, within well-defined boundaries of place and time. Many adults tried to influence what went on within boy culture even though they did not supervise it.

In order to understand boys' world fully we need to understand certain problems that arose at its boundaries: how boys tried to maintain the boundaries; who tried to penetrate them; and how that penetration— when it did happen—affected boy culture.

Of all the forces that threatened the borders of boy culture, the most pervasive was the community at large. The confrontations between youngsters and their communities came usually over minor acts of vandalism. The reasons for these social collisions varied. Acts of trespass and petty theft often grew out of the blithe disregard that boys had for private property. They refused to recognize the lines that separated one adult's possessions from another's.[61] At other times, it was the very knowledge of possible trouble with adults that led to vandalism. Boys, after all, were constantly daring each other to perform dangerous acts. And since a confrontation with authority was one kind of danger, risking that confrontation was a way to prove one's bravery.[62] Thus, the pleasure in raiding a garden or an orchard came from the adventure as much as the fruit, and youthful mischief-makers made a sport of avoiding officers of the law and irate property owners.

Sometimes an angry private citizen took it upon himself to fight petty youth crime in his community, but doing so made him a handsome target for another form of boyish malfeasance—the prank. One Ohio man—a "strait-laced Presbyterian farmer . . . who often rebuked the boys for their escapades"—paid for his opposition to vandalism when he found a ghastly battered corpse in his barn one morning. Although a frightened inspection showed that the corpse was a carefully prepared dummy, the episode had given the local boys an effective way to express their resentment of the farmer.[63]

Pranks, however, were more than just acts of vengeance. They reversed men's and boy's roles, giving younger males the power to disrupt the lives of older males and forcing the elders to do their boyish bidding. There was, for example, a Connecticut doctor who made a favorite target for the local boys. The "queerest man of the town," he had only one eye, spoke in a high falsetto, and possessed the strange habit of dismounting from his horse every time he saw a stone in the road. This made him an easy victim for pranks, as the boys scattered stones in his path and then watched with delight as he got off his horse to throw them away. The boys had found an exciting way to attack the dignity of an adult.[64]

Pranks resembled petty theft, trespassing, and other forms of vandalism in that they served as skirmishes in a kind of guerrilla warfare that boys waged against the adult world. These youthful raids on adult dignity and property gave boys a chance to assert their own needs and values and lay their claim to the out-of-doors as a world for them to use as they saw fit. Acts of vandalism also provided boys with an opportunity to express their hostility toward adult authority—in other words, toward most grown-up men. It was the men (police, constables, irate property owners) who stood in the way of most boys' adventures.[65] Finally, the guerrilla warfare of pranks and petty theft gave boys a moment of power to foil the intentions of grown men and to gain the property they wanted. Vandalism represented a statement of hostility and resentment by the males of one generation against the males of another, and it served also as an assertion of the needs and values of boy culture against the needs and values of adult (male) authority. Grown men could rarely control vandalism—they could only oppose it enough to make it a more exciting pastime for boys.

Neighbors, teachers, and lawmen fought countless skirmishes with the more troublesome boys of the community. Yet if an enemy of boy culture was one who tried to thwart youthful pleasure or who could compel a boy to do something against his will, then its most potent enemies were fathers and mothers. Parents provided a very different sort of enemy from distant figures of authority. Remote adults could be irked at little emotional cost, but parents were (usually) the two most beloved and powerful people in a boy's life. How did boy culture fare in its conflicts with parents? What happened when the borders of home and boys' world overlapped or the values of those two spheres conflicted?

The situation of fathers presents a simpler picture than that of mothers. Middle-class men had fewer points of contact than their wives did with the boy culture of their sons. While the activities of boys often swirled through the yard and into isolated corners of the home, they rarely approached the offices and counting houses where men spent their days.[66] Of course, fathers did intrude into the world of boy culture. In rural areas, a boy was expected to work on behalf of the family even if his father was a prominent lawyer, storekeeper, or politician. Boys might work at home or elsewhere, but it was fathers who arranged the work, and most fathers oversaw it, punishing failures of duty.[67] Fathers also frustrated boy culture by serving as head disciplinarians in their families. They were responsible for punishing the most serious breaches of household rules and, as a result, usually meted out the harshest discipline. For example, when Lew Wallace, the future novelist and Civil War hero, was banished from his Indiana home after long years of truancy and misbehavior, it was his father, not his mother, who banished him. The father also had the duty of punishing his son when someone from outside the home complained about the boy's behavior. For instance, when a Maine boy named John Barnard was caught stealing fruit from a neighbor's orchard, it was his father who sat him down for a stern lecture.[68] These intrusive duties placed the father in the role of arch-enemy to the hedonism that typified boy culture.

But fathers and other men were only the most visible enemies of boy culture, not the most effective ones. In the role of mother, women had more extensive contact with boys than their husbands did. And it was the mothers—not the fathers—who had the duty of responding immediately to situations that arose in the daily ebb and flow of family life. Women were also more effective opponents of boy culture because of their methods of opposition. They relied less than men on bluster or physical punishment and more on tenderness, guilt, and moral suasion—tactics that seemed to disarm the youthful opposition more effectively than a simple show of power. These contrasts between men's and women's tactics grew partly from the difference in their basic social duty toward boys: men were charged especially with the task of maintaining good order; women were supposed to go beyond that and make boys fit for the sober, responsible world of adults. To be sure, young Daniel Beard and his friends spoke from experience in declaring men as the "enemies of boys, always interfering with our pleasure." But Huck Finn saw deeper when he proclaimed that Aunt Sally wanted to "sivilize" him.[69]

Inevitably, then, the home and the out-of-doors came to stand for much more than just two physical spaces for women and boys—the domestic threshold marked a cultural dividing line of the deepest significance. On one side lay women's sphere, a world of domesticity and civilization; on the other side, boy culture flourished and adult control gave way to the rough pleasures of boyhood. Neither space was exclusive—women entered boys' world to deliver reprimands and reminders of duties at home, while boys sometimes established their distinctive culture in the nether regions of the household. But the home and the out-of-doors had powerful symbolic meaning. When boys tracked mud and dirt across clean floors, they did more than create extra housework—they violated the separation of spheres by bringing fragments of their boy-world into a place where they did not belong. And mothers also viewed their sons' priceless collections of rocks, leaves, and dead animals as invasions of a civilized world by a wild one. Thus, women and boys fought constantly over muddy footprints and other relics of the outdoors that found their way into the house.[70]

But mothers did not just struggle to keep the dirt and hedonism of boy culture out of the house. They also fought to extend their moral dominion into boys' world. Fortunately for women, they had more than one tactical weapon to use in this battle for moral influence. Often mothers attempted to control behavior by maintaining close contact with boy culture. The women who lived in small towns—and in all but the largest of cities—were members of social networks that sent information about their sons back to them quickly. Since they tended to run their errands in the same neighborhoods where their boys played, mothers could even conduct occasional surveillance of boy culture.[71] Most women were able to influence their sons' activities in the world outside the home. For example, mothers often played a direct and active role in curbing the physical violence of boy culture. Mary Howells punished her son William when she caught him fighting. He reported in later years that it was the influence of mothers which sometimes forced the boys to use buckshot instead of bullets in their hunting guns.[72] In a similar vein, mothers kept their sons away from impending "boy-battles" when they had advance knowledge of such events.

Women had other avenues of influence besides immediate surveillance and response. Their moral and spiritual authority seemed immense to their sons. Edward Everett Hale referred reverently to his mother's moral lessons as her "gospels." Ray Stannard Baker, a journalist who grew up in Wisconsin, remembered his aunts' religious teachings with less affection. He described these women, who had raised him in place of his invalid mother, as "veritable gorgons of the faith. They knew all of the shalt-nots in the Bible." He summarized their moral instruction as: "You mustn't, you can't. Remember the Sabbath day."[73]

The dire warnings against boyish behavior, though, came not just from the word of God or even from a mother's pleadings. Most of all, they came from the voice of conscience, that "tyrannical monitor" that condemned in a boy's heart every violation of the moral code he learned at his mother's knee. Daniel Beard, for one, felt this inner influence. His heart sank when his mother told him to stay away from the place where his friends were going to battle the boys from the next town. "This was bad news," wrote Beard, "but I never thought of disobeying her." So confident was Mary Beard of her influence over Daniel that she made no attempt to keep him at home. At the appointed hour, he wandered to a spot overlooking the scene of battle: "I stood disconsolately on the suspension bridge and watched my playmates, feeling like a base deserter." Beard's conscience held fast; with no one there to restrain him, he smothered his own urge to run to the aid of his comrades.[74]

There were other boys like Daniel Beard who loved to plunge into

the endless tumult of boys' world but who were held in check by their
own consciences. Lew Wallace's habit of truancy from school was restrained only by "the thought of [his] mother's fears" and his memory of
her "entreaties and tears."[75] Clearly, mothers had an immense influence
which extended beyond their physical presence and stretched as far as a
boy could roam. Yet, as the Wallace example shows, maternal influence
could not halt the operation of the wayward impulses that drove boy culture—it could only curb them. Boys, in other words, could not subdue
their surging desires. They were pulled one way by the power of impulse
and tugged another way by the voice of conscience.

In this struggle, the pressures of boy culture supplied a powerful counterforce to maternal influence. The worst fate a youngster could suffer at
the hands of his peers was to be labeled a "mama's boy." One man wrote
that "the most wicked and wanton song I knew [as a boy] was":

> *Does your mother know you're out?*
> *No, by thunder, no, by thunder!*
> *Does she know what you're about?*
> *No, by thunder, no, by thunder!*

The boys especially liked to sing this song as they performed feats of
daring. The implication was that a mother's control was powerful—but it
was delightful to slip beyond her grasp into forbidden pleasures.[76]

A vignette from a midcentury etiquette book suggests the ubiquitous
influence of peer values on boys. As a mother earnestly tries to tie a rib-
bon in her son's collar, he complains that "the boys'll call me 'dandy,' and
'band-box,' and 'Tom Apronstring.'" The author of the book replies that
Cousin Horace (the local paragon of good manners) "plays very heartily,
too . . . he is no 'girl-boy.'" Even mothers knew the pressures that boys
exerted on each other to ignore maternal pleas and abide by the standards of boy culture. It was a painful insult when a boy was accused
of being tied to maternal apron strings or was reduced to the early-
childhood status of "girl-boy."[77]

Such potent ridicule gave boys a powerful weapon for forcing others
to reject their mothers' influence and conform to the hedonistic norms
of their own cultural world. Under this kind of pressure, boys did much
more than refuse to wear ribbons in their collars. Henry Seidel Canby
remembered from his childhood that "breaking windows on Hallow
E'en, swearing, pasting a cow with rotten eggs, or lining the horsecar
tracks with caps to make the spavined horses run down grade, were
protests against being 'goody goody.'" Daniel Beard and his friends

scorned boys who "never went barefoot, . . . wasted a lot of time talking to girls, took no hikes, bathed often but seldom went swimming, won prizes at Sunday school but never on the ball field, and bought kites instead of making them."[78] Clearly, boys had a fine-tuned sense of who behaved acceptably and who did not, and nearly all of the unacceptable behaviors were ones encouraged by mothers. Boys employed ridicule, ostracism, and hazing to defend the values and integrity of boy culture from maternal assault.[79]

The boys' world was a culture governed by shame. Male youngsters were constantly watched by the eyes of their youthful community. If they violated the rules of their subculture, boys were subject to name-calling, scornful teasing, and even separation from the group. The threat of such painful treatment usually kept boys in line while they were together. But once away from the presence of their group, boys found it easier to follow along with domestic values. Of course, they misbehaved at home, too, but that was in response to their own impulses, not because of what the other boys would want them to do. Accounts of nineteenth-century boyhood show absolutely no evidence that boy culture affected youthful male behavior at home (unless, of course, it was a matter like dress that would in due time become *visible* to other boys). By contrast, the inner controls implanted largely by women were those of guilt. Boys carried the influence of maternal values out into their own world. Their consciences, as we have seen, made them feel guilty at some of their boyish misdeeds and held them back from committing others. Thus, women's sphere and boy culture differed sharply in the way they exercised social control. In this control, as in so many other aspects of values and behavior, the two different social spaces represented two divergent approaches to life.

Some of the most important lessons that a youngster learned from his experience of boy culture were the lessons about living a life divided between two spheres. He adapted to a constant process of home-leaving and return. And he quickly discovered that this process meant more than just a physical change of scene. It meant a constant adjustment to the clashing values and demands of two different worlds—back and forth from a domestic world of mutual dependence to a public world of independence; from an atmosphere of cooperation and nurture to one of competition and conflict; from a sphere where intimacy was encouraged to one where human relationships were treated instrumentally; from an environment that supported affectionate impulses to one that sanctioned aggressive impulses; from a social space that was seen as female to another that was considered male. At the same time that a boy learned to live in a world divided, he was also learning to live with divided loyalties and a divided heart. It was a conflict that would form a basic part of life for middle-class men.

Outgrowing Boy Culture

Boys defended the boundaries of their world zealously. They waged hit-and-run warfare against adults who tried to stifle their pleasures, and they harassed without mercy those boys who called on grown-ups to intervene in their affairs. But there was one boundary that they could not protect—the boundary of age that separated boyhood from manhood. In time, all boys grew up.

The end of boyhood in the nineteenth century did not come as it comes in the twentieth. There was no sequence of events that marked the progress of boys from childhood to manhood, and there were no key ages at which all youngsters reached important milestones. In earlier times, apprenticeship had marked an end of sorts to the boyhood years (though even the ages of apprenticeship might be indefinite). In the nineteenth century, the ages and events that brought boyhood to a close varied sharply with family and personal circumstances.[80]

In spite of these vague age boundaries, there were a few important events that marked the end of boyhood for many youngsters. These often had to do with leaving home or taking a first clerkship or full-time job. One dramatic example comes from the experience of Lew Wallace. When Lew was in his midteens, his father brought his carefree years of rambling and truancy to an end by turning him out of the house to support himself. Lew took on a clerical job, and, while working at it, conceived the literary ambitions that formed part of his work in manhood.[81] Alphonso Rockwell's boyhood also ended with the start of a clerkship, though his departure from home was more amicable than Wallace's— and in that sense was more typical. Looking back from old age, Rockwell realized that his boyhood stopped on the day he left his home in Connecticut to take his new position in New York City:

> The ties that held me to boyhood days and pleasures along old and familiar lines were to be broken forever. Henceforth there were to be no more trips to "Indian Rock" in the company of boy intimates, where we imagined ourselves wild Indians . . . nor would I ever in the days to come sail [the familiar ponds and streams], or swim in them, or walk their banks with the zest or sense of pleasure I had known.[82]

Alphonso was assuming new statuses now—self-support, a home away from his family—which were acknowledged as distinctive marks of manhood.

But these were not the only changes that signified the end of boyhood. A teenager also brought his time in boy culture to a close when he took his first strides toward another signpost of manhood—marriage. The journey toward marriage began with the dawning interest of pubescent boys in the opposite sex.[83] As boys developed an interest in girls, the customs and habits of boy culture started to lose their luster. Daniel Beard recalled in his autobiography the ways in which his outlook changed when an attractive new girl arrived in town: "Suddenly marbles became a childish game which made knuckles grimy and chapped. . . . Prisoner's base was good enough sport but it mussed one's clothes." The rhymes and rituals of boyhood now "seemed absurd instead of natural" while the services at church took on a new interest. Daniel suddenly began to appear in public with his face clean and his hair neatly combed.[84]

The pubescent boy did not, of course, return to the gowns and petticoats of his earliest years, but he did compromise with the demands of domesticity and restraint. He accepted willingly the confinement of clothing that had once seemed like shackles, and he wiped the once-treasured grime of outdoor activity from his face and hands. As he took his first steps toward marriage, a life's work, and a home of his own, he clothed himself in the garb of "civilized" manhood and washed off the marks of "savage" boyhood.[85]

The cares and commitments of manhood now loomed up before teenage boys. At first sight, boys approached manhood eagerly; they were impatient to leave behind them the separate world that they had guarded so jealously. For example, when Alphonso Rockwell left his home in Connecticut to start his first clerkship, he did not reflect on the pleasures of boyhood (as he would in later years). Instead, he felt that he "was taking a step up in the world." Swelling with the sense of his own growing importance, he told his carriage driver on the day that he left home to drive fast, "as it would not do for me to miss the train . . . I [have] an important engagement to meet in New York."[86]

Charles Dudley Warner's observations on the end of boyhood ran parallel to those of Rockwell. He, too, was nostalgic about boyhood later in life, complaining that "just as you get used to being a boy, you have to be something else, with a good deal more work to do and not half as much fun." Yet Warner was quick to admit that "every boy is anxious to be a man, and is very uneasy with the restrictions that are put upon him as a boy." Warner also pointed out that, as much as boys liked to "play work," most would gladly trade it for a chance to do "real work"—that is, a man's work. As we noted earlier, some boy-culture pastimes imitated men's activity or offered direct (if token) participation in the work of male adults.[87] Yet, there were important disjunctions between boys' world and the world of men, gaps of duty and expectation that loomed like chasms before a teenage youth. The experience of facing those gaps and then trying to bridge them produced one of the most trying times in the lives of nineteenth-century men: the treacherous and often prolonged passage from boyhood to manhood.

The contrasts between boy culture and the world of men were sharp ones: boy culture emphasized exuberant spontaneity; it allowed free rein to aggressive impulses and reveled in physical prowess and assertion. Boy culture was a world of play, a social space where one evaded the duties and restrictions of adult society. How different this was from the world of manhood. Men were quiet and sober, for theirs was a life of serious business. They had families to support, reputations to earn, responsibilities to meet. Their world was based on work, not play, and their survival in it depended on patient planning, not spontaneous impulse. To prosper, then, a man had to delay gratification and restrain desire. Of course, he also needed to be aggressive and competitive, and he needed an instinct for self-advancement. But he had to channel these assertive impulses in ways that were suitable to the abstract battles and complex issues of middle-class men's work. Finally, a man—unlike a boy—needed a sense of responsible commitment. He could not throw over his family, disregard his business partners, or quit his job on a whim. A man had to have a sense of duty based on enduring loyalty, not on the strongest impulse of the moment. Manhood presented a young male with challenges for which boy culture had not fully prepared him. With the leap from boyhood to adulthood, a young man gave up heedless play for sober responsibility.

The strain of transition from boy culture to the world of men—coming simultaneously with the painful experience of leaving home—created a stressful and uncertain phase of life. Starting usually in the middle to late teens, a boy (often called a youth by now) struggled to make the transition on his own. There was no rite of passage to help him through. Society left him largely on his own to find his way to an adult identity.

Chapter 3

MALE YOUTH CULTURE

I N the life of the nineteenth-century male, the time of transition from boyhood to manhood was variable in length and loose in the definition of its boundaries. This period of flux, when it received any name at all, was called youth. It began in a boy's teens and lasted until his twenties or even thirties. In youth, a young male might engage in a variety of activities, ranging from education to on-the-job training to menial labor, that prepared him for adult responsibility or gave him a chance to mark time while he chose a course for the future. During this transitional phase, young males lived in settings that ranged from boardinghouses to college dormitories to their own family homes, and they often shuttled back and forth between these settings. A leading historian has aptly called this a period of "semidependence," since a youth's relation to his family was ambiguous and—in some cases—frequently shifting.[1]

Between the Past and the Future

Youth, in general, was ill-defined. Boyhood and manhood, with their clashing demands and their differing styles of behavior, mixed awkwardly. A young man had no standard pattern by which to chart his course through this phase of life, but he did share with his male peers a common set of personal issues that needed to be resolved. These issues reflected the transitional nature of this time of life in the way that they fell into two groups: those that connected to the youth's past and those that concerned his future.

While the circumstances of daily life forced a young man to focus on his future, his inward attention often drifted toward the commitments of his past, and especially toward his attachment to home. He had to loosen that attachment, but to do so was not a simple matter. Leaving home meant much more than sleeping under a different roof and minding one's own money. It meant turning away from a world cloaked in an aura of love, piety, nurture, and dependence; it meant separation from confining moral and spiritual influences; and it meant setting out from a female realm to join a male one. This complex change created many crosscurrents of feeling.

To leave behind a familiar world for a world unknown can be trying under any circumstances, but this departure became more difficult in the 1800s than it had been in the previous century. The known realm of home was now separated from the unknown world of men by a vast, growing gulf of symbolism and beliefs. The actual connection between home and the "world beyond" was looser than it had been in the 1700s. A boy from a family of status in the eighteenth century had left home to work or study among relatives and family friends. As the old ties of community and extended kin weakened in the nineteenth century, however, going out into the world was more likely to mean separation from familiar places and people.[2]

The painful difficulties of the break from home were evident in young men's letters and diaries. Homesickness suddenly became a common topic of discussion in the nineteenth century. The word did not enter the English language until the late eighteenth century, and it did not appear in any of the source materials studied here until 1806. Then, within a few years, comments like "I begin to feel homesick" and "I am a little homesick" became commonplace.[3]

Countless letters and diaries describe young men's separation from home, sorting motives and analyzing feelings. Theodore Russell, a Massachusetts youth, wrote to his sister in 1835 that he was puzzled by the willingness of young men like himself to leave "the warm and devoted friendship" of home for the "cold and heartless applause which is . . . [the best] that can . . . await us in the world." Three years later, when Russell was about to set forth into the world as a lawyer, he again felt caught between personal ambition and the backward pull of boyhood. "I can almost wish," he wrote, "to throw aside the energies of man, the soul stirring scenes of later years, the hope, the cares, the joys, the realities of manhood, again to pass into the sweet dreamy times of boyhood's romance." But Russell resisted this wish, for he believed that self-assertion was natural and manly. "Man," he wrote, "is made for action, and the bustling scenes of moving life, and not the poetry or romance of existence. I am willing, I am earnest, to launch forth into the world." Within a few years, Russell had risen to political and legal prominence in Boston.[4]

When he discussed young men's conflicted feelings about leaving home, Theodore Russell cast the issue as a struggle between attachment and worldly ambition. But the conflict raged at other levels as well. In the moral symbolism of the time, home was sacred. It was the place where a boy's piety and virtue were cultivated, and it was seen as his chief source of warmth and security.[5] Yet, in symbolism and in personal experience, the domestic realm meant restraint, dependence, confinement, and submission for a young man.

Breaking away from home stirred deep feelings of ambivalence. John Barnard, a native of Maine, described the immobility that plagued him from his teens to his early thirties in these terms:

> Two forces act upon me with equal power[:] the centripetal—which draws me towards my father and mother and friends—the centrifugal which acts as a repellant and drives me to seek wealth and distinction in foreign lands[;] these forces being at present equal hold me stationary at a fixed distance from home[,] nor can I tell which way I may be precipitated.[6]

Eventually, Barnard compromised by seeking wealth and distinction near his family and friends in Maine. But his tortuous indecision of more than a decade had made youth a painful time of life. He was caught between the pull of his past and the lure of his future.

Seeking a Future

As a young man tried to shake free from the powerful grip of his past, he faced a host of problems in determining his future. Economic uncertainty, moral qualms, inner restlessness, and the vague requirements of entry into middle-class occupations all created potential problems during youth. But the greatest concern of young men facing the future was the quest for commitment in two fundamental arenas of life: love and work.

Young men wrote to each other constantly about their attempts to attract feminine attention and about their hopes and fears regarding married life. In particular, they shared feelings of sadness and defeat when rejected by the young women they pursued. As they were tossed between elation and despair, young men were often shaken by a sense of vulnerability. At one lull in his romantic life, Daniel Webster asked a friend to "forget all the weakness and vanity" exposed in him by the "unreserved intimacy" of a recent love affair. Young men's feelings about themselves and their future were threatened by the pursuit of love and marriage.[7]

The other key to men's self-esteem and social identity was their work. Here, too, youth was a time of turmoil and uncertainty. As Rutherford B. Hayes wrote during his college years, his profession would be "the passport ... to all that I am destined to receive in life." With so much at stake, young men wrote avidly about their careers—choosing them, entering them, succeeding and failing at them. Much of the anxiety provoked by this choice grew out of a fear of failure. Here is how young M. S. Bailey felt in 1880 when he first tried his talents as a lawyer: "If I had confidence in myself to make a comparative success then I could live on ... with no fears for the future, but as it is I am in continual doubt and full of misgivings." And yet, in the very same letter, Bailey wrote of his adopted Colorado: "I am already filled with visions of riches. ... Here is a vast field for workers and vast amounts of money to be gotten ... I shall work and work to win." Bailey's fears, his doubts, and his determination were all typical at this point in his life, and he vacillated wildly among them.[8]

At the same time that his feelings and his deepest commitments were in flux, a young man was confronted by uncertainty in other crucial aspects of life. For instance, a youth who sought a place in the professions or the upper ranks of business was confronted by a loose, eccentric set of entrance requirements. If he aspired to the professions, a college education might prove helpful. But academy learning could suit him well enough, and a humble education in a village schoolhouse might be sufficient for a youth of talent and ambition. By custom, the final step toward the law, medicine, or the ministry was a period of study or apprenticeship with a member of the profession, but there were men who became professionals simply by hanging out a shingle. The route into the upper ranks of commerce involved even less formal education than that required of a future professional, though some sort of clerical apprenticeship was usual. The upward path in manufacturing was even less clearly defined. Success might reward the man with little formal education but long experience in a particular mode of production.[9]

Even these descriptions of the uncertain routes to middle-class success make the experience of the nineteenth-century youth appear more fixed and certain than it really was. Some young men, for instance, embarked on their life's work before they were twenty, while others did not commit themselves to professional preparation until they were nearly thirty. The pursuit of success might be stalled by any one of a number of factors. Some young men interrupted their educations to help support their parents; some were frozen by indecision in choosing a career, or changed occupations after the initial choice. Many youths marked time by teaching school; other restless young men strayed further from middle-class work, finding employment as sailors, riverboatmen, or cowhands, or even roamed from place to place, searching for any work they could find.[10] These unsettled ways of living could provide excitement, but they could also leave a youth frustrated and despondent. Aaron Olmstead, a young New Yorker, received a letter from his sister about a restless friend who traveled the country looking for a job:

> He has been all through N.Y. Ohio Indiana Illinois pretty thoroughly—went down the river as far as New Orleans, and then wended his way towards home going from one place to another in hopes of finding something better . . . he came home destitute enough I assure you. I know not whether it will satisfy him.[11]

The constant changes of place during youth signified more than a search for employment and adventure; they reflected an uncertain sense of self. This was especially evident in confusion about personal values. Some young men worried that they lacked the strength to maintain moral standards without the daily influence of their parents. One youth who confronted this situation was Sergeant Kendall. As an eighteen-year-old art student in Paris, Sergeant was living an ocean away from his family in New York. He wrote to his parents of a "steady 'blue' feeling about [himself]" that came from his fear of moral weakness: "I feel somehow less noble than I used to be, less thorough and sincere with myself, less firmly resolved to do right at any course, somehow more lax in my feelings and not so determined to draw a sharp line between right and wrong." Such words of moral self-doubt echo through the writing of young men from all parts of the nineteenth century.[12]

While some young men feared that they lacked strength to live by long-cherished values, others were rejecting their families' principles. Hiram Bingham III, the son and grandson of distinguished missionaries, was raised to follow the family calling. But by the time he reached his mid-twenties, Hiram was rejecting God, courting a worldly young heiress, and exploring careers in chemistry and history. In a letter written at this point in his life, Hiram begged for pardon. "Father, forgive me, O forgive me if you can," wrote the young man. "I know that [my] proposed plan of life is not in accordance with your wishes nor your beliefs. I am now more sorry than I can tell."[13]

Bingham at least was grabbing hold of a new moral standard. Other young men were far more confused about their values and their personal lives.[14] Ray Stannard Baker summarized this feeling when he described his life in his early twenties:

> I had not yet learned what I was good for, and I was torn between what I wanted to do, and what I thought it was my duty to do. I was disturbed in my religious beliefs; I was halfway in love with three or four girls; I could see no prospect . . . for years of earning enough money to set up a home of my own.

Baker described these years as "exciting," "adventurous," and "educative," but he also called them a "hopeless" time full of "doubt" and "frustration."[15]

The confusion experienced by Baker and others like him was not simply personal. It grew out of vague expectations. For a male youth occupied a social niche that lacked definition. It was a status without a status: a youth was neither a boy nor man.

There were, as we have noted, few customs or social supports to help a youth through this passage. Male youths could sometimes turn to family, women friends, and mentors. However, a family was often far removed from the realities of a young man's everyday existence, and his feelings of dependence on them at this point in life could make their help problematic. Also, a youth might feel reluctant to turn to a woman friend or to a mentor at work or in the classroom. After all, such people represented the two areas of life—love and personal advancement—that created the most anxiety in the first place.

Lacking all these customary forms of support, the young man turned to a different source—other young men. They were, after all, the people who shared the same hopes and fears, the same daily experience, the same uncertain passage from boyhood to manhood. At no other time in life were males so likely to seek help and reassurance from their male peers as during these turbulent years of transition.

Youth Culture and Boyhood

In the nineteenth century, young Northern men with professional or commercial ambitions congregated in certain places. These places were most visible in the business areas of America's burgeoning cities, where clerks from commercial and professional offices gathered in great numbers; but they also formed smaller groups in countless rural towns where the clerks at local offices and stores mingled with teachers from neighboring hamlets to provide mutual support and diversion. Male youths also clustered together at the many colleges and academies that sprang up across the Northern countryside in the nineteenth century. Even the growing lads who went to sea or headed west found themselves congregated in all-male groups. And wherever young men gathered, a special culture appeared. It expressed the peculiar needs of youth and at the same time provided a means to satisfy those needs. As young men passed through a transitional phase in life, the culture that evolved among them combined elements of the boys' world they had left behind with aspects of the men's life they had not yet attained.

One way in which male youth culture repeated the experience of boys' life was in its emphasis on self-created clubs and organizations. Indeed, young men were elaborating the boyhood experience more than repeating it, for they started associations wherever they turned, and channeled far more of their collective life through their organizations than boys did. Male youth culture was not completely encompassed by these associations, but the organizations founded by young men expressed the needs and fears they felt.

Presumably, informal social groups had always existed among American youth. In colonial New England, a sort of youth culture had appeared where young men were concentrated in large numbers; colleges, in particular, had bred such a culture. Yet there had been few formal youth organizations in the colonial era, and those that had developed were created largely by adults. Formal, self-created associations of youth did not begin to emerge until the late 1700s. In that era, college students formed the first literary societies, while apprentices in the larger cities and towns of the North founded organizations for self-improvement and sociability.[16]

These literary and apprentice societies provided models for many types of self-created youth organizations in the nineteenth century. The direct descendants of the apprentice societies were the young men's associations that grew up during the early 1800s. They were started by young clerks and nascent professionals who sought mutual improvement and shared fun. By the turn of the century, literary societies and debate clubs were also springing up in cities and rural areas as well as colleges, and they remained vital institutions for much of the century. While these groups worked more intensively to cultivate the intellect than the apprentice societies or young men's associations did, they closely resembled those organizations in the way they mixed social life with self-improvement.[17]

Meanwhile, the religious ferment of the early nineteenth century spurred young people to use the format of the young men's organizations for specialized purposes. Zealous converts founded religious societies and reform associations, some of which confined their membership to male youths. Even these groups—narrow though they were in purpose—provided social cohesion in the lives of the young people who belonged to them.[18]

Then, too, there were young men's organizations whose purposes were almost entirely social. Secret societies, lodges, and fraternities grew up like weeds throughout the nineteenth century. They flourished in any place with a concentration of young men—cities, towns, colleges—and they took varied forms. Some were spontaneous, informal clubs that a few young men created for their own passing enjoyment, while other groups sought to perpetuate themselves in institutional form and spread their web of good fellowship to new places. In either case, these societies offered social acceptance at a time of life when other bonds and commitments were in flux.[19]

Some of the functions served by this special subculture met needs that harked back to boyhood. Young men's organizations performed many functions of a family. Since male youths often lived in neutral settings like boardinghouses and residential hotels, their lives lacked the nurture associated with home and family. Thus, they joined (or started) organizations that openly expressed a familial nature. The Young Men's Christian Association in Utica, New York, appealed for funds by pointing out: "Many a young man in this city of yours spends his days at work, perhaps in some mechanics shop, or mill, or office, or in your stores, [and] when at night comes home has nowhere else to go, for at the best the little room he calls his own is no HOME to him." The appeal also referred to the YMCA library as a refuge for "many half-homeless wanderers in these streets." The departed members of one young men's society referred to members who remained as "friends at home."[20]

The male youths who belonged to these groups showed familial feelings in other word usages. They often referred to each other as "brothers," and some of their organizations were called "fraternities" or "fraternal lodges." For some, the term "house" had powerful attractions; college fraternities in particular used that domestic term for their club buildings. And young men's societies of various kinds built or bought homes which they furnished in a domestic style.[21]

Like families, male youth groups provided a setting for common nurture. Literary societies, college fraternities, and friendship clubs rarely met on a formal basis without enjoying a meal together, and when the group was small, one member usually provided food for the others. Shared nurture increased the sense of brotherhood.[22]

Most of all, an atmosphere of friendship and fraternal warmth gave young men's clubs their resemblance to families. Whatever other purposes a young men's association served, it had little future if it did not nourish strong personal bonds. Writing about his years at college, Alphonso Rockwell had "to confess that [his] best friends were . . . obtained" through his fraternity. Indeed, a great many young men's groups had their origins in circles of friends who sought to organize and extend themselves. As a college student, Rutherford B. Hayes participated in the founding of such a club. He and eight friends at Kenyon College started a group called Phi Zeta. The club derived its name from the initials of its Greek motto, *Philia Zoe* ("Friendship for Life"), and it took as its main object the promotion of "firm and enduring friendship among its members." The larger associations of male youth proved fertile ground for these smaller and more intimate friendship groups. For instance, a cadre of close friends from the Boston Mercantile Library Association formed a small club in the late 1830s called Attic Nights. The members were all Boston clerks with strong literary interests who met to read, talk, and eat together on Saturday evening. Warm friendship groups like these helped to bind larger male youth groups in familial feeling.[23]

Male youth organizations, then, provided nurture and warmth that young men had expected from their families, but the young men's organization was emphatically an all-male family. The appeal of these associations lay not only in their resemblance to the family, but also in their links to boys' world. Young men's collective life retained some of boy culture's defining qualities—its emphasis on enjoyment and play, its uneasy mixture of competition and camaraderie, and sometimes its violence and hedonism. To say the least, male youth culture lacked the placid restraint of middle-class family life.

In spite of high-sounding titles like "debating society" and "library association," nearly all young men's organizations provided entertainment. The elaborate banquets and parties which they staged were indeed familial moments of common repast, but they were more than that. They also provided the occasion for jesting and laughter, for song and drink, and for all sorts of rough fun from food fights to wrestling matches. In addition, male youth organizations as diverse as apprentice associations, sailing clubs, and college fraternities produced plays, which were usually open to the general public. Young men's organizations also presented the debates and literary exercises from which so many of them took their names.

Those were not just intellectual performances, however. They usually took place in a social—or even a festive—context. At the meeting of a literary society or college fraternity, a debate or a series of orations and poems would often serve as the evening's entertainment. On some campuses, the contests between rival debating societies took on the partisan atmosphere that later typified football games. In many towns, a literary presentation or debate might be the only entertainment of an evening, and thus a major social event. Even in the larger cities, the lyceum lectures—which as often as not were adjuncts or offshoots of young men's associations—were occasions to see and be seen, to meet and greet one's friends. The conversations and chance encounters before the lectures or during the intermissions spawned many small parties afterward.[24]

An especially popular form of entertainment when young men gathered was the testing of wits. This testing often took the organized form of sardonic toasts which were directed unsparingly at other group members and often built into a competition of witty insults. Many organizations staged spoofs or satiric revues which poked clever fun at the club's members. Above all, the testing of wits happened informally in the ceaseless cut and thrust of daily conversation between ambitious youths. One former clerk recalled the atmosphere of his literary society: "We educated each other by criticizing and laughing at each other."[25]

Clearly, the life of young men's organizations grew out of boy culture. This was an associational world that valued fun and amusement. The surging competitive impulse that typified boy culture also functioned as a shaping force in the culture of male youth. The spirited competition of young men's debates and the heated rivalries between literary societies or debating clubs showed that the combative urge of boyhood still flourished. The verbal thrust-and-parry of male youth groups also expressed the urge to compete. In fact, that ceaseless clash of wits between friends recalled the physical combat of loyal playfellows in boyhood. Although the means of expression changed, the basic principle of mixing affection with attack remained the same.

While competition could unite, it could also divide. Here again, the organized world of young men resembled the boy culture that preceded it. The clubs and gangs that blossomed in boys' world served to exclude as much as include, and the fraternities and associations of male youth had much the same effect. The young men's societies in cities and towns competed for members, prestige, and public attention, and thus set groups of ambitious youths against each other. The divisive effect of this competition was most visible in college settings, where the community was small and closed. There, rivalry loomed large, jealousy fed on exclusion, and personal rejection was hard to conceal. The fraternities that flourished at nineteenth-century colleges guarded their secrecy with tenacious zeal; some early ones even built their chapter houses with thick brick walls and no windows.[26] This practice carried the middle-class passion for domestic privacy to an extreme, while serving the more obvious function of protecting fraternal secrecy.

This ostentatious exclusion enraged the students who were left out, and bitter feuds developed between members and nonmembers or between rival organizations. In 1803, the opponents of secret societies at Dartmouth hatched a plot to destroy those exclusive groups. Operating in deep secrecy themselves, the adherents of the antifraternal faction nearly succeeded in their objective, and set off fierce social and political warfare within the student body. The feelings aroused on both sides were powerful. One partisan of secret societies wrote that "Cataline himself was a saint compared with some of the fellows who plotted this scheme," and, when the plot failed, the same young man wrote angrily, "It is but right that the person who raises a storm should perish in its ravages."[27]

So deep was the antagonism between student groups that college authorities sought to use it for their own purposes. Officials often supported the hazing of new students as a way to instill loyalty to one's college class and to set the classes against each other instead of against the college administration. In fact, some of the earliest football games in the United States were actually contests in which the freshman and sophomore classes of a college made two opposing lines and tried to kick an inflated cow's bladder through the members of the rival class to a goal behind them. The real purpose was not so much to win the game as to inflict violence on the other class, creating group solidarity in the process.[28]

Even while male youth organizations gloried in a rough, competitive, playful spirit that harked back to the ethos of boy culture, their collective activities still carried striking reminders of deep familial needs. We have seen that this yearning for family life showed through in the common nurture of banquets and impromptu feasts, and also in the way that secret fraternities and societies carried domestic privacy to a drastic extreme. It also appeared—subtly and unexpectedly—in the theatricals that were staged by so many young men's societies. These productions varied widely in seriousness and sophistication, but they shared at least one common feature: male youths played all the female roles.[29]

At one level, this gender-blurring reflected mere necessity—there were no women in young men's organizations to take the female parts. And putting teenage boys in women's roles also reflected a time-honored tradition in the theater. There was more going on here than the simple workings of necessity or tradition, however. The thing that some veterans of these productions recalled most vividly in later years was the spectacle of young men pretending to be women. Indeed, these theatrical amateurs wrote plays which required them to act as females.[30] Thus, at a time in life when young men were living without maternal nurture and had to supply each other with some form of substitute, they chose to play-act together as women and men. At a point in the life cycle when males were most separate from female company, they chose to invent it together playfully; and at a moment in their emotional lives when they were coping nervously with romantic intimacy, they used the stage to practice on each other.

Yet the male theatricals were poking fun at the female role even as they allowed young men to occupy it. In fact, they were mocking the whole sex-role configuration on which the family was based, and so were the other rites and practices of male youth organizations. The banquets which recalled family meals also took place in a rude, jesting atmosphere that mocked the genteel restraint of the middle-class dining room. And while the privacy of the young men's secret societies did copy the obsessive seclusion of the middle-class family, it is also true that the thick, windowless walls of the secret societies were a parody (however unconscious) of middle-class domestic isolation.

The rituals of male youth culture expressed ambivalence about family life. Boys liked to flaunt their scorn for the domestic world, but the customs of youth culture conveyed yearning as well as scorn. The life that flourished within young men's associations blended elements of boy culture and family life into its own distinctive mixture.

Youth Culture and Manhood

Young men did not create their world only from elements of the past. The lives they were leading as clerks, students, or professional apprentices called their attention constantly to the future. Their attempts to enter the men's world of work and achievement reminded them daily of ways in which they needed to change their behavior and reshape their character. Because young men's organizational culture was largely a product of young men's own needs and intentions, it nourished many of the skills and attitudes that were needed for worldly success. Thus, even as male youth culture helped young men to integrate valued customs and habits from childhood into adult life, it also aided the same young men in overcoming long-set patterns of behavior that could hinder their quest for manly achievement.[31]

Many male youth organizations helped young men prepare for the rigors of manhood by providing an education. Most youths who were bound for middle-class occupations had limited classroom experience (several winters in a small schoolhouse, maybe a year or two at an academy) and needed to improve at essential skills like reading, writing, speaking, and dissecting an argument. Even when urban schools began to offer a more coherent program in the second half of the nineteenth century, there were still a great many youths from rural areas who lacked a decent education and not a few from the cities who needed to brush up on basic skills required for middle-class work.

Thus, young men's societies served, in the words of one scholar, as "a substitute for college." They had their own libraries. They sponsored debates and offered countless opportunities for public speaking of other sorts, from the presentation of literary papers to the delivery of political speeches to the reading of poems written by the members themselves. The young men's associations also sponsored lecture series. Some were a motley assortment of traveling speakers, but others were courses of lectures given by an expert on a particular topic; these amounted virtually to college courses. Thus, the young men who joined societies and associations were often exposed to broad bodies of knowledge and gained extensive practice in the skills of writing, speaking, and logical analysis. While the young men's organizations offered little formal instruction in these skills, their members taught them to each other through unsparing criticism. In this way, a great many male youths received an invaluable equivalent to a college education through their membership in societies and associations.[32]

Some of these organizations offered a better education than many colleges did. Especially in the antebellum era, college courses demanded little of a student's time or intellect, so students created literary societies to supplement their education. These societies were like colleges in their own right: they taught their own curricula, purchased their own libraries, established their own rules of conduct, and even granted their own diplomas. Usually a college had two such societies, which vied for members and competed in debates on the great issues of the day. These organizations set such a tone of intellectual concern that even the college fraternities that emerged in the early nineteenth century—groups that were far more concerned with sociability than the literary societies were—featured the reading of a paper as a regular part of their meetings. On and off campus, the young men's associations and literary societies were remarkably similar in that they enabled young men to educate each other outside of a formal learning system that was ineffectual.[33]

The young men's societies promoted other useful skills, too. To the upwardly mobile youth in their membership, these organizations offered an education in the social graces. Even the young men from middle-class backgrounds were encouraged to shake off a bit of their boyish crudeness and practice good manners. Moreover, the male youth organizations provided a setting where members could cultivate the fine art of business friendship. The great Boston publisher James T. Fields learned to blend friendship with instrumental skills while he was a member of a young men's society, the Boston Mercantile Library Association. Fields used his influence, his charm, and his good editorial judgment to promote the literary ambitions of his friends within the association, just as he would use those traits to become the preeminent American publisher of the mid-nineteenth century.[34]

Male youth organizations further prepared their members for the world of manhood by strengthening competitive habits learned in boyhood. In urban and small-town settings and on college campuses, these organizations vied for prestige, public attention, and new members. Young men competed with each other for membership in these societies and fraternities.[35] Nowhere was competition more evident than in that quintessential young men's activity, the debate. Self-improvement societies made debating an integral part of their activities, setting friend against friend in verbal combat.

The ubiquitous custom of the formal debate did more than sustain the competitive habits of boy culture, though. It also transformed contentious energies into forms that would be more useful in the middle-class world of work. The debating experience forced young men to think on their feet, to present a convincing argument, and to duel with words and ideas rather than fists and rocks. Debating replaced the physical skills and primal aggression of boyhood with the abstract skills and the verbal aggression that were needed for middle-class work. Still, the debate experience—even as it transformed the talents and tendencies of boyhood—left competitive impulses intact, and even nurtured them. Forensic combat engaged the emotions of young men as fully as physical contests commanded the feelings of boys. Charles Van Hise, a famous geologist and educator, had a place on the debating team of his literary society while he was a student at the University of Wisconsin. After his team won a major victory over a rival society, Van Hise described his "wild elation": "How the body tingles at such times! Every muscle is set like a whipcord. The whole body is in action."[36]

The members of Van Hise's society were enthusiastic about this victory, too, because all of them took an active role in the constant round of organized debates and informal arguments at the society.[37] These encounters sharpened the skills of those involved and eventually produced an agreement about which debaters could best represent the whole group. The process of debate and discussion in young men's societies honed the competitive instincts of the participants even as it nurtured their analytical skills.

The endless process of competitive evaluation that was involved in these verbal clashes represented another refinement of a habit bred by boy culture. Boys constantly evaluated one another on the basis of physical skills. After they grew to be young men, they judged their peers by verbal and intellectual standards instead of physical ones. In other words, young men were learning to weigh and rank the abilities of their fellows just as they would in the world of middle-class work. Henry Dwight Sedgwick, a lawyer and scholar, described explicitly the way his peer-rankings changed as he grew. As a boy and as a college student, he rated others according to physical prowess. During his teens, Sedgwick also began to measure his peers on the basis of their scholastic abilities. By his early twenties, when he had reached law school, his standard of physical prowess had dropped away altogether. Sedgwick now ranked the young men around him on "the scale of success"—first as students of the law and later as lawyers.[38]

Male youth culture also educated its members in the exercise of power. Here again, young men were building on lessons they had learned within their boys' world. Boys exercised power in many ways, from leading gangs to bullying other boys. But these informal, unstructured experiences were not the subject of much conscious attention in boyhood. By contrast, the exercise of power within male youth culture was a focus of vigilant attention, and it happened within formal settings. After all, the young men's societies were founded and run by the members themselves; when one of these societies sustained itself or expanded, it did so through the efforts of the young men who ran it.

These societies began informally, with a group of friends coming together for sociability and self-improvement. The founders set up rules and constitutions, often before the group had ever met. A case in point is the club Rutherford B. Hayes and his friends started at Kenyon College to promote "firm and enduring friendship among its members." Within a few weeks of the initial idea, members were selected; several meetings were held; a name, a motto, and a badge were chosen; meeting formats were adopted; and "several regulations" were established "to secure the prosperity and permanency of the club."[39]

While this club did not survive the graduation of its members, other young men's societies lasted for decades with little but financial assistance from older men. The youthful members of these organizations vied with each other for the powers of office. Those who succeeded in gaining power carried out the rules of their organizations and helped to put new ones in place. They oversaw the scheduling of such group activities as lectures, debates, and banquets; they took charge of upkeep and improvement in libraries, club rooms, and buildings; and they played an active role in recruiting new members and maintaining the organization's financial health. Nor was the exercise of power limited to the elected officers. Key decisions were often hammered out in committees or at meetings of all members. Thus, young men learned to maintain and extend institutions, to make and administer policy, and to persuade and campaign in pursuit of their own goals. As they nurtured their institutions, male youths learned lessons that would prove valuable in the world of middle-class work that lay ahead.[40]

In sum, the self-improvement societies that formed the core of male youth culture played a vital role in bringing their members through the transition from boyhood into the world of men. Young men set aside the physical skills they had relied on in boyhood and cultivated the abstract skills they would need to meet a man's duties. The assertive impulses and competitive drives of boy culture were not so much forsaken as they were redirected—furnished with new channels to follow and new goals to reach.

Youth Culture and the Struggle for Impulse Control

The playful, hedonistic, libidinal quality of the boys' world contrasted sharply with the sober sense of duty attached to middle-class manhood, and as boys approached manhood their quest for gratification and excitement sought new objects. Many found pleasure in strong drink, and some discovered a new form of adventure in gambling. Then, there was the most alluring—and most strictly forbidden—indulgence of all: sex. In nineteenth-century America, boys reached puberty in their midteens, and from then on, they fought a long battle with sexual temptation which extended not only to relations with others but to masturbation as well.[41]

The youthful impulse to seek forbidden pleasures threatened the peace and good order of society in fundamental ways. For instance, the boyish love of brawling and fighting combined with the heedless use of liquor to produce frequent violence between college students and boys from local towns. Furthermore, sexual desire was seen as an especially powerful force in a young man, distracting him from his work, blinding him to his future duties as a breadwinner, and leading him even to disease and insanity. People believed, in other words, that a young man who surrendered to sexual desire also gave up his ability to carry out the man's role.[42] Thus, the pursuit of pleasure among youthful males seemed a threat to the basic integrity of society.

Of course, the male quest for thrills did not begin with the approach of manhood. Boyhood's excitements, however, were a social nuisance, not a social threat. The hedonistic impulses of boyhood could be held in bounds—if not always curbed entirely—by the vigilance of family and community. In times past those traditional institutions had served to limit young men's quest for excitement, too; but in the nineteenth century, the young men who were forming the middle class of their generation often lived far from the vigilant gaze of a family and of a community that knew them.[43] How, then, could these young men be controlled? And, more importantly, how could they be confirmed in their habits of self-control?

Certain youth organizations played an active role in encouraging tighter self-restraint. Some, such as the ubiquitous temperance societies of the antebellum era, were aimed directly at the control of impulse. Many of the more broadly focused self-improvement societies also took a direct role in discouraging the pursuit of "mere pleasure." Simply by the fact that they provided engaging alternatives to vice, the self-improvement societies did much to distract young men from their own wayward impulses. By midcentury, older men were founding male youth societies whose primary purpose was to help suppress vice and promote self-control among those just entering manhood. The YMCA was the most famous and successful organization of this sort, and it emerged as a central part of male youth culture in the second half of the nineteenth century.[44]

Yet, in spite of all these institutional forces, young men's societies did not inculcate self-control to the same degree that they nurtured young men's worldly ambition or developed the skills needed for middle-class work. After all, most young men's societies were aimed at external achievement more than internal restraint. Given their common experience in boyhood, young men who gathered together were bound to be more receptive to lessons in self-assertion than self-control.

There were other social forces arrayed in the battle for the youthful mastery of desire. Preachers and ministers of all sorts waged a holy war to conquer hedonism among youth who came to the city. The evangelists of the antebellum era addressed young clerks whenever they sought to fan the flames of revival in Northern cities. Throughout the century, there were ministers whose mission was preaching to the male youth seeking a place in the urban middle class. Much of the prescriptive literature on nineteenth-century manhood consists of printed sermons delivered to young men in the crusade for their souls (and their libidos). These books of sermons appeared less often during the second half of the century, when they were replaced by a moralistic secular literature (usually scientific or medical) that echoed most of the themes of impulse control that had dominated the preaching of earlier generations. There is no way to measure the effect that these books and speeches had on young men, but we do know that many of the preachers involved—including the young Henry Ward Beecher and Hartford's Joel Hawes—drew large crowds of male youth to their churches.[45] We also know that several books of exhortation to young men went through numerous editions and printings.

Even the most successful advisers in virtue conceded that they were not the primary architects of male self-restraint. Rather, it was the mothers of these young men who laid the foundations of conscience on which the preachers of impulse control sought to build. As we have seen, many young males possessed active powers of self-control by the time they confronted the temptations which came with puberty and independence. These powers, nurtured in boyhood homes and augmented by the institutional forces that arrayed themselves during young manhood, helped middle-class men keep a far tighter rein on their urges for pleasure and excitement than they had kept as boys.[46]

Still, while men held in check many surging desires and perhaps even drove some of them entirely out of consciousness, the task of self-control was not an easy one. Proof of this comes from the lives of middle-class men. There were alcoholics and gamblers and philandering husbands. Probably more common were men who sometimes—though not constantly—gave in to one form of temptation or another. The mastery of impulse was a lifelong struggle, not a dramatic skirmish that was won or lost forever in youth.

Nonetheless, youth was perceived as a turning point in life, a moment of change in a young man's control of inner needs and outward behavior. Male youth culture did much to turn big boys into young men. This distinctive culture nurtured good work habits and taught appropriate forms of self-assertion. It provided valuable experience in the uses of power, illuminated the delicate art of competing and cooperating with the same group of people, and offered some limited aid in impulse control, while fostering the expression of many of those same impulses. Male youth culture—with young men's societies at its vital core—supported its members during a time of transition by mixing elements of a familiar past with preparation for a demanding future.

Chapter 4

YOUTH AND
MALE INTIMACY

W HEN Daniel Webster was eighteen years old, he called his best friend "the partner of my joys, griefs, and affections, the only participator of my most secret thoughts."[1] Four years later, in 1804, young Daniel asked another close friend: "What is this world worth without the enjoyment of friendship, and the cultivation of the social feelings of the heart?" He answered his own question later in the same letter when he told his friend: "My heart is now so full of matters and things impatient to be whispered into the ear of a trusty friend, that I think I could pour them into yours till it ran over."[2]

Webster's statements present a very different concept of friendship from the one that was embedded in boy culture. To boys, friendship meant a stalwart alliance and a boon companionship. It was a bond cemented by loyalty and invigorated by shared enjoyment. As boys in their midteens began to shape their own lives, their notions of friendship changed. This contrasting idea of friendship was based on intimacy, on a sharing of thought and emotion. A friend was now a partner in sentiment as well as action. While boys had had little interest in "the social feelings of the heart," young men like Daniel Webster cultivated those same emotions. The gentle (even "feminine") emotions of the heart replaced the rough aggressions of boyhood. Young men might even express their fondness for each other in affectionate physical gestures. All together, these friendships inverted familiar patterns of male behavior— they were intimate attachments that verged on romance.

In the history of white, Northern culture, these romantic bonds between men were unusual. Certain youths from elite families of the eighteenth century did indulge in loving, intimate friendships with each other. We know, for example, that the corps of young aides that surrounded General Washington in the Revolution exchanged letters of great affection. But this kind of relation between men did not spread to other classes or become a common feature of the social landscape until the turn of the nineteenth century.[3]

These romantic friendships of male youth closely resembled the intense bonds between women first portrayed by Carroll Smith-Rosenberg in her landmark article, "The Female World of Love and Ritual."[4] Yet the intimate ties between young men of the nineteenth century differed from those described by Smith-Rosenberg in at least one fundamental way. Among males, romantic friendship was largely a product of a distinct phase in the life cycle—youth.

Male Friendship in Youth

The intimate, romantic bonds of male youth were intense offshoots of less remarkable friendship patterns. To start with, young men in their late teens and twenties filled their letters and diaries with the mention of a great many casual associates. These fellows—colleagues at work, occupants of the same boardinghouse, classmates at a college or academy—passed through young men's lives in a procession marked by good fellowship and little attachment.[5] Such casual friendships flourished in young men's societies where group activities and a feeling of camaraderie drew together individuals who had no deeper affinity.[6] There were a few males studied here who found their friendships only in casual companionship. Edward Jarvis, a man who formed no close male bonds in his youth, eventually found his medical career blocked by the same rigid and harshly judgmental qualities that had prevented him from making friends.[7] Charles Milton Baldwin, a sculptor and stonecutter from upstate New York, did not develop close friendships as a young man, since his relationships with the opposite sex preoccupied him completely. In fact, this reliance on intimacy with women was a common theme among the young men who were not close to others of their own sex.[8]

Still, theirs were the unusual cases. Most young men enjoyed at least one strong friendship. These warm attachments were built on affinities of many kinds—similar dispositions, common tastes, shared interests, a knack for mutual understanding. Close friendship began with good companionship but it went on into deeper realms of feeling and sharing.

The relationship between Morton Bailey and James Cattell provides a good illustration of a close attachment between two young men. They met as classmates at Lafayette College in the 1870s and maintained a devoted friendship after graduation, while Bailey practiced law in Denver and Cattell studied psychology in Germany. At this phase in life, the discussion of careers formed a vital part of close friendships, and a good portion of the correspondence between Bailey and Cattell focused on hopes and fears about their prospects for success. Was Morton too ambitious? Was Jim not ambitious enough? Was Denver a good place to practice law? How could Jim support himself through long years of graduate training? But Morton and Jim did more than ponder these questions and give advice. They offered (and sought) emotional support that was warm, reliable, and reassuring. The two friends shared congratulations in times of triumph and consolation in times of failure, and reminded each other of their personal strengths.[9]

Bailey and Cattell shared comfort and support so freely because of the warmth and trust between them. Bailey wrote of their openness: "I think you have seen fit to honor me . . . with your confidence—therefore [there is] no good reason . . . why I should not be wholly frank with you, as well concerning yourself as myself." Such candid talk opened up the possibility of stinging criticism, but their frankness was rooted in a powerful sense of loyalty and appreciation. As Morton admitted on one occasion, "It is superfluous for me to assert to you . . . my strong and long continued friendship. Strangely unlike yet . . . strongly drawn toward each other—You little know, Jim, what genuine pleasure and comfort I get from all your letters."[10]

From time to time, a fond male friendship in youth blossomed into something more intimate and intense. Warmth turned into tender attachment, and closeness became romance. Although there is no statistical evidence to tell us precisely how many young middle-class men experienced romantic friendship, we do know that these ardent relationships were common in the nineteenth century. Their expressions can be found readily in the diaries and personal correspondence of the era, and there is no evidence to suggest that this form of relationship was not socially acceptable among middle-class male youth.

One kind of romantic male bond was exemplified in the intense connection between Daniel Webster and James Hervey Bingham. Webster and Bingham became close friends at Dartmouth, and the warmth of their friendship continued past graduation. While they studied law, taught school, and served as law clerks, the two offered each other an intimacy that might otherwise have been missing from their small-town bachelor's lives. Of course, their relationship encompassed many of the same qualities as a close, but less intimate, friendship. They shared dreams and doubts about their careers, and they offered each other honest expressiveness and emotional support.[11]

There were several dimensions of the friendship between Webster and Bingham, however, that gave it an intimate, even romantic tone. First was the way they addressed each other. They sometimes opened their letters with greetings like "Lovely Boy" or "Dearly Beloved," and Webster on occasion signed his letters with affectionate phrases such as, "I am, dear Hervey, your Daniel Webster," and "Accept all the tenderness I have, D. Webster." In between the salutation and the closing, Webster used many other terms of endearment: "my Hervey," "my dearest J. H. B.," "dear Hervey."[12]

The romantic tone extended beyond nicknames and salutations to the way these young men described their feelings for each other. While they were together in college, Daniel described his "dear Hervey" as "the only friend of my heart, the partner of my joys, griefs, and affections, the only participator of my most secret thoughts." After graduating, young Webster wrote to Bingham: "I knew not how closely our feelings were interwoven; had no idea how hard it would be to live apart, when the hope of living together again no longer existed."[13]

When they were together, they talked intimately of daily events, friends, career plans, and college life. But the topic which Daniel and Hervey discussed with the greatest fervor—and which required the most intimate trust—was the subject of women. Like other males in their late teens and early twenties, they were obsessed with the topic. Dreams, fears, and puzzlements about romance held a tight grip on their attention. Like many of their peers, Webster and Bingham needed a special friend with whom they could discuss such vexing, delicate matters.[14] So they wrote to each other constantly about "the Misses." They exchanged advice, rhapsodized about female beauty, cursed feminine wiles, and consoled one another when romantic hopes were dashed.

When a new young woman caught the fancy of one or the other, Webster and Bingham carried on like the future lawyers they were, sifting the fragmentary evidence of passing words, stolen glances, and idle gossip for clues to feminine intentions. Underneath it all lay a childlike anxiety that was deeply embarrassing to a young man, so embarrassing that he could reveal it only to intimate friends. Here is Webster fussing and fretting to Bingham over the latest object of his affections: "I dared not go to see Fanny; though I would not for anything have her know that I passed so near her. Do you ever hear from her? How is she? Does she mention my name in her letters to you?"[15]

While Dan pursued his dream of intimacy with a woman, his bond with Bingham came in many respects to resemble a marriage. The two young men shared the joys and sorrows of life, offered each other emotional support, revealed their deepest secrets, and even spoke to one another in terms of endearment. At a time of great discouragement in his quest for a wife, Webster offered Bingham a vision of their common future that amounted to a marriage proposal.[16] "I don't see how I can live any longer," wrote Webster, "without having a friend near me, I mean a male friend, just such a friend as one J. H. B." And so he announced—only half-jokingly—that he would move in with Bingham: "Yes, James, I must come; we will yoke together again; your little bed is just wide enough; we will practise at the same bar, and be as friendly a pair of single fellows as ever cracked a nut." The picture that Daniel painted of their life together was modest but idyllic:

> We perhaps shall never be rich; no matter we can supply our own personal necessities. By the time we are thirty, we will put on the dress of old bachelors, a mourning suit, and having sown all our wild oats, with a round hat and a hickory staff we will march on to the end of life, whistling as merry as robins.[17]

Dan was not quite offering Hervey a romantic love nest or a vine-covered cottage, but it was a cozy, intimate image of the two men yoked together happily for life, sharing Bingham's "little bed." If Webster's words lacked romance, they surely described the loving familiarity of a happily married couple.[18]

In his more realistic moments, Webster knew that he would marry. Yet it stands as a tribute to the power of his tie with Bingham that he saw their friendship as occupying the same ground as marriage—to the point where the two seemed to be mutually exclusive. In one letter where Daniel told Hervey of his "exultation" that their "early congenial attachments will never be sundered," he promised that his friend would "continue to occupy the parlor of my affections, till Madam comes! Madam, you know, must have the parlor, but even then you shall not be cast off into the kitchen." "Depend on it," Webster continued, "if Madam treats you, or anybody else who is an older proprietor than herself, with prankish airs, we will soon away with her into Lob's pound."[19]

Still, for all the similarities between a marriage and the youthful male intimacy of Webster and Bingham, there was one irreducible difference.

Only within marriage was sexual activity allowed. There is no evidence to indicate that Dan and Hervey ever developed a physical relationship, but there were other intimate relationships between young men which did involve touching, kissing, and caressing. These relationships had the same emotional textures and qualities as many other intimate male friendships, but their physical expressiveness gave them an extra blush of romance.

The friendship between James Blake and Wyck Vanderhoef was certainly one that had a romantic aura. These two young men, both engineers, met in 1848 when they were in their twenties. Their friendship did not blossom immediately, but when it did, Blake wrote of the event as if he had just engaged to be married. In his diary, he exulted: "I have found a *friend!* one upon whom I can repose every trust, and when in trouble and affliction can seek relief." Blake's account of events between himself and Vanderhoef sounds more like the choice of a wife than the start of a friendship: "After an acquaintance of nearly three years I have chosen [Wyck] as my friend, and he has reciprocated; May he live long and happy, and may the tie of pure friendship which has been formed between us, never be severed, but by the hand of death." When James described the place of this bond in his life, he used the rhetoric of nineteenth-century marriage and domesticity: "Long have I desired a friend, one whom I could trust myself with upon this journey of life." It was, wrote James, "a beautiful thing" to "retire from the cold selfish arms of the world, and receive the pure embrace of friendship."[20]

The marital overtones of James and Wyck's relationship were not confined to words and imagery, but extended as well to their actions. Like other devoted young friends of the time, they made a pact of lasting friendship. The arrangement was unusual, though, in that it also included Wyck's fiancée, Mary, with whom James, too, enjoyed a close relationship. The three, who were already "bound together in friendship" and "cemented by affection," now exchanged "a kiss of purity" as a pledge "ever to love, ever to cherish and assist each other." When the "sacred hour" of their pledge had passed, James felt certain "of that confiding love, which will never fade."[21]

Of all the similarities to marriage in the Blake-Vanderhoef relationship, the most striking to the twentieth-century eye is their physical affection. For these two young men, "the embrace of friendship" was not just a figure of speech. As James noted without comment on one occasion, "We retired early and in each other's arms did friendship sink peacefully to sleep."[22] In other words, the two friends not only shared a bed, but they shared embraces there as well. Apparently, this was a common occurrence for them, and James noted their nocturnal embraces in his diary without a hint of apology. The most revealing of these diary entries came just after Wyck and James had parted company, and James was describing their last night together:

> We retired early, but long was the time before our eyes were closed in slumber, for this was the last night we shall be together for the present, and our hearts were full of that true friendship which could not find utterance by words, we laid our heads upon each other's bosom and wept, it may be unmanly to weep, but I care not, the spirit was touched.[23]

This statement is noteworthy for its description of intimate affection between men, but it is even more noteworthy for what it reveals about the limits of acceptable male behavior. James closes his comments with an apology for his unmanly conduct, but his apology is for weeping, not for laying his head on the bosom of his intimate male friend in bed. Apparently, crying violated the norms of manliness more than the exchange of physical affection with another man.[24]

Thus, the range of behavior allowed in friendship did not end with the intimate bonds of youths like Webster and Bingham, but extended further to include romantic and physically affectionate relationships like that of Blake and Vanderhoef. The blush of romance was deeper still in the affairs of Albert Dodd, a Connecticut college student. Writing in his journal in the late 1830s, Albert described his intimate relationships with two other young men, John Heath and Anthony Halsey. To John, Albert never confessed his affectionate feelings. On the surface, the relationship was simply a close friendship, and Albert was left to sort out his unspoken feelings in his journal. There, he wrote, "I love you, indeed I love you" to John, but he kept these words to himself.[25]

In his later romance with Anthony Halsey, Dodd shed his caution. While he poured out his feelings for Anthony in his journal ("adored Anthony," "my most beloved of all," "how completely I loved him, how I doated on him!"), he was also willing to bare his soul to his friend in long hours of intimate talk. More than that, Albert and Anthony had a physical relationship. "Often too [Anthony] shared my pillow—or I his," Dodd wrote, "and then how sweet to sleep with him, to hold his beloved form in my embrace, to have his arms about my neck, to imprint upon his face sweet kisses!" This description differs from James Blake's accounts of his nights with Wyck Vanderhoef in its intimacy, and in its erotic tinge. Not only does Dodd kiss Halsey as they embrace in bed (Blake mentions no such erotic play), but there is an undertone of passion when Dodd mentions his friend's "beloved form" and remembers the kisses, and the nights, as "sweet" ones. All these subtle differences take additional erotic force from Dodd's confession that he found Halsey *"so handsome,"* a confession that has no equivalent in Blake's journal entries about Vanderhoef.

The relationships described in the journals of Blake and Dodd were quite similar, but Dodd's affair with Anthony Halsey seemed to go one significant—and passionate—step beyond that of Vanderhoef and Blake. Yet, as significant as this step appears to the twentieth-century observer, it did not take Dodd and Halsey across any perilous social boundaries. Albert Dodd described his erotic encounters without self-censure.[26]

Another striking feature of Dodd's romantic life was that it mixed male and female love objects as if that were the most natural habit in the world. His rapturous musings about John Heath mingled freely with love poems to a woman named Julia, and the journal entries which glowed with Dodd's passion for Anthony Halsey filled the same volumes that expressed his yearning for his beloved Elizabeth. The mixtures, at times, became even more complex. "All I know," he wrote before meeting Elizabeth, "is that there are three persons in this world whom I have loved, and those are, Julia, John, and Anthony. Dear, beloved trio."[27]

Nor was Dodd alone in blending the love of men with the love of women. James Blake, after all, enjoyed an intense relationship with Wyck Vanderhoef's fiancée, Mary. He exchanged fifteen- and twenty-page letters with her, and the two sometimes talked alone for hours. At this transitional stage in life, the distinction between love objects—and between their genders—sometimes faded to invisibility. Just as the separate spheres were not hermetically sealed but rather leaked their contents one into the other, so, too, a young man's feelings for the dearest members of each sex could sometimes blend and merge.

Channels of Intimate Affection

Albert Dodd and James Blake shifted easily between their love for men and their love for women. They saw nothing strange in their physical relationships with close male friends, and they felt no sense of tension between their intimate lives and the positions of social respectability which they pursued. Yet, to the twentieth-century eye, the words and deeds of these men do appear strange. How can we grasp their undisguised affection for other males and their lack of anxiety about physical romance with their own sex?

People of the nineteenth and twentieth centuries have understood same-sex romance in very different ways. To appreciate the difference, we must start with a statement by historian Carroll Smith-Rosenberg, who wrote that loving ties between women—even ties with erotic overtones—were "socially acceptable" in the 1800s. Furthermore, these relations were considered "fully compatible" with heterosexual bonds.[28] Smith-Rosenberg's observations are as true for men of the nineteenth century as for women. In fact, the romantic friendships between men may have received stronger cultural support than the bonds between females.

The historical models which the nineteenth-century bourgeoisie used to understand same-sex intimacy were predominantly relationships between men. Following the habit of their era, these Victorians turned to classical antiquity, citing the devoted friendship of Damon and Pythias, and quoting the writings of Aristotle and Cicero, who praised pure, spiritual relationships between equal men.[29] Advocates of homosocial love also invoked biblical models such as David and Jonathan, who declared that their love was "wonderful, passing the love of women." Devout Protestants patterned their friendships after the ties that bound early Christian communities, where a kiss or clasped hands expressed intense religious feeling, and words of love between members of the same sex echoed the love they shared for God.[30] These historical models provided sanction especially for romantic friendship between men, but they extended support to intimacy between women as well. Even the most conservative and respectable families accepted loving ties between members of the same sex.

There was another dimension of cultural support for these relationships. The nineteenth-century bourgeoisie had an understanding of homoerotic contact that was very different from that of the late twentieth century. Our forebears did not make clear distinctions between what was *homosexual* and what was not; in fact, there was no such term during most of the 1800s. When nineteenth-century Americans referred to an act that we would now term *homosexual*, they often called it "the crime that cannot be named." The lack of a word for homosexuality is closely tied to the fact that there was no concept of it, no model for sexuality other than heterosexuality. When middle-class Northerners wrote about homosexual acts, they often did not treat them separately from other forms of carnality, such as bestiality, prostitution, or heterosexual buggery. Here again, word usage is revealing. The nineteenth-century term for the legal crime of homosexual intercourse was *sodomy*, but that term could also be used to indicate copulation with an animal, or "unnatural" (oral or anal) intercourse with a member of the opposite sex. It is further significant that *sodomy* and "crime without a name"—the two imprecise labels for homosexual behavior—referred to acts and not to types of persons, social identities, or relationships. Indeed, the one other term which loosely referred to homosexuality was the phrase "unnatural act," which again created the concept of a vaguely defined sexual behavior, not of a personal or a social identity.

The phrase "unnatural act" is useful in one other way for our understanding of nineteenth-century American concepts of homosexuality, for the word *unnatural* implies that the source of the act is inhuman. The desire for erotic play with a member of one's own sex, then, came not from a man's (or a woman's) "natural" passions but from some evil source that was external to human nature. In other words, a man who kissed or embraced an intimate male friend in bed did not worry about homosexual impulses because he did not assume that he had them. In the Victorian language of touch, a kiss or an embrace was a pure gesture of deep affection at least as much as it was an act of sexual expression. The behavior of James Blake and Albert Dodd was understood outside of the strictly sexual context that we would apply to it in the late twentieth century. Those men were in many ways freer to express their affectionate feelings than they would be in the twentieth century.[31]

The physical dimension of romantic friendship cannot be understood solely in terms of sexual boundary definition, however. There were other common experiences that helped to shape patterns of physical affection between friends of the same sex. For instance, nineteenth-century boys expressed their feelings for each other in physical ways much more than verbal ones. As we have noted, fistfights and wrestling matches served as disguised channels of affection between boys. Although they rarely exchanged warm embraces with friends, boys knew the feeling of a friend's body at close range in moments of high emotion.

There were other aspects of daily life in the nineteenth century which provided a context for the physical expressiveness of romantic friendship. One has to do with the meanings attached to the experience of two males (or two females) sharing a bed. In our own time, the phrase "sleeping together" has become a euphemism for sexual intimacy, but in the nineteenth century that phrase still carried its literal meaning. Many middle-class men grew up in large families where children, of necessity, shared a bed.[32] Although the spread of affluence and of modern notions of privacy made the rule of single beds for single persons more common in the late nineteenth century, most middle-class men of the 1800s shared a bed with a brother regularly during childhood. This made the experience of sleeping with another man mundane. It also made the feeling of another male body against one's own quite ordinary—there was no reason for that feeling to cause the tension it can cause in the twentieth century. In an era before central heating, the body warmth of a brother was probably a source of physical pleasure, too. And if the brother was also a beloved friend, the experience could provide emotional satisfaction. William Whittlesey and his brother Elisha realized this when William left their Ohio home in 1838. Elisha wrote to him: "You and I was always together. . . . I never knew what it was before to be separated from a dear Brother." He added significantly: "I miss you the most when I go to bed."[33]

Of course, young men like William Whittlesey did leave home, and when they did, the custom of bedmates continued. Students at colleges and academies often slept together, and impecunious clerks and professional apprentices did the same. For these young men as for brothers at home, the experience of sleeping together was a familiar one that sometimes developed intimate overtones. In 1839, an Illinois storekeeper named Joshua Speed added a few dollars to his meager income by agreeing to share his room and his bed with a man he had never met before—a bachelor lawyer named Abraham Lincoln. This transaction was a common one, but their business arrangement soon blossomed into the closest friendship of a lifetime for the two men.[34]

It was an ordinary experience, then, for men to sleep together. Affection was certainly not a requirement of this simple arrangement, but affection often did come with it. Physical contact was an incidental part of sharing a bed, but it happened—and, in the context of a very affectionate relationship, this contact could express warmth or intimacy. It could even express erotic desire. A wide spectrum of possible meanings—from casual accident to passion—could be felt in the touch of a bedmate. In the absence of a deep cultural anxiety about homosexuality, men did not have to worry about the meaning of those moments of contact.

It should be said that the same thing held true for the romantic friendships of nineteenth-century women. They expressed their intimacy in words and by touch, in the parlor or in bed. Same-sex romances, whether between females or males, were largely bound by the same cultural rules. However, there were some fundamental differences that separated the intimate experience of males and females. The most important difference lay in the fact that the intimacy in women's relationships, once formed, would often endure through life, while the intimacy of male friendship was largely limited to the years between boyhood and manhood.[35]

The distinctive conditions of youth—vague social expectations, uncertain career plans, restless wandering, the transitional nature of youth as a phase in life—all created the conditions for romantic friendship. Adrift in this period of change and uncertainty, a young male cast about for whatever anchor of security he could find. The people closest to him were likely to be of his own age and sex. The offices, countinghouses, and classrooms where a middle-class youth spent his days were sex-segregated. The boardinghouses and dormitories where he lived away from home were all-male environments, and the literary clubs, debating societies, and fraternities where he spent his spare hours were not open to females. His relationship to his parents was in flux (even if he was living at home, he was often eager to prove his independence), and he met adults only at work, usually as his superiors. Present circumstances led a young man naturally to seek other male youths for companionship and security. Moreover, he had long been accustomed to turn to friends of his sex as allies in the face of challenge.

The challenge a young man now faced was different from the battles of boyhood, however, and the needs he felt were deeper than those met by boy-culture friendship. When a young man turned to a male friend, he often needed much more than a boyish ally and comrade. Instead, he needed friendship that would fill some of the emotional space so recently vacated by home and family. In providing love, security, and a sense of being special, these intense attachments gave male youths a substitute for the emotional nurture provided most often in boyhood by a mother. A somewhat older bachelor might also provide the sort of worldly counsel that a young man had once received—or wished for—from his father.[36]

At the same time that the intense attachments between young men harked back to their past, they also carried portents of the future: these intimate relationships offered a rehearsal for marriage. We have already noted many of the similarities between male intimacy and wedlock: the terms of endearment, the pledges of devotion, the sharing of deepest secrets, the emotional support, even the exchanges of physical affection in bed. Romantic friendships gave young men a chance to play-act the trials and the possibilities of marriage, to test their feelings about adult intimacy in a setting where lifelong commitment was not at stake. In a time when divorce was not an acceptable option, young men felt understandably insecure about what lay ahead in marriage—especially when one thinks of the suppression of tenderness that they experienced in boy culture. Intimate friendship offered them a chance for rehearsal. More than that, it was a rehearsal with a member of the more familiar and less intimidating sex. The intimate attachments of male youth served as a testing ground for manhood even as they offered a reprise of boyhood.

"A Fondness I . . . Sometimes Think Almost Childish"

Even as young men were pursuing friendship eagerly, they believed that intimate male attachment was a passing fancy; they were conscious of the fact that these relationships belonged to an era in their lives which would not last. The romantic friendships we have studied offer testimony to the self-conscious segmenting of life and of personal attachment. When Daniel Webster proposed to Hervey Bingham that they should live together forever, he was expressing a strong and genuine wish, but he knew that the wish would not come true. Webster, after all, was obsessed with the pursuit of marriage. He even wrote candidly to Bingham about the limits of their intimate relationship. As he reflected on the pleasure of their confidential talks, he told his friend that they "converse[d] with a fondness I always approve, though sometimes think almost childish."[37] To Webster, then, the warmest, most confiding moments of his friendships were worthy of a child but not a man.

What was it that made the intimate friendships of youth seem childish even to their participants? By using the word *childish*, a young man contrasted the qualities of his own intense attachments to the qualities of manhood. He knew that the tenderness, the dependence, and the expressiveness that these relationships evoked in him were qualities at odds with the independence and emotional austerity expected of a grown man. To Daniel Webster, for instance, it was the "fondness" of his conversations with Bingham that made them seem "childish." Furthermore, there was a quality of play in these relationships, something both passionate and whimsical which set them apart from manhood with its serious, determined tone. A man's life was a life of work, and there was little room in it for heart-to-heart talks late at night.

Indeed, young men showed in many ways their knowledge that the intimate friendships of youth were doomed. When Rutherford B. Hayes and his friends formed their Phi Zeta ("Friendship for Life") fraternity at Kenyon College, they did so in fear that their close bonds would not survive graduation. Their fears were realized in spite of their efforts—the club did not survive, and few of their friendships remained close after college.[38]

Even when a friendship did survive, there were still other perils that threatened its existence. Morton Bailey and James Cattell had a double vision of their attachment. When they looked beyond their current intimacy and viewed the years of friendship that lay ahead of them, their writing turned cool and formal. They described a future day when they would "extend to each other the hospitalities of [their] own homes"— when they might "exchange social courtesies and spend not a few vacation times together in pleasant converse."[39] Even though Bailey and Cattell shared their deepest wishes and feelings for the moment, they expected only "social courtesies" and "pleasant converse" later in life.

There were several reasons why close friends assumed that their ties would be broken by manhood, and all of them were related to the task of taking on a man's duties. We noted earlier, for instance, that many young men thought of their intimate friendships as the functional equivalent of marriage, and they expected that wedlock would threaten those male bonds. Their fears proved accurate: of all the intimate friendships described here, not a single one maintained its former intensity after marriage. Some of them did not survive at all.

A dramatic instance of such a transformation occurred in Abraham Lincoln's friendship with Joshua Speed. The two were ardently close friends as well as bedmates for more than three years. Lincoln and Speed—who both turned thirty during their time together—were living through a period of tentative beginnings in courtship and career. They became so close that when Speed shut down his store and moved away, Lincoln was plunged into the worst depression of his life. As he followed the subsequent triumph of his friend's courtship, though, Lincoln emerged slowly from his depression. Then, once Speed was married, their relationship suddenly lost its significance for Lincoln. His letters to Speed grew distant in tone, and soon they were corresponding only on business matters. There was little anger or bitterness at the demise of the friendship, and once or twice in later years the two men reminisced warmly. Without doubt, however, their intimacy had come to a sharp and sudden halt when Joshua Speed married.[40]

Other changes in a young man's life worked to doom his intimate friendships. Chief among these was a strong commitment to a career. Albert Dodd, noted earlier for his passionate attachments to fellow males, underwent a dramatic change during his time at Yale in the late 1830s. After devoting himself to the study of law, he first went west to practice in St. Louis and then in Bloomington, Illinois. During these years, his correspondence grew impersonal and showed no indication of the romantic passions he had experienced just a few years before. In fact, Albert made self-mastery the dominant theme of a letter he wrote to his brother at this time. He argued forcefully that the control of moods, the government of temper, and a determination to look on the bright side of things were crucial traits in the development of character. Judging by the great changes in his life, young Dodd must have been practicing the self-control he so fervently preached. Then, in 1844, he was accidentally drowned. Although Dodd was only twenty-six years old at the time of his death, he had lived long enough to reshape his own life and temperament.[41]

Albert Dodd's commitment to a career played a central part in the redirection of his passions away from romantic friendship, but that commitment was clearly not the only force at work in the transformation of this young man's life. He had also done something larger in the process of finding a calling: he had gathered and focused his energies and found a use for them within the main currents of his society. He had taken command of his own needs and found a way to connect them with the needs of the social world around him. It appears—to use Erik Erikson's term—that Dodd achieved a sense of *ego identity* during the years after college.[42] In doing so, he sacrificed some of the passions and personal attachments that had given meaning to his days as a student.

The experience of Daniel Webster shows how a young middle-class man achieved his manhood—and how he gave up other modes of feeling and attachment in the process. The ten years after Daniel's graduation from Dartmouth were a time of experiment and uncertainty. These were the years when he sustained and strengthened the intimate ties formed in college with Hervey Bingham. He continued several other friendships with nearly equal zeal. As mentioned earlier, young Webster and his friends engaged in constant exploration of their hopes and fears about marriage and work. Then, gradually, he put together the pieces of his adult life. His hesitation about a career in the law vanished. His beloved father died, leaving him free to practice law wherever he pleased. He began courting a young woman named Grace Fletcher, and, in the process of wooing her, made a confession of faith and became a church member. Finally, in 1808, nearly a full decade after his college graduation, Webster married Fletcher. As a recent biographer of Webster has written, he "had finally taken the last step" in fitting himself for his life as a mature man. "He had committed himself to a profession, made his peace with his family and his God, and taken the kind of wife he needed. The doubting and inward looking were behind him forever."[43]

This transformation—like the one that Albert Dodd experienced—was achieved at a price. For "the doubting and inward looking" that Webster left behind had been the stuff and substance of his intimate attachment with Bingham. In the absence of a wife, a settled career, or a home of his own, Webster had latched onto the security of close friendship. The uncertainty of life in a period of transition had added a special strength to these bonds of friendship. Once that uncertainty was gone, the soul-searching stopped and the basis for intimacy suddenly grew narrow. Letters to friends (which Webster wrote less frequently now) took on a breezy, unreflective tone. Webster continued throughout his life to have warm and pleasant, if intermittent, relationships with the friends of his youth, but their bonds were never again bonds of intimacy.

Webster's experience was a common one. Major commitments—marriage, a settled career, a home of one's own—were the marks of a man's identity. Once those commitments were made, a male became a man, and the romance and carefree play of boyhood and youth were set aside. There was little room for attachments to other men that were tender, intimate, dependent—in short, "childish."

Instead, the identity of a middle-class man was founded on independent action, cool detachment, and sober responsibility. Men aimed to make themselves individual actors, differentiated and separate from all others in a middle-class workplace that was open and fluid. Adult male identity—so detached and independent—contrasted with that of adult females, which was built on interdependence and connection. Women were linked by "supportive networks" and by female "rituals which accompanied virtually every important event in a woman's life."[44]

Of course, it had been this way from the start for middle-class women in the nineteenth century. Growing up in a domestic world where women set the tone, girls built close, expressive relationships with mothers and sisters, and inherited a network of female friends and relatives that provided personal support and a foundation for a woman's identity. As she grew up to be a woman, a girl developed her own network, but it meshed with the network she had inherited; it extended its reach beyond marriage, connecting a woman closely to other women and to her past.[45] For boys, things were different. A male was constantly creating new networks of peers and leaving old ones behind, from the self-made, shifting alliances of boy culture to youthful friendships in the workplace and the young men's associations. Thus, the romantic friendships of young manhood were not part of a lifelong network of intimate bonds. The closeness of these relationships was distinctive to one phase of the life cycle.

Although these intense attachments of male youth did not last into manhood, they did leave a legacy in men's adult lives and provided a rehearsal for the marriage on which nearly every man embarked. Moreover, while friendships between men lacked the intensity of youthful bonds, they often showed a loyal, enduring fondness which must have owed something to earlier and more intimate ties. The special friendships of youth may also have contributed to the cohesion of social relationships in the keenly competitive marketplace where middle-class men spent their days. As men struggled to maintain the balance between cooperation and competition in the workplace, they built on their experiences with the contentious comradeship of boy culture and then added to it the experience in youth of intimacy with another man. By teaching empathy and a sense of appreciation for the interior lives of other men, those youthful relationships helped to provide a readier feeling of trust when men began building bonds with competitors and collaborators.

This process suggests a final legacy of the intimate friendships of youth. Many of the social bonds that men developed with their fellows in the marketplace were nurtured in men's clubs, fraternal lodges, political parties, and various formal and informal business associations. Men tied their loyalties to those groups with a passion equal to that of their youthful friendships. These male institutions may, in fact, have offered their members a viable emotional compromise between connection and autonomy: men could invest their bonds to the group with the same deep relational needs that they had displayed in youth, yet they did not have to develop a particular relationship that might interfere with their professional independence or leave them vulnerable in the harshly competitive world of middle-class work. By absorbing the desire for male attachment and diffusing it over a broad membership, all-male clubs could provide an outlet for deep emotional needs without threatening the individual autonomy or the psychological armor that were basic parts of a man's public identity.[46]

Friendship did not, in sum, disappear from the lives of mature men, but it never regained the passionate intensity of youth. Male friends—*men* friends—came to play a different sort of role in each other's lives.

Chapter 5

THE DEVELOPMENT OF MEN'S ATTITUDES TOWARD WOMEN

IN 1815, a young man wrote of the woman he loved: "Only to think that I should aspire to possess the love of such an *angel*." Little more than two decades later, another bachelor warned a friend about women: "Beware lest the little d[evi]ls with their laughing, swearing eyes, their passions brows, their damask cheeks bedevil your heart, and lampoon you as they do most men."[1] These two descriptions of women were both typical of their time. Young men of the nineteenth century regarded women with deep ambivalence and swung wildly from one extreme to the other in their feelings. Where did these attitudes come from? How did a young man develop his perceptions of the opposite sex?

In all but the most unusual families, a boy's first experience of women came from his mother. She was the first person to provide him with love, nurture, and a sense of human relatedness; she was also the first person to frustrate him, control him, and reject him. This, of course, is true in many cultures. But, as we have seen, the relationship of mother and son in the middle-class homes of the 1800s had more distinctive dimensions. The cultural celebration of maternal love increased the chances that the boy would experience it, and may even have exaggerated the longing for female affection in boys who failed to receive it from their mothers. At the same time, the nineteenth-century expectation that a mother would implant morality in her sons inflated the chances that a boy would experience women as agents of frustration and control. Thus, the boy's first relationship with a woman established a set of expectations in which both love and frustration were firmly embedded. Later experiences built on these early expectations, sometimes adding strength to them and sometimes revising them. New layers of experience were being added even before a boy left home.

Brothers and Sisters

In 1835, when Theodore Russell wanted to reveal his deepest thoughts about his past and his future, he confided in his sister Sarah. Even though she was several years younger, he felt most comfortable sharing his innermost feelings with her. "What [is there]," he asked in a letter to his father, "like a sister's holy love[?]"[2]

Such confidence and trust between brothers and sisters was common in middle-class families of the time. Indeed, the relationship was so important that it served an important symbolic function. In the prescriptive literature of the nineteenth century, the brother-sister bond was exalted as a model of purity in an era when sexual control was a cardinal principle of morality. The authors of advice books held up the sibling tie as a shining example of chaste, Christian love between a male and a female. There were young men and women who actually did use the brother-sister bond as a guide for their own behavior outside the family. Theodore Weld, for instance, pursued his relations with women according to the rules he had established in his extended, intimate ties with his own sister, offering his Christian guidance in return for chaste but ardent devotion. Lu Burlingame, an Indiana writer and lecturer, also used the sibling relationship as a model. She held off the passions of her eager young beau for two years by invoking the bond of brother and sister—"deep and pure and unselfish."[3]

While the brother-sister tie served as a cultural ideal, it also provided important personal experience. For most girls and boys, it was the first peer relationship with the opposite sex, and it served as a bridge between the separate worlds of male and female. After hours of play with others of their own sex, boys returned home to the world where their sisters spent their time. Here, in the evenings and on rainy days, the children of both sexes mingled more freely than they did at school. Henry Seidel Canby remembered quiet card games with the girls, and Edward Everett Hale recalled that brothers and sisters made up stories and drew pictures together. He also noted that sisters and brothers made an effort to "report every evening to one another" on the events in their separate daytime worlds. In this informal atmosphere, and in the

more structured setting at the dinner table, boys had their most extensive contact with girls.[4]

These moments of contact unfolded in the presence of adults. Vigilant and concerned, parents injected their own expectations into the relationships of youthful brothers and sisters. On the one hand, boys were
required to play a protective role in their sisters' lives. By the time they
were eight or nine years old, boys were sent to escort their sisters home
from evening visits. Without prompting from their parents, brothers also
defended their sisters against harassment by other boys. In turn, girls
had their own obligations to their brothers. Catherine Sedgwick wrote in
her popular novel *Home* that parents "early accustomed [their boys] to
receiving household services from their mothers and sisters." The parents, according to Sedgwick, required this service in the hope "of inspiring [their sons] with a . . . consideration for that sex whose lot it is to be
domestic ministers of boy and man."[5]

The duties of sororal service and fraternal protection created a reciprocal kindness in the relationship of sister and brother, but those same
duties also emphasized the difference between the sexes. The male was
strong and knew the ways of the world, the woman was weak and knew
the arts of the home. Out of this careful sorting of gender traits grew a
common pattern of brother-sister relations, a pattern that—as Sedgwick
noted—parents were eager to promote. The girls became accustomed to
serving their brothers, and grew reliant on fraternal protection in dealing with the world; as they did so, many developed a habit of adoration
toward their brothers.[6] For their part, brothers who came to think of
their sisters as generous, frail, and adoring often developed that sense of
loving, fraternal consideration which their parents had hoped to breed in
them. The heartfelt sensitivity of brother for sister is evident in this letter from a beloved brother who was about to be married. As Seargent
Prentiss sought to reassure his sister Anna that she would be no "less
necessary . . . to my happiness" than she had been, he wrote:

> If I thought my marriage . . . would in one jot or tittle, affect my love for
> you, or deprive me of any opportunity of enjoying your society, or con-
> ducing to your happiness, I should shrink from the hour which I now
> look forward to with such joyful anticipations. No my own dear sister, my
> love for you is a part of my existence.[7]

These were loving, generous words, but they cannot conceal the fact
that Prentiss had created a happy situation for himself. He now had two
women of his own age who were committed to love and adore him,

while his sister had to swallow her feelings, share her beloved brother, and wait for fate to deliver her a suitable husband.[8]

The situation of Seargent and Anna Prentiss makes at least one thing clear: The brother-sister relationship among the middle class served as a two-edged sword. It taught inequality and encouraged love at the same time, and nurtured a separation of the sexes even as it fostered intimacy between them. This relationship did not, of course, begin these lessons, but it did drive their message home forcefully. The structure of the relationship was neatly reciprocal and distinctly unequal.

In the bond between brother and sister, the personal was clearly political, but it was not *only* political. The love and warmth between siblings could obscure issues of power; it seeped around and through the formal roles and the official prescriptions to nurture deeply affectionate relationships. These ties often provided young men and women with their first experience of intimacy with a peer of the opposite sex. Aaron and Lucy Olmstead certainly enjoyed such an intimate relationship. They grew up together as part of a large family in Saratoga Springs, New York, but by the time they reached their twenties, they had both left home—Aaron to attend Rensselaer Polytechnic Institute and later to teach at a small Connecticut academy, Lucy to live with a different brother and his family in a small Pennsylvania town. During these years of separation, they wrote long and affectionate letters to each other; it is from these letters that we learn about their relationship.

Aaron Olmstead liked to confide in his sister. He disclosed his feelings about marriage to her and asked for her advice about the course of his career. He made up acrostics to send her, and, in the loneliness of his position in Connecticut, relied on her to raise his spirits: "I wish you would write to me soon. Your letters are the glad rays that cheer me here." By the same token, Lucy depended heavily on Aaron. This reliance reached a peak during the years she lived in Pennsylvania, where she was surrounded almost entirely by strangers and suffered from a crippling case of homesickness. She wrote at the end of one letter: "I cannot close without begging you to write immediately. . . . [Your] letters . . . are always received torn open and read over and over with the greatest eagerness." After the letters came, Lucy thanked Aaron profusely for "his expressions of sympathy and love." As sad as she was at their separation, she also worried about the times to come when other loves would stand between them. "If we meet in after years," she wrote, "it may be with affections centered in other objects, and our time so occupied that it will admit of but a hurried visit. . . . Perhaps absence and time may so change us that a seeming coldness may exist between us." While Lucy fretted like a lover, she affirmed her commitment like one, too. She avowed herself "a Sister who will continue to love you the more dearly the longer she is separated from you," and she signed letters: "Yours with the most sincere love and affection."[9]

Because the letters of Aaron and Lucy Olmstead come from a narrow span of years when they were in their twenties, we have little direct evidence of the longer course of their relationship. Their frequent references to the "many past enjoyments" they had shared and the "many scenes of youthful pleasure of which we had partaken" strongly indicate a bond with a long, rich, and affectionate past. We also know that when Lucy returned to Saratoga and ended her time of crushing loneliness, she continued to write frequent, loving letters to her brother in Connecticut. Indeed, her letters served as a conduit of information and advice to Aaron from the rest of the family. In the eyes of parents and siblings, Lucy was Aaron's chosen one within the Olmstead clan. Whether this relationship maintained its intensity over the course of a lifetime we do not know, but it is clear that their bond offered Lucy and Aaron a special experience of intimacy. They had a chance to test their feelings and their personal skills in an intense relationship with a peer of the opposite sex, in a circumstance where expectations were safely limited and the chances of rejection were minimal. Together, brother and sister had given each other a trial run at marriage.[10]

The Olmsteads offer us an example of genuine sympathy and deep affection between a brother and sister. Still, the same standards that affected other siblings affected this intimate relationship as well. While Aaron wrestled with the choice of which career path he should pursue among a wide range of options, Lucy was stranded in an isolated town where she was sent as a pawn in family plans to help her brother Samuel. As Aaron wrote to Lucy with speculations about when he might marry, Lucy could only stand passively, waiting and hoping that someone she liked as well as Aaron might appear in her parlor and find her suitable. And although the affection between them was mutual, the hard work of committing feeling into words fell to Lucy. Loving as it was, this relationship gave its participants an intimate experience of the imbalance between the sexes. In the era of the Olmsteads, the brother-sister relationship served the sexes as a laboratory of love and inequality.

Boys and Girls Together

Not every relationship between brother and sister was as close as the one between Aaron and Lucy Olmstead. Distant relationships simply passed unnoted in letters and diaries. As for relations that were hostile or tense, the feelings they generated were apparently silenced in the interest of domestic peace. In an era when family ties beyond childhood were largely voluntary and siblings could live far apart as adults, an ill-matched brother and sister could simply bury a failed relationship.

The silence that surrounded bad feeling between brothers and sisters did not carry over to the wider relationship between the sexes in childhood. Indeed, the relations of boys and girls outside the family showed a much broader range of emotions than brother-sister ties did. In particular, these relations offered boys a more comfortable setting for expressing negative feelings about the other sex.

For much of the day, boys and girls were separate. They played apart in the schoolyard, and their daily chores afforded them little contact. When left to play freely, the boys headed for the streets and the fields, while the girls stayed close to the house. Still, their activities brought them together often enough to create a sense of familiarity. In most cases, boys and girls were classmates at school. They attended the same churches and went to Sunday school together. On rainy days, the friends of brothers and sisters might inhabit the same house. When the weather was nice, their outdoor spaces were bound to overlap, especially around yards and porches. Boys and girls had ample opportunity to become familiar, and they developed clear and passionately held images of each other.[11]

The young males held an image of girls that was distinctly two-sided. Boys knew that they preferred the company of other boys, contrasting their own rough play with the gentler pastimes of girls. The opposite sex, they felt, was timid and dull. A girl spent her day in that world of good behavior where dirt and noise were not allowed and where—given middle-class tastes of the time—the sun rarely shone.[12] The most serious damage to a boy's image of girls probably stemmed from the fact that he had recently escaped from that domestic world himself. Boys, after all, spent the first few years of their lives entirely in women's world, closely supervised and dressed in the same clothes as girls. If boys' feelings about girls contained a great measure of scorn, it was a scorn they felt for an old and frustrating identity that they had finally and gleefully shed. Girls were the objects of ill feeling that they had done little to create.

It did not matter to the boys that girls had roused their scorn unwittingly. The boys delighted in the opportunity to attack them. Young Francis Parkman made an electric machine that could give a shock to a whole row of girls at school. More often, boys launched sudden attacks of slapping and scratching. Even more frequently, they pelted girls with mud balls, snowballs, chestnuts, and whatever other small-but-annoying objects came to hand.[13]

The girls, especially when treated as an undefined herd of gentle, frilly things, made a handy screen on which a boy could project many hostile feelings. In one quick attack, a boy could take vengeance on an earlier identity, express his disdain for the clean politeness of domesticity, and vent his scorn for the restraint of impulse that home and women represented. The cruelty of boys to girls was in certain ways similar to their cruelty toward small animals. Both categories of victim appeared to boys as frail, defenseless creatures, and both were targets unlikely to fight back. In either case, boys were conducting an exercise in power by taking advantage of a situation which they could easily dominate.

There is yet another dimension of meaning to the petty violence that boys inflicted on girls. Since boys used rough physical contact to communicate fondness as well as dislike, their attacks on girls signified not only hostility but also its opposite, affection. If pelting another boy with stones could be an expression of regard, a similar assault could transmit the same sort of message from boy to girl. Or at least in the mind of the boy it could. The idea that girls might experience petty attacks in a different way either did not occur to boys or else did not deter them from launching their assaults.

The records of nineteenth-century life indicate that boys' emotions about girls often combined fascinated attraction with the disdain that we have already explored.[14] When a boy was "stuck on" a girl, he might do little more than exchange glances and giggles. A more adventurous fellow might carry a girl's books home from school or exchange tokens of affection. Older boys liked to find clever ways to send notes to their chosen ones during class time at school, and a few even wrote valentine messages to their sweethearts. While these desultory affairs rarely preoccupied the boys, they do indicate a capacity for tender affection toward girls that was totally at odds with the rough, boisterous surface of the youthful male personality.

The same boyish interest in the opposite sex showed through in other, more generalized ways. In the classroom, boys liked to pull pranks that would attract the girls' attention and make them laugh. They were also capable of minor acts of gallantry such as breaking a pencil in half to share with a needy girl or refusing to squirt girls who happened into the midst of a water fight (an odd point of chivalry on the part of boys who liked to splatter young females with mud balls).[15] In sum, boys made it clear that they found girls admirable and attractive, even though they displayed an equally genuine sense of scorn and suspicion toward females. The positive feelings that girls aroused—feelings that the boys seemed to find mysterious and unsettling—may have added a special passion to the boys' feelings of disdain, and thus lent particular vigor to their playful attacks.

In all of this, there is little to indicate that boys were paying attention to specific qualities of individual girls. Young females served as nearly blank screens where boys focused positive as well as negative feelings about the opposite sex. The screen was not perfectly blank, of course; boys looked at girls and saw gentler, quieter people than themselves, people enmeshed in a domestic world and dressed in gowns and curls. These few broad cues were enough to elicit a confusing combination of disdain and reverence that was rooted in boys' early life experience. One common theme that did link these ambivalent feelings was a wish to dominate, either through physical aggression or through the protective gestures of gallantry. The desire to dominate, together with the boyish ambivalence toward girls, formed an important emotional legacy that boys brought with them to the more focused relationships with girls that would come in their late teens.

The "Effects of 'Cupid's Darts'"

In the world of nineteenth-century childhood, boys and girls assumed that a young male "liked best to be with boys" and "would a great deal rather play with a boy than [a girl] at recess."[16] Then, at about the mid-teens, boys took a new and serious interest in girls. Not coincidentally, this was the age at which puberty arrived in the nineteenth century. Boys were conscious of the changing forces that drove their interest. One Massachusetts youth of seventeen or eighteen asked a friend, "[A]t our age when our affections are strongest is it to be supposed that we should not have someone on whom our affections are fixed?" "If it were to be otherwise," said the boy in answer to his own question, "it would be out of the ordinary course of our nature."[17]

What did this dramatic change feel like to a boy who lived through it? Daniel Carter Beard, illustrator and founder of the American Boy Scouts, left a vivid description in his autobiography: "When girl-consciousness entered my young life it swept through it like a tornado." He "fought vigorously" against the change, but "at length . . . threw up [his] hands and succumbed." Yet he felt "ashamed" of himself for abandoning "the things which [he] had heretofore deemed the only ones worth while." These "things" were passions and pastimes like rough games, dirty fingernails, and raucous teasing, which he traded for cotillions and regular baths. He accepted willingly the same "Sunday church clothes" he had resented throughout boyhood.[18] While he might have noted that these were grown-up men's clothes, and signs of increasing power and independence, he did not experience the change in that way. Rather, he framed the situation in terms of gender, not age: he felt that he must choose between a *woman's* way and a *boy's* way. And he surrendered readily to the female world he had fought against for so long. In the words of another love-struck youth, these were the "effects of 'Cupid's Darts.'"[19] Beard and countless other young men gave themselves up to the pursuit of romance.

And how did they pursue romance? There was a wide variety of young people's activities, some involving large numbers of youthful men and women. As many as twenty or thirty might go out on a sleigh ride or a skating party. In a small town, similar numbers might go to quilting or logging bees, while large groups of young city folk would mobilize for outings in the country. In the second half of the century, church socials became common. More formal indoor affairs such as balls and cotillions caused special excitement among the young men and women in a given locale. Then, too, there were events—music society meetings, lyceum lectures, public examinations at academies and colleges—that took place for their own purposes but allowed many young single people to mingle freely. All of these social occasions provided pleasant distractions—skating, dancing, singing—from the tensions that built when eager, nervous bachelors and misses gathered to measure and be measured for romance.[20]

The level of excitement increased at smaller parties and informal get-togethers in private homes. While there was certainly a chance to talk at the large public events, these private parties were more intimate occasions which put an added emphasis on personal conversation. Depending on the mood and the people, the talk could be serious or superficial, polite or flirtatious. Even here there were diversions from the mating games in progress. The young people pulled taffy, read aloud, or gathered about the piano to sing.[21]

Other diversions, instead of offering distractions, served as ritualized versions of the mating game. Dancing, which had abundant overtones of romance even in a large public hall, became a more intimate gesture in a private home with only a few people present. So passionate were the overtones of dancing that it was forbidden as sinful at many small-town parties. Kissing games offered popular alternatives to the sins of dancing. They involved "a great deal of clasping hands, of going round in a circle, of passing under each other's elevated arms, of singing about my true love, and the end was kisses distributed with more or less partiality according to the rules of the play; but thank Heaven, there was no fid-dler." This may seem like an odd way to improve on the "sins" of con-tredanse, but the folks in Massachusetts did not see it that way: "Kissing was a sign of peace, and was not at all like taking hold of hands and skip-ping about to the scraping of a wicked fiddle."[22] Whether the amuse-ment was dancing or kissing games, though, the point remained the same: these diversions let young people play out the romantic dreams and passionate impulses that lay beneath the surface of their tense chat-ting and anxious flirtation.

The balls and parties marked a stunning change for boys who had struggled so long against the world of petticoats and politeness. Reeling already from the new feelings brought by puberty, they felt baffled by the sudden transformation of familiar relationships. In an autobiographi-cal novel of the era, a boy arrived at his first party, and "the sound of . . . girls' voices . . . set his heart in a flutter":

> He could face the whole district school of girls without flinching,—he didn't mind 'em in the meeting house in their Sunday best; but he began to be conscious that now he was passing to a new sphere, where the girls are supreme and superior and he began to feel for the first time that he was an awkward boy.[23]

As a boy crossed the threshold into this new arena of feeling and ex-perience, he dimly realized that he was passing back into women's world. His sense of mastery slipped away from him when impulses he could not deny drove him into a social realm he could not understand. The experi-ence of boy culture left a youth unprepared to grapple with this loss of his sense of mastery and control.

At this dramatic juncture in life, all but the most isolated youths turned to their male friends for help and support. The attempt to under-stand women became a shared obsession, and the pursuit of them be-came a shared crisis. In boardinghouse bedrooms, on long walks home from parties, and in letters, young men traded intensely in the feelings and details of their relationships with women. They reported on their ac-tivities—the dances, the visits, the conversations—and they complained when they did "not drive much of a trade in the *wooing line*."[24]

This correspondence between young men also reveals an elaborate intelligence network, full of codes, secrets, and cryptic messages. Young ladies were referred to by designations such as "L----a," "°°°°," and "a certain blue eyed one,"[25] and veiled communications were common ("----told me a few days since, that when I wrote I might give her love to you, if I thought you would accept it") and so was inside information ("Your sweet-issimus Rebecca has not come to Boston. Her sister will come first.").[26] Young men made baffled attempts to analyze the confused responses of the young women who caught their fancy ("There was a No, and a Yes, and a blush, and a smile, and a blush, and so you may make what you can of them"), and they plotted strategy as allies.[27]

These alliances and networks of intrigue were devices for operating in a foreign country where feeling outweighed reason and grace mattered more than strength. Men faced emotional issues that had played no part in boy culture and that rarely surfaced in their current world of career apprenticeship. Young males found themselves confessing their shyness to one another and fretting together about their problems in attracting women. When Daniel Webster wrote to his friend Habijah Fuller about the experience of entering a ballroom, he exposed a sense of vulnerability that was common to young men:

> About nine [I] wandered "unfriended and alone" into the ball-room. What a congregation of beauty! Whose heart but must flutter a little, at so many pretty faces? . . . attention was so much divided, that it could not fasten anywhere, and though [I] "trod among a thousand perils," came off unhurt.[28]

Feminine beauty (and the feelings it evoked) felt dangerous to Webster, and he wished for the company of a friend to guide him through this peril. A young male knew how to fight back—or at least how to prove himself—if he were mocked or snubbed by other males; but physical self-assertion gained nothing with a woman, and the rewards for unrelenting effort were much less certain in the world of romance than they were in the male worlds of work and play.

To understand their predicament, young men relied on what they knew: they turned to the familiar language of commerce, ill-suited though it was to the problem at hand. In 1802, Daniel Webster, fearing that all the young women of Hanover might be married before he chose one, made the following proposal to a college friend: "It is true . . . that there is a prospect of all the Hanover *Ribs* being sold before you and I can become purchasers. How do you think it would do to forestall the market, and, for the sake of security, to bespeak a Rib in season?"[29] A subtler variant on this commercial style of thinking was also common: men sized up the women of a town or a region as if comparing shipments of goods at market. "I agree with you that the *maids* of *Saratoga* are *unrivalled,*" wrote one youth. "Our New England girls may equal them but *Yankee* as I am give me Saratoga yet." Another young man compared both the number and the beauty of Maine and Massachusetts women:

> You know that the new towns have usually more males than females, and old commercial towns the reverse.... In point of beauty, I do not feel competent to decide. I cannot calculate the precise value of a dimple, nor estimate the charms of an eyebrow, yet I see nothing repulsive in the appearance of Maine Misses.[30]

As this quotation reminds us, there was a market mechanism of sorts involved in the relation of marriageable men and women, that the ratio of "supply" to "demand" varied from place to place. Still, the metaphor reduced women to commodities in supply. For this reason alone, an economic understanding of women could not have been helpful to a man confronting his emotions as he walked into a crowded ballroom or expressed his interest to a special young woman.[31]

Men persisted, nevertheless, in drawing on their commercial and competitive visions of the world as they tried to grapple with their romantic insecurities. The advice they offered each other in dealing with women was no different from the advice they would have offered for success in any other arena. Young Aaron Olmstead gave a friend the following counsel on facing a room full of young women:

> Depend upon it, "a faint heart never won a fair lady." If you would make conquests instead of suffering your eyes to be dazzled by a false splendor and sculking [sic] away in the background you must take a monstrous dose of Col. Crockett's *"go ahead"* ... and well-prepared with self-assurance ... bounce into the midst of the fair [ladies].[32]

With its references to self-assurance, conquest, and Davy Crockett, this statement sounds more like a recipe for victory in the warfare of boy culture than a piece of advice on success with women.

Still, there was one respect in which the competitive model of romance was apt. When a young man sought a woman's attention at a party or a dance, every other member of his sex was a rival. Here was a situation he could understand, and he responded to it with keen enthusiasm. Half a century after winning his wife's hand in marriage, the novelist Lew Wallace could still give a sharp description of his four competitors for the young woman's affection.[33] Young men like Wallace knew intimately the perils of competition, and they knew from long experience how to cope with the pangs of defeat.

What they did not know was the nature of the opposite sex. When they were courting, they feared rejection by a woman far more than defeat by a rival. Women appeared as desirable but mysterious beings whose judgment of a young man could elate him or leave him shattered. Young men tried desperately to understand these females who obsessed them.

Devil or Angel?: Attitudes toward Women

As much as young men relied on competitive and commercial metaphors to make sense of their relations with women, those were not the only distorting lenses through which they viewed their female counterparts. They brought to their romantic experience a set of attitudes which both deified and degraded women. Young men called them "celestial maid," "angelic creature," and "the fair ones." On the other hand, they also made frequent associations between women and the temptress Eve. Men used religious imagery to describe women because their feelings about them were transcendently powerful, and the mixture of good and evil in their imagery shows how deeply ambivalent their feelings were.[34]

Men portrayed feminine evil as a problem with many facets. They doubted female sincerity, especially in the midst of courting. A New Yorker named Horace Leete praised the woman his brother hoped to marry, saying that her love was "one of true sincerity such as is *rarely* to be found" in a woman. Young men like Leete especially feared that females, with their supposed vanity and insincerity, would make fools of them and manipulate them for their own selfish purposes. One man asserted that a boy learned as he grew up that "a spider web is stronger than a cable . . . [and] that a pretty little girl could turn him round her finger a great deal easier than a big bully of a boy could make him cry 'enough.'" Youthful men feared the shrewdness of the opposite sex, and they were frightened by the ability of women to exploit their attractiveness to men.[35]

To some extent, this fear was another expression of young men's anxiety about being lured back into women's sphere. A return to a domestic life meant responsibility, confinement, high virtue, and good manners, none of which appealed to the graduates of boy culture. At a deeper level, the re-creation of a home evoked old memories—of wearing girlish clothes, of being constantly watched, and (most threatening of all) of being deeply dependent on a woman. After years of striving for "manly independence" and now arriving at the verge of it, male youth grew panicky at the thought of a retreat to dependence. Henry David Thoreau, who was a lifelong bachelor, described the domesticated male as a pathetic caged creature:

> His house is a prison, in which he finds himself oppressed and confined, not sheltered and protected. He walks as if he sustained the roof; he carries his arms as if the walls would fall in and crush him, and his feet remember the cellar beneath. His muscles are never relaxed. It is rare that he overcomes the house, and learns to sit at home in it.

Thoreau's depiction of "the civilized man [with] the habits of the house" echoed in Daniel Webster's fearful description of married life: "This said wed-lock is a very dangerous sort of lock. Once fastened it is fastened forever. It is a lock that one can't unlock; you can't break it, you can't pick it."[36]

Young men saw the women who attracted them as lures that drew them back into the cage of domesticity. To describe this aspect of their fear of women, male youths returned to the hunting experiences of boyhood. Only now the situation was reversed; they themselves had become the prey. A young man in love was "like a pheasant in a snare." Another watched the young women of his village search for husbands and vowed: "I will be very careful they do not ensnare me." Other men found in their situation a new sense of empathy for the fish they had caught as boys. John Barnard thought of his two unsuccessful courtships and "resolved aye swore that that bait should not catch me again."[37] Women were at once the fisher and the bait, the trapper and the lure. From one place in their hearts, young men regarded women with the vigilance and fear that the prey feels for the predator.

As deeply as young men feared women, however, those fears represented only one side of their feelings. If their thoughts of women sometimes called up images of devils, hunters, jailers, and the perfidy of Eve, they also evoked images that were reverential and profoundly attractive. Indeed, women would not have looked so dangerous to men if they had not been so appealing, nor would their domestic world have seemed so ensnaring if it had not seemed so desirable.

At the basis of women's appeal lay two characterizations of femininity that survived well into the twentieth century: "the fair sex" and "the weaker sex." Men could not resist the attraction of the female. The "fair ones," as they sometimes called women, evoked such "romantic passion" that men felt they had lost control of their feelings.[38] An incident in the autobiography of businessman Charles Flint shows the way bachelors felt about the appeal of feminine beauty. Flint and some friends stayed up most of one Saturday night celebrating their victory in a sailing regatta. According to a poem written about the occasion by his friends, Flint "whistled . . . brave bachelor airs" full of "brave anti-marital scorning" that night. Yet early the next morning while his fellow celebrants slept, Flint quietly rose, put on his Sunday best, and went ashore to join an attractive young woman at church. His poetic friends noted that "the eyes of the ladies there won us/ As Heaven can't win you . . . or me." They also reached the broader conclusion that "of Beauty Man ne'er knows satiety." In this tale, the loveliness of a woman could move a man to do that which Heaven itself could not. The story shows how, in spite of "brave antimarital scorning," feminine beauty lured men willingly away from the familiar pleasure and security of male culture.[39]

Once drawn out of that protective all-male world, young men found that other feminine qualities attracted them further. Among these traits was what they saw as women's "weakness." This did not refer primarily to women's lack of physical strength, and certainly did not connote a want of moral or spiritual power. Men used the word to describe a set of traits that were the opposite of their own presumed aggression, boldness, and worldly self-confidence. A turn-of-the-century article summed up what men throughout the 1800s saw as the appeal of feminine weakness. "Grace, daintiness . . . are what men like in women," according to author Rafford Pyke. Women also had a "gentleness that appeals to strength," and a "dependence [that] appeals to all that is generous and chivalrous and tender in [a man's] nature. That one he loves should look to him for everything—protection, maintenance and happiness—what else can be so thrilling to a manly man?"[40] To men, feminine dependence dramatized their own hard-won independence and, in so doing, affirmed their sense of manhood.

Feminine weakness attracted men for another reason, too. The word *weakness* directly implies a power relationship, and men had been training themselves in the uses of power ever since boyhood. Women, by contrast, had been taught cooperation and encouraged in the arts of submission. Young men seized eagerly on this cultural difference. They found gentle submissiveness appealing: relationships with women offered them a respite from the struggles for dominance that raged constantly in the world of men.

The marriage bond, moreover, would be the most important self-created relationship of a man's life. If that relationship had involved a constant struggle for power, it would have added—at the very deepest levels—to the uncertainties bred by daily life in the turbulence of the marketplace. Thus, young men *needed* to see young women as weak and dependent; the upbringing of young females conspired with their needs to a great extent.

Yet it was one of the greatest ironies of male-female relations in this era that women were not only weak and dependent: they were powerful in some respects, and men wanted them to be that way, too. A young male did not use the word *powerful* to describe women in their areas of strength, because it would have fed his insecurities to think of women in that way. Instead, he spoke of ways in which a loving female might serve him. The most evident form of service was nurture—something men had been accustomed to receive from women since the moment of birth. The New York bachelor Horace Leete made the following comment on the value of marriage: "I believe that if anything adds to a man's happiness, it is the society and companionship of a noble hearted and confiding woman. The thoughts of becoming old, and [having no one there] to feel a real interest in our welfare, presents . . . a dark and gloomy picture." As one writer put it: "[A man] wants [a woman] to depend on him, because in his soul he knows he depends on her."[41]

The image of woman as a source of strength—a person to depend on—went well beyond the male vision of the female as nurturant and supportive. Men believed that women were transcendently pious and pure. They also believed that a woman had the power to evoke piety and purity in a man. One youth wrote of a woman's ability to rouse his slumbering spirit: "She is to me a guardian angel, ministering to the finer affections of my soul in a manner wholly new to me, and has awakened new life and energy within my dormant breast." Another young man quoted Tennyson, saying, "I know of no more subtle master under heaven than is the [youthful] passion for a maid."[42]

These statements recall the submission and the dependence of early childhood, of small boys learning right and wrong from the women whose love and care was necessary for their survival. Male youth, arriving at the verge of manhood, still associated a woman's love with the stirrings of conscience. When Ulysses S. Grant was an army officer in his early twenties, he told his sweetheart at home about her power over him:

> You can have but little idea of the influence you have over me, even while so far away. If I feel tempted to anything that I now think is not right I am shure to think, "Well now if Julia saw me would I do so" and thus it is, absent or present, I am more or less governed by what I think is your will.

William Lloyd Garrison II summed up this form of male faith in women: "Men would be much better if they acted always as if [women] were looking at them." The young women who inspired men's love also aroused the moral sense, which grew dull in the male worlds of sociability and work.[43]

The contradictions in men's images of women may not have been as clear to the men themselves as they appear to us now. The dense mixture of suspicion and desire had been developing since a boy's earliest contacts with women, and it governed the fearful encounters, the bold flirtations, and the stubborn obsessions with women that typified early manhood.

At some point, however, a young man crossed a magic line: he became involved in a real relationship with a young woman. Now he was dealing with the unique qualities of a distinct human being, not with the abstract traits of a general group. His long-standing ideas about women did not go away; they were emotional ghosts that would continue to haunt him for the rest of his life. But those spirits had to battle now with the daily evidence of a young man's senses as he learned about the distinctive features of a real woman's personality. His old fears and fantasies had to share his attention with the actual traits and virtues of a woman he had come to love.

Chapter 6

LOVE, SEX, AND COURTSHIP

IN colonial New England and its kindred settlements to the west, there were few arranged marriages. From the start, individual preference was the norm in choosing a wife or husband. Paternal approval was necessary, and fathers occasionally used this veto power, but the fundamental choice belonged to the man and woman who wanted to marry. Thus, love—or something like it—must have played a role in the choice. Physical attraction, compatible habits and tastes, and a sense of pleasure in each other's company presumably influenced these marriage decisions. We do have the testimony of colonial husbands and wives that they loved each other.

Yet there were factors that kept love from playing the kind of role in colonial courtships and marriages that it was to play in the nineteenth century. God and community placed heavy demands on the love and allegiance of the individual. Men and women reminded themselves that their emotional commitments belonged to God above all; they sinned in loving anything of this world too deeply. This did not prevent love between man and woman, but it surely inhibited such love. So did the communal frame of mind that dominated colonial New England. Personal relationships were bounded by mutual duties, and individual inclinations had to make a place for themselves within that structure.[1] Only when the demands of God and community began to recede could love in the modern sense come into full flower.

Romantic Love

To understand the historical emergence of modern love, we need to understand the appearance of what some have called the "romantic self." This is the belief that every person has a unique essence, a fundamental core that remains when all social roles and conventions are stripped away. A man or a woman in love shares that essence with his or her beloved as with no other person. This sharing of one's innermost self is vital to modern romantic love.[2]

Before such sharing (and such love) could happen readily, two historical changes had to take place in the Northern states. The first change was religious. The romantic self is the same personal essence as the Christian soul, the chief difference being that a true Christian—at least in the Puritan sense—shares that innermost core with God and not with a beloved human. Before romantic love was possible historically, God's exclusive claim on a person's true core had to recede as a cultural belief. The second historical change that had to take place was social and cultural. As long as the dominant conception of the individual was that of an inhabitant of many roles and statuses, the romantic self was probably unimaginable. At least, it was inaccessible to other people.

As the religious and social beliefs of the Puritans lost their ability to shape individual lives during the eighteenth century, the romantic self became more accessible. By the end of that century, New Englanders were speaking the language of romance. Romantic love was emerging as the main criterion for marriage. By the nineteenth century, romance had become a cultural ideal, the unquestioned essence of love. And love was the sine qua non of the marriage choice. A Pennsylvania man expressed the faith of his time when he wrote in 1850: "Marriage without love cannot fail to be a source of perpetual unhappiness."[3]

Individual men and women who lived out this new concept of romantic love did not experience it in the same terms we have used to describe it here. Instead, nineteenth-century lovers spoke of profound mutual sympathy. One young man wrote that love involved "the appreciation of each other's character and the strong sympathy and similitude of thought and feeling," while another expected that he and the woman he loved would always "sympathize and contrive together and be so happy." A third man used the same language of deep sympathy in this love poem:

There is a breast congenial . . . with all
My views of excellence and worth;
Alive to sentiment and friendship's holy flame.

I will not then forget the mind intelligent
And bright—nor yet the heart
Where sympathy and kindness ever swell;
But think I have a place in [her] affections . . .

The ideal of love was for two people to be as finely tuned to one another as possible.[4]

Because men and women in love felt driven toward a complete and shared understanding, they set an extremely high value on candor. A man named Clayton Kingman told his sweetheart, Emily Brooks: "I want you to be as open and confiding *to me,* as to *any one,* and I will be to you." "Let us," he wrote on another occasion, "be more like one, let us communicate our ideas, our notions to each other." When aspiring doctor Edward Jarvis realized that he had never told his fiancée about the diary he kept, he wrote: "I am very sorry I did not tell her before. I have disclosed all my secrets (except this) to her and she has reciprocated the confidence. I will not be reserved on any other thing to her."[5]

Candor connected two people who inhabited separate spheres. It moved lovers past the stereotypes of the opposite sex and confronted them with the real people obscured by the larger images. For a man, this meant seeing a woman not as devil or angel, temptress or paragon, but as one particular human being. Ideally, he opened up his true self and found the true self of his beloved open in return. With its promises of intimacy and oneness, romantic love offered a grand, irresistible dream to young people of the nineteenth century.

Courtship

For all of its potential rewards, love presented young men—and young women—with a set of problems as well, beginning with the basic structure of courtship. As with many other social situations since childhood, the males were allowed broad initiative, while a woman had very narrow latitude.[6] He could choose a person to pursue more freely than she could. Still, courtship, as a social situation, had unfamiliar and threatening dimensions for a young male. In particular, the quest for love and marriage presented a man with standards of success that were foreign to him. At work or elsewhere among his own sex, a male was judged largely for what he could *do.* In courtship, on the other hand, a woman judged him largely for who he *was.* To be sure, his attainments of occupation and income might affect his eligibility to court a woman, but in the end she accepted or rejected him because of his qualities of person. His whole being was subject to judgment in courtship, and the stakes—marriage and companionship for life—were the highest he had ever played for. Young men were used to risks, but not risks of this kind.

The structure of courtship was such that women could thwart men's dreams, frustrate their plans, and leave them feeling unworthy and embarrassed. Thus, romance and the pursuit of marriage drew out some of men's deepest suspicions about women even as the experience elicited some of their most exalted feelings. Male suspicion focused on the possibility that women could use their attractiveness and their power to say no as a way to make fools of men and gratify their own vanity. A woman who behaved in this way was called a coquette, and men often described their feelings about coquetry in writing. Lucien Boynton, an aspiring lawyer, doubted that "such a person has . . . strict and well-established moral principles." In writing about the woman he was courting, Lucien said bluntly: "She will sacrifice anything, no matter what to the object she may have in view which may be merely the gratification of her vanity." Events proved that Boynton had reason to be suspicious, for the young woman in question suddenly broke off with him when she became engaged unexpectedly to a new suitor.[7]

We cannot know how many women in courtship acted purely out of vanity. What we do know is that young men wrote about coquettes frequently and with fear. The central issue, it seems, was power. Young men were not used to women having control over them, and the females they courted did have personal power over their feelings and fate. The experience roused emotions remembered from infancy and boyhood, when mothers played the unenviable role of archfrustrater to their sons. For some men, this had been the only important experience of submission to a woman, and it left them suspicious of females who had the power to thwart them.

The truth of the matter was that women labored under greater handicaps than men did. Although women did have some power in courtship, it was largely the power to say no and thus to hurt or frustrate a suitor. Women could not do as their brothers did and actively seek out a partner. Instead, they had to wait for an interested male to come along. Early in the century, a young woman named Eliza Southgate pointed out that "the inequality of privilege between the sexes is . . . in no instance . . . greater than in the liberty of choosing a partner in marriage; true, we have the liberty of refusing those we don't like, but not of selecting those we do."[8]

Woman's relatively passive role in courtship was made worse by the fact that the choice of a partner had deeper implications for her than for a man. Her husband would determine where she lived, what level of wealth and status she attained, and how she might structure her life. As a leading historian of courtship has said, "it was men who . . . held the lives of women in their hands."[9] Young men sometimes showed an awareness of this basic inequity. A Connecticut law student observed thoughtfully that the marriage contract was "much more important in its consequences" to women than to men:

> for besides leaving everything else to unite themselves to one man they subject themselves to his authority—they depend more upon their husband than he does upon the wife for society and for the happiness and enjoyment of their lives,—he is their all—their only relative—their only hope—but as for him—business leads him out of doors, far from the company of his wife, and it engages his mind and occupies his thoughts so as frequently to engross them almost entirely and then it is upon his employment that he depends almost entirely for the happiness of his life.[10]

If young men felt that their situation in courtship was dangerous, the reason lay not in a balance of power that was structured against them, but in the fact that their feelings and their self-esteem were so deeply at risk. In a situation like courtship, it did not take a designing woman to hurt a man's feelings. A kind, sincere woman, if she discouraged his interest or refused his proposal of marriage, could plunge her disappointed suitor into depression and tumult.[11] Young men knew that they risked pain and humiliation in courtship, and they defended themselves with stubborn emotional restraint. When John Barnard of Thomaston, Maine, was rejected by his longtime sweetheart, Lucinda, he boasted that "she did not know the strength of my feelings[,] she could not. I had guarded myself with the utmost care, too *proud* to let any one know he or she had the power to mar my peace one moment." This pride in the concealment of feeling was a male custom that dated back to the concealment of pain and gentleness in the play of boyhood. Many men turned to it out of habit when confronted by the risks of courtship.[12]

And yet the open expression of feeling was vital to courtship, so male restraint caused problems. A Midwestern woman, Mary Butterfield, complained that the man who courted her, Champion Chase, was "too cold and reserved at heart." Chase, who was a lawyer, could only reply, "I have endeavored to govern my feelings in all circumstances." The relationship between Butterfield and Chase survived his frosty self-control, but other men were not so fortunate. One woman in the 1830s broke her engagement to a Harvard student because she "felt there was a re-serve in [his] nature" which did not "upon intimate acquaintance be-come the more open and frank."[13] The guarded manner of these men forced women to be more cautious in showing their feelings. The men sensed correctly that the women were holding back and interpreted this restraint as an attempt at manipulation. That, in turn, roused male suspi-cion, and so it went in a vicious circle.

Courtship, then, contained many stumbling blocks to love, to trust, and, ultimately, to marriage. Social expectation threw yet another barrier in the path to wedlock, for people agreed that a man must be able to support a wife before he could marry. The young man knew this not only from common sense, but from the weight of advice which pressed upon him from many directions. Printed counsel told him that he should not marry until he could support a family "in circumstances of comfort." And fathers reminded their sons that love might "achieve a great many things but there are some things it cannot do; it cannot pay your rent Bill or your Board Bill."[14]

When a young male broached the subject of marriage with the woman of his heart, he always conditioned his proposal on his ability to support her. The tone of these statements showed that a man's readiness to serve as a breadwinner was taken for granted as a requirement for marriage. A ministerial candidate named Ephraim Abbott said as much in 1808 when he wrote to his sweetheart, Mary Pearson: "If I am ever in circumstances to make honorable provision for a family, you will then become my companion, my consort." In the final years of the century, a man's ability to support a family remained the central requirement for marriage. Ray Stannard Baker, later an eminent journalist, fell "halfway in love" several times in the 1890s, but—fresh out of college and work-ing as his father's real estate assistant—he "could see no prospect at least for years of earning enough money to set up a home of [his] own." For Baker and countless others like him, these practical considerations only added to the problems created by inner anxiety about love and marriage.[15]

With so many difficulties in the way, it may seem surprising that middle-class men of the nineteenth-century North married at all. And yet most men were eager—and sometimes desperate—to get married. Typically, young men responded to letters from their beloveds much more quickly than the young women responded in turn, and also wrote longer love letters than they received. As one impatient fellow told his intended: "[T]here [is] no sin in declaring that I am *extremely* anxious for our union." A young woman named Annie Wilson understood this male frenzy, describing with wry humor her willingness to set a much-postponed wedding date: "The ostensible reason is that there is no necessity for waiting—the real reason [is] that Frank *won't* wait . . . so I in the most dutiful manner consented to put him out of his misery."[16]

With so much personal ambivalence and so many external obstacles, why were men so eager to get married? First and quite simply, marriage was a mark of full manhood, and manhood was a status to which males urgently aspired. Especially for young men whose careers were starting to take shape, wedded life completed the social identity of a male adult. Second, men's daily condition at this point in the life cycle made marriage look attractive. Frequently (and emphatically), they said that they were lonesome. Most of them had broken away from the warmth and nurture of their boyhood homes, and, as much as they cherished their long-sought independence, they yearned for someone who could offer tender, loving care, and even add a bit of moral ballast to their lives. Above all, they wanted a faithful companion, someone they could always count on to be there.[17]

A young teacher and engineer named Levi Lockling complained that he did not meet enough marriageable women and announced to his friend Aaron Olmstead: "I am tired of being a bachelor, and of being such an isolated being [in] the wide world." Other men made more explicit statements about their desire for a home of their own. Maine bachelor Stephen Tuckerman told his sister that he yearned to "taste the comforts and enjoyments of a home with the society of a bosom companion to solace a portion of [his] time at the domestic fireside and in the bosom of a family."[18] Marriage held out a promise not only of companionship, but of shelter and security.

One additional factor helped to create the urgency that men felt about marriage. Even in the earliest years of the century, the average American male first joined a woman in matrimony when in his mid-twenties. The experience of the men studied here (who are not, to be sure, a scientific sample) suggests that the average age of marriage for Northern middle-class males in the early nineteenth century was a few years older than for the general population of men. Other studies have shown that, in the later years of the century, the average middle-class male did not marry until he was nearly thirty.[19] In an era when puberty came in the midteens and young men entered the middle-class work force in their late teens or early twenties, the delayed age of marriage increased all the pressures mentioned so far—the loneliness, the wish for a home, the need of solace and comfort. It must also have created an almost unmanageable problem for young men in coping with sexual feeling. On the average, a middle-class man lived as a bachelor for ten to fifteen years after puberty, and he did so in a culture with stringent rules against premarital sex. Whether a young man abided by these rules or not, he needed a legitimate outlet for his sexual impulses.

So young men tried to build bridges across the gulf that separated them from women. Those bridges were a long time in the building, but virtually all men did marry. Sooner or later, they summoned the courage for the most perilous step—the proposal of marriage. Most men eventually received an acceptance, even if not on the first try or from the first woman they asked.

Transition to Marriage

In between the shifting moods of courtship and the commitment of marriage, there was a period of transition. It combined many of the uncertainties of courtship with the sense of devotion that belonged ideally to wedded life. During the nineteenth century, this period of transition came to be known as "engagement," and, while it mixed the features of courtship and marriage, it also had distinctive qualities of its own. This was a time of material preparation for married life, a phase in the relationship when lingering doubts were addressed and deeper understandings were sought.

The engagement period, which began officially with the announcement of the couple's intention to marry, was a way for the man and woman to place themselves under the eye of the community. The decision that led to the public announcement, however, was an intensely private one. The woman and the man were deciding to pledge themselves to one another for a lifetime. Thus, engagement marked a deeply personal commitment at the same time that it announced a very public entity—the couple. Marriage was, after all, both an intimate relationship and a vital link in the larger social network.

The relative emphasis on the public and private aspects of engagement shifted during the nineteenth century, and the shift serves as a clear indicator of the changing meaning of marriage. Early in the century, when people spoke of "betrothal" instead of "engagement," the central event was "publishing" the fact that a man and a woman had pledged to marry. The couple posted a notice on the door of the local meetinghouse and then the minister announced their intentions from the pulpit. The basic rituals of betrothal emphasized the bonds between the couple and their community.

By midcentury, a new set of rituals with a private emphasis was re-placing the more communal ones. The engagement was announced through personal channels, not public ones. The families of the prospec-tive bride and groom wrote to friends and relatives to inform them of the couple's pledge. During the second half of the century, in other words, people no longer informed the whole community of an engage-ment, and communal institutions played no role in making the an-nouncement. Another engagement custom that developed during the nineteenth century stressed the private importance of the bond: this was the exchange of tokens (usually rings) to mark the pledge between woman and man. The choice of tokens was personal, and the ritual of the tokens emphasized the distinctiveness of the couple rather than their likeness to other couples. Such rites of engagement were suited to an era of individualism, while the customs of betrothal had been fitted for a time when the community was supreme.[20]

Whether the period began with public or private rituals, there were certain tasks that most couples needed to accomplish during the transi-tion to marriage. They had to make material preparations for wedded life, and wedded life meant the creation of a home. Although the tasks were often shared, the man took chief responsibility for finding a place to live and conducting the business needed to secure it. The woman had the job of turning that house into a home. She furnished it and added domestic touches that gave it a feeling of security and comfort. She also spent a great deal of time making or buying the linens and clothing that comprised her trousseau.

As the century progressed, these items were more likely to be given as gifts to the prospective middle-class bride; still, even as the burden of the trousseau lightened, another duty grew heavier. Weddings became increasingly elaborate during the course of the nineteenth century, and a woman shared with her family the responsibility for planning the event. Her future husband usually managed to avoid the details of wedding preparation. Once a house was found, his main task was to build the ca-reer and earn the money that would provide the base for their married life. A couple's first negotiations over money frequently took place when the woman, in the process of setting up the household, had to ask her fi-ancé for money to use on furnishings. The wedding might be months in the future, but the couple was already establishing married roles for the husband-provider and the wife-consumer.[21]

As they began to work at the material tasks of marriage, the betrothed man and woman continued the process of deepening their intimacy. The basic issues remained the same as they had been in the earlier stages of romance. They sought, as one man put it, an "entire sympathy and confidence." The means to that end was still candor. Clayton Kingman of Connecticut affirmed the doctrine of candor to his fiancée: "May we be frank and open, and with all, kind and forbearing, then we can be happy."[22]

If the betrothal was a time to deepen intimacy, then the opportunities to do so were extensive: nineteenth-century engagements lasted much longer than their twentieth-century counterparts. Two-year engagements were common; a Concord, Massachusetts, couple endured nearly eight years from the time they were pledged to marry until the day of the wedding. Why did engagements last so long? The primary reason was the requirement that a man should be able to support a household before he married. This obligation linked a young man's urgent desire for wedded life to the unpredictable progress of his career. The unfortunate couple from Concord began their eight-year engagement just after the prospective husband, Edward Jarvis, graduated from Harvard in 1826. At the time, Edward had not even chosen a career. Once he decided to pursue medicine, he had to complete his professional education and endure a major failure as a small-town doctor before he was ready to support his beloved Almira Hunt.[23]

Although a man's breadwinning ability was the first factor in determining the length of an engagement, other causes could increase the time in subtle but significant ways. In the families of certain women, parental reluctance slowed the arrival of the wedding date. The parents sometimes disapproved of their daughters' choice of husbands, but more often they were simply loathe to part with cherished daughters. The Reverend Eliphalet Pearson, for example, had watched with approval as Ephraim Abbott courted his daughter, Mary. Pearson served as a mentor to the young minister, who became a virtual member of the Pearson family during five years of courtship. Then, when Ephraim finally gained a pastorate that could support Mary in suitable fashion, Eliphalet Pearson began to hesitate. He told Ephraim that they should "wait for decency" to get married. Since the couple had already been courting for more than five and a half years, it is hard to imagine when more "decency" might have arrived.[24]

Prospective brides, for their part, often balked as the wedding approached. They felt the same reluctance to leave their families that their parents felt about their leaving, for marriage meant "the relinquishment of those nameless ties which render *home* so delightful in early years." The delight of early years grew not only from loving bonds at home but also from the relative freedom to learn, to visit, to meet new people, that women enjoyed while single. As Alexis de Tocqueville put it, "the amusements of the girl cannot become the recreations of the wife." Indeed, a young woman could expect few recreations in marriage. Her life would be circumscribed by her domestic duties and her well-being would depend heavily on the efforts of her husband. On top of all that, she faced the dangers of nineteenth-century childbearing. Young women expected such a sharp and painful transition to wedded life that many suffered from a kind of "marriage trauma," which one historian describes as "a withdrawal of emotional intensity from the too-burdened marriage choice."[25]

This withdrawal of emotion appeared to the young men who courted these women as an endless series of excuses for delaying the wedding day. Confronted with these sudden hesitations, the eager husbands-to-be responded in the mode they knew best: aggressive action. They pressed constantly for an early wedding date, and the more their fiancées hesitated, the harder they pressed. Usually (but not always), the woman relented.[26]

Thus, the couple arrived at the altar, with each probably happy and excited but also often harboring misgivings. Years of hope and frustration, of dreams and fears, were focused on that moment of union. It was a union of two separate individuals in search of love, companionship, and comfort, and a symbolic union of two separate spheres that wove together the complementary talents and values of male and female to strengthen the social fabric.

Finally, this was a union of two bodies to express love and to produce new generations of men and women. It was, in other words, a sexual union as well as a personal and social one. As a young man and a young woman courted and then committed themselves to marriage, they had to confront their feelings about sexuality. Ideally, they made an effort to align their sexual needs and wishes as nearly as possible. Before we explore middle-class marriage in the nineteenth century, we need to understand the clashes and the compromises over sex that took place previous to the wedding day.

Sex before Marriage: Attitudes and Experience

Throughout the twentieth century, historians have treated Victorian sexuality as a contradiction in terms. Students of the nineteenth century have delighted in accounts of pianos dressed to cover their naked legs and therapies designed to suppress masturbation. Only in the past generation have historians begun to explore the relation between public prescriptions and private norms, between expressed ideas and actual behavior. While middle-class ideas and experience took different forms in the nineteenth and twentieth centuries, recent research has shown that there was far more to the history of Victorian sexuality than a reign of repression.

The repressive reputation of the nineteenth century grew out of ideology more than behavior. Middle-class moralists preached the doctrine of sexual restraint from the pulpit, in the medical press, and on the lecture circuit. They started from the assumption that nature had endowed men with tremendous sexual passion while leaving women with little or perhaps with none at all.[27] Working from there, the preachers of purity urged manly self-control. They called not only for premarital chastity but for complete mastery of sexual feeling.

One important step in this process was the suppression of masturbation. The missionaries for self-control insisted that this "solitary vice" would lead to the breakdown of intellect and the destruction of will, and thus to effeminacy, to insanity, and even to premature death.[28] Even if he never touched a woman, a man's sexual desires could ruin him: he had to cut them off at the source to save his own body and soul. Clever men, concerned with the welfare of youth, invented tools to help young males tame their impulses. One such device, when worn by a man, would cause a bell to ring every time he got an erection.[29]

Even with such technical help, the individual male bore the burden of responsibility for suppressing his sexual desires. Sylvester Graham, one of the leading missionaries for self-control, declared that "LASCIVI-OUS DAY-DREAMS" amounted to "unchastity of thought." He warned that "this *adultery of the mind,* is the beginning of immeasurable evil to the human family." Such fantasies, by their very nature, were subject *only* to self-control. Graham and others like him set an immense task for men: to master their behavior by subduing their feelings and even by suppressing their daydreams. One historian has rightly called the ideal of the nineteenth-century sex advisers an "athlete of continence" who was constantly "testing his manliness in the fire of self-denial."[30]

This stringent code developed in the early nineteenth century, when the expansion of commerce lured young men away from the traditional values and communal vigilance of small towns. The ideology of sexual repression offered an alternative to the unchecked selfishness of the marketplace; it provided a sense of personal control and a form of moral discipline at a time when ethical chaos seemed imminent.[31] This doctrine of self-control hardened into a public orthodoxy once the migration from country to city became a steady, permanent flow. The twentieth-century view of nineteenth-century sexuality is based largely on that repressive Victorian orthodoxy.

But historians have begun to uncover a different set of male sexual values. In fact, the very existence of the ideology of self-control—and the vehemence with which it was asserted—might have suggested long ago to historians that an opposite doctrine existed. The quiet, powerful opposition to the orthodoxy of self-denial came from an ethic of male aggression. Although this doctrine was rarely articulated on paper, it made its power felt in many ways. We can guess that such an ethos of sexual aggression existed at the start of the nineteenth century simply by looking at the premarital pregnancy rate. Between 1761 and 1800, roughly one American bride in three went to the altar pregnant. The rate for the next forty years dropped to one in four.[32] Even with the rate in decline, it is clear that many young men were ready to engage in coitus before marriage. Presumably, some of those young men were from the Northern middle class.

Another kind of evidence for the doctrine of sexual aggression comes from the testimony of those who opposed it. Many evangelicals complained of the widespread pressure on young men to experiment with sex before marriage, and a late-century American physician railed against fathers who tickled the penises of their baby sons into a state of erection to assure themselves that their sons were "robust."[33] Purity advocates pointed out time and again that the ethos of sexual aggression had its roots in two widespread assumptions—that nature had endowed the male with an immense sexual appetite, and that it was necessary for him to satisfy that appetite. A physician who joined the purity movement of the late 1800s denounced "those among the males of our generation, who attribute to men an inherent natural need to gratify passions, claiming that the weaker sex understands it to be necessary to man's nature, and willingly tolerate lustful ante-nuptial and post-nuptial practices."

Observations of a general tolerance and encouragement of male sexual aggression came from individuals in their private writing as well as from public advocates in books and speeches. Maud Rittenhouse, an Illinois woman, lamented in her diary that "boys are taught all their lives that purity is only for women (*some* women) and vice a necessity to them and 'natural.'" The assumption was widely held in nineteenth-century America that males had urgent sexual passions; the next logical step was the belief that it was natural and necessary for men to *express* those passions. An assumption like this may not be quite the same thing as a moral imperative, but its effect on behavior (by discouraging opposition to male sexual expression) was probably much the same. It provided a basis in belief that encouraged aggressive sexuality in men.[34]

The existence of an ethic of sexual aggression is also consistent with the experience of males during boyhood. Boys certainly learned from each other that aggressive expression of impulse was appropriate male behavior. This vital lesson could easily be applied to sexual drives. Since boys often expressed their affectionate feelings toward each other through physical aggression, the experience of boy culture helped prepare a growing male to accept a code of sexual conduct that stressed the aggressive expression of impulse. There were no tracts that taught this ethic of assertive sexuality, and no preachers who urged its virtues, but its strength is clear by evidence and by inference.

Middle-class men, in sum, were confronted by two ethics of sexual conduct, one urging the "natural" expression of aggressive impulses and the other demanding stringent self-control. Charles Rosenberg, who was the first historian to identify these conflicting codes, has observed that "few males were completely immune from the reality of both."[35] How did these two codes develop within the life of a young male? To what extent did they conflict during boyhood? The evidence about the sex education of middle-class boys is thin, but there are enough fragments of data to permit a few informed guesses.

A boy's exposure to contradictory sexual attitudes probably began at an early age. The rise of moral motherhood in the late eighteenth and early nineteenth centuries must have focused women's attention on the nascent sexuality of their children.[36] The masturbation phobia that gripped the middle class during the 1800s would have provided special encouragement for mothers to stop children from stimulating their own sexual pleasure. On the other hand, we have already seen that purity advocates complained of fathers who tickled their infant sons' penises into a state of erection to assure themselves of the next generation's virility. By the time a boy reached the age of six or seven, he was also subject to a constant and increasing influence from boy culture, which persistently stressed the expression of aggressive physical impulses.

If this cursory sketch of boyhood sexual influences is correct, the forces of suppression and expression were already dividing up along gender lines during boyhood. As was so often the case in middle-class culture, "female" meant restriction and "male" meant release. Long before adult sexual feeling had surfaced, conflicting pressures—with strong overtones of gender—were building up around sexuality.[37] Then puberty arrived and brought these emotions to the surface. A male youth encountered an intense barrage of sexual advice from ministers, purity crusaders, and an abundant advice literature. This barrage added public anxiety to the forces that already bore upon a young man's burgeoning sexuality. By the time such a young man approached his first romantic relationship, he had been assailed by pressures and counterpressures of great strength.

Given the welter of feelings and the tangle of advice attached to sexuality, how did young men actually govern their sexual behavior? What happened when they were confronted by a real relationship with an actual woman? Some simply ignored one line of sexual counsel and followed the other. This pattern was sufficiently common that "neat categories of 'clean men' and libertines" seemed reasonable to thoughtful people. One man wrote about the kind of "boy who was not afraid to trifle with the most forward of girls," and who was thereby "esteemed above his years and almost [as] a man." These were the "libertines," the young men who ignored counsels of purity and responded to the social encouragement of aggressive male sexuality. The "clean men" defined themselves in contrast to the sexually active ones. These "athletes of continence" took pride in being "those who practiced [sex] not at all." They constructed barriers of self-denial which Daniel Webster referred to as "the restraints which youth, with infinite pains, imposes on its passions."[38]

Young men who embodied the pure types of self-denial or sexual aggression were distinctly visible to their peers, but it may have been the exceptional nature of their behavior that made them stand out. Very little evidence survives to help us make judgments about the frequency of sexual activity among middle-class youth, or about what percentages of this group held various attitudes about sex. The limited testimony available does suggest that the young man who heeded only one extreme of sexual counsel was exceptional. Most seemed to search for a way to obey one sexual ethic without violating the other.

As they struggled with this conflict, young men developed different patterns of thought and behavior to help them abide by both codes at once. These strategies—for, unconsciously, they were strategies—were distinct but not mutually exclusive. Young men might use any or all of them, depending on their needs and inclinations.

One of the ways in which male youth reconciled the conflicting codes of sexual behavior was by thinking of love in a way that drained its erotic content. Charles Van Hise, the aspiring geologist who would later serve as president at the University of Wisconsin, gave full expression to this idea in a letter to his fiancée, Alice Ring. "A man becomes acquainted with a woman," he wrote, "[and] finds her character pure, her thoughts chaste." The two discover "something in each other which answers a vague restless longing of their higher natures. The two minds are harmonious; they have the same general hopes, tastes, aspirations." Van Hise carefully contrasted the exalted love of this hypothetical couple with that love "which unites the bodies of man and woman." He noted scornfully that "this grosser [bodily] love . . . is but a . . . refined form of sensuality."[39]

Van Hise's contemporary, Sigmund Freud, would have called this pure, ethereal attachment a form of sublimation. Other men who described spiritualized romance recognized it as a way to exalt love above its unseemly beginnings in instinct. Dio Lewis, who was a leading purity advocate in the late nineteenth century, wrote about the relationship between love and sex to a man who had just married: "Your enjoyment of the courtship was intense. It grew out of the sexual instinct. . . . Subordinated to mind and soul, this passion is a great source, not only of the sweetest delights of our earthly life, but of the deepest and most enduring love." When literary critic Henry Seidel Canby reflected in the 1930s on his youthful experience of romance in the 1890s, he recalled "falling in and out of love" as a youth "with never a crude pang of sex, though in a continuous amorous excitement which was sublimated from the grosser elements of love." This ethereal concept of romance flourished because it provided men with a way to reconcile the counsels of erotic aggression and sexual restraint. By allowing people to think of love as an out-of-body experience, the idea of spiritualized love offered deliverance from the contradictory demands of male sexual values.[40]

This ethereal view of romance could be combined readily with another strategy for reconciling the conflicting codes of sexual behavior. Certain young men found that if they pursued spiritualized love and practiced self-restraint with one class of women, they were still free to enjoy erotic pleasures and give vent to their natural passions with another. In his autobiography, Henry Seidel Canby offers a striking description of this practice of the "double standard." The boys that Canby knew in the late nineteenth century divided girls into two categories: "nice girls" and "chippies." The nice girls came from good families—that is, from families of the business and professional classes of Canby's hometown. Canby reports that he and his friends "were familiar by hearsay or experience with the sexual in every sense, yet did not think in those terms of the girls of our own class for a simple reason—we did not want to. That came after marriage." The young males built their relationships with girls of their own class on spiritualized love instead of sex, and, as Canby puts it, their notion of "romance was incompatible with our quite realistic knowledge of sex." He writes that "sex, naked and unashamed, with no purpose but its own gratification, was kept in its place, which was not friendship, not even the state of falling in love."[41]

For Canby's friends, sex had its place not in love, but in relations with young women of other, lower classes. Male youth from middle- and upper-class backgrounds "raided the amusement parks or the evening streets in search of girls that could be frankly pursued for their physical charms." Canby writes openly about the exploitative, impersonal nature of these liaisons. With a "chippy," a young man could turn loose his passions. "It was the old woman hunt," writes Canby:

> her pretty face, her shapely limbs, were all there was to a "chippy"— companionship, friendliness never entered to complicate a simple and exciting relationship except in surprising moments when a plaything struggling against a last and not too determined assault, became suddenly a human being pleading to be aided against the ardors of her own blood.[42]

Here was a way for a youth from a middle-class background to heed the pressure for sexual adventure and yet remain true to the code of purity. He tested his passions on women of a different class whose humanness he recognized only fleetingly and with surprise.

The pursuit of chippies created many problems. For one, it did not nurture good feelings about sex. Canby confessed: "We learned to associate amorous ardors with the vulgar, or, worse, with the commonplace, and to dissociate them sharply from romance." These young men found in their experience with chippies a confirmation of what they had believed from the start: that sex and nice girls should have nothing to do with each other.[43] Furthermore, the pursuit of chippies required not just a denial of humanness, but a denial of humanness based on class prejudice.

This sexual adventuring could have come easily to a male youth schooled in the rough classroom of boy culture. The very language with which Canby describes youthful encounters with chippies—a language of play and playthings, of raids and the hunt—bears the imprint of boy culture. The seduction of a chippy as described by Canby sounds like the story of a boy hunter who takes pity on a squirrel when it screams for its life in his trap. Even the undertone of class antagonism carries an echo of the sharp clashes between boys from different neighborhoods and social orders. Moreover, since the hunt took place outside of their middle-class world, it enabled male youth from comfortable families to feel as if they were obeying the bourgeois code of self-denial. It was the women from "good families" who seemed to generate the call for sexual purity, and it was they who were spared sexual aggression by the boys who sought out chippies.

For the male youth who wished to avoid lustful activity with "nice girls," another sexual outlet was available. Prostitution resembled the encounter with chippies in many ways: it safely removed sex from one's own social world, dehumanized the experience (which may have made it feel like less of a moral violation), and bore overtones of worldly adventure. There were differences, though. Prostitution was illegal, it was a business, and it meant buying sex instead of earning it by conquest. A paucity of evidence keeps us from knowing how many middle-class youths had sex with prostitutes or how frequently they did so. We have enough fragments of information to hazard a few broad statements, however. Given the constant and growing presence of prostitution in American cities through the nineteenth century, there must have been some percentage of middle-class youth that frequented brothels. We know that the price structure of brothels late in the century suggests a disproportionately affluent clientele. It seems fair to assume that at least some of these bourgeois clients must have been young bachelors. A visit to a prostitute gave a middle-class bachelor another way to straddle the conflicting demands for sexual assertion and purity.[44]

One more—and very different—way for a young man to handle these contending pressures was to turn the duty for sexual control over to the woman he loved. For engaged men, this strategy seemed to be the most common of the three. One historian has observed: "In general, couples became involved in sexual 'boundary disputes' only when they were well on their way toward marriage."[45] The negotiation of sexual limits, that is, happened within the larger context of engagement.

Young men showed no hesitation in setting up their fiancées as their consciences. "*Your will shall be my law,*" wrote one man. "You shall help to cleanse me," said another. The correspondence of a New England youth, Elias Nason, with his sweetheart, Mira Bigelow, shows the feeling that lay behind men's desire to share the burden of sexual restraint. During one absence, Elias confessed: "Oh Mi how intensely do I long to see you—to feel you—to put these very hands . . . in your bosom—that soft delicious bosom . . . I shall tear you to pieces." Elias knew that these feelings needed control, and he knew how he wanted them controlled. He wrote to Mira: "My passions are terrible and none but you could master them." The division of labor was clear—men expected to be the sexual aggressors, women were supposed to contain their aggression.[46]

It is impossible to determine how often this strategy failed in restraining couples. There is evidence—sometimes oblique—of specific bourgeois couples engaging in coitus before marriage.[47] Since the bridal pregnancy rate among white Americans did not fall much below fifteen percent during the nineteenth century, it seems safe to guess that at least some middle-class Northerners who left no private records were engaging in premarital intercourse. There is no evidence, though, to suggest that couples who defied the official norms predominated among the middle class. Indeed, some of the data suggest that the official code of restraint may have had a powerful effect on behavior. The most exhaustive study of the subject has been made by historian of courtship Ellen Rothman. Through her research in letters and diaries, she found that middle-class couples, starting in the early nineteenth century, defined romantic love "so that it included sexual attraction and gratification but excluded coitus." Rothman calls this change in customs "the invention of petting" and asserts that "intercourse was posted as not only 'off limits' but as an altogether separate territory, accessible only to married people."[48]

A striking piece of anecdotal evidence from the end of the nineteenth century supports Rothman's contention. In Henry Seidel Canby's account of the male pursuit of chippies, he recalled that the "not too determined assault" of the young men was "restrained by a moral taboo on seduction and fear of results if one went too far." These boys limited themselves to "what the next generation called 'petting.'"[49] If a male youth—in this setting where he was unconstrained by bonds of class and where he was out to vent his sexual aggressions—still found himself inhibited by "a moral taboo on seduction," then that taboo must have taken deep root in his conscience. The calls for male purity did not prevent petting, nor did they prevent some young men from pressing the sexual boundaries of even the "nicest" young women, but the doctrine of self-control apparently worked as a counterforce to the pressures for sexual aggression. If young men could resist the temptation to intercourse even in the most inviting situations, then they had learned to curb their impulses. Such behavior represented a compromise between sexual purity and sexual conquest.

Engagement—a testing period in many respects—offered its sharpest challenge to a couple in the area of sexual adjustment. Young men (and young women) harbored conflicting passions and fears about sex; to reach an understanding based on such deep ambivalence was difficult and occasionally impossible. For the man, the sexual negotiations with his fiancée posed crucial questions. How well did his conscience function? How effective was he at enlisting the aid of a woman to control or focus his passions? And could he do all this without losing the aggressive thrust which he needed to succeed as a breadwinner? In short, could he purify his impulses without destroying them? No two bridegrooms could answer these questions in precisely the same way, but there was no doubt that the sexual negotiations of a betrothed couple laid open fundamental issues for young men. These were issues that would be crucial to their marriages, and crucial to their manhood.

Chapter 7

MARKRIAGE

THE modern wedding ceremony is so elaborate and so fully enveloped by myth and custom that it seems to be centuries old. The ceremony as we know it, however, did not exist in 1800. Northerners of that day married in a civil ceremony which followed Puritan tradition. Performed by a local magistrate, the wedding was held in a private home before a few witnesses. In the world of 1800, marriage created a household, which was the basic unit of society. The community had a vital interest in the stability of every marriage, and so each wedding united a couple in mutual duty and bound it solemnly to the community through the presence of legal authority.[1]

During the first third of the nineteenth century, a new ceremony emerged. It focused not on the place of marriage in the community but on the two individuals being wed. The bride and groom stood together at the center of the ceremony. They dressed in clothing they chose especially for themselves and for the occasion. Each of them was flanked by a few attendants of the same age and sex—the people who were closest to them in their own individual worlds of friendship and support. Larger numbers of relatives, friends, and associates formed an audience to watch the bride and groom in their special moment. A minister presided over the ceremony, which—by the 1830s—was usually held in a church. Instead of invoking the legal authority of the community over this marriage, he united the hearts and souls of two individuals into one couple.[2]

The new focus of the wedding ceremony reflected the new focus of marriage. In the nineteenth century, matrimony was viewed increasingly as a union of two unique individuals. As this ideal gathered strength, the actual occurrence of intimacy within marriage became more common, but it never became the dominant experience of middle-class husbands and wives. The ideal was too difficult for many people to achieve, and the social conditions of nineteenth-century marriage—the distribution of power and the separation of spheres—proved too much of a barrier.

Concepts of Marriage

Nineteenth-century marriage, with its emphasis on the individual husband and wife, was based on two different ideas about the fundamental nature of the bond. In one of these concepts, wedlock represented a union of two persons. Though this was an old idea, it had new resonance in a world where the individual had become the basic unit of society. The second concept was one of marriage as a power relationship based on male dominance. In the era of hierarchy that was now fading, this second idea of marriage had been the prevailing one. During the nineteenth century, the idea of marriage as a union of individuals mounted steadily in importance. It grew up alongside the hierarchical concept of marriage without really supplanting it. The two could be quite compatible—but during the century, as people began to develop the egalitarian possibilities of marital union, the two concepts sometimes came into conflict.

In an era when love was a matter of full and lasting sympathy, marriage was easily cast in the same terms. The "right idea of marriage," according to Elizabeth Cady Stanton, was a bond of "deep fervent love and sympathy." And it took only one intellectual step to turn fervent sympathy into total union. The letters of Richard Cabot, a young doctor, to his future wife, Ella Lyman, show how one might take this step. "All that concerns you," wrote Cabot in 1888, "I want to have concern me too . . . I want to see your world and have you see mine." Such complete empathy made one lover an extension of the other, in action as well as in thought. As Cabot said, "I want . . . your certainty of my interest and sympathy and love for you and your concerns so that you will never need to stop to consider even before you call on me for anything I can and ought to do."[3]

Thus, the common notions of love and empathy created a constant pressure toward oneness. This notion of unity had roots in religious belief. Men and women of the nineteenth century saw "holy matrimony" as a sacred arena where man and woman practiced the Christian virtues of love and self-denial, where spiritual union transcended selfishness and lust. The shift from civil ceremonies to church weddings made a statement: marriage was a hallowed union, not merely a business contract. Daniel Wise, an author of advice to young women, defined his ideal of matrimony in spiritual terms: "Marriage, properly viewed, is a union of kindred minds,—a blending of two souls in mutual, holy affection,—and not merely or chiefly a union of persons."[4]

Even the most secular of people spoke in terms of union when they described the ideal marriage. In 1809, Massachusetts bachelor George Tuckerman described with envy the marriage of his newlywed brother, Joseph. Writing to their sister, George pronounced Joseph "a fortunate man" and said of the new couple: "Their thoughts, and feelings, dispositions and inclinations, and almost every throb of the Heart, appear to move in unison." George asked wistfully: "*Am I* ever to ever to enjoy anything like this—[?]" Tuckerman's yearning expressed the dominant ideal of wedlock in his century.[5]

Still, it is important to stress how the ideal of union rested on the foundation of nineteenth-century concepts of gender. Charles Van Hise stated the gender issue clearly in a letter to his fiancée, Alice Ring. "Man and woman will love," he wrote, "because the mind of one is the complement of the other." Thus, when Van Hise said that each lover "harmonizes the life of the other" and that there are "deep, sweet harmonies" between them, he meant that love brought together natures of very different construction and made of them an agreeable whole.[6]

Van Hise was writing about two individuals who were complementary opposites in many ways. The notion of woman and man as creatures with opposing qualities was, after all, the very essence of nineteenth-century bourgeois thinking about gender. Marital oneness was more than a merger of two kindred spirits—it was a union of opposites.

The gender differences which blended in marriage were familiar ones. Midwesterner Champion Chase explained to his fiancée that "true female character was perfectly adapted and designed by its influence often exerted to soften and beautify the wild rough and turbulent spirit of man." But men saw marriage as more than a way to make up for their lack of self-restraint. They saw it as a way to remedy their own clumsiness in matters of love and tenderness. One man wrote that women possessed "affection and all the finer sensibilities of the heart and soul . . . needed for comfort and consolation." Men imagined that they could turn to women for a kind of nurturant understanding that other males would not provide. As the hero of Francis Parkman's novel *Vassall Mor-*

ton put it: "I would as soon confess to my horse [as to a man]." Men turned to women to make them whole, to provide them with means of living and being which they believed they could not provide for themselves.[7]

Some women resisted parts of this doctrine of complementary traits. In particular, they opposed the idea that they should take on moral burdens for men when they were not certain they could manage the same burdens for themselves. Augusta Elliot, a young New York woman, scorned her fiancé's attempts to place her on a pedestal: "As to my being your superior in every respect and my mind's being of a more lofty order than yours—*I don't believe one word of it.*" In general, though, women believed with men that the traits of the two sexes were complementary and that the union of husband and wife created a whole out of opposite parts. Mary Poor, in letters to her husband, expressed the belief that marriage could remedy her defects. "How feeble is a family without a head," she wrote. "Females have intuition but are destitute of judgement." She admitted once to feeling like an "unprotected female" when Henry was gone and complained during another absence that she yearned "for somebody to lean on." Mary Poor believed in marriage as a union of two distinctly different kinds of people.[8]

The concept of marriage as a union of two people was a romantic— even spiritual—notion. The other dominant view, which envisioned wedlock as a relationship of power and duty, was decidedly earthbound. As different as these two conceptions were, though, they shared one important quality: both rested on common beliefs about the fundamental traits of manhood and womanhood. These common assumptions about gender kept the two dominant concepts of marriage closely linked even when they seemed to point toward very different sorts of relationships.

The structure of power and duty in marriage, as nineteenth-century men and women thought of it, began with basic characteristics. The belief that women were clean and domestic suited them by nature to maintain a home, and the assumption that they were pious and pure fitted them to raise the children and act as a conscience to their husbands. A man's duties in marriage were envisioned by a similar process. Since men were considered naturally active and courageous, it followed readily that they should go out into the world to play the role of breadwinner. Byron Caldwell Smith, a young college professor, stated the basic expectation: "A home is the work of husband and wife, but the unequal positions of women and men make the husband responsible for the support of this home."[9]

Among the middle classes, supporting a home meant something

extra, though. It meant not only food, clothing, and shelter, but a certain degree of luxurious ease. When, in 1845, Alexander Rice explained to his beloved, Augusta McKim, why he was not ready to marry her, he phrased his argument in terms of comfort, not support. "Would it be showing any affection," Rice asked, "to take you from your present comfortable home to a situation of less comfort and one of privation and anxiety to us both[?]" If he could have "[settled] down in some lucrative and comfortable situation" with Augusta at the moment, he would have, but Alexander had neither the money nor the job to support a middle-class way of life. As bourgeois advice writers put it, young men should not marry until they could provide for a family "in circumstances of comfort."[10]

Beyond this sex-typed division of labor, there lay another vital question: In this marital arrangement, who held ultimate authority? Middle-class men and women had no doubt as to the answer. James Jameson, an early nineteenth-century writer on the family, put it flatly: "In the domestic constitution the superiority vests in the husband; he is the head, the lawgiver, the ruler . . . he is to direct, not indeed without taking counsel with his wife, but to his decision the wife should yield." By giving the power in marriage to the husband, middle-class culture was passing on a traditional arrangement. The very language Jameson used betrays his adherence to the time-honored notion of the man as the head of the household.[11]

There was another traditional source on which the husband's authority rested: the Bible. The letters of John Kirk illustrate the powerful role the Bible still played in the nineteenth-century understanding of marriage. An abolitionist and an evangelical Christian, Kirk turned to the words of Saint Paul to support his views on man's dominion over his wife. Writing to his cousin Sally in 1853, Kirk referred to her husband as her "liege lord, to whom the Holy Apostle enjoins you to submit in all things." He then quoted Paul to explain why submission was necessary. "For Adam was first formed, then Eve. And Adam was not deceived, but the woman being deceived was in the transgression."[12]

Of course, most middle-class men in the nineteenth century were not evangelicals like John Kirk. Still, the Bible was the best-known and most widely read book in the United States, and the women of the middle class knew its precepts even better than the men. Before a woman defied her husband or dealt with him on equal terms, she had to struggle with the force of biblical injunction and with the centuries of marital tradition that were justified by those injunctions.

While women generally knew the Bible better than men, letters invoking the Bible or tradition to support the husband's power were more often written by men. Men had more to gain by this arrangement, and so they had reason to issue reminders about it from time to time. Women more than men focused their sole attention on marriage as a union of persons or souls. This conception of marriage offered a woman the hope of deep satisfaction. As for the conception of marriage as a duty-bound relationship of power, women responded in varying ways that suited their personal needs and situations: with Christian submission, with quiet subversion, or—more rarely—with open struggle. How husbands and wives actually lived out the two dominant conceptions of marriage is itself a complex subject.

Married Life: Roles and Realities

Henry Poor, the business publicist, believed that women gave up every-thing when they married.[13] This fact helped to form the basis for the in-equality in nineteenth-century marriage. By marrying, a woman lost her name, her home, and, in most cases, the control of her property. She surrendered her social identity and put in its place a new one: essen-tially, that of her husband. Much of who she was became submerged in who her husband was.

Young men and women knew this even when they were single. A Connecticut law student, George Younglove Cutler, wrote in his diary that "besides leaving everything else to unite themselves to one man they [women] subject themselves to his authority."[14] The structure of the marriage relationship also empowered the husband to determine his wife's social status. Elizabeth Hill, a young Ohio woman, realized that "a lady could not shape the future . . . she went down or up as her husband did . . . he led the way, made the reputation, the fortune of both."[15] A man's power to shape a wife's fortune gave him the upper hand in decid-ing matters of mutual concern. We can see this process at work by exam-ining two domestic issues: where the family would live, and who would manage its finances.

Choice of residence was an issue even before the wedding. The expe-rience of an engaged couple, Augusta McKim and Alexander Hamilton Rice, shows how a man used his breadwinner's role to make this decision his own. As Alexander's college graduation approached, he accepted a job in Virginia. Augusta, his fiancée, lived in Boston. She did not want him to move so far away and accused him of being "too ambitious for worldly distinction." He replied by pointing out to her that a good first job was important to his future, and that the position in Virginia was the best that he could find. Then, he reminded her that he was the "one upon whose arm you are to lean thro' life, upon whose reputation your own will also rest and upon whose effects your happiness as well as his own will mainly depend." As long as the wife depended on her husband's economic support and all that came with it, he could treat his needs as those of the entire family and demand prime consideration.[16]

The same balance of need and power existed at every stage of a middle-class marriage, so men continued to make the decisions about place of residence. Charles Van Hise pondered this issue after a train ride in 1891. He had overheard a conversation between two women returning to their bleak Kansas farms after visiting their families back east. "Thus it is and always will be," reflected Van Hise. "These two women have left home and friends and the pleasant and beautiful East, each to follow a man to fortune." Van Hise's suggestion that this was eternally true shows how deeply people assumed that men must inevitably choose the family's place of residence.[17]

Family finance was another area in which a man's right to decide was undoubted. Men, we know, wrangled with their fiancées over the expense of setting up a household. Typically, the future bride did most of the shopping herself, but, as long as the groom provided the money, her purchases needed his approval. This pattern continued into marriage. The Poor family of New York City and Massachusetts dealt with earning and spending in a revealing way. Henry signed blank checks and gave them to his wife; she then used them to buy goods and services for the household. This system provided Mary with daily flexibility but left Henry with final oversight.

The example of the Poor family also shows the persistence of this form of gender arrangement. For all his acumen as a business analyst, Henry turned out to be a thoughtless manager of household finances. He was slow to pay bills, he often put too little money in the family checking account, and he gave Mary too few signed checks for the purchases he expected her to make. Mary protested this behavior frequently, but she never moved to take over Henry's role. Although he demonstrated his lack of fitness for the task and even showed an "unmanly" want of rationality in the process, it was unthinkable that he should be replaced.[18]

Beyond these specific tasks, the larger pattern of mundane duties and behaviors in a marriage reflected male power. The experience of Will and Elizabeth Cattell shows how this power expressed itself in the lives of one couple. Will was a minister, a college president, and an official of the Presbyterian Church, while Elizabeth was the organizing force that made Will's professional life possible. A letter from Will to their son James makes this dynamic clear. Writing on a Sunday morning, Will noted that the hour had come when Elizabeth ("dear Mama," as he referred to her) always told him to hurry so they would not be late for church. A few sentences later, he interrupted himself: "Yes!—there's the call from dear Mama!! So goodbye till after church:—and Mama is calling to Harry 'Would you see that Papa has his cuffs!'"[19]

This telepathy in the Cattells' marriage took place on the common ground of Will's needs. It was Elizabeth who knew that Will wanted a reminder about the time before church, it was she who knew that he would forget his cuffs. She monitored his health, his work hours, and his sleeping habits as well. As she said, "I know you so well . . . you need someone to watch you."[20] For his part, Will accepted his wife's help with childlike passivity ("dear Mama"). He waited happily for her call, instead of stirring himself to activity at the right time; he counted on her reminder about his cuffs instead of taking his own responsibility for them. While the details of these interactions played themselves out through the individual personalities of Elizabeth and Will Cattell, the fact that their thoughts merged around Will's needs is a sign of the power in the husband's role. A woman depended on her husband's income, and she cleared a path for him through the mundane business of life so that he could concentrate on his work.

Yet, as much as patterns and expectations in marriage were heavily skewed in favor of male power, those factors did not determine the outcome of any one decision, nor did they set the habits of authority in any given marriage. Rather, they established conventional limits within which the unique needs and distinctive traits of particular wives and husbands determined their own routines for the exercise of power.

Perhaps the most revealing statements on this subject come from passing remarks made by husbands and wives about decisions in their marriage—remarks that are tossed off so casually that they suggest a description of daily habit. In 1848, Theodore Russell, a prominent Boston lawyer, wrote to his father about the vacation he was going to take. "I suppose I am little tired out," he wrote. "I dislike to go away just now but my wife presses me hard to do so—and I have concluded to."[21] This brief comment shows three revealing facts about power and choice in the Russell's marriage. First, Sarah Russell felt free to give her husband advice. Secondly, Theodore listened to her advice and took it seriously. Third, the ultimate power to decide lay with Theodore. She may have pressed him hard to take a vacation, but he was the one who "concluded" to do it.

William Dall, a scientist in Washington, D.C., wrote to his mother in 1887 about a job in Massachusetts which she sought for him but he did not want. He started by mentioning the poor pay that came with the job, and then he mentioned his wife's wishes: "I am sure that, unless the circumstances were very favorable, . . . Nettie would very strongly oppose leaving Washington where all her friends and some of her relatives are fixed. The matter would have to be managed with great tact so far as she is concerned."[22] The last sentence is ambiguous; it is not clear whether William would have to manage Nettie tactfully, or whether she would have to manage the announcement of the move tactfully with friends and relatives. Whichever way one reads that sentence, William evidently took his wife's opinions into account in making major family decisions—but those opinions were one factor (and not necessarily the most important) in a decision *he* would make.

To put this in somewhat more abstract terms, social expectation gave husbands most of the power to make decisions for the couple and the family. Depending on the individuals and their own unique needs and arrangements, a wife could have an influence on her husband's decisions. The degree of influence could vary from minimal to overwhelming; the influence of most middle-class wives fell well between those two extremes. Even in cases where the wife's influence was overwhelming, however, she had to overwhelm her husband because he was the one empowered to make the decisions.

It may be misleading to characterize a wife's influence over her husband in general terms, because her influence probably varied from one specific issue to another. The marriage of Mary and Ebenezer Gay provides a good example of this. In matters of family finance, Ebenezer made the decisions without much apparent influence from Mary. Their correspondence with their children reflects this pattern: the chief reason Ebenezer had for writing his children was to oversee their finances, but money was a minor topic in Mary's letters to her children. Where place of residence was concerned, Mary exerted some influence over her husband. At one point in their marriage, she lobbied him heavily for a move to Boston from the little coastal town of Hingham, Massachusetts; although her wishes did not prevail, they did force his serious consideration of a subject he did not wish to consider at all.

In matters of child-rearing, Ebenezer was not simply influenced by Mary—he ceded most of his power to her. In 1827, when their grown son Charles became embroiled in a disciplinary matter that threatened his naval career, Mary proposed to her husband that he go the next morning to Boston in the hope of saving the situation. Ebenezer thought that "there was no use in going," but, in the middle of the night "when no sleep visited us," Mary made up her mind to go herself. Ebenezer did not utter a word of protest against her decision. As long as he did not have to go himself, he was quite content to give Mary her own way in responding to a crisis with their children.

So it went in the Gays' marriage. Depending on the issue at hand, Mary might have no influence, a moderate influence, or even an outright grant of power. Still, the influence was influence on her husband's decisions and the grant of power was a grant from him.[23]

What happened when men ceded large amounts of power to their wives? Some people viewed this practice with tolerance and a few even admired it.[24] More generally, social convention worked to discourage such violations of prevailing norms. In his diary, New Englander John Barnard denounced a woman who "told me how she managed her husband and a great deal of nonsense which was interesting only as it was not pleasing." Barnard asserted that this woman was "sowing the seeds of strife." While Barnard criticized only the wife in this case, some men also belittled husbands who let their wives make the decisions.

In 1846, Massachusetts shoe manufacturer Arial Bragg described a couple in which the man took orders from his wife. Bragg wrote that "she wore the breeches, as the vulgar saying is." That phrase is revealing in many ways. Most obviously, it points out the fact of a gender role reversal with the most dramatic symbolism possible. The saying poked fun at women, especially in an era when women could never wear pants. It also degraded the husband. The word *the* in "the breeches" stresses the notion that there was *one* pair of pants to be worn in a marriage. If the husband was not wearing the pants, then he must have been wearing the dress. The clear meaning is that the man was a woman, which implied that he was foolish, confused, and (like a woman) not worthy of respect. He was, in short, a contemptible figure.[25]

In the context of nineteenth-century gender meanings, there was a second layer of contempt in saying that a man did not wear the breeches in his marriage, as it recalled the attire he had worn in earliest boyhood. At that point, he was small and powerless. He was dominated by other people, most often his mother, and was dressed in a fashion that made him indistinguishable from a little girl. Thus, to say that a man's wife wore the breeches (and Bragg's use of the phrase makes clear that it was a common saying) was not simply to belittle him by calling him a woman; it was to call him a little boy, which meant, in turn, a powerless creature who resembled a little girl. This popular phrase hit a man in many spots at once. It served as a forceful reminder that a man made himself contemptible if he let his wife exercise the power in their marriage.

Thus it was that norms of proper gender behavior were enforced. Yet there were counterpressures toward allowing women greater influence in a marriage. When a husband was usually gone from the household and the wife was there running it, men must have found it difficult to avoid turning over power to their wives. Moreover, the ideal of union in marriage may have encouraged men to share their power with women. A man who identified deeply with his wife was bound to appreciate her needs and her point of view more than a man who was content to be distant from his wife. Such empathy on a husband's part might readily yield a process of marital decision making in which the wife took an active part.

But the social force that played the largest role in increasing a wife's influence was the rise in woman's moral stature during the nineteenth century. The very way in which young men pleaded with their fiancées for moral guidance indicates that the new valuation of a woman's character gave her increased leverage in dealing with her husband. The wife's replacement of the husband as the parent who would mold their children's character offered her another source of power within the marriage.

The growing power—or at least the decline in submissiveness—that was expected of wives showed publicly in certain key settings. In divorce proceedings, the moral stature of women's sphere provided new, effective grounds for attacking a husband's performance of his duties. By the middle of the nineteenth century, witnesses were testifying that male vice posed a threat to the moral sanctity as well as the economic stability of their homes. Such charges built the foundation for successful divorce suits of wife against husband.

Meanwhile, the female reform societies that arose in the 1830s publicly attacked the behavior of many men toward their wives. The New York Female Reform Society, through its newspaper, *The Advocate*, charged some husbands with a "tyranny . . . in the HOME department, where lordly man . . . rules his trembling subjects with a rod of iron, conscious of entire impunity." The assault continued: "Instead of regarding his wife as a help-mate, . . . an equal sharer in his joys and sorrows" such a husband exercised "a despotism which seems to be modeled precisely after that of the Autocrat of Russia." The fact that women dared to make these claims in public—and used a model of emotional equality in marriage as part of their case—suggests that women were gaining new power in dealings with their husbands. But the fact that female reformers found so many tyrannical husbands to attack shows that the bulk of authority within middle-class marriage still lay with the man.[26]

The power relationship between husband and wife seemed at once changed and unchanging. In describing spousal roles under the new domestic-relations law of the nineteenth century, legal historian Michael Grossberg has noted that courts and commentators came to recognize "separate legal spheres in the home" with "enlarged . . . rights" for the wife and mother. Yet there was no doubt as to who held the final power. "Patriarchy," writes Grossberg, "retained its legal primacy." While a new "domesticated concept of patriarchy . . . distinguished between male authority to govern the household and female responsibility to maintain it and nurture its wards," such new distinctions "perpetuated patriarchy in republican society."[27]

In the law, in printed counsel, and in the actual behavior of men and women, the nineteenth century marked a change but not a revolution in the power relations of husband and wife. Man's primacy in the home was modified and circumscribed but not denied. All parties recognized the man as head of the household—and one dimension of his power was his dominion over his wife.

Married Life: Alienation and Distance

If married couples varied widely in how they lived out the concept of marriage as a power relationship, it stands to reason that they would differ in fulfilling the less traditional, more ethereal concept of marriage as union of husband and wife. Couples spread themselves across a broad spectrum from total alienation at one end to warm, empathetic, abiding intimacy at the other. To gain some sense of the ways men and women sought to fulfill the ideal of marital union, we need to look at different points on this spectrum.

Total alienation is an easier experience to identify than enveloping intimacy. Divorce and abandonment are as close to absolute statements as one can make in a human relationship, and recurring violence makes its own chilling comment on alienation. All of those signs of marital estrangement existed in the middle-class world of the nineteenth century. There was certainly physical abuse in some marriages, though its presence as a part of bourgeois life appears in the source materials largely in

murky shadows. In an era when divorce was rare, abandonment punctu-
ated the end of a marriage more frequently. A man's departure could
take the form of an utter disappearance, of the virtual abandonment (or
separation) that could result when a man moved west, or in the absence
of the husband who rarely came home except to sleep at night.[28]

Most middle-class couples (even those with great emotional distance
between husband and wife) maintained an active working relationship
that included regular daily contact. The marriage of Ebenezer and Mary
Gay provides a clear example of a couple who played their roles faithfully but with little warmth and scant affection. Theirs was the most
common form of alienation in wedded life.

The offspring of two prominent Massachusetts families,[29] Mary and
Ebenezer married in 1800 and spent their forty-two years together living
separate lives that were bound by law, custom, and a sense of duty. As
with most husbands and wives, Mary expressed happiness at the start of
her marriage. Less than a year after their wedding, Mary referred to
Ebenezer as "a friend nearer than all the world beside," but, even as she
praised him, she conveyed her awareness of the painful results of a bad
marriage: "Had Heaven in this friend given me other than that I have
most happily found, the sun would not have shown on a wretch more
miserable."[30]

After this early letter, Mary Gay offered few words of affection for her
husband. She appreciated his hard work, respected his efforts to support
their brood of ten children, and showed sympathy for his feelings at
times when his life was difficult, but the spark of affection and the
warmth of companionship were absent from her writing about him. Instead, she complained that he tracked mud across the clean carpet, and
she struggled with him over their life in the dying port town of Hingham. Generally, they were yokemates without intimacy. He stayed out of
her way when it came to the children, and she left money matters to
him. As for the mud, Ebenezer usually left that outside the house, along
with his interests and worldly concerns.[31]

While Ebenezer Gay built his life around work, Mary built hers
around her children. She fought fiercely to give them every advantage
that a lawyer's income could provide, and they in turn were her primary
source of love and happiness. Even in her sixties, with the children
grown and mostly gone, Mary's offspring were at the center of her life.
After a long illness in 1841, she consoled herself with the fact that "I
have had kind children to alleviate [my troubles]—and I think now if the
weather should be pleasant *even* I might gain some strength and not be
so troublesome to my dear children." She went on, "I sometimes have

wept over the wreck of what I was—but [my children] decorate my chamber with what grows [that] they can find and I *try* to be satisfied with my prison—for such after all it is."[32]

Two points need to be made about this statement. One is that Mary Gay's "prison" seems to be not just her sickroom but her life. She had become a troublesome, dependent person, full of despair, a "wreck of what [she] was." At best, her marriage had not lightened her feelings; at worst, it was the structure of her prison. The second point is that Mary Gay was still married to Ebenezer when she wrote this letter, but one would not guess it from the contents. It was her children who cared for her, brightened her room, provided her with strength in her time of need. She never mentions Ebenezer—not as a helper, not as a problem, not in any way. Mary Gay constructed her world around her children. Her husband was irrelevant.

The married relationship of Mary and Ebenezer Gay is nicely summarized by her response to a small professional victory in his later life. After serving for many years on the board of a local bank, Ebenezer announced at age sixty-eight that he did not wish to be reelected. His colleagues reelected him anyway, and he glowed with pride. Mary reacted with a sympathy and respect that nearly forty years of drab marriage had not shaken: "I am sure [if he hadn't been reelected] he would have been far less happy than now, when he feels as if he was still of importance to the community . . . the truth is there is no one to make good his place." She also observed that "it would have been unfortunate for himself and not well for us had he retired from the business—his time would have been a heavy burthen."

Mary clearly meant that her husband's time would be a heavy burden not just for him but for those at home who would have to cope with his restless, unaccustomed presence. It is also revealing that Mary Gay measured the effects of Ebenezer's retirement on "himself" and "us," thus dividing the family not between generations, sexes, or husband and wife, but between the man she married and the domestic unit she constructed with her children. Ebenezer and Mary Gay stayed together out of mutual sympathy, respect, and, above all, a sense of duty. Their marriage was a construct of laws and obligations more than a haven for nearness and warmth.[33]

One final comment about the Gays tells a good deal about men's place in a distant marriage: we know about the Gays through the testimony of the wife. In the nearly half a century that Ebenezer and Mary were together, he rarely wrote to her or about her. His cryptic Yankee phrases were reserved for matters of money and business, even in family correspondence. This seems typical in distant, duty-bound marriages. The wives—trained to explore their states of being and express their feelings—recounted painful experiences. The husbands retreated into silence.[34] And into activity.

A man with an unsatisfying marriage could withdraw into a variety of activities. In the antebellum years, long hours spent at the tavern and the coffee-house with colleagues, clients, and competitors mixed pleasure liberally with business. Debating societies stimulated the mind, Masonic gatherings stirred the spirit, and both kept husbands away from home. In the last third of the century, this organized camaraderie played an even larger role in men's lives. Athletic clubs sprang up in growing cities all over the country. Fraternal lodges proliferated to the point where, by the turn of the century, their membership comprised one-eighth to one-quarter of the adult male population; the proportion of members among middle-class men was even higher. At the same time, elite men's clubs with roots in the pre–Civil War era enjoyed a great expansion of membership in the last third of the century, and new ones appeared in every large city. These clubs included in their ranks many leading members of the upper middle class. Numerous men belonged to more than one of these organizations, and each membership represented extra time away from home.[35]

The importance of clubs, lodges, and taverns as alternatives to marriage lay not only in time spent beyond the company of one's wife, but also in the structure and content of the new institutions. Recent historians have pointed out that fraternal orders posed "an alternative to domesticity." One scholar, Mary Ann Clawson, has studied the form and the ideology of these lodges and observed that fraternalism was based on "the same overarching metaphor of the family" as the domestic model, but that it created "fictive fraternal bonds" in place of the blood ties and marriage bonds of the home. Historian Mark Carnes analyzed the content of fraternal ritual and found that, at one level, it had the function of "effacing" a man's real kin (especially mothers and wives), replacing them with an all-male family that provided love, intimacy, nurture, and support. Wives recognized their competitors, and they organized a national campaign against the fraternal movement.[36]

Men's clubs, too, posed a self-conscious alternative to home. As a magazine article noted in 1876, men went to their clubs to "seek the comforts of a home." A club provided domestic advantages without the confining responsibility of home and hearth:

Each member is as much at home as if he were in his own castle; the building . . . is kept with the same neatness, and exactness, and comfort as a private dwelling. Every member is a master, without any of the cares or troubles of a master. He is always obeyed with alacrity. He can come when he pleases, and stay away as long as he pleases.[37]

Club relationships deepened the appeal of the club as an alternative to marriage. A critic put the matter directly: "Every club is a blow against marriage, . . . offering, as it does, the surroundings of a home without women or the ties of a family."[38] From the club or lodge, a man could seek as much or as little emotional involvement as he wanted. To some men, an arrangement like this was more attractive than wedded life.

But these were not the only modes of escape from wife and wedlock. Men often hid from marriage in their work. It was a legitimate pastime, one that most middle-class husbands enjoyed. More than that, men had a marital duty to work, and this soothed men's consciences even as the work kept them from their wives. Of course, men worked hard for reasons other than marital disaffection, but there were certainly those who worked constantly because they liked it better than spending time with their wives (Ebenezer Gay comes to mind here). In spite of widespread male adherence to the belief that home was a shelter from the world of work, the sheltering role was reversed in the lives of some husbands.

In an era when romantic love was exalted, when the pressure for a happy home life was strong, and when young men sought marriage so ardently, why did husbands pursue so many avenues away from their wives and homes? The simplest response is that men were freer to do so than women. Men were the ones whom duty called away from home; they were the ones on whom the pressing daily business of child care rested lightly; they were the ones experienced with aggression, with adventure, with the habit of risky initiative; they were the ones encouraged to cherish independence and chafe at restriction. Opportunity and experience combined to make men more likely than their wives to retreat from marriage.

These were not the only reasons, however. Wives were more comfortable and experienced than husbands with the language of intimacy and with the skills needed to mend and sustain a relationship. In addition, marriage loomed larger in a woman's social identity, so she felt a greater sense of responsibility for it than a man did.

All of this can help us understand why, given a problem in a marriage, men were more likely than women to retreat. That still leaves the question of why married people wanted to retreat at all. What were the sources of this estrangement? Some of the answers are obvious and perhaps universal. Any system of marriage is bound to produce poor matches. Even where individuals choose their own partners and are wedded for love, there is no way to predict compatibility or lifelong patterns of personal change. The nineteenth-century middle class certainly had its share of mismatches.

In different places and times, though, these mismatches take different forms and are the product of varying cultural pressures. The chief pressures in the northern United States were ones that, by now, are familiar to us. The dominant belief structure presented the sexes in sharply polarized terms: women were pious, pure, submissive, domestic; men were active, independent, rational, dominant. This neat division of traits, in turn, affected personal development and shaped views of the opposite sex so powerfully that it undermined the common ground between the sexes and raised barriers to understanding. Women came to find the company of men rough, loud, and demanding, while men found female company tepid, restrained, and excessively refined. Even without the formal institutions of fraternal orders and men's clubs, men and women (especially after the days of courtship) chose to segregate themselves socially. Henry Seidel Canby described this with clarity in his memoirs. He said that a typical dinner party unfolded in this way when the meal was done:

> Afterwards, without that separation for coffee practised in more formal societies, the guests flowed into the living room and even in flowing separated into austral and oriental currents while the tides of talk rose and took on different notes. With an obvious relief the men gathered around the fireplace dropping facetiousness, while the women's conversation . . . sought human values around my mother's coffee table.[39]

With their values, aspirations, sensibilities, and social worlds so different, many men and women must have found it hard to meet on common ground.

One cultural distinction that played a special role in the estrangement of married men from their wives was the treatment of women as moral exemplars. The social expectation that marriage would help a man control his passions was largely a statement about a woman's restraining influence on a man. This expectation comes through clearly in a letter from General William Pender to his wife, Fanny, during the Civil War. Pender wrote: "Whenever I find my mind wandering upon bad and sinful thoughts, I try to think of my good and pure wife, and they leave me at once. My dear wife you have no idea of the excellent opinion I have of your goodness and sweetness. You are truly my good Angel." Though some women felt uneasy with their moral deification, the weight of cultural and spousal pressure made it easy for wives to fill the role of the virtuous monitor. Harriet Beecher Stowe told her husband, Calvin, that she saw the "terrible temptations [that] lie in the way of your sex" and gave him frequent advice on matters of sexuality, religion, and personal habits. Calvin received his wife's counsel in virtue with respect and gratitude if not always enthusiasm.[40]

Here lay the rub. For men accepted their wives' moral governorship and often encouraged it, but that did not mean that they enjoyed it. The voice of conscience, after all, is not an easy voice to love. By insisting that their wives monitor their progress in virtue, men threw an obstacle in the way of marital intimacy and affection. "A man must get out of drawing room society into some other where he can put his mind so to speak in a shooting jacket and slippers," said one elite gentleman.[41] Another compared favorably "the social ease and freedom from restraint" of male company with "the refined charm of female society."[42] Men expected—even demanded—virtue of women, but they found it dull, confining, and probably disturbing to their own feelings of self-worth.

These conditions did not always produce a fundamental alienation for men in married life. Just as boys fled domestic restraint in the daytime and came home to seek love and nurture at night, so there were men who cherished the freedom of male worlds even as they maintained a warm and lasting affection for their wives. This combination of love and separation was a common one in middle-class marriage—a kind of midpoint between alienation and intimacy.

Married Life: Love and Separation

The economic changes that swept the United States in the first third of the nineteenth century had a direct impact on the structure of marriage. We have seen how those changes moved the work of middle-class men out of the home and how men followed their work, with the result that adult males were often scarce figures in the household. The growth of national markets and the revolution in transportation had another effect, as the business trip became increasingly common and kept men away from home for days and weeks at a time. This sort of absence was less common than the daily trip to the office, but it produced a larger bulk of historical evidence, because it required that husbands and wives write to each other if they wished to stay in touch. These extended absences throw into bold relief the issues raised in a marriage by the regular separation of husband and wife. Such separations, in the context of a loving marriage and a work-obsessed manhood, created a form of wedded life that was full of contradiction.

A case in point is the marriage of Henry and Mary Poor. Henry was a young lawyer when he and Mary Pierce, a minister's daughter from Brookline, Massachusetts, fell in love. Henry's affection was undeniably deep. After a long visit from Mary during their courtship, he wrote of the desolation left by her absence. They were married in 1841 and made their first home in Bangor, Maine.[43]

The first weeks of marriage fulfilled their hopes of intimacy, but Mary was complaining of a change in the relationship less than a year later. She noted that Henry "makes himself scarce at home" and said that he was gone so often that she felt only "half-married." During his first year of marriage, Henry had added a lumber business to his busy legal practice, and had become involved in local politics. Mary found herself "restless" when he was gone.[44] Within months, one of the central themes of their marriage was set: Henry's absence and Mary's consequent loneliness.

After eight years together, the Poors moved from Maine to New York City. There, Henry was more absorbed than ever in his work. Mary had plenty of company at home—she gave birth to six children during these years—but she could not accustom herself to Henry's absence from home. He was in Europe on a long business trip when she wrote: "The longer you are away, the worse I feel about it. It sometimes seems as if I *must* see you . . . I can think of nothing to tell you, because when I sit down to write, I have but one thought, and that is, how much I want to see you. That overmasters all others."[45] Even when the Poors took summer vacations on the farm in Maine where Henry grew up, he could not pull himself away from work to join the rest of the family. By 1864, Mary felt so isolated that the Poors moved to Brookline. Mary now enjoyed the company of her relatives, while Henry commuted home from New York as often as he could. Although she had more adult companionship in Brookline, Mary saw Henry less than ever. Her letters were forlorn, as she begged him to "come away from New York and take a vacation. Life is more than meat."[46]

During the 1870s, Henry's travel schedule eased up gradually, and by the time of his seventieth birthday in 1882, he was working mostly at home in Brookline. In this period of their marriage, Mary said they were "as happy, as two lovers." Although Henry still worked steadily on books and railroad manuals during the day, the couple was often united for the evening. For the last twenty years of marriage, they lived together happily where Henry worked.[47]

Mary Poor, it should be said, was not an emotional or intellectual weakling. She raised four children to maturity, survived the death of two others, ran a large and busy household, read avidly, pursued an active social life, worked for various charitable groups, and, in later years, cared for her elderly sisters. Still, she longed for a more complete and constant relationship with her husband. That longing was not just a product of Henry's absence. It was also a result of their great love for each other.

Given his chronic absences, Henry's love may be less evident than Mary's, but he expressed his affection constantly in his letters to her. When she left to visit her parents in the early years of their marriage, Henry wrote: "I do *miss* you beyond power of description." He added: "The truth is I never felt you so completely necessary to my happiness as since you have been absent." More than a decade later, during a long absence, he wrote to her as his "dearest partner [and] friend," expressed his "love and affection" for her, and confessed that he often wrote to her "in thought" during the day.[48]

Still, although Henry Poor loved his wife deeply, his recurrent absences cannot be attributed simply to the necessary press of business. Poor made a lifelong habit of piling one venture on top of another until his books, manuals, journals, securities work, and publicity jobs all but obscured his family from sight. Even when his projects were well in hand, he skipped family vacations, and he worked so much after his retirement to Brookline that Mary wrote to one of their children: "Your father sits in his usual seat with a pen in his hand—I really wonder why he does not take a pen to bed with him."[49] The work that kept this husband away from his wife went far beyond the demands of external circumstance.

The truth is that Henry Poor felt a deep emotional need to be working. He confessed to nervous anxiety when he was idle. He took pride in being constantly "on the go" and loved to compare himself to powerful, hardworking animals. Also, there were other forces within Henry that made home life awkward for him. He struggled with his own clashing feelings about love and tenderness, and treated issues of sentiment as women's province. He tried to avoid such issues even when they were unavoidable. As he told Mary, he preferred to deal with the embarrassments of intimacy when they were separated because "we can at the distance we are apart, talk of love matters without blushing."[50] Yet Poor clearly needed to love and be loved. Once he knew Mary Pierce, he was desperately eager to marry her. By all evidence, he felt a deep affection for her. Although Henry could, as he wrote, "go into the world where in the business and bustle of life, he [could] forget his troubles," he expressed loneliness for Mary when they were separated for more than a few days.[51] He wrote at the end of one such separation, "I should be completely miserable did I not know that I *possessed* a *wife* and children, and that they are soon to be united to me."[52] Henry Poor wanted love deeply, even if it perplexed and disabled him.

Confused about intimacy but clear about work, Henry invested himself tirelessly in the problems of railroads, stocks, bonds, and business legislation. James McGovern, the historian who has studied Poor's life most closely, has summed up the man's contending needs and passions in this way:

> Activist . . . attitudes . . . took precedence over his insistent though subdominant needs for love and sympathetic reciprocity. Being home too much where he could release the shy, tender, and idealistic feelings with which he approached love could only threaten his primary goals. Though beset with conflicting needs, Henry subordinated his softer and gentler ones to those leading to . . . productive achievement.[53]

Henry Poor's arrangement of needs fitted closely with the ideas of gender that dominated his era: a man focused his energies on the world, while a woman concentrated on the emotional needs of her family.

With this division as the ideal, the physical separation of man from wife became pervasive. Midcentury advisers to young men tried to balance the trend by urging husbands to stay home as much as possible. As often happened, these authors indicated the prevailing trend by advising against it.[54]

Marriages like the Poors'—full of both separation and affection—existed on emotional ground that stood somewhere between alienation and intimacy. This middle ground was crowded with bourgeois couples in the nineteenth century.[55] Such marriages were born in love and nurtured with the hope of lasting affection: they were based on contrasting spousal roles, and extended traditions of unequal power between husband and wife, yet they were inspired by the ideal of a union between souls. Couples like these were kept apart by the demands of the middle-class workplace and often by male ambivalence, but there was enough love between husband and wife that they regretted their separation.

Still, these middle-ground marriages did not fulfill the yearning for

intimacy that swelled in the nineteenth century. To understand where
such couples stood in the spectrum of marital experience, one remark by
Daniel Webster is worth considering. After years of marriage to his
beloved Grace, Daniel wrote his friend George Ticknor about Ticknor's
wife, Anna. Repeating with approval a comment that John Calhoun had
made about the Ticknors' marriage, Webster wrote: "He talked to me
. . . about your good fortune in picking up a *companion* on the road to
life." Grace was a good wife and a staunch support, but she lacked
Daniel's education and did not understand the rarefied atmosphere in
which he operated. Anna Ticknor, by contrast, was cultivated, worldly,
and well informed. She was more than helpmeet and cherished partner
to her husband—she was truly a companion.[56]

The Websters' marriage did not lack for affection or regard; it was not
an arid affair of duty like the match of Mary and Ebenezer Gay. But it
was not intimate, not a full meeting of souls. It was probably the usual
middle-class experience; but pairs like the Ticknors were common
enough to keep the ideal of union alive and flourishing.

Married Life: Intimacy

We associate marital intimacy with the presence of many conditions—
congenial companionship; shared values and tastes; deep trust; an intu-
itive sense of one another's feelings; and a knowledge of one another's
unique personal needs. Still, the essential part of intimacy lies beneath
these phenomena. The word itself comes from the Latin *intimus*, meaning "inmost" or "deepest," and that is the key to its meaning in relationships.[57] Intimacy is the aim of romantic love, the sharing of that innermost core which is one's truest self. It is the opposite of estrangement in
marriage.

In her account of romantic love in Victorian America, Karen Lystra
describes three "sensations" detailed by nineteenth-century lovers,
sensations which correspond closely to the experience of intimacy as
it is meant here. Two of these are self-disclosure and self-expression.
The deep mutual involvement of intimacy was based on the unmask-
ing of the true self, getting to know the other "beyond social conventions and roles." This revelation of one's essential self came through
sincere, candid emotional expression. As the process of expression
and self-disclosure went forward, the intimate couple experienced a
third sensation: the development of a shared identity. Through this
experience, man and woman transcended their individual selves. By

deep, mutual immersion, they "assimilated a part of each other's subjectivity." This, in different terms, is the ideal of union, and it was a much-desired aspect of intimacy.[58]

Viewed as a cultural phenomenon, the pursuit of intimacy was a tribute—positive *and* negative—to the ascendancy of the individual in nineteenth-century America. It was an expression of unique individuality through the exposure of one's distinct core of selfhood. At the same time, intimacy was a quest to overcome the isolation of individuality through the merger of two selves into one.

The existence of intimacy, as an ideal and as an experience, was not just a product of cultural history. It was also the outcome of changes in family relationships. In particular, the closer, more direct, and more sustained bonds between mother and child that were typical of the nineteenth century left the child with a desire for such intimate connection later in life. The flourishing of intimacy as a cultural phenomenon required the proper worldview among men and women, and the right pattern of common experience in early life.

Romantic love and intimacy played a part in the formation of virtually all middle-class marriages in the nineteenth century. What would happen after the wedding day was far less certain. We have seen that the emotional gap between husband and wife grew wide in many marriages; yet, for other couples, intimacy endured and even flourished.

One such couple was Charles and Persis Russell. Married in 1815, they lived for the rest of their lives in the small town of Princeton, Massachusetts, where Charles was the local merchant and a leading political figure. He spent most of his time in Princeton, but he made occasional trips to Boston to buy goods for his store. Intermittently, he also represented the town in the state legislature, and this led to longer absences from home.

Charles's letters make clear, though, that he was devoted to domestic life—and especially to his beloved Persis. When he was away from home he wrote to her frequently and urged her to do the same, even if the letters "contain but a few lines." Charles often complained of homesickness, and sent Persis a stream of letters detailing his physical health.[59] The most touching of these came late in life during a role reversal of sorts; this time it was Charles who was left at home while Persis visited their children and grandchildren. He wrote to one of his sons:

> I write a line at this late hour just to say that I am as well as usual. I supposed your Mother would be rather anxious to hear. I have been so afraid [sic] of being sick since your Mother went down that I have almost

fancied myself, at times, not quite well. I thought yesterday morning that
I should certainly be attacked with a lame back and put on a plaster,
again I thought my old trouble of a pain in my stomach was certainly ap-
proaching and took freely from your Mother's pill box, but am inclined to
think it was at least in part my imagination.[60]

Charles's health formed an important part of his bond with Persis. It
provided him with an acceptable way to ask for nurture—for mothering—from his wife without discarding his formal authority or violating
conventional norms of gender. Women, after all, were expected to act as
doctor and nurse to their families.

This illustrates the division of labor between Persis and Charles,
which followed gender customs closely. The conventionality of their
arrangements showed through when Charles went to Boston, leaving behind a variety of "male" tasks. When the Russells' sons were small, these
jobs (running the store, doing chores on the farm) fell largely to Persis;
but as soon as their elder son, Theodore, reached his teens, Charles
turned the work over to him. There was no indication that Persis had
performed these tasks poorly. Charles certainly trusted her to supervise
Theodore's performance; Persis was, in fact, the conduit of his orders.[61]
But Charles viewed these tasks as a man's work: better that Theodore
should learn to do them than that Persis should be kept from her
women's work to get them done.

The Russells, then, subscribed to the customary assignment of tasks
by gender, along with all the beliefs about the nature of men and women
on which such custom rested. Still, their intimacy was undeniable. In
this context, that intimacy appears as a kind of bridge between two people who saw their basic natures as fundamentally different. One letter in
particular evokes the feeling of shared selves that typified the Russells'
marriage. During the legislative session of 1836, a letter from Charles
described the hardships of spending the Sabbath alone and away from
home. Aching for "the pleasure of which I am deprived," he sought to
create the feelings he missed by conjuring familiar scenes in his letter.
He entered not only his wife's activities but even her dreams:

> While I am writing these lines I suppose you are in bed with Sarah [their
> daughter] close up to your back and wrapt in sweet sleep and perhaps
> dreaming some pleasant thoughts that might have passed through your
> mind on this holy day ... or perchance you may have sat up later this
> evening than usual and are now, with Tom and Sarah, chatting about the
> absent members of the family (as we have been wont to do when all were
> present but Theodore).[62]

The palpable sense of detail and the tenderness of its rendering show that Charles was intimately and warmly familiar with his wife's routines. They also suggest a knowledge of her feelings and thoughts, a knowledge which is underscored when Charles adds: "But my dear, whether asleep or awake, or however the day may have been past, I know these things have been upon [your] mind and separated as we are at this moment, I can read your thoughts in my own feelings." Charles wrote as if his inner life and that of Persis were the same. In their intimacy, Charles felt as if they shared innerness in other ways: "Let us bless God for so uniting our hearts as to make them susceptible of the happiness he bestows."[63]

Of the three sensations that Karen Lystra places at the core of romantic love in the nineteenth century, self-disclosure and self-expression are much easier to locate in the letters of married couples than the third. But that "subjective feeling of being immersed in and assimilating a portion of someone else's interior life" is certainly evident in Charles Russell's letters to Persis.[64] Indeed, this intimate feeling of union was not merely evident but flourishing in the Russells' marriage after more than twenty years of wedded life.

Among intimate couples, the Russells were unusual in one respect: their kind of marriage was more common in the last quarter of the nineteenth century than in the earlier years when the Russells lived.[65] In the later era, couples wrote to one another in a way that separated their individual selves more distinctly from the roles they occupied. Whereas Mary Gay referred to her husband as "Mr. Gay" early in the century, Frank Kendall, a New York businessman, called himself "Your affectionate and loving Frank" in 1882. Married couples at the end of the century seemed prone—more than their earlier counterparts—to continue discussing each other's individual quirks and weaknesses decades into the marriage. Alice Van Hise noted to her husband, Charles, that "you and I are not backward in suggesting improvements to be made in each other. We know each other's corners and weaknesses." In a tone of greater worry, Elizabeth Cattell wrote to her husband, Will, in 1880: "I know you so well, as soon as you feel a little stronger you will attempt to do things you ought not to do, you need some one to watch you."[66]

Many late-century couples expressed affection readily after years of marriage. "Good night my darling. I go to dream of you," wrote Frank to Elizabeth Kendall. And Elizabeth Cattell liked to remind her "dear old man" Will how much her happiness depended upon him. The Cattells also possessed an ability to read each other's thoughts that resembled a mental union between them. The couple did their best to avoid overnight separations, because Will could not sleep when they were apart.[67]

Of course, these late nineteenth-century men and women did not invent marital intimacy. Still, the signs which we might expect of an intimate marriage show through more readily in the correspondence of couples late in the century. These men and women gave themselves to a process of self-expression and self-disclosure that was ongoing. Their letters suggest that marriage sustained a growing knowledge of self and other. This was the direction in which marriage was tending.

The experience of Charles and Alice Van Hise was somewhat different from that of other late-century couples described here. In its difference, the Van Hises' experience reveals some of the historical forces that were pushing toward intimacy in marriage, for they seemed to have an awareness of gender that contrasted with that of other couples in similar marriages.

The two of them met in 1875, when Charles was a freshman at the University of Wisconsin and Alice was living with her family nearby. After they married in 1880, Charles became an eminent geologist, teaching at the university and ultimately serving as its president. Alice bore and raised their three children.

Even before they were married, Charles and Alice showed signs of a keener awareness of gender than did other intimate couples of their era. In 1879, when they were already engaged, Alice's mother asked Charles a difficult question: Would it be a problem that Alice knew little of the technical subjects which he studied? Her question prompted him to write Alice a revealing letter. First of all, Charles posed the issue differently from the way Alice's mother did. He added his ignorance of music (Alice was a skilled pianist) to Alice's ignorance of mathematics as part of the problem that could arise. In doing so, Charles was consciously placing his fiancée's special skills on the same plane of importance with his. Such a symmetrical view of talents and significance in a marriage was unusual.

Having framed the question in this way, Charles searched for an answer. He concluded that having different skills was more conducive to harmony in a marriage than having the same ones. He reasoned that "if our intellectual works were exactly in the same line, . . . in an unguarded moment of defeat of one by the other, envy might creep in." Here, Charles was imagining that husband and wife could be, in his own word, "competitors" in the same sort of work. His conclusion, of course, was quite conventional: that their marriage would benefit by the clear separation in their spheres of activity. Still, the mere fact that Charles discussed the possibility of their working in the same field shows that he (and presumably Alice, too) lived in a far different world of thought and action than the other intimate couples studied here.[68]

At the start of their marriage, the Van Hises handled the conventional separation of spheres in an unusual fashion. Alice did not have a career, but she joined Charles on his geology field trips. Eventually she missed the comforts of home and decided not to go again; but she had a choice in the matter, a custom which was common in their circle of friends. Charles liked to tell the story of a colleague whose wife came along on all of his field trips. One day in camp, the husband sat on top of a tree, "claiming that at last he had got to one place [his wife] could not come." At that very moment, she was "shinning up [the] tree, taking off her shoes to do it." This woman stopped coming on the trips only when she began to have children. Like the Van Hises, this couple resolved their question of spheres in a conventional way, but the wife clearly had a choice through a significant portion of their marriage about whether to join her husband in his work world.[69]

The Van Hises' self-consciousness about gender arrangements in their marriage shows through once again in a comment made by Alice in 1891. Writing about a couple they knew, Alice said: "L. M. has some disagreeable traits as a husband that you are free from. He seems to be running things in her department most too much to suit my taste." This man, it turns out, was taking over decisions in household management— decisions his wife thought were hers to make. As Alice saw the division of labor in their marriage, the household was her "department" and she was glad that Charles did not interfere with her authority there.[70]

The Van Hises, then, were a conventional couple when it came to gender arrangements, but, unlike the other couples studied here, they were aware of other possibilities. And occasionally—as when Alice joined Charles on field trips or when Charles put her musical talents on the same plane with his mathematical skills—they thought and acted in unconventional fashion.

We cannot be sure why this was so, but at least one possibility seems likely. The world of the University of Wisconsin in the last quarter of the nineteenth century was quite different from the world of any other couple in this study.[71] At the university, advanced ideas on many subjects gained a hearing, and in some cases gained favor as well. It is clear that the Van Hises' friends often deviated from the usual arrangements between man and wife, and Charles and Alice certainly knew women who chose to make their careers in the academy or the professions instead of in marriage. These experiences did not make them a radical couple, but the Van Hises were transitional figures who lived by old ideas while understanding something of the new.[72]

Crucial among these new ideas was the concept—potent in its implications—that woman was an individual equivalent to man. Emerging from the midcentury women's movement, this new view saw women not as bearers of generic female qualities, but as unique selves whose qualities could include the "masculine" alongside the "feminine." Such a conception of womanhood gave females as legitimate a claim to a career and the vote as to motherhood and domesticity. Under the influence of this notion, the separation of spheres was laid open to question and the division of labor (and power) within a marriage became a problem to be solved, not an arrangement to be assumed.

In the late nineteenth century, this idea of womanhood was radical. Solid, middle-class couples certainly knew of it and probably found it both ridiculous and threatening. For the Van Hises, the new notion of womanhood was a present reality. They rejected much of it in making their life choices, but they were conscious of its possibilities, accepted parts of it, and knew people who lived according to its precepts. The new idea had moved into circulation and was starting to affect individual lives.

Underlying this new concept of womanhood was another idea, the same one that was creating changes in marriage. Before the nineteenth century had dawned, the notion was already growing that a person's sense of well-being was best fulfilled not through the exercise of social roles and duties but through achievement and experience as an individual self. The emergence of the individual from the enclosure of social roles—begun in the late eighteenth century and proceeding through the nineteenth—led to the new conception of a man as someone who created his own status and identity through his own personal efforts. Even as it was reshaping male self-conception, the new individualism was fostering change in marriage. Once, matrimony had been viewed in terms of communal obligation. Now, in a society where the individual was the fundamental unit, marriage had become a bond between two people who sought a transcendent sense of well-being through their relationship. This raised the stakes in marriage. Formerly, intimacy had occurred as a happy accident in wedlock. As the nineteenth century progressed, intimacy became the goal of marriage. Under these circumstances, it occurred more often, and when it did not occur, there was a greater sense of failure and disillusion. Thus, the late nineteenth century saw both an increase in marital intimacy *and* an increase in the divorce rate.

Of course, marriage at the end of the century was not a purely personal relationship. It was still a legal contract encumbered with traditional assumptions about gender, assumptions that accepted male authority as a governing principle of relations between the sexes. Nor was the personal relationship itself free of traditional belief. Man and woman might be individuals detachable from their social roles, but male and female selves were viewed as fundamentally different, and that difference was construed in such a way as to justify male authority in worldly matters. In other words, men and women were viewed increasingly as selves but not as equal selves. The idea of the autonomous individual was applied to all white males, but its application to women had only been partial. The hope of intimacy in marriage was growing, and equality was not seen as a necessary ground for intimacy.

Sex in Marriage

Just as new ideas about the self began to affect ideals of marriage, they also began to change people's feelings about the purposes of sex. In eighteenth-century society, with the individual's identity embedded in carefully rank-ordered roles, men and women saw the aim of sex as reproduction. Sex not only reproduced the race but reproduced the source of identity: the family. Then, as the individual's identity emerged from the enclosure of ascribed roles, reproduction of the family lineage lost its meaning. The bond between man and woman now created a personal relationship and a domestic world of care and nurture, while their social identity was generated by the man's efforts in the marketplace. In this context, sex between husband and wife expressed personal as well as social needs; increasingly, it signified intimacy between two unique selves.[73]

As many nineteenth-century men and women thought of it, marital sex united the bodies of two people already joined in love. One writer on marriage said in 1882 that the sexual relationship of married people "vivifies [their] affection for each other, as nothing else in the world can."[74] Thirty years earlier, an adviser to young women had asserted that the "physical aspects" of marriage, "pure and necessary as they are, . . . derive all their sanctity from the spiritual affinity existing between the parties." Sex in marriage was an emanation of love.[75]

Procreation, of course, was still closely associated with sexual intercourse in the minds of most people. A study done by Dr. Clelia Duel Mosher just before and after the turn of the century bears this out.

Mosher asked fifty-two women, most of them highly educated, about their experience of marital sexuality.[76] Roughly two-thirds of her respondents said that the principal goal of sex was reproduction. There is reason to suspect a certain amount of lip service in their answers, however. Certainly, "reproduction" was the polite traditional answer that a woman would feel most comfortable giving to a stranger. Indeed, many of the thirty women who gave this answer then qualified it—often to the point of downright contradiction—when they elaborated on their responses. One such reply said that intercourse was "necessary to complete harmony between two people." Other women in the study argued against the notion that procreation was the chief aim of sex. One asserted that "the first and highest reason for intercourse" was "the desire of both husband and wife for the expression of their union," adding that the "desire for offspring is a secondary, incidental, although entirely worthy motive, but could never . . . make intercourse right unless the mutual desire were also present."[77]

In fact, people were beginning to see children not as the mere outcome of procreation but as a result of their love and intimacy, expressed through intercourse. In her study of courtship and marriage correspondence, Karen Lystra found that middle-class men and women commonly wrote of their children as, in Lystra's phrase, "love tokens." One such correspondent called her daughter a "little pledge" of her love for her husband, while another described a child as a "tie to both our hearts." A third told his wife: "You are my life Darling, *and* I cannot look upon our baby, except through you. My love for him does not arise from consanguinity alone, [but has its] roots deepest in the soil of the love I bear my wife."[78] As the purpose of sex was changing from procreation to intimacy, the purpose of procreation itself was changing from the embodiment of lineage to the embodiment of love.

There was an emotional logic in all of this. For the middle class of the nineteenth century, the highest ideal of marriage was the union of opposites—a union of opposite kinds of people, opposite spheres, and opposite sets of moral principle. Sexual intercourse was the ultimate symbol and the supreme ritual of that union, joining bodies of opposite parts. Sex was the dream of union made flesh, and children were its lasting embodiments.

Large problems stood in the way of husbands and wives as they tried to realize these ideals, however. To begin with, men experienced powerful cross-pressures on matters of sex. Peers, proverbs, and popular counselors taught a male that his drives were fearfully strong.[79] He learned that the fate of his soul was tied to his control of that surging impulse, and he was encouraged to enlist the woman he loved in that effort at self-control. Thus, the object of his desires became the agent of his frustration. Some of the pressure for restraint subsided with marriage, because marriage made intercourse legitimate. Yet even then, the need of middle-class men to limit the size of their families introduced new constraints. Two of the most widely used methods of contraception—continence and coitus interruptus—required a man to exert self-control.[80]

Women, meanwhile, brought their own conflicts and concerns to marriage. Their training made them reticent about sex. They were taught that they had little or no passion, which made them mistrust their own erotic impulses. They knew as well that controlling male sexuality was their responsibility, and such a burden could not have made sex seem appealing to them. Moreover, as the person who bore the physical burdens of reproduction, a wife might well develop other negative associations with marital sexuality. As one historian has written, the prospect of pregnancy "threw a dark shadow over every act of intercourse" for a married woman.[81] And yet, there may have been more ambivalence than antipathy for most women. A wife's duty to please her husband would have lent social sanction to her own erotic desires. Indeed, there were nineteenth-century women who looked at sex as a source of gratification.[82]

Still, with so much emotional conflict attached to sexuality, it is hard to imagine that new husbands and wives could approach their lovemaking with an attitude that was intimate or relaxed. Clearly a woman and a man were arriving at the marriage bed with different needs, different feelings, and different inner struggles.

Apparently, husbands were more likely to resolve their inner conflicts in the direction of desire, and wives to resolve theirs in the direction of restraint. This pattern certainly fits with the popular nineteenth-century notions of male and female behavior. More than that, it shows through in the evidence we have about sex in middle-class marriages.

One source of this evidence is nineteenth-century writing about sexuality. A wide variety of authors described the same conflict in marriage between the husband's initiative and the wife's reluctance. Doctors testified that husbands tried to "overpersuade" their wives into sex. In the same vein, a feminist marriage reformer asserted that "the majority of married women are slaves to excessive sexual passion in their husbands, and . . . any attempt on the part of the wife to assert her own rights in this respect is productive of . . . much domestic infelicity." The sexual radical Victoria Woodhull, adopting the same metaphor, said of marital sexuality: "I would rather be the labor slave of a master, with his whip cracking continually about my ears, than the forced sexual slave of any man a single hour." Henry Clarke Wright, a conservative opponent of Woodhull's sexual radicalism, learned of the same sexual conflict in marriage by talking to women on the lecture circuit. In response, he wrote that "woman alone, has the right to say when, and under what circumstances, she shall assume the office of maternity, or subject herself to the *liability* of becoming a mother." The fact that Wright and so many other writers of differing viewpoints referred to the same struggle over sex indicates a common pattern of behavior.[83]

The Mosher study of sexuality and married women provides more evidence of the conflict between male initiative and female reluctance. One respondent, who wished to have sex about once every other week, told Mosher that she and her husband had intercourse three times a week, and that they would do it "oftener if she would submit." Men, one woman complained, "have not been properly trained about sexuality." The negative tone of these comments indicates an atmosphere of conflict surrounding differences of sexual desire.[84]

Difference does not necessarily mean conflict, however. The very same study by Mosher also turned up clear signs that cooperation and empathy were possible in the sex lives of married couples. Some of Mosher's respondents described their physical relations with their husbands in satisfied, and even ecstatic, terms. One woman, who had found a happy compromise with her husband on sexual frequency, wrote of their relations: "Simply—sweeps you out of everything that is [commonplace?] and every day. [Gives] a strength to go on." Others wrote of their husbands' kindness in a context that suggested their sexual frequency was a compromise between differing male and female wishes. These women, in achieving sexual mutuality, offered rapturous descriptions of their experience. One said that her years of physical relation with her husband had had "a deep psychological effect in making possible complete mental sympathy, and perfecting the spiritual union that must be the lasting 'marriage' after the passion of love has passed away with years."

The respondent who was most precise about the link between agreement on coital frequency and happiness in marriage was a woman whose first marriage had ended in divorce. Wed a second time at age fifty, she described sexual adjustment in the later marriage this way: "My husband is an unusually considerate man; during the early months of marriage, intercourse was frequent—two or three times a week and as much desired by me as by him." Through this experience, the woman had learned that sex was vital to "complete harmony between two people."

Her statement that her husband was "unusually considerate" is a reminder that many men were unwilling to compromise on the issue of
sexual frequency or that they did so only after rancorous conflict with
their wives. Still, enough women were happy with their sexual frequency
(and with their husbands) to leave the impression that the ideals of mutuality and spiritual union were approached in some nineteenth-century
marriages.[85]

Of course, the Mosher study can only tell us about sex and marital
happiness from a woman's point of view. We do not know that the men
whose wives were pleased felt the same way. It is even possible that a
male version of the Mosher study would show that husbands who ignored their wives' wishes were happier with their marriages and sex lives
than men who took their wives' needs into account. There is some cor-
roborating evidence, however, to suggest that the sexual experiences of
married men and women were running on parallel paths.

Nineteenth-century women who were pleased with their erotic experience in marriage recounted a particular feeling that was central to
their pleasure: the feeling that sex was an experience of spiritual oneness, that love found a natural outlet in physical affection which in turn
exalted that love to higher realms. This experience, described by wives
in the Mosher study, is also clearly visible in the correspondence of
nineteenth-century husbands.

There are, for example, the letters Edward Eaton wrote to his wife,
Mattie. Edward was a Congregational minister from the Midwest who
served from 1886 to 1917 as the president of Beloit College in Wisconsin. He and Mattie were devoted to each other, and his letters to her
blended thoroughly the languages of intimacy and eros. Once, after
twenty years of marriage, Edward's travels kept him away from home on
Thanksgiving Day. Weary and alone, he let his feelings of intimacy and
physical affection for Mattie overflow. He thought of the many evenings
they had spent together:

> . . . so full of rest and joy in each other's presence, in such full trust in
> each other, each heart beating tranquilly close to its loved fellow. Dear
> love what a garden of the heart you are to your boy, a sweet and sacred
> enclosure, all fragrance and refreshment and utter comfort; all this and
> always this.[86]

The intensity of Eaton's love fused body and spirit. When he and
Mattie were separated, his yearning was at once emotional and sexual.
He wrote on another occasion: "How I longed this noon for the soothing

touch of your loving hand on my forehead. . . . When I am away from you it seems as if the one most desirable thing were to get within touching distance of you."[87] Edward Eaton's words show how his love for his wife spilled over easily into the pleasures of touch and sensual fantasy.

A letter from Charles Van Hise to his wife, Alice, shows the same fusion of love and erotic feeling. Alice had asked Charles, who was on a geology expedition, to kiss himself on the back of the neck for her, and he replied: "I don't know just how to do the kissing asked of me; so I will wait until I can get home and not only kiss you there but everywhere, my love, my darling." For Charles Van Hise as for Edward Eaton, sexual desire merged with tender affection in his love for his wife. Men experienced this feeling just as women did.[88]

The sexual relationship of intimate couples was an expression of love in more than a symbolic sense. The process of bridging the gap between sexual desire and reticence—without force or resentment—required that couples learn compromise and understanding, and then practice those skills repeatedly. Indeed, the commitment of a couple to this process of empathy and mutual identification showed in itself that a common purpose and sense of caring already existed. In other words, the route to mutual happiness in sex was the same as the route to happiness in other realms of married life. Good sexual adjustment betokened good marital adjustment.

Thus, even without the simultaneous testimony of the wife and the husband, we can guess that where the process of sexual adjustment was proceeding with satisfaction—where tenderness flowed smoothly in erotic channels—mutual intimacy must have been present. While it is true that such union is not visible in the majority of Mosher's cases nor in the correspondence of a majority of the husbands studied here, neither is it a rare occurrence in either of those sources. Marital intimacy was not the *predominant* experience for middle-class couples—in bed or out—but it was still a common one, sufficiently common to nurture the romantic ideal and keep it growing.

The moments of sexual wholeness enjoyed by fortunate couples were not shared equally throughout the century, however. The men whose letters provide evidence of a fusion between the erotic and the affectionate were all late nineteenth-century husbands.[89] Similar expressions in the writing of men from earlier in the century are fragmentary and much harder to find.[90] The Mosher study also contains hints of change over time. Mosher's respondents who were born before the Civil War differed noticeably in certain sexual attitudes from the women born later. They were, for instance, more likely to see procreation as the aim of sex and less likely to see enhancement of the relationship as a main purpose. This is an oblique measure of behavior from a very small sample of the female population, but it does point in the same direction as the men's letters: it indicates that the joining of love and sex in marriage became more common in the final decades of the century.[91]

This historical timing ran parallel to another trend—the growing presence of marital intimacy in the late nineteenth century. The common pattern of these trends was not accidental. Both were following the upward arc of the importance of the self. After all, intimacy was present when two people disclosed their true selves to one another, and it reached its height at the moments when the two became so immersed in each other that they experienced a sense of union. In this context, sex was the physical counterpart of intimacy.[92]

In a heavily draped society, even a partial disrobing was an act of self-disclosure. And the entry into or envelopment by another body was a process of mutual immersion. As intercourse reached its climax in the mingling of substances from each body, two individual bodies achieved a moment of union. When a nineteenth-century woman wrote of sex, "It seems to me to be a natural and physical sign of a spiritual union, a renewal of the marriage vows," she was voicing a belief that was widely shared within bourgeois culture.[93]

Sex embodied intimacy, intimacy expressed selfhood. The increasing incidence of intimacy and sexual harmony in marriage could not have happened without the growing importance of the self as the cultural and social measure of things—but this growth alone was not enough to produce intimacy and sexual harmony. They required a match of personalities, which is difficult to achieve in any era, and a sense of mutual understanding, which was hard to attain within the gender arrangements of the nineteenth century. Intimacy and sexual harmony in marriage had become more common by the end of the nineteenth century, but they were still the experience of a minority of middle-class couples.

Continuity and Change in the History of Marriage

Historians in recent years have debated the nature of marriage in the nineteenth century. Some claim that "companionate" marriage came into existence during the 1800s, bringing with it a sense of supportiveness, affection, and mutual dependence.[94] Others have argued that such closeness of husband and wife was not a reality until the end of the nineteenth century.[95] Part of this debate may actually hinge on the distinction between cultural ideals and personal behavior. There is no question that intimacy and affection were marital ideals through most, if not all, of the nineteenth century. The testimony of correspondence, diaries, court records, and advice literature all point to the powerful influence of this vision of marriage. It was not the only model available; older standards based on duty and hierarchy appear in personal letters and in the presumptions of law. Still both marital ideals existed side by side throughout the century, with the companionate exerting a strong and growing power.

The patterns of *behavior* in marriage present a much more elusive problem. The standards for historical comparison, for one thing, are not as clear as they may seem. It is possible to find intimate marriages in any historical era before 1800; so, in the strictest sense, companionate marriage existed before the nineteenth century, before the ideal itself. On the other hand, it is not clear that love and intimacy are the dominant behavioral realities even in the late twentieth century. The divorce rate alone shows how difficult it is to live and sustain the companionate ideal—and the divorce rate only counts the couples who decide not to live together. It does not count couples who choose to accept their alienation as a fact of their marriage and avoid divorce; nor does it indicate how many men and women carry out their wedded life with respect, duty, perhaps even warmth, but very little intimacy. Neither does the divorce rate tell us about couples whose marriages go through distinct cycles of involvement and distance. The dominance of companionate marriage as a lived reality in the twentieth century may be less certain than it seems.[96]

Recognizing all these limitations, the evidence gathered for this book permits some speculation about changes in marital intimacy during the nineteenth century. It seems that loving, companionate marriages were in the minority throughout the century for middle-class couples, but it seems as well that this minority grew as the century went along. Indeed, the growth of companionate marriage may have accelerated in the last third of the century. Certainly, the written evidence of marital intimacy is easier to find then than in the previous decades.

These trends leave us with a further question: Why did the reality of companionate marriage arrive so slowly when the ideal was so widely expressed? First, the particular kind of change we are discussing here is a personal adjustment, which is difficult to achieve under any circumstance. To endure for a lifetime, companionate marriage needs flexibility, trust, commitment, empathy, and two compatible personalities. Men probably found the many compromises and accommodations of such a marriage especially difficult. As "head of the household," a man had a right to expect his wife to do as he said. Surely, this was easier and more comfortable than endless negotiation and compromise, especially when a competing concept of marriage held that a husband's power over his wife was his male right.

Of the factors that made the ideal of companionate marriage difficult to realize, though, the one most distinctive to the nineteenth century was the ideology of separate spheres. Raised on the idea that they were completely different beings, a man and a woman started their relationship with a sense of alienation. Although the romance of courtship did much to close that distance, the intensity of the romance was hard to maintain through years of marriage. The lives of husbands and wives ran in very different channels, and the values espoused in their separate daytime worlds encouraged the old sense of estrangement. As we have seen, it was possible to realize the ideal of companionate marriage in the nineteenth century, and it became increasingly so as the century went along, but the gender ideals of the era made a challenging form of marriage even more difficult to realize.

Middle-class men themselves seemed largely unaware of the slow changes in the institution of marriage, but they were keenly attuned to the differences in married life among themselves. Charles Russell reflected on these differences one night when legislative business kept him in Boston:

> Were I to consult my own inclination, ... I should fly, at once, to the bosom of my family, and there ... remain in the enjoyment of ... domestic happiness. ... How unhappy must that person be who does not find in his own domestic circle, by his own fireside and in the presence and company of his dearest earthly friends that enjoyment, comfort and pleasure ... [that] this blessing [of home] is so admirably calculated to afford. When I see a man that can take more pleasure in the company of others than he can find at *home* I should think that ... all was not right and that far better would it have been for him had he forever enjoyed the lonely comforts of "single blessedness."[97]

By dividing men into those who enjoyed home and those who stayed away, Russell was recognizing the choice that middle-class men of his time were often called on to make: home or the world. Some men felt enervated or trapped by domestic life, while others were drawn to its warmth and security. Still others—perhaps the largest number—felt themselves attracted to and repelled by each world at the same time.

Men's conflicting feelings about marriage shaped the choices they made between home and the world. Some of the ambivalence they brought to married life transcends the nineteenth century, but the cultural forces of the time structured men's feelings—and their images of marriage and women—in ways that heightened inner conflict for men regarding wedlock. Men came to this relationship with desires to dominate and to be nurtured; with views of woman as angel and as devil; with the fear that marriage and domesticity were a trap and the hope that they were a sanctuary; with the expectation that a wife would be a source of morality and the assumption that she would be a source of restriction; with the wish that marriage would offer him intimacy and an end to loneliness, and the fear that marriage would smother him and put an end to his freedom.

Looking back from the twentieth century, we cannot know in any statistical sense how men arranged themselves along the spectrum of commitment to home and the world. We do know what cultural terms structured their choice, and we know what inner conflicts pressed upon them in choosing. Within these confines, men made their own personal commitments.

Chapter 8

WORK AND IDENTITY

WHEN historian Arthur Cole explored the lives of eighteenth-century merchants, he made a surprising discovery. These leading businessmen spent much of the day away from their businesses, investing large amounts of time in the public and religious affairs of their communities. From a larger perspective, Cole's unexpected discovery certainly makes sense. This was an era when a man's identity came as much from his family and its place in the community as from his own achievements. A merchant enjoyed a position of prominence in his community, so it was his duty to lead in matters of governance and religion.[1]

Cole observed of the eighteenth-century merchants: "As yet, perhaps, business had not become so much an end in itself and success in business did not become so adequately a basis for self-satisfaction, as was to become the case in the next centuries."[2] This did not mean that a merchant's work was unimportant to him. It represented a part of his public usefulness along with his political and religious leadership. His contribution to the common wealth blended seamlessly with his other contributions to the good of the community. Only in the early nineteenth century, when the individual emerged in importance from the communal context, did a man's work take on a separate meaning and provide the chief substance of his social identity.

Work and a Man's Identity

In the nineteenth century, middle-class men's work was vital to their sense of who they were. "Man is made for action, and the bustling scenes of moving life," wrote Theodore Russell as he sought a place in the world of middle-class work.[3] This self-perception was constantly reinforced by those who made up a man's social world. As Mollie Clarke told her suitor, Willie Franklin, in 1868: "I often think it is so different for men from what it is with us women. Love is our life our reality, business yours."

If a man was without "business," he was less than a man. In 1844, a New York college student made the gender connection explicit in a letter to his fiancée: "It is so unmanly so unnatural to spend a lifetime in the pursuit of nothing." "*Suitable* employment," to use his phrase, was vital to a man. After a week of unemployment, young Lucien Boynton described his inner emptiness and depression: "The week has left a painful vacancy in my mind, and the 'Blues' seem to be already gathering around me. My soul feels as tho it had been feeding on wind and vapor." A man's life had little substance or meaning when he lacked work.[4]

Work was not just a personal matter, however. It helped to connect a man's inner sense of identity with his identity in the eyes of others, and the expectations of others were bound to larger social conditions. As the nineteenth century opened, the United States was becoming a nation where no formal barriers prevented white men from achieving positions of wealth, power, or prestige. Now, a man could determine his place in society through his own efforts. Of course, positions of high standing were limited in number, and informal barriers made access to these positions difficult for much of the male population. Still, a man could thrill at the prospect of improving his own position and becoming the master of his own social fate through personal energy and determination. Again and again, men described their personal goals as the outcome of their struggle—through their work—for a desirable social position. Certain phrases recurred when men set forth their goals: "arrive at eminence and fame"; "rise to wealth and honor"; "[get] on in the world"; "prepare myself for some station of respectability and usefulness."[5] A man's social position depended, in theory, on his own efforts. Thus, men identified themselves closely with their work.

Of course, male identity took its shape partly from its relation to female identity. In the gendered division of labor of the nineteenth-century middle class, the woman made the home and reared the children, while the man earned the money to make the woman's efforts possible. But men's desire for position and fame was not just a residue of the breadwinner's role. The division of tasks between the sexes gave a man the power to determine the social status of his whole family. It was *his* work that marked the place of his wife and children in the world. In other words, the self-made man of the nineteenth century made not only himself, but his family as well.

This awesome power of social creation added weight to the already great importance of work. As we have seen, men and women were keenly aware of this male prerogative when they approached marriage. Alexander Rice reminded his future wife that he was the person "upon whose arm you are to lean thro' life, upon whose reputation your own will rest and upon whose effects your happiness as well as his own will mainly depend."[6] The power to create the social position of one's family raised the stakes for the nineteenth-century man. No wonder he identified himself so fully with his work; in a social sense, he was what he achieved—and so were those he loved.

The Meaning of Career Choice

Ambitious young men of the nineteenth century filled their private writing with the anxious buzz of hope and fear. As Rutherford B. Hayes began his study of law in 1842, he wrote in his diary: "I have parted from the friends I loved best, and am now struggling to enter the portals of the profession in which is locked up the passport which is to conduct me to all that I am destined to receive in life." Hayes felt that his entire future hung in the balance as he began his career. Other men shared that feeling, writing in their letters and diaries of wild oscillations between "black discouragement" and "the most ardent hopes, the most glowing ambitions."[7]

Getting to the point of entry into a career was not, in itself, an easy task. Many obstacles lay between a male youth and the professional portals that Rutherford B. Hayes described so auspiciously. Poverty, family obligation, complications of courtship, and conflicts of intention with fathers were all common factors that slowed the progress of a youth toward a career in business or the professions.[8] But of all the elements that delayed the launching of careers, none caused so much youthful philosophizing or contained such latent gender meaning as the choice of an occupation.

This decision was not only the necessity and the prerogative of a man;

it was, above all, a decision about what *sort* of a man one wished to be. This aspect of the decision contained its own dimension of gender, for Americans viewed different professions as more or less manly. Politics, for instance, was seen, even by its detractors, as a masculine pursuit. Aggression, deceit, competition, and a spirit of self-interest—all traits that middle-class culture associated with men—were vital elements in the quest for the manly goal of power. William Dean Howells confronted this phenomenon as a young man. He arrived in Columbus, Ohio, in 1858, a political journalist who loved literature. He quickly discovered that politics in Columbus was a man's world, while the arts were the province of women. To pursue his interests, he had to divide himself into male and female halves that could only flourish in different social realms. Not only was politics marked "male," but a career in the arts was marked "female." Other professions were sex-typed, too. Teaching, for instance, carried an aura of femininity, although a college president was manly.[9]

In general, male callings rested on power, pride, and public eminence, while female careers involved nurture and sentiment, an understanding of human feeling used to cultivate and ennoble the human spirit. Given the middle-class ambivalence about both male and female values, the choice among professions posed difficult problems for a young man.

These difficulties were evident in the contrasts middle-class folk loved to draw between the law and the ministry. In some ways, the two callings were similar.[10] They were considered the most learned of professions; they required a mastery of precedent and tradition; they demanded a cultivated faculty of reason, even as they obliged a man to master the less rational arts of persuasion; and they encouraged their practitioners to join a knowledge of theory with an understanding of human nature. Yet, for all of these likenesses, the two professions appeared to nineteenth-century men and women as diametric opposites.

Reuben Hitchcock, a prominent Ohio jurist, returned from church one Sunday in 1848 and wrote to his wife: "As [the minister] stood in the pulpit today, I could not but contrast the high and noble character of his profession, with any worldly pursuit, and particularly with law and politics." Focusing on the legal profession, Hitchcock wrote:

The lawyer racks his brain over knotty and difficult questions, and . . . is constantly harrassed, . . . the slave of the public . . . [who] is required to exercise a liberality and practice a style of living, which will consume all his income, and give to him for all his effort . . . the occasional applause of some of his fellows for his ability.

Worldly matters demanded a lawyer's time, but his counterpart in the pulpit was occupied by higher concerns: "The faithful minister of the Gospel acts for the highest moral and spiritual interests of his fellow-men, and is laboring directly for the happiness of his fellows, and when he shall rest from his labors, his works shall follow him." Hitchcock ended his comparison with this wish: "If our dear boys are spared to grow up, and their education, habits, piety, and qualifications of mind shall fit them for the sacred desk, it will be to me, and I doubt not to their mother, a cause of devout thankfulness and gratitude to God."[11]

As a young attorney, Henry Varnum Poor made a similar comparison between the ministry and the law. Poor was practicing law in Bangor, Maine, and the experience filled him with so many second thoughts that he pondered a change from the bar to the pulpit. He found that his legal practice threw him in among "men actuated by passion, prejudice, and desire for revenge," men who offended his sense of Christian goodness. At another level, he disliked the law because it was "based upon force, a principle diametrically opposed to that by which the conduct of man to his neighbor should be regulated— . . . the principle of love." Poor felt that if he pursued a minister's career, he would live more consistently with "the theory of [his] life that man . . . should live for his fellow man and adopt that profession . . . which can best promote their happiness in the world."[12]

Although Poor's grounds for contrasting law and ministry were not precisely the same as those of Reuben Hitchcock, they were very close in their moral basis—deeply rooted in the nineteenth-century division of virtues and vices into gender categories. In the minds of Hitchcock and Poor, the legal profession stood for passion, self-seeking aggression, and a constant capitulation to worldly lures and pressures. The law, in other words, represented the classic male weaknesses.[13] The clergy, by contrast, symbolized the great female virtues. A minister's work was governed by moral and spiritual interests, by love, and by a concern for the happiness of others.

Since Hitchcock and Poor echoed the judgment of their culture about feminine virtues and masculine flaws, their words seem to suggest a lofty prestige for the clergy and a dominant influence for the standards women represented—but matters were not this simple. First of all, one must remember that Hitchcock and Poor themselves both chose to be lawyers. Hitchcock's letter expressed a wish that his sons might become ministers, but he made no disavowal of his own career; and, although Poor's statement was occasioned by his doubts about life at the bar, he ultimately expanded his work—not to the ministry but to publicity and analysis for the railroad industry. Poor's actions belied his adherence to the principle of love in vocational choices.

Indeed, the statements of other men show that, if the ministry stood for the female in middle-class culture, that symbolism did as much harm as good to the profession's image in the eyes of men. A damning midcentury essay ("Saints and Their Bodies") by Thomas Wentworth Higginson indicates the ministry's problems with public perception. Searching for the "causes of the ill-concealed alienation between the clergy and the people," Higginson found "one of the most potent" to be "the supposed deficiency [in the clergy] of a vigorous manly life." He noted that many parents "say of their pallid, puny, sedentary, lifeless, joyless little offspring, 'He is born for a minister,' while the ruddy, the brave, and the strong are as promptly assigned to a secular career!" Even when people praised a favorite minister, they often did so in terms befitting a woman. An admirer of William Ellery Channing described his "native sensitiveness of organization" as "almost feminine" and lauded his "womanly temperament." Another Unitarian divine, William Thacher, possessed a "winning and almost feminine gentleness of demeanor."[14]

Just as the feminine traits inhering in the ministry could lower its status in the eyes of men, so too the manly associations of the legal profession could add to its appeal. Alexis de Tocqueville expressed a common perception when he wrote: "In America . . . lawyers . . . form the highest political class and the most cultivated portion of society."[15] Lawyers—as men—could use their "natural" sense of reason to guide the great republican experiment and to wield power wisely in protecting the rights and freedoms of Americans. What better use could there be for such proverbially male traits as dominance and reason?

In the end, the gender-linked valuations of the bar and the pulpit did not prevent either profession from replenishing its ranks with each succeeding genration. As we shall see, however, the gendered associations did affect the relative prestige of the two callings. At some level, young men seemed to be aware of these considerations as they chose careers. The gender meanings of different professions probably led to a self-selection in the kinds of young men who entered various lines of middle-class work, although the evidence here is not sufficient to confirm the point. At the very least, the link between gender and profession created identity problems for certain men—problems that cried out for solution.

Men found one solution to this problem through a strategy that merged the worldly with the godly, the "male" with the "female." The strategy centered on the notions of Christian warfare and the Christian soldier. By waging Christian warfare, a minister could act with manly aggression while pursuing the sacred goals of love and goodness that his culture linked to women. A lawyer or businessman, by taking up arms as a Christian soldier, could purify his wealth and power by using it to godly ends. The chief arenas for this holy warfare were the revival and reform movements that flourished throughout the nineteenth century. As evangelical fervor swept into the Midwest in the 1820s, an Ohio scholar and teacher named Elizur Wright rejoiced: "How exhilirating [sic] the thought, that an efficient army of vigorous Christian soldiers are in the act of preparation, and will soon stretch [in all directions] . . . inspiring 'life and motion and joy through all our ranks.'"[16]

Wright recommended this "constant, vigorous, and persevering warfare" as a way to sanctify the energies of men in the worldly professions. One capitalist crusader of this sort was John Kirk, a salesman and a zealous abolitionist. Speaking to a group of evangelical converts in 1853, Kirk reminded them: "You have enlisted in the Christian warfare for life, under Christ, your King." With slavery in mind, he advised the converts that "we wrestle . . . against principalities, against powers, against the rulers of the darkness of this world, against Spiritual wickedness in high places." In his own work, Kirk wrestled for profit with his competitors, but he made time for the greater and more holy battle for the soul of a nation.

The idea that a man of the worldly professions might enlist in holy warfare carried on through the century. In 1888, Richard Cabot, a young reformist doctor, asked his fiancée, Ella Lyman, to "stand side by side . . . in mutual help and understanding as we fight God's battles." For Cabot's generation, this urge to wage holy warfare against worldly evil crystallized into the collection of social movements that we now call "progressivism." Historian Robert Crunden has observed that many notable progressives came from religious families that cultivated stern Protestant consciences. Resisting pressure to follow careers in the ministry or missionary work, these devotees of reform found secular channels for their evangelical impulses, launching crusades to save society from its worldly sins. Progressivism offered men of worldly callings the opportunity to respond in manly fashion to the dictates of their Christian consciences.[17]

Throughout the century, ministers also enlisted readily in Christian warfare. The great reform movements and revivals gave them suitable opportunities to apply assertiveness, energy, even masculine hostility to the cause of Christian goodness. J. L. Tracy, a young teacher trained for the evangelical ministry, wrote to Theodore Weld in 1831, urging him to bring the work of revival to the Ohio Valley, which he called "the great battlefield between the powers of light and darkness." "Why not," asked Tracy, "train the soldiers of the Cross within sight of the enemies camp?" And young Henry Ward Beecher, in his earliest days as a minister, crowed that he was "waxing mighty in battle" as he penned an abolitionist editorial.[18]

By freeing up the aggressions of the clergy and purifying those of the businessman and the lawyer, the image of the Christian soldier in sacred warfare liberated vast quantities of male energy.[19] Without this spiritually charged assertiveness, the great antebellum and Progressive reform movements would have been unimaginable. Moreover, this sacred combativeness made career choice possible for many young men by adding toughness to "feminine" professions and lending virtue to "manly" callings.

Men at Their Work

Some men chose their careers easily and some chose them with qualms about the manliness or the morality of their choice, but the time came when each of them "first [made] trial of [his] talents" in a profession. Many years of hard work and even more of grand dreams had been spent in preparation for this moment. Young men often felt as if an audience of friends and family watched their first efforts at success. One youth even imagined an arena full of "spectators" waiting "in expectation."[20]

Although there were some who could claim immediate and encouraging victories, young men were more likely to report a mundane, discouraging reality. They lacked connections among clients and fellow professionals, and they had no record of proven success to attract business. Given the sharp, constant fluctuation of the American economy in the 1800s, there was always a good chance of starting out at a time of contraction when even established firms were going down. With so many initial problems to confront, young men often achieved little success at first. Some simply failed.[21]

Not surprisingly, self-doubt flourished in the writing of new businessmen and professionals. Morton S. Bailey, as a beginning lawyer in Denver, wrote a letter in 1880 to his close college friend, James Cattell, pouring out his fears: "I am in continual doubt and full of misgivings lest the future be darker than the past, and with this feeling of dread do you wonder that I hesitate to make the advancing steps or that I would almost rather not take them at all." Self-doubt was a disease of the novice at the start of the century as well as the end. When Daniel Webster wrote to congratulate a friend who had just preached his first sermon, he confessed anxiety about his own career. He felt the "conflicts . . . between the rival powers of Hope and Fear," and, as he expressed full confidence in his friend's success, he realized that he did not have the same feeling of certainty about himself: "Poor human nature! How entirely sure we are and easy about everybody's fortune but our own."[22]

Perhaps the aspect of the novice's self-doubt that was most distinctive to the nineteenth century was the way in which men chose to cope with it. When Allan Gay, an art student, wondered in a letter to his father in 1839 whether he had enough talent for painting "to make it necessary and proper for me to continue," he responded to his own fears as if by instinct: "I have learned it is not so much genius as an untiring perseverance that determines to conquer every obstacle." Talent, in the minds of nineteenth-century Americans, mattered less than persistence. The proper antidote to male self-doubt was not self-examination but "untiring perseverance" and a redoubling of effort.

Ray Stannard Baker, an aspiring journalist, took the experience of being "jobless, hungry, and (briefly) homeless" as an invigorating challenge. He refused to "confess defeat," and he knew that he "could and would stand a considerable degree of starvation before [he] surrendered." "Curiously enough," Baker recalled, "it did not seem at all hardship. Something about it even lifted one's spirits. It was an adventure in hard realities; it aroused everything a man had in him. It was in short to be enjoyed—almost!" From boyhood onward, a male learned that it was shameful to walk away from hindrance or defeat without fighting back.[23]

Thus, young men responded to the initial doubts and frustrations of their careers with intensified effort. A student named Mary Butterfield noted in 1846 that "it is a common and a great fault with young men . . . when they enter upon active life to become entirely absorbed by business." At the very start of their professional lives, then, young men began the habit of pouring heart and soul into their work. This habit, spread out over a lifetime, became a defining mark of American manhood.[24]

It was a common observation in the nineteenth century that American men had a passion for work. In 1820, a Connecticut law student noted that business "engages [a man's] mind and occupies his thoughts so frequently as to engross them almost entirely and then it is upon his employment that he depends almost entirely for the happiness of life." Another commentator wrote in 1836 that the American man "is never . . . so uneasy as when seated by his own fireside; for he feels, while conversing with his kindred, that he is making no money. And as for fireside reading, . . . 'he reads no book but his ledger.'" A third critic warned at the start of the twentieth century that there was "a masculine disease in this country": the "habit and fury of work, unreasoning, illogical, quite unrelated to any [economic] need."[25] As young Boston physician Richard Cabot wrote of his work, "I wouldn't for the world be free of my harness; I put it on and keep it on myself." Work may have been a harness to Richard Cabot, but it was a harness that he loved to wear.[26]

Any phenomenon as widespread and deeply felt as this male passion for work was bound to be—in Sigmund Freud's term—"overdetermined." In other words, one can locate many reasons for men's prodigious appetite for work. Most of these reasons, taken individually, might be sufficient to explain the masculine zeal for productive activity. Taken together, they provide an explanation with many interconnected sources.[27]

Some sources of men's passion for work we have already examined. In the nineteenth century, a man's primary duty was to support his family through his efforts in the workplace; a man determined his own social position and that of his family through work; work provided men with an acceptable outlet for aggressive action in a society where such action was a crucial component of manhood; it also gave men an arena in which they could exercise their manliness through dominance.

In addition to these motives, there were other, gender-related forces that gave men their passion for work. We have seen how life in a middle-class household taught children to associate the female with nurture, interdependence and restraint, while linking maleness to power, independence, and freedom of action. When a boy left home to join the company of his fellows for part of the day, his experience established the male world even more firmly in his mind as a realm of liberty and adventure—and the female world as a realm of quiet confinement. This web of gender associations extended readily into adulthood. Most middle-class men seemed to enjoy their work. Their jobs in the male domain of the marketplace provided them with a more inspiring challenge than they could find elsewhere in their lives. Just as the absorbing play and the stimulating games of boyhood became the focus of boys' days, the feverish competitions of the marketplace excited men's interest.

Historians have accepted the word of nineteenth-century ministers, moralists, wives, and mothers that home was a haven in a heartless world.[28] Certainly there were bourgeois men who felt this way; but there were other men who experienced home as a dull lodgement or even as a threat to personal independence and individual manhood. Women sensed this feeling at times. In 1869, Serena Ames asked her beloved,

George Wright, if he "sometimes [had] uneasy feelings about a time to come when a weak, childish woman will cling too closely, impeding your progress, and by too much coaxing, thwart your desires, making you less free to go your way in the full liberty of manhood?"[29] Even if the woman herself were not "weak" and "childish," a man could readily associate home—the female realm—with his own experience of weakness, child-ishness, and restraint as a small boy. A man for whom these associations were especially strong and unmanageable might well become compul-sive in seeking out the world of work in order to experience more of "the full liberty of manhood." Work could serve to reassure a man about his manhood and about the freedom and power that manhood betokened. More positively, it provided many men with a compelling challenge and engaged their sense of play.

Beyond these gender-linked motives, there lay still another source of men's passion for work. In the words of a contemporary, men over-worked "to escape ennui or unwelcome thoughts."[30] Men's testimony makes clear that the use of work to avoid painful feelings was a common male habit.[31] One person who understood this was Charles Van Hise. The letters he and his wife, Alice, wrote to each other after the death of their twenty-year-old daughter, Hilda, reveal a clear contrast in the way men and women treated work as part of the grieving process. When Charles set out on a business trip a few months after Hilda's death, Alice wrote despondent letters. Charles replied with great sympathy for her plight. "I know your desolation," he wrote. "I wake up in the night and it comes over me. In the morning it is always there with me." He also knew that he had a much easier way to escape from sorrow than Alice did. "The only possible thing to do is to think of the things to be done and do them. I am aware that this is far easier for me who have thus far been full of business, and who is moving from place to place."[32]

Van Hise's statement offers us a key to understanding why work seemed to comfort men more than it did women. It certainly was not be-cause women lacked for things to do; all but the most privileged middle-class women had their days full of domestic and social duties. Rather, it was because activity had long since taken on a reassuring quality for men. Trained from boyhood to associate action with male worth, doing *something* (but especially doing familiar tasks with many past satisfac-tions attached) reassured men about their own worth as male human be-ings. Since doubts about one's personal value lie at the heart of feelings of grief, men naturally turned to work for succor at times of loss. Also, work—being a prime source of enjoyment for some men under normal circumstances—could function effectively as a temporary distraction from the weight of grief. Activity could lift a man's spirits even as it soothed his hurts.

For women, the balm of action was not so comforting.[33] The virtues they had learned to identify with female worth—piety, purity, and submission—are all states of being more than of action. Because she associated her human value with "being" more than "doing," a woman coping with grief lived with her feelings instead of acting against them; she acknowledged them and sifted through them with family and friends. Thus, when Alice Van Hise filled her letters to Charles with expressions of grief and statements of her shortcomings as a mother, she was doing the work of mourning in her "woman's" way. But Charles misunderstood. He saw feelings of grief and self-doubt as ones to banish—even to vanquish. Thus, when he told Alice that the "only possible thing to do is to think of the things to be done and do them," he was giving Alice the best advice he knew. When she sorted through her feelings about Hilda's death, he urged her to "cease trying to solve the riddle of the Universe."[34] He did not understand—it was not a "possible thing" for Charles to understand—that Alice was doing her own grief work, trying to find a way to be at peace with her loss, to accept her feelings and live with them. For Alice, work was an avoidance of the issue. For Charles, it was a balm, maybe even an elixir.

Many other men used their work, as Charles Van Hise did, to assuage grief and "escape unwelcome thoughts." Indeed, work had a kind of magical aura in the world of bourgeois manhood. Beyond matters of duty, power, identity, and escape, many men worked constantly because it gave them pleasure. The middle-class world of work provided them with a male environment that was both familiar and stimulating.

The Measure of a Man: Failure and Success

Middle-class manliness was defined by notions of success at work, yet an understanding of failure is also vital to an understanding of bourgeois manhood. Failure was a fact of life even for those men who might be considered successes. It visited some successful males in the early years of adulthood; it was a temporary companion to all; and it entered every family through the disappointments and disasters of sons, brothers, uncles, and cousins. Many men had to learn how to grapple with failure, and the *fear* of it was a common experience among males of the middle class. To understand these men, we must understand their attitudes and feelings about failure.

Family correspondents handled this unpleasant subject quickly, with curt phrases. The New York merchant Sylvester Lusk said of his hapless brother's attempt to start a business in Texas: "I hope William will get better out of the Texian advanture [sic] than we have previously reason to expect." Writing several months later about the career choice of a different brother, Sylvester observed, "I hope whatever he undertakes he will not share the fate of William." George Dryer, business manager at a Minnesota sanitarium, discussed the failure of his brother in similarly vague terms: "I am sorry you cannot report to me more favorably of Charlie. From his conduct and from the good resolutions he expressed I had great hopes that he would assist you and by a more manly course wipe out some of the unpleasant memories that are associated with him." With such cryptic phrases and glancing allusions, families discussed the failed men in their midst. These men, and the references to them, drift through the pages of nineteenth-century letters and diaries like silent, unwelcome ghosts.[35]

Failure was a want of achievement where achievement measured manhood. Moreover, failure was viewed as a sign of poor character. The deficiencies of character that were thought to cause failure were of two sorts. One was laziness. Again and again, we have heard men exhort one another to "industry," "persistence," "hard work," "unflagging effort," and "the wise use of time." Each of these popular phrases stood not only as an exhortation to positive behavior, but as a warning against negative behavior. Typically, men were prone to write about desirable traits, but when they did discuss undesirable ones their disapproval was sharp. They urged each other to start "breaking up all . . . tendencies to indolence" and to "quit loafing."[36]

The other deficiency of character that men held responsible for failure was a tendency to vice and debauchery. Just as people wrote about failure in veiled allusions, they referred to the vices that bred failure in vague obscurities. Samuel G. Stevenson, an aspiring businessman from New York, told an uncle close to his family that his father's "habits are so bad, that he is unfit to mingle in respectable society." Young Stevenson added candidly his reasons for not identifying his father's vices: "To give you a history of his conduct, would only add pain to my thread-bare feelings on this subject. To say the least [his habits] are too bad to reduce to writing." Even after his father had conquered his bad habits, Stevenson felt such pain about them that he still could not bear to give them a name: "Father is quite a new man. His habits are good, and he enjoys perfect health, having more than one year remained without the least interruption from his old habits."[37]

What habits were so shameful as to be unmentionable and so devastating as to prevent success? We get a clue from a letter about Ebenezer and Mary Gay's son Charles, whose "follies," "debaucheries," and "dissipation" were the subject of many pained and obscure references in his family's private writing. One letter specifies the sources of Charles's accumulated debt, chief among them being drink, billiards, and new clothes. Of these vices, one suspects drink as the primary culprit behind Gay's failures, and also behind the many glancing references to "vices" and "follies" in the correspondence of other worried families. Certainly liquor was the favorite target of authors who advised young men. More than any other common vice, it ate away at personal judgment and physical health.[38]

Of course, alcohol was part of the collective life of male youth and of many workplace cultures. In some all-male settings, the pressure to drink was so strong that liquor consumption became a badge of manhood. Ironically, then, the flaws of character that led to failure came either from an excess of manhood or a deficiency of it: in a symbolic system that identified the aggressive passions as male, an unusually strong desire to drink or otherwise debauch oneself was both masculine and a hindrance to success. On the other hand, the traits associated with habitual drinking—passivity, submissiveness, and a want of energy and self-assertion—were marks of insufficient manhood and a hindrance to success. Being a man, then, meant more than suppressing "female" qualities and encouraging "male" ones. It also meant strict control of some "male" impulses and encouragement of others. A man who failed at this task paid a high price, which a nineteenth-century newspaper described with unsparing candor: "If we have not the will to avoid contempt, misery and disgrace, we deserve neither relief nor compassion."[39]

This was the cultural understanding of failure. How did men cope personally with the "contempt, misery and disgrace" attached to it? Men who failed (or felt that they had) were helped by the fact that the harsh code of failure was not quite as monolithic as it may appear. When Samuel Stevenson tried to explain the ruin of his father's business, he said that it was "owing to misfortune . . . and bad habits." The distinction suggests that, behind the belief in character as the determinant of failure or success, there was some sense that factors beyond a man's control could affect his fate in the workplace.

This distinction between bad luck and bad habits in explaining business failure is evident in a Massachusetts minister's diary entry in 1807. The Reverend John Pierce of Brookline noted that a local club had held a debate on the question: "Whether it be expedient for legislators to make a difference between bankrupts by misfortune and bankrupts by knavery?"[40] The law at the time did not separate business failures on this basis; in its eyes, a bankruptcy was a bankruptcy, and a man simply had to live with the harsh consequences of his failure. Still, the fact that men publicly debated the distinction between bad fortune and bad character suggests that people could at least separate the two in their minds as possible causes of ruin.

The existence of this conceptual difference shows us that there were cracks of mercy in the great wall of condemnation. When individual men tried to understand their own failures, they often sought comfort in the thought that uncontrollable fortune had led to their downfall. Daniel Webster's son Fletcher blamed the demise of his land management project in Illinois on the economic collapse of the late 1830s. Young Massachusetts doctor Edward Jarvis explained the failure of his medical practice in Northfield, Massachusetts, by the treachery of his rivals, accounting their "falsehood and defamation of [his] character" as the reason for his disappointment. Certainly, it was the common custom of the time for politicians to blame their defeats on the dishonesty, fraud, and "corrupt bargains" of their opponents. By claiming that factors beyond their control led to their ill fortune, some men tried to justify the disgrace of failure.[41]

Many men learned another way to deal with setbacks, however, a style of coping that was more consistent than analysis or explanation with the active values of manhood. Such men drove themselves to shake off failure, rise above despair, and plunge back into action headlong. This approach to hardship was deeply embedded in middle-class culture. In an essay quoted earlier, young Will Poor enumerated all the usual habits and virtues that would lead to triumph. The crowning rule of successful behavior was this: "Above all, . . . [do] not be discouraged by any adverse circumstances." In later years, Will's own successful father observed him with admiration: "[Will] is different from me. If he meets with a repulse he will not be cast down, but continues to fight with unabated courage the battle of life."[42]

Will may have learned this lesson from his father's incessant activity or from his own experience in the world of boys. Certainly he could not have avoided the homilies about adversity that fell from the lips of so many Yankee sages in this era. Henry Ward Beecher said: "It is defeat that turns bone to flint; it is defeat that turns gristle to muscle; it is defeat that makes men invincible." On the same subject, Wendell Phillips wrote: "What is defeat? Nothing but education, nothing but the first step to something better."[43]

Such precepts echoed far and wide, providing a language of hope and determination that shaped the private thoughts of middle-class men. Reflecting in 1878 on the qualities needed to succeed in business, Charles Van Hise summarized his ideas in this way: "In short, [the man of business] must not know the word 'fail'; all things must be bent to one thing—success."[44] Taken literally, Van Hise's advice was a prescription for denial: succeed by ignoring failure, pretending that it does not exist. Apparently, this was the most potent strategy that middle-class Americans could find for dealing with such a painful issue. When they discussed the failure of family members, they certainly pretended "not [to] know the word" and avoided the subject as deftly as they could. When it was their own failure, they tried to deny it by ignoring their feelings of discouragement and pressing onward.

Maine native and future politician John Barnard took this strategy to its highest degree. On his thirty-fourth birthday, he reflected in his diary on the wayward course of his adult life. By his own ready admission, he was not a success; as he put it, " I [have] . . . but little to show for my labours." Although ambitious, he rarely held a job for long. He never trained for a career, and his most frequent occupation was the classic time-marking activity of educated youth: schoolteaching. In his mid-thirties, he was past the age where most young men needed such holding actions.[45]

Yet Barnard's birthday reflections were buoyant, optimistic, almost sanguine: "In the main I have been a happy man—blest with a mind not too easily cast down by changes of fortune. Always buoyed up by hope." He then described his hopes—and habits—in classic words of nineteenth-century determination: "How much we count on the future. Lay plans and anticipate riches—honour and happiness—disappointment cools our ardour but little. We alter our plans and drive on as briskly as ever and so I presume I shall continue to do till death shall summons me from all earthly scenes."[46] Barnard steadfastly refused to be shaken by his own failure.

Or, more accurately, he refused to admit that he was shaken. For his own account of his adult life belies his cheery words and reveals the depth and strength of his denial. In nearly two decades after leaving home, John Barnard resorted to many strategies common to frustrated men who suffered through their own repeated failures. Barnard moved constantly. His personal relations were tumultuous: he engaged in feuds and fistfights with his male peers and treated women with extravagant faithlessness. He "drove about into all the wild company [he] found." He also, in his own words, "tried *spirit* to keep [his] *spirits* up" and he "used opium sometimes."[47] These are not the habits of a man "always buoyed up by hope" and "not too easily cast down by changes of fortune." They seem to be the actions of a man pained by his own inadequacy.

The distance between Barnard's image of resilience and his actual experience is revealing in two different ways. First, it shows the cultural power of denial as the accepted strategy for coping with failure. Here was a man who described his own suffering vividly and remembered his depressions of spirit with painful clarity. Yet, when he tried to step back and summarize his life, he resorted instinctively to the standard formula that reconciled his experience of failure with dominant ideals of manhood and success. As a way to describe defeat, the formulaic language of resilience and denial was inadequate, but, as a way to rationalize the "contempt, disgrace . . . and misery" of failure, this formula clearly had usefulness and strength that made it popular.

In the end, it may have proved effective for Barnard. After marrying happily in his mid-thirties, he gained the stability that had eluded him for so many years. He began to keep a diary as a way to deal with the pain of a long separation from his wife. It turned quickly into a sifting device, one that enabled him to describe his past, sort it out and come to terms with it at a time when he was clearing away the financial debris of his turbulent life and securing his personal commitments. In this context, the cultural formula of "pressing on past failure" became a kind of incantation; it reminded him that he could still succeed, and linked him ritually to other men who rose from ruin to success. Whether he had lived according to its dictates in the past mattered less than his attempts to abide by them in the present. Barnard went on from this moment to achieve success in Maine politics. Thus, a cultural article of faith became a self-fulfilling prophecy.

Still, this understanding of Barnard's attempts to change himself and cope with failure does not help us to understand the decade and a half of his life in which tumultuous behavior and worldly defeat ran side by side. Did personal habits cause failure or were they a behavioral response to the pain of ill fortune? Or did the two create a spiral of despair, shiftlessness, and failure? Barnard's life poses these questions without providing any effective answers. Certainly, his contemporaries believed that bad habits contributed to many ruined fortunes; and it is true that rootlessness, constant interpersonal turmoil, and chronic inebriation are all hindrances to success in most professional and business occupations. Yet the annals of success in the nineteenth century are full of men—Andrew Jackson comes to mind—whose lives were marked neither by regular sobriety nor by peaceful personal relations.

Even if such habits were in part a cause of failure, it is very hard not to see them also as a response to worldly setbacks. It must have been a painful experience to fail in a society where failed men "deserve neither relief nor compassion." Whatever other motivations men had to drink, carouse, or run from responsibility, the sting of defeat must surely have been one. We have John Barnard's direct testimony that—during his long period of failure—he sought wild company and used liquor and drugs to raise his sagging spirits.

Failure was a painful experience. In addition, the fear of that experience cast a long shadow over men's lives. In a competitive, burgeoning economy the chances for failure were great. While men were reluctant to discuss their own chances directly, their anxieties were drawn into the open by the prospect of love and marriage.

In 1822, a young man named Benjamin Ward connected his thoughts about his fiancée with his fear of failure. He wrote, "If I should sink in my professional efforts . . . how would that friend be wounded, how would her days be embittered. . . . If I were wholly independent, . . . my fear of . . . defeat would be far less terrible." Another young man, George Rudd, wrote to his brother in 1858 about failure and its connection to marriage, using language as strong as Ward's. Rudd recognized that there would "be another" who would "share in the embarrassment of failure . . . —and that very fact . . . will only make the burden to be borne the more crushing." If these two men are an accurate indication, men were acutely aware of the price of failure and feared it greatly. "Embarrassment," "burden," "crushing," "terrible"—these strong words suggest the dark underside to the hope of success. It is not surprising that men felt reluctant to discuss this underside.[48]

Yet, despite the frightening prospect of failure, most men focused on their dreams of success and plunged ahead. Whatever their ultimate degree of success or failure, they believed in the game enough to play it. The unbelievers—who thought the game was not worth playing—might retreat into drink, self-abasement, and failure. There were, however, more constructive alternatives. For a few self-conscious rebels, the communal movement of the antebellum years provided an escape from the heavy costs of manhood in an era of individualism. For a larger number, the security of evangelical Christianity may have provided a solace against the pain of failure and the anxieties of the open market. In a different vein, the popularity of such heroes as Natty Bumppo and Davy Crockett may have reflected the need for a fantasied retreat from the bruising defeats and artificial demands of men's lives in the marketplace.

Still, fantasy could offer, at best, partial comfort, while evangelism and the communal movement never absorbed more than a limited minority of men from the comfortable middle class—and had, in any event, run their course as movements of significance by the last third of the century. By those final decades, though, a cultural device had evolved that buffered men from the demands of the marketplace. Middle-class males for whom work was an ordeal increasingly found shelter in vague, debilitating illness. Actively tolerated in some circles, male neurasthenia was a common phenomenon in the late nineteenth century.

The Cultural Meaning of Male Neurasthenia

Will Cattell was a Pennsylvania native. Trained as a minister, he rose to the presidency of Lafayette College. Then, in 1883, Cattell's ill health forced him to resign. The pressures of the job had broken him down mentally and drained his physical energy. Free of responsibility, Cattell rested for several months. Then he took a part-time job in Philadelphia with the Presbyterian Church. The new situation worked well at first. Will wrote to his son James that he had "more *really* troublesome things to settle [in his new position] in the last two weeks than [in] . . . two average months at Lafayette" and yet he was "hopeful and happy."[49]

Within six months, however, the vague, enervating symptoms of his earlier collapse reappeared. By May 1885, his wife, Elizabeth, feared that he was "breaking down again." Will suffered from a downward spiral of tension, insomnia, fatigue, irritability, and depression. Although his work provided the ultimate source of strain ("After the meeting of his board on Tuesday, he came home completely broken down. Dr. Harper and Dr. Reid had both annoyed him, and made him very angry."), Will Cattell's tensions came to focus on his obsession with the noise of the streetcars that rumbled past his home. His son Harry observed that his father could not rest "on account of the noise grating upon his nerves. When Papa is home he talks of nothing else but the noise when there is any and in anticipating its coming when there is none." Will finally resorted to extreme measures. Upon discovering that the sound of the cars did not penetrate an isolated closet on the third floor of their home, he retreated there at night in search of undisturbed rest.[50]

Cattell's nervous obsessions were very much his own, but he shared the larger pattern of illness with a substantial portion of comfortably situated middle-class men in the late nineteenth century.[51] These neurasthenic males described an odd lot of symptoms: blurred vision, indigestion, restlessness, backache, constipation, disorientation, headache, throat irritation, colds, dizziness, loss of appetite, palpitations, and spitting up blood. The most common complaints of all were those suffered by Cattell: insomnia, tension, depression, and (especially) fatigue accompanied by an utter lack of energy.[52] A salient quality of the illness was its episodic nature. Although some men suffered only one bout of neurasthenia, it was common to have recurrent breakdowns. Even when the symptoms ebbed, the men plagued by this illness watched anxiously for signs of its return. Their lives swung between periods of productivity with nervous good health and periods of illness with restful recuperation.

The disease did not occur randomly across the life cycle. Its most prominent contemporary student, Dr. George Beard, noted that his neurasthenic patients were largely aged fifteen to fifty. Its most assiduous historian, F. G. Gosling, reports that the illness struck 68 percent of the people he studied when they were between the ages of twenty-five and forty-five.[53] Although the episodes often continued into later life, neurasthenia—in its onset and its greatest severity—was especially a disease of youth and early middle age.

George Beard gave the label *neurasthenia* to the disease in 1869, but the phenomenon of recurrent breakdowns, accompanied by the strange variety of symptoms later typed as neurasthenic, is evident in the historical record from the early years of the century. Francis Parkman and Henry James, Sr., were among the prominent sufferers in the antebellum era. Such problems as fatigue, blurred vision, indigestion, headache, and depression were commonly associated complaints among evangelicals and reformers as early as the 1820s. Lesser-known men, such as Boston lawyers Thomas and Theodore Russell, described symptoms, diagnoses, and cures that closely resembled those experienced by men late in the century.[54]

Thus, George Beard was giving a name to a familiar collection of symptoms when he identified the disease in 1869. By the 1880s, neurasthenia reached near-epidemic proportions in the northern United States. Eventually, its male sufferers included Theodore Dreiser; William Dean Howells; Charles Evans Hughes; Henry James, Jr.; William James; John LaFarge; Louis Sullivan; and Woodrow Wilson. Only after 1910 did the disease begin to disappear.

Neurasthenia lumped together under one heading a variety of emotional disturbances, neurotic tics, psychosomatic illnesses, and organic maladies. Yet, when the symptoms are seen in relation to the central problem of chronic exhaustion, they take on a coherent meaning. This, in fact, is how neurasthenic middle-class males saw themselves. These people believed that men broke down when, like Will Cattell, they suffered from the strain of overwork. One Massachusetts woman expressed the common wisdom in this way: "C. [her husband] goes early to his office every weekday and returns late, quite 'used up.' I do not think he will give up his usual office hours before August unless he quite 'breaks down,' which I sometimes fear will be the case."

Again and again, men repeated this connection between overwork and breakdown as a way to explain neurasthenic health problems. William Dean Howells described his most serious breakdown as "the result of long worry and sleeplessness from overwork," and Will Cattell's son James attributed his own neurasthenic decline to the fact "that my constitution is not very strong and I at times overstrain it." The common perception that too much work caused breakdowns was spread and reinforced by doctors, who saw overwork as the chief source of neurasthenia in professional men.[55]

This conclusion rested on a belief that was widely shared by doctors and neurasthenics alike: the human body was a closed system containing a finite amount of energy. Different activities drained energy at different rates, with the "brain work" that typified middle-class occupations providing the most notorious drain on the system.[56] Some people, it was thought, had less energy enclosed within their systems and so were more susceptible to exhausting their supply and collapsing into the chronic lethargy of a breakdown. In the phrase of the time, too much brainwork "used up" a man.[57]

George Beard and other doctors who studied neurasthenia did not denigrate its victims or view it with alarm. Rather, they saw it as a symptom of progress. In this medical view, the human race had developed more complex societies in the course of evolution, and these societies moved at a faster pace. The human nervous system pressed to keep up with its own external creations, and some men who worked at the pinnacle of social evolution (that is, in professional and executive work) broke down from the strain. This self-congratulatory theory found echoes in the writing of nonspecialists. James Cattell, for instance, asserted that the "men who do most in the world are seldom quite healthy—those who try to do all they can use themselves up."

As we shall see, there were men who disagreed with Beard and looked askance at neurasthenic males; but the doctors who treated the illness and those who theorized about it showed respect for the men who suffered from it. This contrasts sharply with the case of hysteria, another disease common at the same time as neurasthenia. Although the two ailments were similar in their mix of psychological and physiological symptoms, hysterics were mostly women, and the (male) doctors who treated them took a condescending—and sometimes condemning—attitude toward them.[58] Neurasthenia was not a source of pride, but it did not become a badge of shame until the very turn of the century.

A specially important fact about neurasthenia is that it was treatable. Physicians, friends, and relatives often recommended exercise for relief from neurasthenic symptoms. It was important, however, that the exercise should be moderate. James Cattell summarized the common opinion about exercise as a cure, saying that a man who "spends a month exercising out of doors . . . gets himself in good health and good spirits, too. But when he continues taking a good deal of exercise . . . he gets into about the same condition as before he took too much."[59] There was such a thing, then, as "too much" exercise. As a cure, it needed to be regulated carefully. Moreover, when physicians and patients wrote about exercise, they did not mean strenuous workouts but long daily walks.[60] This regimen was often combined with a vacation. In the larger scheme of contemporary therapeutics, the most important thing about exercise may have been that it forced the neurasthenic away from work.

In fact, the most widely accepted remedy for neurasthenia was rest and relaxation. S. Weir Mitchell, a well-known Philadelphia neurologist, made the rest cure famous, and one of his patients, Charlotte Perkins Gilman, has made it notorious through her story "The Yellow Wallpaper." In this thinly fictionalized account of her treatment with Mitchell, Gilman described an enforced passivity in which her will was almost totally surrendered to the doctor and her confinement nearly reached the point of sensory deprivation.[61] Most physicians did not define rest in such extreme terms, especially not for men. Some ordered extensive bed rest without the severe isolation of Mitchell's cure. Others simply prescribed a cutback in work hours to be replaced by frequent breaks for sleep and repose. Still other physicians took rest to mean relaxation, not time in bed. Long vacations with fresh air, mild exercise, or simply an absence of care satisfied the demands of such doctors.

In practice, a physician might combine these forms of rest in different ways. When the president of Beloit College, Edward Eaton, broke down in 1891, his doctor ordered him to leave work entirely and go to bed. As Eaton improved, the doctor said he could return to work, "*provided*, he uses care and discretion, and will take sufficient rest and exercise during the twenty-four hours to offset the amount of work done." Apparently, Eaton did not follow his physician's advice to use care and moderation, because eight months later he was under medical orders to take a long vacation.[62]

The importance of relaxation as a vital component of the rest cure for men is emphasized by the materials in Edward Eaton's case. The fact that the ultimate prescription when bedrest failed was a trip to Europe suggests that Eaton's doctor saw a separation from the cares of life as more important to recovery than physical inaction. This supposition is borne out by the physician's direct advice to Eaton *"don't worry, rest whenever fatigued, . . . and feel that whatever happens is all right."* Eaton received similar advice from the people close to him. A good friend wrote before the European trip: "Forget that you have any cares." When Eaton fell sick again in 1900, his son Allan urged him "to take a month or two off and find just the right place to rest and recuperate in. You ought not to have much to worry over; and it's the pressure of such uneasiness that keeps one from really getting the most from an attempt to build up."[63]

The rest cure for male neurasthenia meant a separation from the emotional strain of work as much as it did a recovery from physical debility. It was combined with other measures in endless variety. Physicians mixed rest not only with mild exercise but with dietary change, hydrotherapy, or one of a vast range of medicines.[64] At its core, though, this was a disease of fatigue and its chief cure was rest and relaxation.

Neurasthenia as a historical phenomenon was rediscovered by women's historians, and apparently it was equally common among males and females. When F. G. Gosling studied the cases of over three hundred neurasthenics reported in medical journals between 1870 and 1910, he found that male and female sufferers presented doctors with the same symptoms but received different diagnoses. Physicians attributed the symptoms of middle-class men to voluntary behavior; they named "overwork or mental labor" most frequently (34 percent of all cases) as the cause of neurasthenia in men of the professional classes. On the other hand, doctors were more likely to attribute female neurasthenia to biological causes, citing "genital/reproductive disturbances, including exhaustion of childbirth" as the most common cause (31 percent of all cases).[65] This sex-typed interpretation of the same symptoms reflects the common medical wisdom about gender in the nineteenth century: men were active and created their own fates by assertions of individual will; women were passive, imprisoned by the demands of their bodies.[66]

In spite of these cultural assumptions (or perhaps because of them), the doctors may have been correct in sensing the underlying problems of neurasthenics. Male sufferers were getting sick by fulfilling social expectations of work, "mental labor," and "ambition"; women were falling ill because they had met the social expectation of childbirth. Some men and women, in other words, may have made themselves sick by performing their social roles. Viewed in this way, neurasthenia was a matter of sex-role strain.[67]

To follow out this line of thinking more completely for men, we should return to the precipitating cause of male neurasthenia: work. The basic structure of the illness, with overwork, tension, fatigue, breakdown, and extended rest, amounted to a rejection of work. The fact that this cycle was repeated over and over in so many lives only adds to the sense that neurasthenia involved men's negative feelings about work. The comments of male neurasthenics and their doctors and friends also make it clear that the sickness could be a response to the worry and strain associated with work as much as to the excess of work or the nature of the work itself.

One gets a stronger sense of the connection between work and male neurasthenia by noting that breakdowns often happened at times of vocational crisis. William James suffered a serious collapse in his twenties when he reached an impasse between his father's wish that he practice medicine and his own desire to pursue philosophy. The first of Francis Parkman's periodic breakdowns happened when, in accordance with his father's wishes, he began to practice law instead of following his own ambition to be a historian. Earlier in the century, the great abolitionist Theodore Weld had suffered from two mysterious illnesses that liberated him from careers that did not satisfy him; in both cases, his health returned with equally mysterious speed once he was freed from the disagreeable work. Weld, like James and Parkman, found himself trapped in what Erik Erikson calls an "inauthentic identity"—one unsuited to a person's needs and values and chosen to please someone else. Neurasthenic symptoms allowed men to withdraw from undesirable callings, while avoiding direct conflict with fathers or other beloved figures.[68]

Men's breakdowns justified other forms of proscribed behavior. When Edward Eaton's "nervous collapse" in 1891 sent him to bed for many weeks, he wrote to his mother: "I hope I can go on gaining at home, as father says. I can now be justified in greater care of myself."[69] In a society where a man had to offer justification for taking good care of himself, neurasthenic illness provided a valid excuse for rest and relaxation. Of course, it was quite possible that a man might enjoy relaxation for its own sake, whether he needed better self-care or not. The symptoms of nervous exhaustion also provided a socially acceptable explanation for such self-indulgence.

Biographer Howard Feinstein noted, after careful study of the James family, that "energy and capital flowed freely for healing, while the sluices were clanged decisively shut for pleasure and idleness."[70] Young men like William and Henry James not only found conventional careers repugnant, but relished the stimulation of European travel and the pleasures of reading and reflection. Each brother engaged in a complex process of invalidism and cure requiring enough recovery to justify the family's expenditures and their own idle time, but not so much recovery that travel and rest might end too suddenly. This process, partly conscious and partly submerged, engaged the brothers for much of their youth and early adulthood.

There is no evidence to suggest that neurasthenics ever composed a numerical majority of the population of middle-class males. If they had been that numerous, little professional work would have been completed in the late nineteenth century. Still, neurasthenia provided an outlet for that minority of men who found their work an ordeal, who were repelled or intimidated by the pursuit of success, who balked at strenuous exertion or took pleasure in a restful life. As Howard Feinstein has said, "Work was a problem for these Americans, and illness was one solution."[71]

Work, however, lay at the heart of man's role; if work was a problem, so was manhood. Male neurasthenia, in other words, contained a profound element of gender meaning. Looked at in terms of gender, male neurasthenia amounted to a flight from manhood. It not only meant a withdrawal from the central male activity of work, but it also involved a rejection of fundamental manly virtues—achievement, ambition, dominance, independence. A man who steered away from the middle-class work-world was avoiding a man's proper place.

Moreover, the neurasthenic man was retreating into the feminine realm. By going home to rest, he was seeking out the domestic space of women. He was also finding refuge in roles and behaviors marked "female": vulnerability, dependence, passivity, invalidism. Even a man who traveled to recuperate was pursuing the life of cultivated leisure which was associated with women. Unwittingly, a neurasthenic man was inverting the usual roles of the sexes, rejecting "male" and embracing "female."

The gender dimension of male neurasthenia becomes more clearly visible when one looks at the professions where male invalids clustered.

Of the fifteen neurasthenic men studied here, all but one were engaged in callings—the ministry, the arts, scholarship—typed as feminine. In medical case studies of male sufferers, there were, to be sure, many businessmen—but, since that was the numerically the dominant occupational group within the middle class, their presence is not surprising.[72] To find neurasthenia in biographies and autobiographies of businessmen takes some doing, but to explore the annals of the clergy, scholarship, or the arts in the late nineteenth century is to find nervous exhaustion rampant. Although no claim to statistical accuracy can be made here, it seems at least a sound working hypothesis that neurasthenics were exceptional among men of business but common (if not predominant) in the academy, the church, and the world of the arts.

There is another dimension of male neurasthenia that involves age as well as gender—for the behavior of nervous invalids represented a retreat from manhood to boyhood.[73] When a man returned home to rest and be nursed, he was repeating the boyhood experience of nurture and dependence in a place sheltered from the world. When he took an extended vacation to recover at the seaside or in the mountains, he was immersing himself in certain classic values of boy culture: play, the rejection of care and responsibility, the pursuit of pleasure. As surely as male neurasthenia represented an embrace of femininity, it also meant a symbolic return to many aspects of boyhood.

Neurasthenia was not the only common form of male regression. The masculine culture of liquor, saloons, clubs, lodges, rituals, games, and prostitution was another avenue of return to boyhood. As a regressive pattern of behavior, though, it differed sharply from male neurasthenia. It bore no trace of a return to the domestic dependence of boyhood; on the contrary, it harked back to boy culture's rejection of home life and its emphasis on collective male enjoyment. The men's world of play returned a man to boys' world in its hedonism, its boisterousness, its frequent cruelty and competition, and its disdain for polite, "feminine" standards of behavior.

It is important to stress that few of the men who suffered from "nervous exhaustion" availed themselves of this other, more assertive form of regression. For Christian gentlemen who rejected such worldly pleasures, however, neurasthenia offered the most socially acceptable escape from the strain of work and the burdens of a grown man's responsibilities.[74] This more "feminine" form of retreat must also have held attractions for men uncomfortable with the rough style of camaraderie that typified masculine culture.

Neurasthenia differed from the masculine culture of escape in one other significant way: it was a full retreat, not a momentary one. The masculine world of relaxation and pleasure existed in a symbiotic relationship with the workplace, nurturing its friendships, mimicking its competition, and rooting itself in close physical proximity to marketplace activities. Neurasthenic breakdowns represented a sharp rejection of work, complete with physical separation, the loosening of business relationships, and the abandonment of the usual pace and style of work activity. The man who broke down was making a statement, however unconscious, of his negative feelings about middle-class work and the values and pressures surrounding it. In doing so, he made a gesture of serious opposition to manhood in his own time.

Chapter 9

THE MALE CULTURE
OF THE WORKPLACE

A nineteenth-century businessman would have felt out of place in the world of the eighteenth-century merchant. The pace would have made a Victorian man restless. In the eighteenth century, information moved slowly and transportation was unreliable, so the tempo of a merchant's work was languid and uneven. The setting, too, would have seemed unusual to a man of commerce from the nineteenth century. A merchant's office occupied the same building as his home, and, although his work spilled onto docks and into shops, those sites were always close to a man's home. This meant that men conducted business near their wives and children. In addition, men's business partners in the eighteenth century were their brothers and cousins, their fathers and sons.[1] Men who entered this world through connections of family and community were the norm, and those ambitious men who burst in from the outside were viewed as exceptions.

The dynamic marketplace of the nineteenth century reversed this pattern. Recruitment into the commercial arena became more open and competitive. At the same time, dramatic improvements in transportation and the flow of information speeded up the pace of work. With the legitimacy of self-interest also now established, the business world of the early nineteenth century suddenly appeared to be hurtling forward in chaos and strife.

Inevitably, this new workplace culture attracted critics. The most influential critique was the ideology of separate spheres. According to its principles, the true value of home was measured by its contrast with the cruelties and disappointments of the world and the corruption of the workplace. As one magazine article portrayed it, the public arena was a place where "we behold every principle of justice and honor, and even the dictates of common honesty disregarded, and the delicacy of our moral sense is wounded; we see the general good, sacrificed to the advancement of personal interest." Other critics described the middle-class work world in more figurative language as a place where "the dark clouds" yielded "the 'peltings of the pitiless storm.'" However it was described, the world earned a reputation as a harsh place where cruelty and deceit held sway.[2]

It is from such descriptions that we have drawn our image of the nineteenth-century marketplace. Yet we need to recognize that the authors of these descriptions were people who spent their days outside the arena of middle-class work, and that their vision does not fully measure the feelings of the men who worked there nor completely represent their experience.

Many middle-class men enjoyed their work and, indeed, often relished it. These men, after all, made up the most powerful class in their society. To the extent that work satisfaction is based on a sense of the efficacy of one's efforts, they had every reason to enjoy their work. Besides, men enjoyed a certain kind of protection: years of immersion in the cultures of boyhood and of male youth accustomed them to the ceaseless competitive striving, the uncertain fortunes, and the assertions of self that were typical of their work world. The "peltings of the pitiless storm" left many men damp but undeterred.

The language of the separate-spheres doctrine can mislead us about the texture of men's work experience in another important way. By portraying men as solitary figures pounded by the worldly storm of rivalry and deceit, the imagery of separate spheres leads us to think of men in the marketplace as isolated beings. In so doing, it has deepened the impact of the figurative language of another cultural doctrine: the cult of the self-made man. The image of the lone male rising steadily by his own effort from a humble cottage to the mansions of wealth and power has profoundly shaped our notion of a successful man's work life in the nineteenth century. Of course, this image expressed a real perception: a man in the marketplace was judged by his own behavior.

Still, it is a mistake to confuse individual action with solitary action. The work world created by the market economy was a fundamentally social one. A man there was rarely alone. The work of the merchant, the lawyer, the politician, and the banker was usually interpersonal and some of it was unrelentingly so. Many men had partners, most had sub-ordinates, some had face-to-face rivals, all had clients, and, in differing degrees, all of them were clients themselves. By the later years of the century, growing numbers were working in the offices of large organiza-tions.

This deeply social world was completely dominated—in numbers, power, and cultural influence—by men. As a subculture, it was a dis-tinctly male arena. Historians who have studied the structure and habits of the middle-class workplace have always approached it as a product of economic rationality, class interest, or professional imperatives. We also need to understand it as a product of its own masculinity. A brief look at three types of work settings—the midcentury publishing business, the antebellum judicial circuit, and the world of high finance at the end of the century—can demonstrate the male sociability of the middle-class work world.

Male Sociability and Men's Work

A book publisher in the middle decades of the nineteenth century prob-ably did more solitary work than the average businessman. He wrote let-ters, worked his account books, and read manuscripts from prospective authors. Yet his social contacts were frequent and sometimes intensive. His intercourse with his partners (if he had them) and his clerks was constant. He had to be in touch frequently with printers, binders, ship-pers, and local booksellers. He saw authors and periodical editors and visited the publishers' trade shows, which had their origins in this era.[3]

A lot of this social business contact took place by prearrangement in offices and other formal meeting places, but a good deal of it happened casually, or at least outside of business offices. The biographer of Boston publisher James T. Fields describes some of Fields's time away from the office evocatively:

> Frequently he visited newspaper editors to consult about advertising, a book notice, or merely to maintain good relations with chit-chat. Always there was Mrs. Abner's Coffee House just around the corner. Here he took buyers, authors, reviewers, and friends and often spent many hours with them over steaming buns and cups of fresh-brewed coffee. There were after all many compensations for dull periods over the account books.[4]

Fields lived in an era when the business areas of a city could still be covered on foot, so the amount of incidental contact and the number of brief visits "merely to maintain good relations with chit-chat" was large. Also, there were eating and drinking places where businessmen would gather. In addition to visiting coffee-houses, publishers went to hotels, restaurants, taverns, and private clubs to mix work with sociability. Finally, Fields and his wife, Annie, excelled at a form of business entertainment which grew steadily in importance throughout the century: the carefully arranged dinner party. Although some such parties included the men's wives, many dinners were "stag" parties, and others allowed only the hostess to join the men.[5] Even at the mixed-sex dinner parties, men and women kept separate company before and after they came to the table. Here as throughout a publisher's day, male work and sociability mixed promiscuously, while men's and women's worlds were scrupulously kept apart.

The business life of a publisher was quite staid compared to that of most antebellum lawyers. Outside the major American cities, lawyers before the Civil War "rode the circuit." A judge and a troop of lawyers left a central town or city and, for months at a time, would travel together from one place to another to hold court. One contemporary described a circuit court as having "the ravishing beauty of a circus, the majestic grandeur of a caravan, the spiritual fascination of a camp meeting and the bewitching horror of a well conducted dog fight." The lawyers of the circuit made up a vivid social world of their own. They shared wagons, work, food, and even beds. Most of all, they shared each other's days and lives for months on end. When odd moments presented themselves during the day, they would quickly sit down "to enjoy a game of cards with more or less drinks by the side." And when the workday was over, the lawyers gathered in a nearby tavern or hotel room, where they ate, drank, told stories, recounted the day's events, argued law and politics, and even held mock trials. As the judicial caravan rumbled slowly onward to the next town, the men continued to entertain each other with "long discussions and exchanges of professional talk."[6]

This subculture had its own important social distinctions. The judge or perhaps an eminent attorney presided informally over the after-hours life of the circuit, and if he found a lawyer wanting in personal or professional qualities, he would cut the man out of the group. Like any other fraternity, this one was exclusive.[7]

Back home in the county seat, the structure of work life and personal commitments did not allow for the fraternal culture of the circuit in its fullest form. Still, even in the sedentary life away from the circuit, the bonds forged on the road linked the local attorneys, and the mores and habits that governed itinerant legal society shaped the culture of the bar.[8]

This was especially true of the alternating rhythm of competition and kinship that bound lawyers in the same locale. In his autobiography, Lew Wallace reminisced about his friendship with another young attorney, Daniel Vorhees. The two men were courthouse rivals in Covington, Indiana: "Our bouts, usually in some justice's court, were frequent. They were rough-and-tumble, or, in wrestling parlance, catch-as-catch-can; sometimes almost to the fighting point." But Vorhees and Wallace established clear distinctions between professional enmity and personal regard. As Wallace recalled:

> I can yet hear the creak of the door of my office as, without a knock, [Dan] threw it open and walked in—generally, the night of the day of an encounter. . . . I can hear the greeting with which he threw himself on a chair: "Well, Lew, I got you to-day," or "you got me," according to the fact. "Come, now, put your work up and let's have the fiddle."[9]

And Wallace would oblige with Voorhees's favorite tunes. So close were their personal bonds that Wallace even helped Vorhees and his new wife when they entertained for the first time. The courtroom rivalry and the personal friendship were thus different elements in a complex form of relation, based on careful management of hostility and affection. Local fraternities of the bar maintained their strength and solidarity because men learned to gather up their hostilities and redirect them through barbed humor, sharp debate, and the closing of ranks against undesirables.

We have already seen pointed exclusion at work in the banning of ill-suited lawyers from the fellowship of the circuit; there were other forms of exclusion as well, which built solidarity and channeled divisive anger toward safer targets. Historian Robert Wiebe has described this process in his analysis of Abraham Lincoln's experiences on the circuit in Illinois. A crucial part of the Lincoln mythology holds that the man was an inveterate storyteller and a master of droll, folksy humor, and Wiebe affirms that this was indeed a part of Lincoln's behavior. He also fills in an unexpected detail: Lincoln's stories were, in the words of one contemporary, "generally on the smutty order."[10] Well known for his shyness with women, Lincoln made himself comfortable in mixed company, according to his law partner James Herndon, by drawing men into a corner to hear one of "his characteristic stories." As Wiebe says, the fact that Lincoln "never told lewd stories in front of women merely underlined their fraternity-binding function."[11]

The close fellowship of the antebellum bar depended, then, on exclusiveness for its cohesion. An incompetent or unscrupulous lawyer or a bad fellow was cut out of the fraternity and could even be frozen out of business. The exclusion of women linked the bitterest of rivals in the solidarity of a male profession. And, unlike the ubiquitous clubs of boyhood and youth, this club had real power.

At the end of the century, many of these qualities were still present in the world of mergers and high finance. Charles Flint, an industrial financier who was known as "The Father of Trusts," describes in his autobiography the all-male world where he spent his days. Flint alternates between tales of cleverness and manipulation and stories about the loyalty and conviviality that bound the nation's most powerful businessmen. He recounts his own deceptions lovingly and explains how his quick-witted trickery kept others off balance in negotiations. Throughout the memoir, Flint offers tips on where to situate the parties to a mediation while talks are in progress and how to convince someone you are shifting your bargaining position when you are really not.[12]

Still, for all of his competitive tricks, Flint insists on the fundamental importance of trust between men. "In no place in the world," he writes, "does more money pass on oral agreement than in Wall Street. If a man's word is not as good as his bond, the high finance of Wall Street is no place for him . . . the man who breaks his word is done, and done forever." Faith in a man's word loomed large in this world because so much significant business was done privately, man-to-man. As Flint explains, "Many of the most important transactions [on Wall Street] are completed long before the papers are drawn; they are consummated during informal talks that do not rise to the dignity of conferences."[13]

These informal talks happened within the context of male sociability. They took place in train cars, on station platforms, in hotel lobbies; often they happened at formal social occasions. One setting that Charles Flint favored was the dinner party. The dinners were times when men (for these *were* segregated occasions) gathered to joke and chat about politics, sports, and friends while sometimes talking business as well. Of the few rituals at these dinners, the most important was after-dinner speaking. Guests were called on to say a few "good words," each hoping to match the other in eloquence or—more often—in cleverness and wit. In this convivial atmosphere, men made new business contacts and entered discussions that might lead to significant transactions.[14]

Another setting where Flint blended business with pleasure was the hunting trip. Compared to dinner parties, such trips contained more of close friendship and less of new acquaintance. The long hours of walking, riding, and waiting allowed for relaxed conversation that often turned to business. Flint's hunting companions appeared repeatedly in other contexts as partners in artful schemes and high-pressure deals; the expeditions in the wilds confirmed alliances as much as they produced new strategy.[15]

As these glimpses of various work worlds show, the shared activity of middle-class men was not limited to the workplace. There was also a male world of play and relaxation, a sociable realm that was physically separate from the sites of business but still tightly connected to the life of the marketplace. This masculine recreational culture flourished in many settings. Early in the century, it flowed in and out of taverns, coffee-houses, and men's boardinghouses. By the last third of the century, this culture of play found new homes in restaurants and exclusive saloons, in fraternal lodges and elite men's clubs, and (for younger men) in the new athletic clubs that were also a part of the collective life of male youth.

Men shared a variety of activities when they mingled in these settings. They played cards or billiards together, and some men enjoyed wagering on these games. A smaller contingent developed a passion for gambling on any activity or event. Many clubs staged ambitious dramatic productions or satiric revues; in the antebellum era, formal debates and readings of literary works were popular.[16]

After the Civil War, sports became a dominant passion shared by men of the comfortable classes. Baseball and rowing were especially popular among the younger men, while hunting and fishing attracted males of all ages. Spectator sports were also a growing preoccupation in postbellum America. Horseracing and boxing had devoted followers, but it was baseball that truly caught the fancy of middle-class men. Some said that baseball was a male obsession second only to business.[17] Meanwhile, the rapid growth of fraternal lodges made formal ritual a common activity within men's world. Throughout the century, there were also middle-class males who engaged in socially proscribed activities. The urban demimonde of prostitution and drug use, of heavy gambling and homosexual nightlife drew a portion of business and professional men, though they were probably small in number compared to the devotees of card games or baseball.[18]

Two activities formed the core of men's recreational culture: drinking and conversation. Liquor was the universal solvent of male play. It helped to relax men as they took a break from the intensity of work. It accompanied almost every activity in this male recreational world; it helped to lower inhibitions about socially proscribed activity; and, above all, it encouraged men's personal expressiveness.[19]

In the latter connection, liquor eased the way for the most important of pastimes in the male culture of play—conversation. Men clearly enjoyed their talk with one another. They told stories and shared the latest jokes. Men seemed especially to enjoy the cut and thrust of clashing wits, sometimes in serious debate but especially in teasing, playful humor. Verbal jousting gave men a way to prove their shrewdness, entertain their fellows, play a competitive game, vent their hostilities, and express their affection in the same rough fashion that had typified male interaction since boyhood. These battles of wit brought bourgeois men most deeply into the realm of play, unbound by formal rules and full of spontaneity.[20] Verbal jousting, then, was a popular style of conversation between men, and its content was usually a playful contempt for one's fellows.

Of course, there was more to men's conversation than just mutual disparagement. They bantered about anything that caught their fancy: politics, sports, common acquaintances, the economic climate. One topic that especially held their interest was women. Men sometimes rhapsodized about the charms and virtues of the "fair sex," writing songs and poems together to hymn their praises; but the talk about women was often much less flattering. At men's clubs, members complained to one another about the dullness of mixed company and the limits women placed on the enjoyment of life. They bemoaned their domestic trials and, like young bachelors in love, sought to divine the whims of the women in their lives. In the company of their own kind, men felt safe to vent tension about their sexual feelings. We have seen that sexually charged humor was much in demand among circuit-riding lawyers and that Abraham Lincoln used such jokes as a way to keep the men together in mixed company. The same ribald humor also served as a common bond among the members of men's clubs.[21]

If one can take ritual as a stylized form of conversation among its participants, then women also served as a chief conversational topic in the fraternal lodges of the late nineteenth century. The rituals of the Masons and other orders completely dominated lodge meetings, and they were focused in great measure on men's feelings about women. In particular, these rites dwelt implicitly on men's discomfort with their female-dominated upbringing and expressed the wish for an all-male family—a wish that was fulfilled both in the outcome of the ritual and in the fact of lodge membership. Like the simpler, more direct forms of conversation about women, fraternal rites expressed negative feelings that rarely found an outlet in other arenas of everyday life.[22]

Even on a subject that tapped deep, common feeling, though, talk did not always come naturally for middle-class males. Given the seriousness of their work and the pressure on males to *do* things, the idea of simple conversation without larger purpose was not an easy prospect. It was here that liquor helped most in lowering inhibitions; and the many popular men's activities—a dinner, a hand of cards, a visit to a sporting event, a preparation for a debate or dramatic production—offered contexts for conversation. A man might feel freer to banter if he was *doing* something else at the same time. Middle-class men valued these devices for loosening up and engaging in spontaneous conversation, because sociability was the vital heart of the world of shared play, which they enjoyed passionately.

As much as this was a world of relaxation and amusement, it always existed in relation to the world of work. In fact, the two worlds were intimately entwined. The restaurants, taverns, and coffee-houses that men frequented were close to their places of work, and business spilled readily from one setting to the other. In larger cities, men who were engaged in certain forms of work, such as law or finance, gathered themselves into specific districts, and this made it likely that men who met on the street or over a drink were rivals and friends from the same line of work. In smaller cities and towns, too, most commerce and professional business was located in the same neighborhood. Physical proximity and the chance encounters that resulted served to blur the boundaries between men's worlds of work and play.[23]

When the culture of male recreation organized itself in fraternal lodges and men's clubs, the new institutions tried to make the boundaries between work and play more distinct by enacting rules banning the discussion of business at the club or lodge. While this may have had an inhibiting effect, we know that men did discuss their work at men's clubs, and one can scarcely imagine that it was never a topic of conversation at fraternal lodges. The temptation to continue a discussion from the workday in the moments before a lodge meeting must have been impossible to resist.[24]

Clubs and lodges served business needs in one other way. When a man searched for new clients, for a contact in another line of trade, or for a new lawyer or doctor, he would naturally begin among the men he knew—and many of the men he knew were his friends and associates from the lodge or the club. Thus, even if a man obeyed the rules and never discussed business, he would still turn to a lawyer who impressed him at the club before he sought out a stranger.

The male worlds of play and work were both together and apart. They had separate physical locations and moved at different paces. The primary purpose of one was serious accomplishment, the chief end of the other was enjoyment. Yet the two worlds flowed readily into one another; they were distinctly male realms, based on the same shared values, customs, and styles of behavior. Together, they formed a sharp contrast to women's domestic realm. When people spoke of "the world" in nineteenth-century terms, they were casting a broad net over the marketplace and the male culture of recreation with which it was so closely integrated.

Middle-class men did not create this all-male world out of whole cloth. A close look at the culture of the workplace and the social world attached to it reveals how much this world resembled the cultures of boyhood and male youth that formed important phases of men's earlier experience. The connections between the work world and the earlier worlds of boyhood and youth were sometimes quite concrete and personal. The main bookbinder for James T. Fields, the publisher, was George Fields, his brother. Like many brothers of this era, they had both moved to the same locale as adults.

Even where kin connections did not link boyhood to the world of men's work, one's place of origin could fasten the bond. For example, men from New Hampshire who moved to Boston tended to settle in the same neighborhoods and boardinghouses. They provided each other not only with friendship but with ready business connections. And where family, town, and neighborhood did not tie boyhood to manhood, college and fraternal connections could provide the link. The pioneering neurologist Alphonso Rockwell tells of how he met his renowned partner, George Beard, in medical school during the 1860s. They had been brothers of the same fraternity at different colleges "and our badges brought us together. Had it not been for this tie the acquaintance probably never would have been formed, and the work of Beard and Rockwell . . . would never have taken form."[25]

Of course, nineteenth-century America was a mobile nation, and most middle-class men did not live out their adult years in the company of childhood companions. Still, the broad similarity of experience in male groupings earlier in life laid a common foundation on which the all-male workplace could be constructed in later years. Most obviously, those earlier male cultures provided models of sex segregation to which men turned by habit in building and sustaining their public world.

Men's domain was also notable for the clear contrast it posed to the female world of the home. Its combative energy, its free expressions of hostility and self-assertion, and the casual cruelty of its rivalries differed widely from the manners and values of the domestic realm to which men returned every night. These very same qualities betrayed a close similarity between the culture of the middle-class workplace and the cultures of boyhood and male youth. Men in the marketplace engaged in endless small competitions—for business, for advancement, or in the playful, competitive testing of wits that formed a cornerstone of male sociability. These constant competitive tests resulted in continuous judgments by peers that, more than anything else, determined a man's status in his profession.[26] A man had to make his own way, looking after his needs in a world of shifting alliances, yet each participant was an individual actor who needed the help of other actors in pursuit of his own good.

These difficult circumstances for personal relationships produced one of the most striking resemblances between the social culture of the marketplace and the all-male worlds of earlier life: a man had to maintain a judicious balance between cooperation and competition. In more personal terms, he needed to channel his aggressive impulses in a way that would not tear the social fabric of which he was part. Relationships developed much as they did in boyhood and youth, mixing combat with friendship, rivalry with nurture, competition with camaraderie. The joys of sociability became almost indistinguishable from energetic contentiousness, and even the warmest of friendships contained an important measure of professional self-interest. Although loyalty was perhaps less passionate and more enduring than it was among boys, men in the marketplace viewed their friends also as allies. They counted on the fidelity of these bonds, and, when alliances shifted, men often felt greater anger at the treachery of old friends than at the rivalry of foes.[27]

One should not, of course, understand the masculine culture of the marketplace as a simple replica of boyhood and youth cultures. There were profoundly important differences between them. Boys' shared world was one of pure play, and, although the world of male youth had more conscious elements of preparation and study, it was still a domain that existed largely to serve its own purposes. By contrast, the world of men was serious business. There was money to be made or lost. There were wives and children to be supported. The status and reputation of a whole family and not just an individual man were at stake. There was power to be gained for its own sake and also for the sake of setting public policy or commercial strategy, which in turn affected many other lives. In its seriousness of purpose and consequence, the male culture of the workplace was emphatically different from the cultures of boyhood and male youth. Still, those earlier worlds served as models, precedents, and realms of shared experience for men to draw upon in building and sustaining a common culture in the marketplace.

This male domain, although it was based on the individual as the unit of action, was a world of profound interdependence. Historians have long recognized this as an economic fact, but we also need to understand it as a social fact. Men's days were often spent in intense social interaction, and they did their work within dense networks of collaboration, contest, and mutual influence. They accepted—and believed devoutly in—personal responsibility for their own success and failure, and yet their preparation for careers, their daily conduct of responsibility, and the effects of their actions were all part of a tight web of social contingencies. The experience of boy culture and male youth associations prepared a man for individual action, but they also accustomed him to mutual influence, cooperative ventures, and regular social interaction with his male peers.

Work Life in the Ministry and Medicine

The energetic bustle and competition of the marketplace provided the dominant model of middle-class work in the nineteenth century. In this arena, men of commerce, law, and finance struggled for success. Politics, though not precisely a marketplace activity, operated on the same competitive model, drew its population largely from men who worked in the market, and had constant exchanges of influence with the domains of capital and law. There were, however, two substantial professions that operated outside the marketplace: medicine and the ministry. These professions were overwhelmingly male, and they demanded both "manly reason" and book learning. However, they conducted their activities away from concentrations of men and power, and they directed their activities as much at nurture as at competition. Finally, they conferred lower status on a man than other nineteenth-century professions. Medicine and the ministry provide object lessons in the role played by gender in the culture of middle-class work.

The minister plied his calling far from worldly rivalry and commotion. This isolation from the self-seeking aggression of the marketplace was part of the appeal of the ministry when compared to law as a profession.

In 1821, Reverend Joseph Tuckerman of Massachusetts described his typical workday in the small-town parish that he served. In the morning, he would go "from the breakfast table to [his] study, remain there till one o'clock,—then dine,—then pass the afternoon with [his] parishioners,—and return to enjoy the hours till bed time, in reading with [his] dear wife and children. This [was] indeed a very simple course of life, but a very happy one."[28] There was no rivalry in Tuckerman's self-described day, no apparent struggle, no aggressive assertion of self-interest.

Work for Tuckerman consisted of two components, each of them distant from the activities of the marketplace. One component was the time he spent in his study reading, writing, and reflecting. The other was the visiting that he did with his parishioners. The social interactions of the minister were different from those of the lawyer or merchant. First of all, most ministerial visits took place in people's homes. The minister rarely approached an office or a countinghouse to pay a clerical call. Secondly, the content of the minister's visits had less to do with self-advancement or competitive advantage than with matters of the soul and the heart, with emotional or spiritual nurture. Finally, in an era when women formed a large majority of active Protestants, these ministerial calls were paid to women more than to men.[29] Thus, nineteenth-century ministers spent their days at home alone or in predominantly feminine company, plying such womanly qualities as sympathy and nurture for the good of others.

Clearly, the minister's tasks placed him at a great distance from the men who subjected themselves to the daily pressures of the market. The decline in the status of the ministry from the late eighteenth century and through the nineteenth derived from many causes, but the daily association of the clergy with women and with the traits and cultural spaces allotted to women must surely have had an impact on the popular view of their profession.[30]

Still, even the ministry bore some imprint of the free-market model and partook of some of the goals and habits that were culturally appropriate to men. Throughout the century, local churches competed for membership, sometimes fiercely and sometimes in a low-keyed, friendly rivalry. The doctrinal wars that erupted periodically in the first half of the century added another competitive element to the minister's job.[31]

The marketplace model emerged as an influence on the ministry in another way. In this period, ministers were employed increasingly on a contract basis, instead of enjoying the virtual lifetime tenure of their colonial predecessors. The new arrangement subjected ministers to many of the same pressures that would have come with an open competition. Now, a man of the cloth had to be a self-salesman and a politician; neither role was compatible with a minister's duty to be a candid spiritual adviser and a sympathetic support in times of trouble. While this situation did not subject the clergy to the same daily pressures as work in the marketplace, it at least created the potential for a similar kind of struggle in pastoral employment.[32]

Finally, the growth of church bureaucracies in the nineteenth century created a new competition for clerical office. Leading divines had always carried on spirited rivalries for influence and prestige, but now there were ministers contesting for positions of formal power in many large denominations. A late nineteenth-century physician wrote of his pastor that "he missed the prize for which all good Methodists who are in any degree eligible are always fighting, a bishopric."[33]

Thus, even a profession as separate by nature from worldly strife and aggression as the ministry felt the influence of the dominant marketplace metaphor. The daily life of a nineteenth-century pastor was distinctly different from that of a merchant or lawyer, but the pastor was still not free in his aspirations from the effects of his own time and place.

Like ministers, doctors plied their trade outside the personal nexus of the nineteenth-century marketplace. They were not directly men of commerce, nor did they live on their services to merchants and manufacturers as many bankers and lawyers did. Moreover, their primary social contacts in a day's work were with patients and their families. Until hospitals began to pull physicians into constant relation with each other late in the century, a doctor in a town or a small city could go for days at a time without seeing others of his profession.

His work did create a good deal of social interaction. Alphonso Rockwell recalled his boyhood doctor in the small Connecticut town where he grew up in the 1840s: "He went around on horseback with his old-fashioned medicine cases balanced across his horse's back." His social style differed from that of the twentieth-century physician: "Unlike the doctor of today, he was never in a hurry. Every movement was deliberate and he had time to talk over the news of the day."[34] The physician, like his contemporaries in business and law, mixed work and sociability.

Still, a doctor interacted less with men than with women. The female sex played the dominant role in the physical care of the family, and—especially in the households that could best afford the attentions of a doctor—women were far more likely than their husbands to be present when a physician visited the home. Moreover, as the medical profession insinuated itself deeply into the process of childbirth, its practitioners confronted themselves with a growing proportion of women.[35] Thus, most nineteenth-century doctors conducted their business at a significant distance from the male ambience of the commercial district and courthouse.

This segregation did not mean, though, that physicians were removed from the influence of the marketplace. They performed on a fee-for-service basis, and their business was openly competitive. In any given locale, a known group of doctors vied for a limited number of patients. In a small-town setting, a new physician had to build a practice slowly, relying on word-of-mouth and on his own connections. In this context, the doctor's character and personality became crucial to his success. To put it differently, he had to sell himself as well as his abilities in a competitive market.[36]

Physicians commonly built a practice by establishing a reputation that mixed professional competence with personal care, but there were other, less scrupulous competitive methods. In an age of uncertain medical standards, many doctors resorted to "heroic" treatments that threatened the lives of patients more than the diseases from which they suffered. According to one historian, "the practitioner who most impressed an ordinary community was apt to be the man who came in, administered overdoses of dangerous chemicals, then was lucky enough to have his patients pull narrowly and therefore dramatically through to recovery." Local rivalries also led established physicians to resort to "falsehood and defamation of character" in discouraging newcomers on their turf.[37]

The irony is that this ill feeling might have been diminished by greater social and professional contact between physicians. Among lawyers, who were drawn together in the courthouse or on the circuit, the sense of fraternity was generally greater than it was among local doctors. By contrast, physicians were isolated rivals who lacked the chance to share experiences, offer professional stimulation, or vent their rivalrous feelings in ritual combat.[38] Locked into the metaphor of the marketplace but lacking its forms of male sociability and struggle, nineteenth-century doctors had a strange relation to the middle-class work world of their era, being neither quite in it nor outside it.

In this way, the medical profession and the ministry of the nineteenth-century North were alike. Although medicine stood in closer proximity to the culture and pressures of the marketplace, the two professions shared important qualities. The essence of each was the work of nurture. Both claimed to offer special wisdom about ministering to human needs. In performing this work, the practitioners of both professions entered the company of women at least as often as they did the company of men; and they were, as we have just noted, isolated from the fraternity of combat and conviviality that typified the male culture of the marketplace.

The nineteenth-century professions of divinity and medicine shared one other trait: each conferred a lesser social status on its practitioners than did the callings of business, law, finance, and politics.[39] One common dimension of this status problem was surely gender. Nurture and care were women's tasks, while men were expected to wield power and wealth—elements that characterized the higher-status vocations. Also, doctors and ministers kept female company far more than did men of law and commerce. In a world where power belonged to men and being male conferred a certain prestige, it is not surprising that professions linked to women conferred lower status than the callings in which males engaged with other males. All of these professions, of course, belonged to men, but some were seen as more manly—and thus more prestigious—than others.

Defending the Boundaries of Gender

By cultural fiat and the preference of individual men, the middle-class workplace was a male realm. As such, it had boundaries that needed defending. In other words, men needed ways to keep women out or to keep them isolated. Men wanted not only to protect their power but to defend the integrity of their cultural world as they conceived it. The male defense of gender turf is an important aspect of the culture of the middle-class workplace.

There were three ways in which women breached the boundaries of men's public domain. First of all, women entered this realm with full social sanction as consumers of the goods and services sold by men. Indeed, "social sanction" may not be a strong enough term. Increasingly as the century passed, women were *expected* to shop for their families, so they had to buy these goods and services in order to supply their households and meet their personal needs; and men had to sell these goods and services to women or they would fail in business.[40] Merchants devised a shifting set of tactics for structuring these constant and utterly necessary female incursions into the male domain. Men reacted very differently to the two other forms of turf invasion by women: the crusade to end men's monopoly of the vote and the quest for a place in the learned professions. Most middle-class men deplored these female intrusions and reacted to them with hostility.

Men had intricate and varied strategies for dealing with the presence of women in their world as customers. These strategies were aimed at two problems that female customers created for a man. First, as a matter of power, the merchant-client relationship put male and female on roughly equal footing, with each needing something from the other. For the merchant as a man, it was not usual, comfortable, or socially acceptable to have approximately the same face-to-face power as a woman.

A merchant's strategies for handling female customers also addressed a second problem: the manner in which a storeowner and his client dealt with each other. Especially in the era before fixed prices were the expected custom, merchant and customer bargained. In these self-interested negotiations, each used guile, wit, and rational calculation to extract the best possible deal from the other. The structure of life in small towns and city neighborhoods may have sometimes suppressed the crudest elements of bargaining, but they probably never lay too far beneath the surface. For a man to engage a woman in such a relationship, however, violated the polite norms of conduct between the sexes and flatly contradicted a man's conception of femininity.[41] A man could feel comfortable in a bargaining relationship with another man because he had been engaging other males all his life in friendly contests for personal advantage; such a combination of rivalry and good fellowship formed the structure of relationships between men. No equivalent existed for a man's relationships with women, and it was this absence that a merchant's strategy of customer relations had to confront.

One aspect of this strategy was to drape one's dealings with female shoppers in elaborate courtesy. Such courtesy hid underlying negotiations from view, even as it paid ceremonious homage to the conventions of gender that those negotiations violated. When Henry Dwight Sedgwick described the manner of a floor manager at a fabric store, he was portraying this strategic courtesy. Exaggerating for effect, Sedgwick had the man bowing politely and effusing: "Yes, Madam, lightweight, flowery chintz, this way, Madam! Here, Madam! Mr. Snooks, will you be so kind as to attend to this lady, a very valued customer? I am sure, Madam, that Mr. Snooks will be able to satisfy your wants. Good day, Madam." He took his leave, noted Sedgwick, with a "respectful bow, and a stately walk away." Unctuousness in this degree would have driven away as many customers as it drew, but Sedgwick's burlesque presented a core of reality: one treated one's female customers with fullest courtesy.[42]

Another element in the merchant's strategy for dealing with women was to "satisfy [her] wants." Of course, this was simply good business. But if one could anticipate a female customer's wishes, one could achieve an additional benefit: short-circuiting more elaborate dealings and thus limiting their inherent discomfort. A good salesman had "to know the personal interest of each customer." One such man, a book-seller, could even predict the kind of book a new customer would buy simply by gauging the person's appearance and manner of speech. Of course, these techniques applied to male as well as female customers. But merchants relied on them more heavily in dealing with women, since they had no preexisting model of how to deal with them in busi-ness situations.[43]

Better yet, the successful merchant with a large enough store and a big enough income could retreat to his office and leave customer contact to salesmen. Merchants did not hire a sales force to buffer them from fe-male customers; the practice began for reasons of business efficiency. But a layer of salesmen did have the happy side-effect of leaving the un-comfortable and anomalous relationship with the female customer to other men of lesser power and rank.

In the final decades of the century, when department stores and other giant emporia emerged as a revolution in retail merchandising, the rela-tion of merchant to female customer changed. The great retail houses created vast women's worlds, environments based on an understanding of the needs and pleasures of female shoppers. These were feminine en-vironments not only in their merchandise, their appurtenances, and their predominance of customers, but also increasingly in their sales forces. Department stores became female enclaves in the public realm, places where women could feel comfortable together in the midst of a man's world. Their isolation helped to preserve a sense of separate spheres even where women invaded the arenas of commerce in massive numbers.[44]

Viewed from a male perspective, the growth of a female sales force behind the counters buffered men from the discomforts of a public, in-strumental relationship with women. The merchant was left with a rela-tion to his women employees, but it was not the same kind he might have had with his female patrons. A customer and a retailer were mutu-ally dependent in a roughly equal relationship; a merchant (or store manager) and his sales clerk were employer and employee, a clearly un-equal power relation. A businessman could feel more comfortable in this connection because its rules were familiar and well established and (not coincidentally) because it left him in a superior position to women in-stead of floundering for comfortable behavior in a situation of relative equality. Literally and figuratively, a female employee was easier to dis-miss than a female customer. Thus, even though a nineteenth-century retailer could not keep women out of his world, he discovered a device that made him feel more comfortable with a feminine presence.[45]

Lawyers faced no such problems with their female clients.[46] First of all, they had far fewer such clients than a retailer did. Also, attorneys (unlike merchants) had command of an arcane body of knowledge that tipped the businessman-client relation heavily in their favor. As the nineteenth-century feminist Antoinette Brown Blackwell wrote, the law was "wholly masculine," and its language expressed the "thoughts, feelings, [and] biases of men."[47] Finally and most dramatically, many of the important professional contacts between women and the legal profession in the nineteenth century took place in that most masculine of settings, the courtroom.

The courtroom was a highly structured arena. The actors in it were there only by invitation. A patriarchal figure, cloaked in robes (and in the mystique of wisdom and power that came with them) presided; this judge was always a man. The chief actors under his purview were lawyers, who were male with virtually no exceptions. The method by which the court arrived at truth and justice was adversarial: a lawyer competed with every allowable device to prove his own case right and that of his opponent wrong. Certainly, the use of fierce struggle to achieve justice was a masculine strategy, far removed from the collaborative, consensual style that women learned in their mutual dealings.

The courtroom was made even more alien to women by the mode of communication favored there, mixing florid oratory with quick, slashing wit. The successful lawyer flourished not by tenderness and kind words, but by clever tricks of language and reason, and by harsh, direct assaults on the credibility or character of those who stood in the way of his case. These were emphatically not the modes of social intercourse that women learned to master and enjoy. With its resemblance to a men's debating society or a verbal wrestling match, the courtroom alienated and intimidated women. Likewise, a male lawyer could be at ease there with women. Their relationship was highly structured, and it granted all the power to the attorney. The presence of female clients was no threat to the masculinity of a lawyer's work.[48]

The real threat to the male culture of the public world came not from female customers or clients. Rather, it came from aspiring female professionals who sought to open male enclaves like law and medicine to both sexes, and from women determined to end the masculinity of political citizenship.

During the last third of the nineteenth century, a small number of determined women tried to gain membership in the bar. Historian Michael Grossberg has summarized the reaction of male lawyers to the efforts of these women as "one of disbelief, coupled at times with 'horror and disgust.'"[49] When called on to justify their opposition to women lawyers, male attorneys drew naturally upon deeply held cultural beliefs about the female sex. Women, they claimed, lacked the nerve, the reason, and the physical stamina to practice law. Exposure to the rough words and rough treatment of the courtroom would strip away a woman's feminine refinement and render her unfit for her role at home. It was true, of course, that men were better socialized for this masculine environment, but the defenders of a segregated profession in the late nineteenth century were not simply trying to spare *some* women a distasteful experience: they were trying to prevent *all* women from practicing law, especially those who were determined to practice.

The late-century decisions about women's entry to the bar were made in two arenas—the courts and legislative bodies. Women gained very different degrees of satisfaction in these these two domains. The courts rarely supported their admission to legal practice. In the most notorious such case, a Virginia appeals court refused attorney Belva Lockwood the right to practice in that state. A Virginia law granted the right to practice to "any person" licensed in another state or the District of Columbia, and Lockwood was licensed in the District. But the state court denied her right on the grounds that "any person" meant "any man." In 1894, the United States Supreme Court upheld this ruling. No other court went so far as to deny women their personhood under the law, but several others did refuse women entry to the bar in their own states.[50]

Frequently rebuffed by the courts, women aspirants took their cause to the state legislatures and the Congress in the late 1800s. Although the legislative record is not uniform, it shows that representative bodies were far more receptive to women's arguments than the courts were. For instance, Belva Lockwood—before seeking the right to practice in Virginia—had gained from Congress the right to serve as counsel in federal courts, a right which the federal courts themselves had denied her. Before the century was over, most states had guaranteed women access to the bar.[51]

However, the legal guarantee did not change the fundamental nature of the bar as a male fraternity. Men managed to isolate women within the profession in a way that preserved male dominance, limited their contact with males as professional equals, and sustained the masculine culture of the bar. In larger firms, women were assigned to clerical and research tasks that would have been unusual for a male attorney. Within the broader profession, certain "female" specialties emerged, such as domestic relations or legal aid—areas closely related to women's established duties in the family and in charity work. Commercial fields such as property or contract law remained bastions of manhood.[52] Just as the department store became physically a female enclave isolating merchants and managers from business contact with women, "female" specialties within the law created ghettoes that separated most male attorneys from the professional presence of women. Even within these specialties, the female presence may not have been very large, for the proportion of women in the bar as a whole had barely reached 1 percent by 1910.[53]

At the end of the century, the medical profession was also struggling to promote its maleness, but its struggle was different in nature from that of lawyers. As we have seen, medicine was perceived in less masculine terms than the legal profession; this perception was affirmed between 1850 and 1880 by a small but significant influx of women into the profession. During those years, the old apprenticeship system of training physicians was decaying, and most states abandoned legislation that governed medical licensing. Under these circumstances, doctors could not effectively defend the entrances to their profession, and those who were inclined to keep women out found it difficult to do so.[54]

Institutional factors were not the only ones that aided female entry into medicine at midcentury. The links between the purposes of medicine and the virtues of domesticity were so clear that many male physicians supported female attempts to enter the profession. Women and their allies argued on behalf of their natural female sympathy and their tender, God-given nursing abilities. They also contended that female doctors could protect the "natural" modesty of women patients better than male doctors could. These arguments combined with the fluid situation of the medical profession to give women a small foothold in medicine.

Still, male doctors spoke forcefully against the admission of women. They put forth the same kinds of arguments that lawyers used in denying women professional status. A female, they insisted, lacked the rationality needed to practice medicine and the courage needed to function in the face of blood, gore, and naked male bodies. Women's opponents also held that men—physicians and patients alike—were full of brutal instincts and that prolonged exposure to bestial male behavior would unfit a lady doctor for her fundamental domestic duties. Some men even argued that the female sex lacked the physical stamina needed for special tasks like surgery.[55] Like the nearly identical arguments against women lawyers, these notions arose as if by habit from the deep fund of middle-class beliefs about gender—the very same fund that supplied the arguments in favor of female doctors.

The opposition to women practitioners did not stop the slow, steady trickle of women into the medical profession; but there were changes in the world of medicine after 1880 that created new problems for female physicians. One was the emergence of scientific medicine as a system of practice and belief that vanquished many of the alternative models to which female doctors adhered. At the same time that medical thinking coalesced around one set of ideas, the structure of the profession crystallized into a network of closely linked institutions—hospitals, dispensaries, medical schools, and professional societies.[56] In this new world, opposition to women doctors could organize and take institutional root more easily than before.

At medical schools, this opposition took effect in a largely incidental way, through chance remarks by professors, negative judgments by fellow students, and the intimidating effect of men's great predominance in numbers and power. Many female practitioners remembered moments of public humiliation that symbolized the burden of being a female medical student. Dr. Dorothy Reed Mendenhall recalled one such incident that took place during her education at Johns Hopkins. She and another woman decided to attend a lecture for students on diseases of the nose. They took their seats directly in front of the speaker and proved to be the only women there. The lecturer that evening had planned to make his presentation entertaining by establishing—and maintaining—a comparison between certain tissues in the nose and the corpus spongiosa of the penis. He sustained this scientific double entendre for an entire hour. Again and again, the audience roared with laughter and the women squirmed in humiliation. This performance was not prepared with the presence of women in mind, but Mendenhall was sure that "the added fillip of doing his dirt before two young women" increased the speaker's "sly pleasure." Given Victorian standards of feminine delicacy, his performance was extraordinary, and Mendenhall cried "hysterically" all the way home. "Part of my trouble," she wrote, "was that I couldn't face my class, many of whom I had seen thoroughly enjoying themselves at the lecture."[57] Whatever the intended point of the talk had been, the experience had an underlying gender message: This is a man's world and we won't change that for you—accept it or be gone.

In fact, the new network of medical institutions (starting, for the aspiring doctor, with medical school) made possible a major change in the culture of the profession. Through the linkage of institutions across space and along the professional lifespan, this network made possible the development, spread, perpetuation, and empowerment of a male culture within the medical world, based on constant contact between men in an environment they dominated. With the emergence of this masculine culture, the medical profession moved closer in its inner nature to commerce and law, with their sociability and their modes of male interaction.

The network of institutions and their culture threw new barriers in the way of female medical careers. When local and national medical societies sprang up in the 1870s, they became the chief mechanism for professional sociability and the discussion of new ideas and common problems. Thus, when they denied membership to graduates of women's medical colleges, medical societies isolated many female physicians from the growing cohesion of the world of medicine. Even the women who graduated from coeducational medical schools were at a disadvantage as they sought to establish private practices, because their isolation in medical school left them limited in the kinds of connections needed to get patients and obtain useful consultations. In an environment where such ties were increasingly necessary to success, some male doctors refused to consult with female colleagues and ostracized male colleagues who did.[58]

Given the foothold women had already attained in medicine and the likenesses between the profession's purposes and feminine domestic ideals, the male culture of the new institutions did not drive women out of the medical world. In 1910, 6 percent of the physicians in the United States were women; but female doctors, like their counterparts in the law, were increasingly shunted into specialized enclaves. They tended to practice specialties such as gynecology and pediatrics, which focused on women or children. Female physicians also found a welcome in the emerging field of public health, where their work resembled the work in such women's fields as teaching and charity.[59]

Not only were female enclaves developing among physicians, but other forms of gender segregation were appearing within the medical world. The emergence of the nursing profession divided the delivery of medical care along a line that separated gender, status, and function all at once. According to this new division, male doctors commanded the high ground of power and status by immersing themselves in specific fields of medical science and making the primary decisions about the care of each patient; the female nurse accepted a subordinate role, carrying out the doctor's orders and providing most of the actual contact and care for each patient. Thus, as doctors' most important professional contacts came increasingly with other physicians in the late nineteenth century, they were able to limit their formerly extensive contact with patients. In some degree, doctors were able to do what merchants and store managers did at department stores: exchange the uncertainties of direct dealing with clients for the certainty of structured relations with female subordinates. This created an aura of distant authority for physicians while giving their workplace relations with women a more secure structure.

In the end, women were not excluded from the medical profession, and they were actually welcomed into the larger world of medical work; but in terms of institutional power, patient-care decisions, and occupational prestige, male physicians isolated and marginalized their female colleagues. In the late nineteenth century, men not only gathered the growing power of the medical profession into their own circle, they also created a more distinctively male professional culture than had ever existed before.

Nineteenth-century women attacked the sanctity of the male public sphere in one other fundamental way: a number of them demanded the right to vote. In defending their political realm, men used the same arguments that were offered to counter women's entry into the professions. Women, it was said, were too physically and emotionally frail for the rough competition of politics. Inherently, they were illogical and emotional, and government demanded steady reason; they were idealists and dreamers, and political decisions required practical common sense. A group of antisuffragists, addressing the Illinois legislature in 1897, put it this way: "We believe that men are ordained to govern in all forceful and material matters, *because they are men*, physically and intellectually strong, virile, aggressive."[61]

Was politics really a "forceful matter"? Some opponents of suffrage believed that it was, and this belief provided them with another grounds for their opposition. Force, they reasoned, was the ultimate basis for government. Even in a democracy, the minority acquiesces in the will of the majority because it knows it cannot physically impose its will on the larger group. According to this line of thinking, women's suffrage contained the seeds of disaster. If women were able to build a majority for a policy that most men bitterly opposed, what would keep the stronger sex from rebelling against the physically frail majority? What if a government dominated by females tried to send its (male) army off to fight in a war that most men opposed? Antisuffragists feared the demise of lawful order. As one of their number, Francis Parkman, expressed it, "Law with no power to enforce it is futile and sometimes ridiculous."[62]

Fears of social chaos reached their peak among the opponents of women's vote when the focus moved from sex difference to the separation of spheres. This familiar symbolic system was applied most often to the division of home from the marketplace, but it expressed America's sense of its political system as well. To understand men's fear of women's suffrage, we need to understand how nineteenth-century Americans applied the doctrine of spheres to politics.

Cast in political terms, the doctrine of the spheres was concerned with the issue of self-interest. It denied that a woman could have self-interest, conceiving of her instead as the embodiment of self-sacrifice. In this moral universe, woman exerted her efforts for the best interests of her family, devoting herself to the development of her children and submitting to the will of her husband. Since she took her social identity from her husband's position in the world and since he provided her with the necessities of life, she took his self-interest as her own.

This political application of the doctrine of the spheres gave continued life to a traditional belief: the family, not the individual, was the basic unit of society. The family's interest was embodied in the male who was its head, who provided it with income and with its social standing. Thus, it was natural that the man should represent the family in the public realm of politics. In politics as in economic life, the male sphere ("the world") was an arena governed by the competition of unchecked self-interests.[63] This principle of self-interest was expressed in the Constitution, which assumed the conflict of selfish motives in political life and made that conflict the fundamental source of its own strength and stability.

By the 1820s, this political system based on competing self-interests had reached its fullest flower in the development of a new male political culture. The emergence of universal white male suffrage stimulated this development. Now that gender was a prime criterion of political participation, a fraternal system of party competition emerged. This system channeled individual self-interest into a male political culture of partisan combat.[64]

Party membership was the key to this culture. Less a matter of choice than of male social identity, party affiliation passed from father to son. Campaigns were mass entertainments which not only celebrated great causes of the past and present but also exalted the shared manhood of its participants. As fellow members of local party organizations, men praised the manliness of their partisan heroes and denounced as effeminate the nonpartisan reformers who opposed the party system. Together, loyalists joined in such masculine campaign activities as military-style parades, torchlight rallies, electoral wagering, barbecues, and logpole raisings. All of these activities were drenched in the free flow of liquor, which the nineteenth century associated with men. Masculine sites such as saloons and barbershops served as polling places. Politics was clearly a masculine world, both in its population and in its favored symbols and rituals.[65]

Since this style of politics was based on fervent partisanship and heated conflict, there was always a possibility that the whole noisy enterprise would fly apart in an explosion of animosity. More than anything else, the exclusion of women sustained the unity of this contentious cultural world. As historian Paula Baker has noted, women provided men with a "negative referent." As much as political partisans clashed over other issues, they shared their manhood in common. To be a political actor, one was necessarily a man. Then, too, in a broader sense, it was women's virtue that supported male political culture in this form. Assured that women would infuse society with their virtuous regard for the good of all, men felt free to set their selfish motives loose in political combat. Just as they expected women to curb male passions in personal life, men believed that women would balance male self-interest in society at large with their female regard for the interests of others.[66]

In a sense, nineteenth-century women did do this. They developed an alternative political culture that carried the moral values of the home aggressively into the world. Women's networks, formed in the church, grew into local reform organizations as women attacked public evil— failure to observe the Sabbath; prostitution; intemperance; slavery. By the last third of the century, these local associations of women had knit themselves into national organizations, of which the most powerful was the Women's Christian Temperance Union.[67] Male reaction to these movements was mixed. Some men, as we shall see, reacted with hostility. Others joined the movements and still others accepted the growth of this kind of female politics, since they believed in the moral stewardship of women.

When women pressed for female suffrage, however, men reacted with vehemence. Grover Cleveland summarized men's feelings when he wrote that granting suffrage to women would destroy "a natural equilibrium so nicely adjusted to the attributes and limitations of both [men and women] that it cannot be disturbed without social confusion and peril."[68] The right to vote would allow women—delicate and pure—to enter the sordid, selfish, and well-liquored fraternity of politics. This would disrupt the cohesion of that fractious culture by ending its male unity, and set selfish rivalry loose on the world.[69]

Worse yet from the traditional viewpoint, women's suffrage would bring chaos to the domestic sphere as well. In Francis Parkman's words, "To give the suffrage to women would be to reject the principle that has thus far formed the basis of civilized government": that "the head of the family . . . [is] the political representative of the rest." If a woman voted, it meant that her husband no longer represented the interest of the household. It meant instead that a woman represented her own interest. To men (and some women as well), this prospect had frightening implications. First, it affirmed that women *had* self-interest and should pursue it. Second, if women pursued self-interest, there would be no one left within the nineteenth-century moral scheme to preserve and extend the fundamental virtue of unselfishness. Moral chaos threatened.[70]

The antisuffragists also argued that if women shared the vote with men, their action would undercut men's authority as head of the household. Suffrage would place a woman on an equal footing with her husband, and their self-interests would weigh against each other. The potential for the destruction of marriage seemed grave. Antisuffragists also worried about who would mind the children if women became politically active. One New York man, asserting that the purpose of women's rights petitions was "to overthrow the most sacred of our institutions," asked: "Are we to put the stamp of truth on the libel here set forth, that men and women, in the matrimonial relation are to be equal?"[71] To men, women's suffrage meant the destruction of marriage, the family, and "the basis of civilized government." It dissolved the separation of spheres, blurred the distinction between the sexes, and abandoned the existing means for teaching virtue and controlling vice.

It is no wonder, then, that men opposed women's suffrage so fiercely. By the end of the century, after more than fifty years of agitation, women had gained full voting rights in only four states. As men created enclaves within the professional world for women doctors and lawyers and within the commercial world for women consumers, they also allowed women a realm of political participation that was consistent with the feminine role of moral stewardship. While these female reform enclaves recognized the formal presence of women in the public realm, they kept women isolated from the male cultures that were the true seats of power. As far as suffrage was concerned, nineteenth-century men staunchly refused women entry into their world of electoral politics, where power itself might have to be shared.

Nevertheless, during the last third of the nineteenth century, a growing number of middle-class people were refusing to abide by the prescriptions of separate spheres. Female temperance crusaders, suffragists, and club women began to pour into the public sphere in ever-growing numbers. Aspiring female professionals, beginning with doctors at midcentury and followed by lawyers and academics in later years, sought acceptance in men's realm. Meanwhile, a less conspicuous troop of middle-class men headed in the other direction. Male neurasthenics returned home during the day, looking for a place to rest and relax away from their proper sphere. Some men even sought a quiet moment with their children from time to time. The old cultural map of the spheres still provided the official version of how the terrain should look, but its prescriptive power was weakening. The proliferation of female enclaves within men's public space offered proof of this looser grip.

At the same time, a different sort of gender change was underway. Men were revising the codes that governed their behavior and their sense of who they should be. In some respects, they were elaborating old ideas, but in other respects, they were drawing on once-forbidden sources for new ideals. Along with the changing cartography of the spheres, this reimagining of manliness would create cultural stress and personal strain for middle-class men as the end of the century approached.

Chapter 10

PASSIONATE MANHOOD

A Changing Standard of Masculinity

MANY of the cultural forms which give shape to manhood in the twentieth century emerged in the late nineteenth. In that era, bourgeois manhood embraced new virtues and obsessions. The male body moved to the center of men's gender concerns; manly passions were revalued in a favorable light; men began to look at the "primitive" sources of manhood with new regard; the martial virtues attracted admiration; and competitive impulses were transformed into male virtues. These cultural shifts did not happen overnight. Some of them began as early as the 1850s, and none were complete by the turn of the twentieth century, but the moment of greatest change came in the 1880s and 1890s. Our lives a century later are still bound by this reshaping of manhood.

The Embodiment of Manhood

In the three-quarters of a century after the American Revolution, bourgeois Northerners showed the deepest concern for manhood in its moral, social, and political meanings, while placing a lesser emphasis on the male body. Then, in the second half of the nineteenth century, this relative emphasis began to change. Daniel Eddy's popular advice book, *The Young Man's Friend*, said little about physical strength or health when it was first published in 1855; Eddy's true concern was a young man's strength of character. The second edition of his book, appearing ten years later, had a wholly different focus. Eddy had come to see physical strength as the foundation of male character: "What mud sills are to a building, muscular development is to manhood." Men were conscious of the changing emphasis. As early as 1858, Thomas Wentworth Higginson lamented the popular assumption "that a race of shopkeepers, brokers, and lawyers could live without bodies." In the 1890s, Edward Everett Hale denounced "the absolute indifference" of Americans "in the first half of this century to matters of physical health."[1]

By the time Hale was writing those words, however, middle-class men were paying assiduous attention to the male body. A vogue of physical culture, beginning in the 1850s, became a mania during the century's final third. Gymnastics, cycling, and skating all enjoyed waves of popularity, but it was body-building especially that absorbed men's energy and attention.[2] Henry Dwight Sedgwick recalled how, as a fourteen-year-old, he admired the muscles of a youth who spent his spare time working with weights: "There he stood, putting up dumb-bells to increase his biceps, and his biceps justified his assiduous care. His muscle was magnificent; when he doubled up his elbow, it stood out like a great ostrich egg, hard and round, unrivalled in school."[3] As Sedgwick's statement shows, this fascination with body-building found its reflection in a concern for muscular body image. A study of magazine articles has revealed that, by the end of the century, heroes were most often described in physical terms, with an emphasis on their impressive size and strength.[4]

As much as they were concerned with the bodies of other men, late nineteenth-century males were most concerned with their own. Men of all ages noted their weight with care and precision, while young males in their teens and twenties recorded changes of body dimension in rapt detail. As a graduate student in 1884, psychologist James Cattell placed himself on a program of exercise. He announced the results precisely and with pride: "My breast increased in circumference 4¼ inches in three months, and the rest of my body in proportion. I had not supposed this to be possible. I am not fatter—my stomach measures only 31½ inches, whereas my hipps [sic] are 38¼." In letters and diaries, young men like Cattell watched for changes in body size with the obsessive attention of a Puritan tracing the progress of his soul toward grace.[5]

Indeed, men of the late nineteenth century went a step beyond Daniel Eddy's assertion that a strong body was the foundation for a strong character; they treated physical strength and strength of character as the same thing. One commentator complained of the boy whose "flabby muscles are no less flabby than his character." Another man equated physical development with moral development: "The only way to become an athlete is by continued exercise, one never did it yet by staying away from the Gym because one couldn't do the Giant swing, and I suppose moral strength grows in much the same way." Hiram Bingham, an early twentieth-century politician and explorer, carried the equation one step further. In arguing for the necessity of military might, Bingham drew an analogy between the development of the individual and that of the nation. A military buildup would strengthen the country's moral force, just as "the development of a man's body gives him strength of mind and self-control."[6]

This embodiment of mind, spirit, and character reached a peak of absurdity at the turn of the century in the doctrine of Muscular Christianity. Using metaphors of fitness and body-building, Christian thinkers imagined a strong, forceful Jesus with a religion to match. In 1896, *Century Magazine* called for a "vigorous, robust, muscular Christianity . . . devoid of all the etcetera of creed," a Christianity "which shows the character and manliness of Christ."[7] This hardy Jesus with rippling muscles was "no prince of peace-at-any-price." He was an enforcer who "turned again and again on the snarling pack of His pious enemies and made them slink away."[8] The key to Muscular Christianity was not the idea of the spirit made flesh, but of the flesh made spirit. In proclaiming that the condition of character follows from the condition of the body, the advocates of Muscular Christianity were creatures of their time.

If physical strength was a source of character in a man, what were the specific virtues that it bred? One of them is evident in the call for a "vigorous, robust, muscular Christianity . . . devoid of all the etcetera of creed." This statement expresses a growing sense of opposition between action and thought. Increasingly, middle-class men saw action—even unthinking action—as manly and viewed "the etcetera of creed" as a sign of effeminacy. Throughout the century, of course, middle-class men of the North had devoted themselves to practical accomplishment. Yankee businessmen had for years harbored a suspicion of educated men who "thought too much." But what was once a harbored suspicion became gleeful public scorn late in the century—and no one was more scornful than educated men themselves. As Charles Francis Adams said in 1883: "I think we've had all we want of 'elegant scholars' and 'gentlemen of refined classical taste,' and now I want to see more University men trained up to take a hand in the rather rough game of American nineteenth-century life."[9]

Reflectiveness appeared explicitly as a gender issue in a 1904 *Harper's Bazaar* article by a woman writer, Marion Foster Washburne.

She contrasted paralyzing female doubt with single-minded male certainty in these reflections on the fears of a new mother:

> No woman can fail to wish that the husband, instead of falling . . . into the wife's mood, [would insist] upon throwing open the blinds, kissing the baby too hard for comfort, doing likewise to the mother, and going off in a gale of hearty happiness that would rock her safely into port. The elemental simplicity of the average masculine mind is exactly what we women need.

A new concept of manly reason was emerging here. In this view, male rationality was not a capacity for deep, logical reflection but rather an absence of complex emotions—an absence which freed men to act boldly and decisively.[10]

Men as well as women expressed admiration for the strong-minded, forceful man. Charles Van Hise described the presence of an army general in such terms:

> In action his blue-gray eyes are full of fire; indeed the first impression was of his eyes, and then with the firmly set jaw may be understood somewhat his force. Of course he is a man of power, but not only so, he produces this impression in a marked degree.

Men were also alert to a lack of vigor or command in another man's character. The naturalist John Burroughs, for instance, wrote of his aging father that his "force and authority as a man were feeble."[11]

Where strength and force were so highly valued, it was only natural that men admired fighting virtues and often endorsed violence. When Sergeant Kendall heard from his parents in 1887 that his brother had a fight with some boys in his class, he told them: "I should like to have seen Franklin lick the boys. Bully for him! Do it again every time—'sic' him. I feel like doing something of the kind to a fellow in our class." That his parents bothered to mention the fight and that their twenty-year-old son felt free to react with such ferocity indicates that the Kendall parents approved of such tussles.[12]

Indeed, bourgeois Northerners did more than endorse interpersonal violence: they now believed that fighting helped to build youthful character. The students at Phillips Exeter Academy were urged to "plunge into it, and be bare fists and wits your only weapons."[13] Of course, scraps between boys were not new in the late nineteenth century. What was new was the change in the meaning of these fights to adults. Early in the 1800s, men and women had seen youthful brawls as a badge of evil and a sign that manly self-control was not yet developed. The same sort of fight was seen late in the century as an emblem of developing character, a means to manliness.

By the end of the 1800s, men were prone to view struggle and strife as ends in themselves. On many occasions, Theodore Roosevelt preached "the doctrine of the strenuous life." In his words, "Nothing in this world is worth having or worth doing unless it means effort, pain, difficulty. No life is worth leading if it is always an easy life."[14]

Oliver Wendell Holmes, Jr., shared Roosevelt's belief that struggle was a virtue in itself. The great justice, in fact, made this belief into a high philosophical principle and considered it explicitly a matter of gender. Speaking to the Tavern Club of Boston in 1896, Holmes analyzed the act of a man who went over Niagara Falls in his own specially constructed boat and was killed:

> Precisely because it was not useful it was a perfect expression of the male contribution to our common stock of morality. Woman, who is the mother, contributes living for another—the ideal of unselfishness. Man who is the breadwinner and the fighter, contributes what boys used to call doing a stump.

To nineteenth-century boys, "doing a stump" meant doing a dangerous deed for its own sake. It could also mean competition in performing useless but daring acts. Thus, when Holmes asked, "Why do we send expeditions to the North Pole?" he answered his own question: "It is nothing but nations doing stumps to one another."

The justice then took this issue of pure struggle to a higher level. He said in praise of men's useless acts: "An ideal is a principle of conduct carried to its abstract absolute and therefore useless expression, and when you find such an expression in life it has the final charm." Holmes added with passion, "This uselessness is the highest kind of use. It is kindling and feeding the ideal spark without which life is not worth living." Holmes was equating manliness with struggle for its own sake and giving it the highest moral value.[15]

The notion of manhood as high strife was not the sole possession of men. The grand-niece of William Dean Howells wrote to her famous relative to bemoan the lack of virility in his novels. By "virility," she meant: "very strong . . . ; and mistrustful; and relentless; and makes you feel as if somebody had taken you by the throat; and shakes you up, awfully, and seems to throw you into the air, and trample you underfoot."[16] Admittedly, her definition of virility was extreme; but it shared with other views a sense of struggle and strife, of violence and force. In the eyes of educated men and women, these qualities were becoming synonymous with manhood at the end of the nineteenth century. As this notion of manliness emerged, there was a growing tendency to look at men as creatures of impulse and passion, even as animals or savages.

Primitive Masculinity

Throughout the nineteenth century, middle-class culture had identified "passion" as a fundamental quality of the male sex. Lust, greed, selfishness, ambition, and physical assertiveness were all seen as distinctively male traits. What changed in the century's final decades was the valuation of these passions. Once they had been viewed as dangerous sources of evil that threatened both soul and society. Now, as the century drew to a close, a man's "animal instincts" were seen in a positive light.

Men compared themselves readily to "primitive" peoples. John William DeForest noted that Civil War soldiers passed their "time like Comanches and New Zealanders," and—as he crawled across a grassy knoll that was raked by Confederate fire—DeForest's thoughts ranged "from an expectation of a ball through the spine to a recollection of Cooper's most celebrated Indians." Some women thought of men in similar terms. A turn-of-the-century magazine writer urged her female readership to provide a den for the man of the house. "Make it a place," she urged, "where he can lie and growl over his bones when he feels like it. . . . One lucky man of my acquaintance has such a den, which is to him as a cave to a primitive man."[17]

When late-century men were not being likened to "primitives," they were urging one another to act like them. Thomas Wentworth Higginson encouraged a Boston audience to tramp through the woods and hills south of town on the trail of game, "and camp where you find yourself at evening, and you are as essentially an Indian on the Blue Hills as among the Rocky Mountains." As if in response to his suggestion, more and more affluent men ranged further and further into forest, jungle, and prairie as hunters in the last decades of the century. One such man, according to a friend, "was never so truly himself as when looking into the bright face of danger."[18]

When men of the era could not imitate "primitive" men directly, they urged one another to learn from them. The lessons to be learned varied a great deal. Health reformer John Harvey Kellogg hoped that men of his kind would be chaste like Indians and other "primitives." Critics of

"American nervousness" encouraged victims of overwork to learn relaxation from "Oriental people, the inhabitants of the tropics, and the colored peoples generally." In the final quarter of the century, it became common for affluent young men to strengthen themselves by spending time in the "Wild West." Of Theodore Roosevelt's experience in the Dakota Territory, Daniel Carter Beard wrote: "By wearing the buckskin clothes, by mixing with ranchers, hunters, and savages, . . . [Roosevelt] consciously imbibed the energy, frankness, and fellowship of the wilderness." Beard hoped to teach the same lessons to city boys when he joined the Boy Scout movement.[19]

Men identified themselves with primitives in the rituals and plays of the clubs and lodges that were so popular late in the century. Athletic organizations and elite men's clubs wrote and performed their own theater pieces. Usually humorous and playful, one of the insistent themes of these shows was the transformation of the players into the "lesser" people whom they excluded from membership—women and people of color. Time after time, these performances turned affluent white men into black-face minstrels, tribesmen of "Darkest Africa," and "cannibal choruses."[20]

A similar phenomenon developed in the ubiquitous fraternal lodges of the late nineteenth century. The new rituals, which lay at the heart of fraternal activity and appeal, drew proudly and self-consciously on the customs of "savage" peoples. The noted jurist Roscoe Pound said that Masonic rites had their origins in the "development of societies out of the primitive men's house." Men who saw themselves as the pinnacle of civilization were zealous to play the parts of those they considered primitive.[21]

Of course, this fascinated kinship with other peoples had also been visible earlier in the century. The popularity of Cooper's Leatherstocking novels, Davy Crockett's yarns, Melville's South Sea tales, and a slew of books about American Indians had expressed the avid curiosity of the white antebellum middle class with those who lived beyond their self-drawn lines of civilization.[22] Avid curiosity was one thing, however, and identification was quite another. Francis Parkman's classmates at Harvard in the early 1840s laughed at his obsession with the people who inhabited America's forests and plains and made fun of him for having "Injuns on the brain." In the decades after the Civil War, such a fascination with "primitives" was considered normal, even in a grown man.[23]

In their desire to penetrate the boundaries of civilization, postbellum men sometimes blurred the distinction between the "savages" and animals. The turn-of-the-century writer Hamlin Garland did just that in the following poem, which he posted over the fireplace of a friend:

> Do you fear the force of the wind,
> The slash of the rain?
> Go face them and fight them,
> Be savage again.
> Go hungry and cold like the wolf,
> Go wade like the crane.
> The palms of your hands will thicken,
> The skin of your forehead tan—
> You'll be ragged and swarthy and weary
> But—you'll walk like a man.[24]

Savages and animals fade together in this poem into one rough-hewn "other." The lack of distinction did not bother the middle-class men of Garland's era. They were drawn to both groups for the same qualities.

The identification of men with animals, unlike their identification with primitives, had no precedent in the cultural tradition of middle-class Northerners. John Burroughs reflected on this change as he described his feelings about Darwinism in 1883:

> It is a new sensation to come to see man as an animal—the master animal of the world, the outcome and crown of all the rest. We have so long been taught to regard ourselves as something apart and exceptional, differing not merely in degree, but in kind, from the rest of creation, in no sense a part of Nature, something whose origin and destiny are peculiar, and not those of the commonality of the animal kingdom.

The animal nature of the human race was no longer an occasional poetic fancy but a scientific certainty.[25]

A flood of animal metaphors poured forth in the post-Darwin era. Man was now "a brave animal," and battle made "the wolf rise in [his] heart." Jack London's 1903 novel *The Call of the Wild* drew much of its immense popularity from its message that beneath the veneer of all human training lurks a wild animal. The mere fact that an animal could be the hero of a book so eagerly read by men was revealing in itself.[26]

Men spoke of their animal nature in phrases like "animal instincts" and "animal energy." They believed that this nature was their male birthright and that it demanded expression. Thomas Wentworth Higginson summarized this position: "The animal energy cannot and ought not to be suppressed; if debarred from its natural channel, it will force for itself unnatural ones." Such "unnatural" channels included "war, gambling, licentiousness, highway-robbery, and office-seeking." Left to its own course, animal energy "not only does not tend to sensuality in the objectionable sense, but it helps to avert it."[27]

It is significant that, when Higginson named the results of suppressed animal energy, he listed a series of antisocial activities connected almost exclusively with men. For the concept of man's "animal nature" was not without its gender politics. Darwin's theories—which supplied the dominant metaphor in this area for late nineteenth-century thinking—provided an animal inheritance to men and women alike. Yet, while men applied the idea of a bestial nature liberally to themselves, they applied it to women only in highly selective fashion. Men preferred to think of women as completely civilized creatures, free of passion and full of moral sensitivities. When they did think of the female as an animal, they were usually considering her as the child-bearing sex—and then men tended to use her beastly nature against her. For example, when segments of the Victorian medical profession grew alarmed that too many women were seeking education and an active role in the world beyond the home, doctors announced that the inherent qualities of the female reproductive system dictated that women should stay home and have babies. Generally, however, men were reluctant to grant an animal inheritance to women, even though they were eager to claim one for themselves.[28]

For their part, women seemed less excited about applying "animal" labels to humans. Most of them shared in the belief that the female sex was more civilized, which may explain why they lacked men's fascination with finding bestial traces in human behavior. But there was one subject that inspired them to attribute animal nature to people, and that was sexuality. The turn-of-the-century movement for social purity was rooted in the belief common to most women "that man is bestial" when it comes to his sex drives. One seventeen-year-old girl decided that "man, from the mightiest king to the humblest laborer is impure throughout— more animal than true man." An older woman believed that even "the slightest departure" from sexual reticence by a woman would turn men "into 'wild beasts.'" Even if experience taught a woman that a man could control his desires, her surprise affirmed the prevailing view of man's animal nature. One such woman testified that her mother had given her "an abnormal idea of men by her own sex attitude. . . . I thought most men must be beasts."[29]

Men generally agreed with women that they were driven by "animal instincts" in sexual matters.[30] The difference between men and women on this topic lay not in any dispute about whether the male was a "brute" or not, but in the meanings men and women attributed to man's sexually animal nature. Within the framework of middle-class culture, a man's carnal instincts were nothing but trouble to a woman. For a late nineteenth-century man, though, his "animal" impulses toward women seemed at worst a mixed blessing. They disturbed his relations with the opposite sex, and they could also lead to inner confusion about sexuality. But this "brutish" side of his nature also expressed his manliness. As one woman summarized the common belief, the sexual "passions of manhood ally [a man] to the forces of the universe and [so] justify themselves." In this view a man's animal drives gave him a "natural" power and not only "justified themselves" but verified his manhood.[31]

Whatever the gender politics of men's animal nature, it is clear that men in the last third of the nineteenth century were changing the moral value that they set on their "natural" passions. Talk of man's "bestiality" was largely a figurative language to discuss the passions that were ascribed to him. If men were showing a newfound pride in the animal within them, it was really a way to express positive feelings about male impulse.

An ardent spokesman for the value of male passion was Theodore Roosevelt. He extolled "the great primal needs and primal passions that are common to all of us" and quoted British minister Sydney Smith as saying: "The history of the world shows that men are not to be counted by their numbers, but by the fire and vigor of their passions." Roosevelt repeated Smith's words on the uses of passion in men's lives:

There are seasons in human affairs when qualities, fit enough to conduct the common business of life, are feeble and useless. When men must trust to emotion for that safety which reason at such times can never give. . . . God calls all the passions out in their keenness and vigor for the present safety of mankind . . . —all the secret strength, all the invisible array of the feelings—all that nature has reserved for the great scenes of the world when the usual hopes and aids of man are gone, nothing remains under God but those passions which have often proved the best ministers of His purpose and the surest protectors of his world.

Wrapping passion in this divine endorsement, Smith (and Roosevelt) included anger, revenge, and "a readiness to suffer" among the impulses they approved for manly use.[32]

Other men were willing to give an even freer rein to passion. In 1885, psychologist James Cattell explained his neglect of his own health by saying, "We have put reason in the place of instinct, and are going to no good end." A young man named Walter Fisher had even stronger feelings. He believed that obeying impulse was "Life's best slogan," that "the basis of ethics is instinct."[33] Fisher's beliefs moved manhood far from the eighteenth-century conception that the passions were dark and destructive forces in a man, forces that had to be controlled by the divine gift of male reason. In the late nineteenth century, men took a second look at their "animal nature" and found it just as useful—and just as necessary to their manhood—as reason.

Of course, men like Fisher and Cattell did not believe that passion should simply rule their behavior; civilization still had its place. But they worried that modern males—particularly themselves and their sons— had become so civilized that their relationship with their own primal needs was now dangerously disrupted. Such cultural spokesmen as these felt a burning need to preach the existence of the masculine primitive, to remind men of the professional and business classes that they indeed *had* a deep reservoir of savage drives and instincts—passions which men needed in order to be men, to struggle, survive, and dominate. They feared that civilization had so fully repressed their passions that their very manhood—their independence, their courage, their drive for mastery—was being suffocated. Thus, they clamored and boasted about their "animal instincts" and their primitive needs in hope of establishing a better balance between civilization and the inner savage. In so doing, they gave passion a new and honored place in the bourgeois definition of manhood.

Manliness and the Military Ideal

As men of the late nineteenth century sought to connect themselves to primitive impulse and to define their lives in terms of passionate struggle, they often turned to martial ideals and images as a way to focus their vision of a manly life. The new male language of struggle expressed the idea—rare in female usage—that existence was battle. The image surfaced in many realms of life during the later years of the century. Fraternal ritual was rife with descriptions of the warfare of existence. A clergyman prominent in the Knights of Pythias resorted to this figure of speech in explaining why Pythians wore military outfits: "Human life is not a playground but a battlefield, in which individuals may make their lives sublime." "From the cradle to the grave," he added, "our life is a scene of unending conflict." A speaker at the 1898 convention of the evangelical Student Volunteer Movement declared that:

> we may liken this [convention] to a council of war, in which we take account of the field to be won, the opposing forces to be met, the agencies we are to employ, the enlistment that is needed, the equipment we must have, and the spiritual authority which must be recognized.

And when the *New York Herald* eulogized Cornelius Vanderbilt in 1877, it did so by adopting the figure of life as a battle: "He had no advantages in his battle, no political, social, educational aid. It was one honest, sturdy, fearless man against the world, and in the end the man won."[34]

The Civil War was unquestionably a key force in shaping this male perception of life as warfare, but the war's cultural influence worked slowly. In the years after 1865, many people recoiled in horror from fresh memories of combat. By the 1880s, though, the memories dimmed, and the benefits of war stood out in bolder relief. As Oliver Wendell Holmes, Jr., told Harvard students in 1895, "War, when you are at it, is horrible and dull. It is only when time has passed that you see that its message was divine." Two years earlier, another Civil War veteran, Francis Amasa Walker, had observed to another Harvard audience that the Civil War had transformed the way the whole nation viewed life. It had produced, he said, "a vast change in popular sentiment and ideals."[35]

What was the "divine message" of the war that brought such "a vast change in popular sentiment"? The war's interpreters varied widely in their understanding, but they agreed on one point: the courage and self-sacrifice demanded by that great struggle contrasted sharply with the soft, pampered life of the business and professional classes after the war. Most men believed with William James that some means must be found to revive the "martial virtues"—"intrepidity, contempt of softness, surrender of private interest, obedience to command"—amid the easy peace enjoyed by the more prosperous classes. Theodore Roosevelt was perhaps the leading advocate of "the fighting virtues" in his generation. He preached:

> We need . . . the iron qualities that must go with true manhood. We need the positive virtues of resolution, of courage, of indomitable will, of power to do without shrinking the rough work that must always be done, and to persevere through the long days of slow progress or seeming failure which always come before any final triumph, no matter how brilliant.[36]

The "divine message" of the war, then, was the virtues it taught: courage, strength, endurance, duty, principled sacrifice. And the men who praised the fighting virtues equated them with manhood. Older traits of manliness such as independence and reason were not supplanted but they were cast in shadow by more physical, "primitive" qualities.

If these martial qualities were part of the divine message of war, the question for men in the closing years of the century was how to nurture those values in a time of comfortable peace and "ignoble ease." Men offered widely varied answers. Oliver Wendell Holmes, Jr., preached a philosophy of strenuous stoicism, "a reverence for men of action." Since he exalted the inherent virtue of activity and struggle, he even praised the world of business: "It hardens the fibre and . . . is more likely [than contemplation] to make more of a man of one who turns it to success."[37]

William James sought different means to bring the "tonic air of battle-fields" into the stale peacetime environment. He expressed his concern about the pallid selfishness of "gilded youths" in 1910 in his great essay "The Moral Equivalent of War." With the model of the Civil War clearly in mind, James proposed that the nation's youth be conscripted into "an army against nature." This corps of youth would work at physical labor, from coal mining to road building, with this ultimate purpose: "To get the childishness knocked out of them, and to come back into society with healthier sympathies and soberer ideas." James's peaceful army would perform useful service, but the real benefit of their work would be the creation of the moral energy and vital purpose that James's generation felt the Civil War had provided for them.[38]

While men like James and Holmes sought peaceful activities that would build manly character as well as war did, there were many others who saw no need for a substitute. This group believed that men could best derive the benefits of war simply by having one. Throughout the 1880s and 1890s, veterans spoke to each other of the nobility of their sacrifice and of the fraternity of courage which they had been fortunate to share. They aired these feelings at conventions, encampments, and battlefield reunions that grew steadily in frequency and size. At the same time, veterans became the centerpiece at the newly popular Memorial Day celebrations, where they and their dead brethren were held up as exemplars of utmost virtue.[39]

The lesson could hardly be lost on the male youth who came of age in these years. Veterans compared the younger generation's easy life with the heroic sacrifice and hardship of the war generation. Could the sons be equal to the fathers? Would they have a like opportunity to test their manly worth in the fires of war? These questions developed a growing urgency during the 1890s. In 1894, a writer in the *North American Review* taunted men for going "flabby" with "idleness and luxury" and suggested that "a great war" might help them "to pull themselves together." Theodore Roosevelt agreed. "This country needs a war," he wrote in 1895. "We feel . . . that the men who have dared greatly in war, or the work which is akin to war, are those who deserve best of the country." Younger men like Roosevelt wanted that chance to dare greatly. As Carl Sandburg, who was twenty at the time, observed, "Over all of us in 1898 was the shadow of the Civil War and the men who fought it to the end." In that year, the sons of the Civil War generation finally got their chance. The "splendid little war" with Spain provided ample chances for glory and an overwhelming victory for the nation.[40]

After its men had gotten their special chance to prove their manly, fighting virtues, however, the nation discovered that the war had left an unpleasant residue. When the United States defeated Spain, it conquered Spanish colonial territories. Now the nation had to decide what its relationship to those conquered areas should be, in particular, whether the United States should suppress a revolt in the Philippines, or withdraw and leave the Filipinos with the independence they sought. The argument over these questions uncovered a generational cleavage.[41] The cleavage centered on issues of imperialism, but looked at more closely, it can also be seen as a clash over the military ideals of manhood.

The opposition to an imperial policy was led by men of the older generation who remembered the Civil War clearly; the younger men, raised on the splendor and necessity of the fighting virtues, favored an assertive global role for the nation. This debate on imperialism provided the context for Theodore Roosevelt's famous "Strenuous Life" speech of 1899, in which Roosevelt treated the martial ideals for the individual man and for the nation as barely distinguishable from one another:

> If we stand idly by, . . . if we shrink from the hard contest where men must win at the hazard of their lives and at the risk of all they hold dear, then the stronger and bolder peoples will pass us by, and will win for themselves the domination of the world. Let us therefore boldly face the life of strife, resolute to do our duty well and manfully. . . . Let us shrink from no strife, moral or physical, within or without the nation, provided we are certain that the strife is justified, for it is only through strife, through hard and dangerous endeavor, that we shall ultimately win the goal of true national greatness.[42]

Just as Roosevelt believed that the individual man could only prove his manhood through strenuous endeavor, so he believed that nations could only prove their greatness by facing strife.

Beneath the circular logic of personal manhood and national greatness lurks another of Roosevelt's pet concerns: dominance. The end result of all the strife, the manliness, and the national greatness would be "the domination of the world." To Roosevelt, this was a worthy goal—indeed, it was the ultimate goal. One can see dominance as the implied project of the whole martial ideal of manliness. After all, war is an attempt to impose by force that which cannot be arranged by peaceful means. If, as so many middle-class men believed at the time, life is a battle, then the purpose of life must be that form of dominance we call victory. The martial ideal was a cult of manly conquest.

But the cult had its opponents. In the "Strenuous Life" address, Roosevelt's chief enemies were not "primitive" peoples or competitor nations but anti-imperialists in his own country. Roosevelt scorned them as men who had "lost the great fighting, masterful virtues." Whether this was a fair criticism or not, one thing was clear about Roosevelt's opponents: they tended to be of an older generation. Their lives were lived by an older set of values and an older standard of manhood. As good, bourgeois republicans, they were not believers in a warrior ethic. They abhorred standing armies as threats to liberty, and their military ethic was a belief in a citizen militia, ever ready to defend freedom. Their deepest concern was independence—to determine their own fate, achieve their own status, choose their own governors, exercise their own economic options. The warrior ethic that appeared at the end of the century disturbed them deeply.

Their concerns were effectively expressed by Ernest Howard Crosby in his 1901 article on "The Military Idea of Manliness." Crosby observed that the United States, because it had always been "a nation of mere tradesmen and farmers," had "never assimilated the ideals of honor, manliness, and glory which distinguish the military peoples." This military ideal was, said Crosby, a "change in the idea of manliness to which we must adjust ourselves." He found the new idea troubling on many counts. It encouraged "deception" and "pillage," and its reliance on rank order encouraged the powerful to prey on the weak. Crosby was also troubled by the petty vanities which he saw in military life. He made this point as scornfully as he could by likening military men to women:

The new idea of manliness involves a high degree of sensitiveness. . . . No other profession except that of actresses, can compete with the army and navy in feline amenities. We used to think such behavior effeminate. It is a mistake. Such behavior is manly.

This military vanity, said Crosby, demanded that "the humble citizen [bow] prostrate."[43]

This last image disturbed Crosby the most. Ever since the American Revolution, the refusal to honor position for its own sake had been a mark of manliness. A man who bowed down to rank was expressing dependence, and, in doing so, he threatened his own freedom and that of the nation. Crosby described his concern about submission in typically ironic tones:

> There is another false conception which we must get rid of before we can appreciate the new manliness, and that is the ancient belief in freedom and independence which prevailed before the recent repeal of the Declaration. Absolute obedience, readiness to obey orders, to do anything, these are necessary military qualities.[44]

Crosby's comment on the "repeal of the Declaration" referred to the recent Senate ratification of the Treaty of Paris, which made the Philippines, Puerto Rico, and Guam possessions of the United States instead of giving them independence. This reference shows how much his concerns about military manliness were based on events in the political arena, and it also suggests the degree to which the new manliness threatened the republican principles that had helped form the foundation of the older conception of manhood.

Crosby's greatest concern was not imperialism abroad but deference and blind obedience at home. There was ample reason for a man of older republican values to be concerned in Crosby's day. Talk of duty and subordination were everywhere. The most famous hymn to deference was Oliver Wendell Holmes, Jr.'s, 1895 speech, "The Soldier's Faith." Holmes said, in the most quoted lines of the speech:

> the faith is true and adorable which leads a soldier to throw away his life in obedience to a blindly accepted duty, in a cause which he little understands, in a plan of campaign of which he has no notion, under tactics of which he does not see the use.[45]

No statement could have strayed further from republican belief than this paean to blind obedience, yet it was simply a resonant echo of a belief that was widely and loudly proclaimed at the end of the century.

This noble submission took two main forms: the surrender of personal aims for those of the group, and deference to a heroic leader. Individual compliance with the group was a basic value of the boys' organizations that flourished at the turn of the twentieth century. These groups, which ranged from church associations like the paramilitary Boys' Brigade to outdoor organizations like the Boy Scouts, shared vital qualities: they were founded and run by adults with adult concerns in mind, and they placed a heavy emphasis on subordination of the boy to his larger group. As historian Joseph Kett has noted, such groups featured "rhetorical glorifications of strenuosity and will power [that] coexisted with the thrusting of youth into positions of extreme dependence."[46]

This emphasis on submission to the group was not just an adult agenda for boys. It became part of a new emphasis in public discourse on the obligations of citizenship. National figures like Theodore Roosevelt spoke gravely of a man's "duty to the State and to the nation," and cast off much of the language of suspicion in which republicans had once described the proper relation between the (male) individual and the state.[47]

The most dramatic instances of male submissiveness involved the cult of the leader that emerged at the end of the nineteenth century. In his study of heroes in American magazine articles, Theodore Greene has described the typical hero from 1894 to 1903 as an "idol of power." Greene found that the traits most often depicted in presenting these men were those used for the mastery of others or of the physical environment. Half of all the heroes' relationships were portrayed in terms of their dominance (as opposed to love, help, cooperation, and so forth). Greene described these idols of power as Napoleonic men of ambition, force, and determination.[48] Even in the next decade, when popular heroes in magazines gained a social conscience, they were still portrayed most often in terms of masterful qualities such as forcefulness and vigor.[49] Greene's evidence shows that this cult of the great man represented a historical change: a century earlier, magazine heroes had been measured in terms of their contributions to the social good.[50]

By the dawn of the twentieth century, then, old prescriptions for manhood were being replaced. Since the colonial era, ideals of manliness had expressed a concern with the government of passions; since the revolution, manhood and independence had been closely linked. Now, male impulse was nurtured, manly reason was redefined, and bonds of dominance and submission between men became respectable. How could the new masculine values be integrated with the old? How could manly passion and strong leadership flourish without threatening civilization or democracy? Advocates of the new manhood found answers to these questions in the vogue of competitive athletics.

Competitive Sports: A Model for Manhood

Northern men had engaged in physical games and contests almost from the time that British settlers came to New England. Wrestling matches and informal team games were played on special occasions under the loosest of rules. Boys did not wait for special occasions; from the colonial era to the nineteenth century, they enjoyed physical contests and indulged in them as often as they could. The Puritans and their Yankee descendents approved of such games, which they considered wholesome exercise, as long as they were not played on the Sabbath or at times that interfered with work. In the middle of the nineteenth century, however, these games took on new meaning and heightened importance for Northern men.[51]

By the 1840s a new game called "baseball" was spreading rapidly. With roots in several ball games that were common in the Northeast, baseball became a vehicle for expressing rivalry between towns, neighborhoods, and businesses. These rival groups organized their best players into teams that championed local honor in hotly contested "match games." In the large cities of the 1840s and 1850s, baseball rivalries focused especially on work-based groups. The teams, at first a middle-class phenomenon, spread later to working-class men as well, but the spectators for the games continued for many years to be middle class.[52] Meanwhile other sports were finding favor. During the 1840s and 1850s, rowing enjoyed a great vogue, with clubs springing up in business and professional circles. The first great intercollegiate contests were the rowing regattas of the late 1850s.[53] During the antebellum years, fencing and boxing lessons even became acceptable for aspiring clerks and well-bred students.[54]

The significance of sport went beyond its growing popularity as a pastime; it was also important as a cultural phenomenon. This dimension was what gave athletics its special significance for the redefinition of manhood at the turn of the century. Before the Civil War, athletics was seen as a form of physical culture that strengthened the body, refreshed the soul, and increased a man's resistance to luxury and vice.[55] In the postbellum period, on the other hand, athletics came to mean competition and not mere exercise. At Phillips Exeter Academy, for instance, late-century students demanded more of the school than simple physical training. Student sentiment urged "the boy to drop his chest weights, and don boxing gloves; to stop jogging on the track, and race; to quit signal practice and scrimmage. There is a difference between physical culture and athletics, and that is it."

The same rage for competitive sports was emerging at Exeter's rival academy. In the 1890s, the letters written by Andover students showed an "exultation in the fanfare surrounding each contest with Exeter." Andover boys at the time often dressed for the Sunday chapel service in their athletic uniforms. By the close of the 1800s, team sports had taken on a moral and social significance that far outstripped their old relationship to physical culture.[56]

Between 1860 and 1890, baseball moved beyond local rivalries to become the national pastime. At the same time, collegiate rivalries spread from crew races to football games, baseball matches, and track meets. Golf became a popular pastime for businessmen at the end of the 1800s, and tennis emerged in the 1870s as a new passion for male youth. The traditions of one affluent family claim that when a daughter in the house wanted to meet young men, she had a tennis court built in the backyard. The story may be apocryphal but the basic point remains: young men were preoccupied with sports, often to the exclusion of romance.[57]

What was the meaning of competitive athletics to those who advocated them? Men seeking a peacetime equivalent to war often turned to team sports with hope. Francis A. Walker believed that the manly traits inspired by Civil War experience were best taught in peacetime by "the competitive contests of our colleges." Cultural confusion between military combat and athletic combat was widespread, especially in the last two decades of the century when the Civil War experience was valorized. Walter Camp, the father of modern football, wrote at the turn of the century that there was a "remarkable and interesting likeness between the theories which underlie great battles and the miniature contests of the gridiron." Camp's contemporaries referred to quarterbacks as "field generals," and called linemen "soldiers" (after World War I, lineman would be said to "battle in the trenches"). Perhaps the most dramatic instance of this confusion between team sports and war came from a conversation that poet Hamlin Garland had with novelist Stephen Crane. The author of *The Red Badge of Courage* had never gone to war, so Garland asked him how he knew about it. Crane responded that he had played football and that its strategy and emotion were like a war, with the other team serving as the enemy.[58]

In a cultural setting where war and athletics were equated and war was thought to breed a new, forceful manhood, people readily came to the position that athletics, too, fostered the new form of manhood. At the start of the new century, the president of Princeton praised competitive sports as tests of manliness, "gentlemanly contests for supremacy." And, in 1901, an education writer insisted that "manly social games, like football, basket-ball, baseball, are our best resources in developing . . . almost every characteristic of virility."[59]

The claims for athletics as a source of manhood were so vast and varied that they can best be understood in several categories. First of all, athletic contests were praised as breeding grounds for the fighting virtues. These included determination, "coolness, steadiness of nerve, quickness of apprehension," "endurance against hunger, fatigue, and physical distress," and—above all—courage.[60]

Through the experience of team play, athletics were also credited with the development of social, cooperative, and even submissive virtues. In 1905, Cunningham LaPlace wrote in a magazine called *The Outlook* that team contests taught a youth "the subordination of the unit to the total, the habit of working with his fellows, of touching elbows." Luther Gulick, a noted leader in work with boys, made the point most emphatically in 1899: team sports bred "heroic subordination of self to the group."[61] To most middle-class men in the nineteenth century, the phrase, "heroic subordination," would have been a contradiction in terms. To men like Gulick at the turn of the twentieth century, the phrase made fine and noble sense. Courage, strength, and endurance meant more to them than independence, especially if a man subordinated himself to the right cause.

If the traits encouraged by team sports contradicted some of the republican values that infused nineteenth-century manhood, they did support some others. Competitive athletics, according to their advocates, counteracted one of the greatest sources of worry for republicans: those "dangerous tendencies in modern life" that often "produce neurotic and luxury-loving individuals." Team contests demanded a strength, vigor, and physical assertiveness that undermined the ease and debility of modern affluence. Other proponents of sports, concerned with the greed of Gilded Age tycoons and politicians, claimed that the experience of team contests restrained "the selfish, individualistic tendencies of the age."[62]

According to popular belief, athletics also served as a moral force by thwarting those habits that the nineteenth century labeled collectively as "vice." As one historian has argued, athletic training required precisely the sort of ascetic self-denial that might stop a youth from masturbating.

Organized sports seemed to check other forms of vice as well. Henry Dwight Sedgwick recalled a group of schoolmates who swore, gambled, lied, and did very little work. He observed that none of the four played football, and speculated that the game would have had an "educational effect" on their moral tone.[63]

When supporters insisted that competitive athletics built character, then, they were claiming more than just the development of martial virtues; they were arguing that organized sports taught self-control, which would enable a boy to govern selfishness or sensual impulses. This line of thinking had an undertone of gender politics; luxury and self-indulgence—"effeminacy"—were considered quintessential female flaws which athletics could counteract. More than that, advocates of sport were claiming new cultural and social ground away from women. For a century, moral instruction had been regarded as a woman's task, but now men asserted that all-male competition could do the job. Beneath this assertion lay an implied complaint that young males were reaching their teens and twenties without the moral training that they should have received from their mothers.

Even as the advocates of athletics were making dramatic new claims about sports and morality, they pointed to academic benefits as well. Many agreed with Theodore Roosevelt that "those boys who take part in rough, hard play outside of school will not find any need for horse-play." While sports siphoned off "animal spirits" so that boys could concentrate in the classroom, they could also teach a new respect for intelligence and cultivated skill. Ellery Clark, a former Harvard track star, testified that "a great light . . . burst upon [his] mind" when he realized that, in athletics, "skill was greater than strength, brain than muscle; and that the man who once thoroughly mastered the method of performing an event could thereafter hold his own with those infinitely his superiors in strength and size."[64]

By the start of the twentieth century, then, the claims on behalf of the athletic experience were broad. Team sports seemed to offer benefits in every aspect of life. In fact, the men of the time treated athletics as a metaphor for life, or as a mirror that reflected the situations of life with a peculiar clarity. Here we find the historical roots of a cultural habit that, at the end of the twentieth century, seems timeless. For example, financier Charles Flint, recalling his years as a hunter, "observed an indifference to sports on the part of men of leisure as compared with the intense delight of those who are transformed from business hustlers into hustlers after game." This facile equation of business with sport, so familiar in later years, was a product of the turn-of-the-century era. It was an equation commonly made. Essayist Rafford Pyke used common athletic imagery to make a different sort of point about manly honesty: "Fair play and the rigor of the game is a masculine ideal; men will trust and like and honor those who live up to its strict requirements." The most famous comparison of life to athletics in this era came from that master of aphorisms, Theodore Roosevelt, when he said: "In life, as in a foot-ball game, the principle to follow is: Hit the line hard; don't foul and don't shirk but hit the line hard." Sport, in sum, both reflected and illuminated men's lives. It also served as "a means of preparation for the responsibilities of life" because it taught "qualities useful in any profession."[65]

Most of all, athletics seemed to teach the qualities men needed in life because it was a competitive endeavor. Cunningham LaPlace, reflecting in 1905 on his son's college experience, turned a favorable eye on intramural sports. LaPlace wrote that student fun "should take the form of a contest, since life is so constituted that this is its law. Every man who obtains a position of responsibility and of corresponding remuneration does so because some man or group selects him from a field as the one who is considered to be best qualified." "A young man," wrote LaPlace, "can best learn" this phase of life from competitive games. Henry Sheldon, a scholar of student customs, shared LaPlace's view of life as inherently competitive. Commenting on college sports, he wrote:

Athletics have flourished in proportion as the competitive feature has been emphasized. In many colleges the chief motive power is not an interest in physical training, but a craving for distinction, an ambition to beat some one. Among nations of Anglo-Saxon descent the desire for exercise is chiefly the result, not the cause, of competitive contests.

Whatever the source of this "ambition to beat some one," everyone seemed to agree that athletics took their value and their appeal from their reflection of life's "inherently" competitive nature.[66]

Increasingly, the appeal of the athletic contest exerted its sway over spectators as well as youthful participants. In the last quarter of the nineteenth century, middle-class males provided a mass following for professional baseball and college football.[67] The popularity of these spectator sports was intimately related to the fact that they were competitions. Historian Leonard Ellis has analyzed their deep structure in a way that links their appeal persuasively to their rivalrous nature. Football pitted one team against the other in the conquest and defense of territory. It emphasized teamwork, an elaborate division of labor, a hierarchy of roles, and intricate strategies in the service of team competition, thus rendering the experience of bureaucratic work—which was just emerging at the end of the century—in dramatic physical form.

As Ellis analyzes it, baseball had a very different sort of structure. The two teams did not engage in direct combat, but rather took turns in an exercise at home-leaving and successful return. From the safety of "home," one individual after another attempted to enter a hostile territory and negotiate a safe arrival back at home. The constant repetition of home-leaving and return mirrored the daily journeys of men into the world and back again.[68] Baseball embodied not just the competition of nineteenth-century manhood but also the organization of male life into zones of striving and safety. Sports seemed to mirror men's lives, and that was the greatest source of athletics' appeal as public drama, as a teaching device, and as a means for building manly character.

Competition and the Evolution of Manhood

If contests mirrored life, life at the end of the nineteenth century seemed more and more to mirror a contest. Repeatedly, men of this era described their lives, and especially their work, in the language of competitive games. Morton S. Bailey, as a young lawyer in the boom town of late-century Denver, described his future in terms of winners and losers: "Here is a vast field for workers and vast amounts of money to be gotten, if I am only equal to the contest I shall win, if weak then some other and stronger one will carry off the spoils." We have seen also that Charles Francis Adams used the metaphor of contest to describe life in his time, calling it "the rather rough game of American nineteenth-century life."[69]

An underlying structure of competition had, in fact, been built into men's work lives for some time. The marketplace of Adam Smith and the political framework of James Madison both relied on competition as the mainspring that made them function. Their models had a formative impact on the way men understood and continued to shape the public world. The metaphor of separate spheres can also be understood as a kind of cultural fantasy about the way in which the impact of competition on society—and on men in particular—might be softened.

By the late nineteenth century, however, middle-class Americans had gone beyond the element of competition inherent in their economic and political systems. They had begun to *import* competition as a motivating device into activities that were basically solitary. Sunday schools by mid-century were offering prizes to their best pupils in the hope of hastening salvation of souls and increasing student interest at the same time. Spelling bees were a handy tool to make the lone drudgery of memorization more appealing, and art competitions grew common. Competition was invested with magical powers to inspire the utmost personal achievement and to lend drama to life's work.[70]

For men, competition became an obsession. They even imposed it on situations where it was entirely out of place. George Dryer, the business manager of a mental institution in Minnesota, brought a note of gratuitous competition into the birth of his first child in 1870. The letter that announced his daughter's birth also pointed out to his father that, "this being the first child of its generation, [it] seems to me [she] ought to have the 'prize cup' 'family premium' or something else to commemorate the event." No such contest had been organized and no prizes were announced, but, in a society where a man's life was increasingly conceived as an endless round of competitions, George Dryer's call for a reward made natural sense.[71]

Indeed, the phenomenon that needs explanation may not be behavior like George Dryer's, but rather the fact that competition had no part in the ideal traits of manhood until the late nineteenth century. As a vital structuring element of male culture from the play of boyhood to the serious business of the public arena, competition was certainly a central process in the lives of nineteenth-century men. Why did the competitive element have no place among the virtues that defined middle-class manhood through most of the century? A large part of the answer may lie in the historical context that produced those ideals of manliness. They emerged in the early nineteenth century, when society was moving away from hierarchy and stability toward a dynamic world of individual liberty and achieved status. Yet, while people disdained the static, role-bound deference of the old order, they also feared the destructive potential of the new, competitive one. Rivalry and contention had created social chaos in the past; how could a new society be maintained with those qualities at its core? Certainly not by treating them as precious skills or desirable traits in a man.

Rather, men's contending passions were treated as a necessary evil in the new social order of the early nineteenth century. Because they were the engines of prosperity and political life, they were not suppressed; but these competitive impulses were carefully channeled by customs and values of male peer groups, were criticized by women and clergymen, and were symbolically quarantined by the separation of spheres.

Indeed, our current notion of a competitive person is a recent historical development. The word *competitive* did not even enter the English language until the early nineteenth century. When it did, it applied to situations ("competitive examination") or institutions ("competitive societies"), not to individuals.[72] Nineteenth-century men and women did not have a language to describe in positive (or even neutral) terms a person who relished contest. They had only words like *contentious* (which had negative, disruptive connotations) and *rivalrous* (which had negative overtones of personal animosity, not generalized competition). In this world, the words did not exist to make a man feel good about being competitive.

By the 1880s and 1890s, the doctrine of separate spheres—the official model of gender relations—had lost some of its coercive power over bourgeois families. From one direction, women were entering many public worlds and demanding entry to others. From the other direction, men were assaulting the doctrine in ways that were less visible but still crucial. By devising male mechanisms like athletics for building character, men were challenging female sovereignty over the moral instruction of boys. By asserting the positive value of competition and competitiveness, they were undermining the moral foundation on which the separation of spheres was built.

Of course, men still supported the doctrine of spheres in many respects. Most, for instance, continued to favor the separation of women from public power. What men rejected were the notions that competition was morally destructive for men and that women were better qualified than men to nurture all aspects of male character. This rejection offers us a clue as to why standards of manhood were changing in the late nineteenth century. Bourgeois men felt increasingly that the notions of "civilization" that lay embedded in the doctrine of the spheres were insidious and even socially destructive. The new manhood was in part a male rebellion against cultural standards that middle-class men of previous generations had helped to sustain.

Chapter 11

ROOTS OF CHANGE

The Women Without and the Woman Within

IN the mid-1890s, Ray Stannard Baker went to a dinner of the Hamilton Club, a group of Republican loyalists in Chicago. A young Eastern politician spoke to the club that night, and he galvanized Baker with his ideas and his manner. Baker later recalled: "I was greatly impressed by his vigor, his directness, and his fearlessness." The speaker was Theodore Roosevelt. He was, said Baker, a "cowboy, hard rider, straight-shooter, bold speaker, champion of the people, gifted in telling the rich old fellows, many of whom were present on that evening, to say nothing of the cultured 'mugwumps,' where they got off!" In the years that followed, Baker became a leading progressive journalist and a "friend and loyal supporter" of Roosevelt. In his devotion to Roosevelt's style and principles, Baker belonged to a large segment of men in his generation: "I was not the only youngster who believed in the 'strenuous life': there were thousands of us who had recently come from the frontier, and the farm, and the plains. Not a few of us felt that we had something to do in saving an America that seemed to us to be going astray."[1]

Baker's generation included a wide variety of middle-class men who were drawn to the strenuous passion and primitive vigor embodied by Roosevelt. Some of these men, like Baker, were progressives, but others were cool to Roosevelt's political views; some, like Baker, were rural entrants to the middle-class world, but more of them had roots already in bourgeois America. Regardless of background or political views, all of them were drawn to Roosevelt's personal portrayal of a new style of masculinity. As Baker describes the attraction, this bold manliness was an antidote to something in "America that seemed . . . to be going astray." But what was this problem? To what social ills was the new masculinity an antidote? What caused the emergence of this energetic form of manhood?

Changes in Men's Sphere

The standards of manhood that guided middle-class men during the nineteenth century emerged in a rapidly developing commercial economy and in the wake of a republican revolution. By the end of the nineteenth century, these standards had survived into a very different era. The changes in the economic environment were especially sharp. An industrial economy had emerged, and the development of national markets in the late nineteenth century propelled businessmen into a quest for economies of scale. Sprawling new firms that served huge markets spawned bureaucracies which employed armies of executives, salespeople, and clerical workers. The number of salaried, nonpropertied workers (virtually all white-collar) multiplied eight times between 1870 and 1910. Twenty percent of the total male work force was white-collar by 1910. Even more important for the men studied here, corporations hired their own corps of experts from new professions such as engineering and accounting, and retained the services of law firms whose entire practice was devoted to corporate interests.[2]

The expanding bureaucracy had a significant effect on manhood. The largest number of jobs appeared at the lowest levels, where work was routine and required skills were limited. The biggest proportional increase of jobs came in the middle-level positions such as bookkeeper, supervisor, and salesman. The lower-level posts were filled with growing numbers of women. Employers assumed that these female workers, mostly young and single, would stay with the firm only until they married; thus, they promoted men to the midlevel jobs. This discrimination did little to open up long-range prospects for those men, however. Top management posts were filled increasingly by college graduates, men with connections to other firms and lines of work. Midlevel workers were likely to be graduates of the new high schools; they were trained by the company and rarely made lateral moves to other firms. In short, a glass ceiling separated middle and upper bureaucrats. Their horizons inside and outside the company were distinctly different.[3]

These patterns of employment marked a dramatic change from the ones that had prevailed through most of the century. The clerk, no longer an apprentice for business leadership, was now a service worker with little chance of making it to the top. The route upward was much longer, and the barriers along the way were largely insurmountable. Even the men who entered an organization in its upper ranks confronted a new definition of opportunity. The mark of success had once been prosperity as an independent owner; now it was victory in the struggle of executives for the top spot. Ultimately, the winner was still an employee. In the new order, every businessman had to submit—the successful one was the man who submitted to the fewest others.

As a larger proportion of business and professional work moved into big cities, the scale of urban life compounded the trouble created by massive corporations. Public distinction was much harder for a man to achieve. One urban businessman with small-town roots summarized the problem in a colloquial paraphrase of Julius Caesar: "What does Caesar say, somewhere? I think he said he'd rather be first in a tank town than second in Rome. Well, I ain't second here. I ain't even five hundred thousand and second. But I could have been first back there [at home]." As men were funneled into large organizations in large cities, they had more competitors for fewer prizes.[4]

Even in the legal profession, where most practices were still small, there was a widespread feeling that the chances for distinction were waning. One lawyer recalls the transformation of the late nineteenth century in these terms:

Law was changing; the old order, when distinguished orators deemed their most important moments spent in arguing before court or jury, was passing away; now the important lawyers were closeted in inner rooms, guarded by office boys, clerks, stenographers, who only admitted officials of great corporations—for organization, for mergers, for bond issues, for any schemes to obtain wealth.[5]

This comparison romanticized the past, ignoring the avarice and brutal self-concern that often typified nineteenth-century lawyers. Still, the view was widely shared in the legal profession; it expressed a concern that public distinction and masterful independence were vanishing. The question that haunted the profession has been phrased in this way by a legal historian: "Could a lawyer on retainer to a corporation . . . still be a manly advocate?"[6]

Worries of this sort were common throughout the business world and the professions. In the nineteenth century, middle-class men had believed that a true man was a self-reliant being who would never bow to unjust authority or mere position. The new structures of work and opportunity in the marketplace did not support such a concept of manhood.[7]

The new work world of the middle class threatened manhood in a second way. Through most of the nineteenth century, the people with mercantile or professional responsibility were men. The public world, after all, was the male sphere. As we have seen, however, women began to breach men's domain late in the century. Even though men held onto power and prestige, their sense of manly prerogative was threatened. Women's presence made a symbolic statement to men that the world of middle-class work was no longer a male club. To the extent that a place in the professions or business served as a badge of manhood, manhood was now being undermined.

Of course, men in the lower levels of bureaucracy were threatened more directly. Women became an established part of their work world by the early twentieth century.[8] Males and females were colleagues and even competitors. The promotions did go chiefly to the men, but a triumph over feminine rivals was not a great boost to a man's sense of manliness.

As women came to dominate clerical positions, they also had an effect on the middle-class work environment. Even top executives and senior law partners had women entering their offices as secretaries and stenographers. The female presence feminized the middle-class workplace by more than sheer numbers. Symbolic changes of atmosphere marked their presence. Spittoons—a ubiquitous feature of the male office in the nineteenth century—disappeared soon after women arrived. The ideal workspace, as depicted in advertisements and catalogues, took on the trappings of a parlor, with carpets, plants, and paintings. Now a man had to be genteel in his language at work as at home. No one, to be sure, would have confused the office with the domestic world; but the subjective reality for men was that their workplace was not masculine in the same sense that it had been.[9]

If men had responded rationally to the situation, they could have altered their standards of manhood to fit their circumstances. Indeed, both the cult of athletics and the model of military manliness included a high regard for teamwork, group loyalty, and respect for authority as manly virtues. Still, gender is not a subject easily treated with reason, especially not in a culture that regarded it as a matter of high moral principle. Thus, when changes in the workplace caused men to feel uncertain of their manhood, their primary response was to seek new forms of reassurance about it. Strenuous recreation, spectator sports, adventure novels, and a growing cult of the wilderness all served this need; but the need was most fully served by the new ideas about manliness. These ideas reaffirmed the importance of manhood and asserted a new pride in traits that had previously been attributed to men—and roundly condemned.

The changes in the middle-class workplace cannot by themselves account for the growth and spread of the new, more primitive emphasis in manhood. Some of its most vigorous proponents were artists and small-town professionals who worked outside of the emerging urban bureaucracies. The changes in the work world did play a key role, however, in preparing the way for fresh ideas about manliness. As the transformation of the marketplace threw old ideals into question, men of that world listened eagerly to new ideas about manhood.

Gender and the Perils of Civilization

In the late nineteenth and early twentieth centuries, bourgeois males worried about the dangers of civilization. One man fretted over boys who lived "in a quiet city, . . . leading an unambitious, namby-pamby life, surrounded by all the safeguards of civilization." Another warned that men "must be on our guard to see that modern conditions do not soften our fiber until, when confronted with hardships, we become as helpless as a hermit crab without a shell." Men of the late 1800s even helped to bring a new word into the American language—*overcivilized*.[10]

In some ways, this collective anxiety was as old as the nation itself. The revolutionary generation had feared that luxury, ease, and idleness would subvert the republican experiment; but something more was bothering men in the late nineteenth century, and it involved the connections between gender and the definitions of civilization.

To understand these changes, we need to know something about the history of the word *civilization*. It entered the language in the eighteenth century. At the time, it referred to a condition of society that was raised above barbarism; it also referred to the institutions and arts of living which accounted for that elevated condition.[11] Men of the eighteenth century were happy to take credit for the enlightened and refined developments that constituted civilization. The postrevolutionary generations in the United States changed the gender meaning of *civilization*, however, when they developed the notion of the separate spheres. While men were expected to toil in a cruel, barbaric marketplace, women were to maintain the moral values that kept men civilized. Thus, civilization developed female connotations.

By the late nineteenth century, men were rebelling against the implications of a civilization that was not manly. Male commentators wrote that society in the United States was becoming "womanized" or "feminized." The most famous of these laments comes from Henry James's 1886 novel, *The Bostonians*. In it, the male protagonist, Basil Ransom, declares:

> The whole generation is womanized; the masculine tone is passing out of the world; it's a feminine, a nervous, hysterical, chattering, canting age, an age of hollow phrases and false delicacy and exaggerated solicitudes and coddled sensibilities, which, if we don't soon look out, will usher in the reign of mediocrity, of the feeblest and flattest and the most pretentious that has ever been.[12]

The anxious hostility of this statement grew out of male fears about women's role in shaping late nineteenth-century society.

These fears were several in kind. Many men bemoaned women's dominance in the process of raising male children, and they pointed to a rising generation of boys who seemed spoiled and dishonest, a pack of "flat-chested cigarette smokers with shaky nerves and doubtful vitality."[13] They worried that women's growing dominion over the teaching profession was ushering in "a regime of sugary benignity."[14] They noted with concern that women now set the standards of appearance and decorum. Women established the sentimental tone of bourgeois Protestant religion, and their values and sensibilities played a major role in forming literary tastes. In private, women enforced sexual virtue. By carrying out their role as the guardians of "civilized morality," middle-class females affected men as agents of unreasoning restraint.[15]

For most of the century, men heard these voices of restraint in public exhortation, in private talk, and in the accents of their own consciences. Then, during the last third of the nineteenth century, a new and forceful voice—another female one—joined this chorus of control. Through various social movements, women attempted to change men's public habits. The largest of these movements was embodied in the Women's Christian Temperance Union (founded in 1874). A proliferation of other related movements was led in importance by the crusade for sexual purity, but it included campaigns against a variety of masculine pastimes from fraternal lodges to boxing matches.[16]

Of course men had encouraged women in their role as the guardians of civilized morality since the start of the century, and some men even played an active role in the social crusades of the late 1800s. As a growing company of bourgeois males began to have second thoughts about the definition of civilized morality, however, they started to criticize those campaigns. A middle-class critic of the antiboxing movement wrote in 1888: "Let thinking men who value their manhood set themselves in array . . . against . . . those who, . . . caught by such specious watchwords as 'progress,' 'civilization,' and 'refinement,' have unthinkingly thrown their weight into the falling scale." The enemy, then, was not only the misguided people who joined the causes but the notion of civilization for which they fought:

> Has mawkish sentimentality become the shibboleth of the progress, civilization and refinement of this vaunted age? If so, then in Heaven's name leave us a saving touch of honest, old-fashioned barbarism! that when we come to die, we shall die, leaving men behind us, and not a race of eminently respectable female saints.[17]

For the first time, men were openly rebelling against the fundamental principles embedded in the doctrine of separate spheres. Rather than civilize themselves according to a feminized definition, men took the negative labels affixed to their character and made them into virtues. *Primitive, savage, barbarian, passion, impulse*—the underside of male character that bourgeois culture had stigmatized was now brought to light for fond inspection.[18] The obsessions of male writing about manhood in the late nineteenth and early twentieth century—competition, battle, physical aggression, bodily strength, primitive virtues, manly passions—all were inversions of "feminized" Victorian civilization.

After nearly a century of accepting the moral terms of separate spheres, why did men suddenly offer public resistance? The answer to this question is complex, but an important piece of it lies in the growing penetration of the public sphere by women. Men had endorsed women's moral stewardship as long as it did not extend to their public sources of power and pleasure, but they began to balk when women attacked taverns, lodges, and brothels. This threat helped to set off the male reexamination of civilized morality and primitive manliness.

Men also turned to assertions of their own "barbarism" in response to a second kind of female incursion into men's sphere. As we know, women in the late nineteenth century were pouring into business offices, fighting for a place in the learned professions, running settlement houses, and graduating from secondary schools and colleges in record numbers. Most threatening of all to men, they were campaigning for the right to vote. Few middle-class men were eager to share their power and prerogatives with the opposite sex, and to some extent the new talk of male passion and savagery came from their attempt to defend the sanctity of their sphere. As women tried to enter the rough arena of money and power, men defended their turf by stressing gender contrasts that had been articles of bourgeois cultural faith for most of the century. They emphasized the same rude passions for which their sex had been commonly criticized—greed and combativeness, selfish drive and brutish instincts, a lust for power and a love of crudeness.[19] These, they reminded women, were the reasons why men occupied the harsh world of economic and political struggle. As men repeated these masculine traits over and over in defense of their worldly dominance, the traits became a source of male pride. Standing in the shadow of the Civil War, it made even more sense to boast—not apologize—about the fighting passions.

We need, of course, to be clear about what these bourgeois males did and did not want when they asserted their primitive nature. Men did not want American society to descend into barbarism; they were still content to cede significant moral authority to women; and they did not wish to challenge the prevalent cultural division of traits between the two sexes.

What they did wish to do was to keep their sources of power and pleasure undisturbed. More than that, they hoped to impose a new metaphor for understanding human endeavor—a metaphor that would exalt "male" passions and fighting virtues to a place of honor that they lacked in the metaphor of separate spheres. In this light, Social Darwinism can be seen as more than a justification for the ill-gotten gains of robber barons. It becomes an alternative to the genteel definition of civilization contained in the doctrine of the spheres. In the Social Darwinist's vision, civilization was not just a matter of reason, complex institutions, and refined manners. It was the triumph of man over man in primitive struggle—a triumph won with fierce, fighting virtues by men not afraid to face the strenuous life. True, reason and self-control gave the man at the pinnacle of civilization a competitive edge over those who were more "barbaric." But reason and restraint were only helpful if they were attached to a core of combative strength and vigor. In this view, civilization could not exist without the male passions. They were honorable, they were creative, they were the primitive base on which all else rested—and, while they needed control and direction, they could not be lost or severely confined without enfeebling the civilization that rested on them.[20]

As we have seen, this ennoblement of manly passion expressed male rebellion against the "feminizing" influence of the separate spheres doctrine. It was also a reminder to women that life in the world of business and politics required the rough masculine virtues, and that world was not a suitable place for the delicate feminine sensibility. When men exalted male passion, their behavior had unexpected implications for the way in which manhood was defined. Through most of the century, a man had understood himself as the opposite of two people—a woman and a boy. He overcame the boy in himself by putting a tight rein on the male impulses that ran loose in a boy. With the revaluation of male impulse in the later years of the century, men were rethinking the relationship of manhood to boyhood.

The Manly Embrace of Boyhood

At the surface, the nineteenth-century middle class regarded boyhood fondly. The views of Rousseau and the romantic poets invested all children with innocence and spontaneity, and these views were reflected in popular sentimental images.[21] Boys and girls in the earliest years of life were portrayed alike as sweet, innocent lambs, just as their clothing marked them as fluffy, soft, and indistinguishable. Then, at about the same point in childhood when boys stepped into trousers, their image was changed. Now invested with a strong will and a full complement of physical skills, boys in pants were seen as rowdy, rude, and irresponsible.

The change was probably the result of deeper feelings about boys coming to the surface, feelings that expressed themselves in various ways: the father twiddling his infant son's penis into erection, for example, or adults giving "large-motor" toys to male toddlers and "small-motor" toys to females.[22] Underneath the sense—the hope—of childhood innocence, the nineteenth-century middle class believed deeply in sex difference. Ultimately, adults attached the new idea of the unblemished child to the girl (thus connecting her to female passionlessness), while attaching older notions of original sin to the boy (thus connecting him to men's passionate "nature"). In a sense, bourgeois culture cleansed Eve of her original sin, while letting Adam be Adam.

This negative valuation of boyhood showed up in many forms during the first three-quarters of the nineteenth century. Henry Coit, the first headmaster of St. Paul's School in New Hampshire, believed that boys were "possessed, in a greater or lesser degree, by the devil." A graduate of another boarding school, Phillips Academy in Andover, recalled that

Dr. Samuel Taylor—who headed the school from 1837 to 1871—was convinced of "the total depravity of the great majority of the boys . . . he ruled as if he believed they were far gone from righteousness."[23]

Casual word usage also suggests the negative image that boys carried. Thomas Wentworth Higginson, for instance, wrote of "a certain stigma of boyishness." In 1835, when men of all ages took to the streets in Utica, New York, to riot against the meeting of the state's antislavery society, the mob was denounced as a group of "vicious boys." Historian Mary Ryan has also noted that the "term 'boy' was often synonymous with prankster in the pages of the Utica press."[24]

It was these attitudes about the rough, impulsive nature of boyhood that led people to contrast it with the reason and restraint of manhood. Boyhood and manhood were distinct in another sense, too, since, for the urban middle class, men's world and boys' world were separate. Geographically, their realms did not overlap, except at home in the evening and on Sunday. And as phases of life, manhood and boyhood had little relation to each other. There was no career ladder or rite of passage to mark the change from boy to man.

Then, in the late nineteenth century, these patterns changed. Boyhood was glorified, boys' vices suddenly became men's virtues, and the two phases of life developed a more natural connection to one another. Men embraced boyhood at the same time that they were learning to value savagery, passion, and the embodied manhood of the athlete and the soldier.

The rising estimation of boyhood began with the growing regard for those childish traits that people considered more boyish than girlish—exuberance, spontaneity, a love of free play. In the middle to later years of the century, a negative image of tame children developed. The scornful terms that framed this image—"very odd old-mannish little boys," "not wild enough for a child"—suggest a positive new regard for the kind of energetic abandon that had made boys a target of criticism for so many years. Parents now grew anxious when their sons turned away from play.[25]

By the turn of the century, adults were endorsing boyish behaviors that they had once condemned. G. Stanley Hall asserted that a boy in his early teens "whom the lady teacher and the fond mother call a perfect gentleman must have something wrong with him." According to Hall, this was "the stage of roistering and youth must have a certain fling."[26] With such attitudes, bourgeois culture of the late nineteenth century was not really cleansing the sons of Adam of their sins, as it had already done for the daughters of Eve. Rather, it was turning those sins into virtues.[27]

In the process, another crucial image changed. For the upgrading of boyhood contrasted with the downgrading of adult manhood. Grown males were deemed not only ignorant but pompous, greedy, and egocentric as well. As Daniel Carter Beard entered adulthood, he "planned a world in which the boys might get together and make known their wants and ambitions, not a world of gray-headed philosophers or a world of money-getting baldheads or of selfish middle-aged people." Thomas Wentworth Higginson condemned adult men even more harshly, accusing them of trying "to bring insanity, once the terrible prerogative of maturer life, down into the summer region of childhood, with blight and ruin."[28] Boys may have always had such feelings, since they were small and powerless next to grown men; what was new in the late nineteenth century was that these feelings were expressed by their targets: adult men. Men of the comfortable classes were apparently growing up without renouncing the perceptions or the pleasures of boyhood.

These men were doing more than complaining about manhood. They intended to reform it, to rid it of its pomposity. They proposed to do this with massive infusions of boyishness. Beard's cure for "a world of gray-headed philosophers" and "money-getting baldheads" was "a world filled with men who still retained some of the urge of boyhood." In Beard's turn-of-the-century generation, men favored the saying that age is "simply 'a quality of the mind'" and praised the man advanced in years who "is still a young man." Thomas Wentworth Higginson complained of those who exalted "full-grown men" and "the dignity of manhood." "Full-grown men?" he wrote. "There is not a person in the world who can afford to be a 'full-grown man' through all the twenty-four hours." If men would only throw themselves "with boyish eagerness" into "games and sports" or "mere physical exertion," they would transform themselves.[29] Boyhood, in all its spontaneity and vigor, would embrace drab, overcivilized manhood. The child would be the savior of the man.

As men sought to transform themselves with an infusion of boyhood, they looked at their own sons and saw that they too were suffering from an excess of civilization. Rather than watch the sources of manliness stifled in boyhood, men devised new institutions to nurture and protect male impulse in the boy. Elite boarding schools were transformed from a model based on the patriarchal family to one based on boy culture. Moved from the antebellum boardinghouse into the postbellum dormitory, the student was now confined with a large number of other boys

under minimal supervision. He encountered competition, shifting hierarchies, cruelties, loyalties, and pranks, as he would have in boys' world
at home. Instead of returning to his family at night for peace and nurture, however, he had only more of "the crowding pressure, the weight
of numbers, the incessant chatter and clatter, remorseless and unending" in a boys' dormitory. This heroic dose of boyhood would cure overcivilized lads and turn them into men, or so the thinking went.[30]

Middle-class men, for the most part, did not send their sons to elite
schools; but they prescribed a similar medicine in the hope of curing
boys of the disease of feminized upbringing.[31] The doses for middle-
class boys were small and carefully measured, and they were to be administered by men and not by other boys. In the late nineteenth century,
a wide variety of organizations began to work with boys. The churches
started organizations like the Knights of King Arthur, while outdoor
groups like the Sons of Daniel Boone and the Woodcraft Indians proliferated, and the YMCA plunged energetically into activity for boys. The
ultimate organization, of course, was the Boy Scouts of America, which
was founded somewhat later in 1910. These organizations meant to in-
troduce coddled boys to the wilderness, to competition, to hardy play
and strenuous virtue. In these boys' groups as at boarding schools, men
were intervening to provide "boyish" experiences so that boys would not
lose touch with the sources of manhood. A new and very positive vision
of the relationship between boyhood and manhood was emerging.[32]

As men exalted boyhood and questioned the restrictions placed on
middle-class manhood, the two phases of life seemed to converge in
concept. One indicator of this convergence comes from the fact that, in
the second half of the nineteenth century, grown men were ever more
likely to be called boys.[33] The impetus for this habit of speech may have
come from mothers who still thought of adult sons as boys. It was common in the late 1800s for women to call grown sons their "boys" or even
their "babies." The habit spread from that relationship to courting and
married couples. Women boasted of their familiarity with "the little
child that lies hidden in the manhood of our husbands," while some husbands and fiancés liked to call themselves "your boy" when writing to
the women they loved.[34] Men also identified themselves as boys in contexts far removed from the male-female bond. On his forty-fifth birthday
in 1882, John Burroughs boasted in his journal that he was "much of a
boy yet at heart." In 1892, Edward Bok wrote in a *Ladies' Home Journal*
editorial that "We men are after all, but grown up boys."[35]

The great appeal of boyishness to men is evident in some of America's
greatest turn-of-the-century heroes. After the closing of the frontier, the

nation's veneration of the independent Westerner focused on a man identified as a child: the cow*boy*. This hero was a man in his exploits but as heedless of civilized restraint as a boy. The era's greatest idol, Theodore Roosevelt, embodied many of the traits associated with boyhood: energy, candor, curiosity, impatience, combativeness, impulsiveness, a keen sense of fun, and even a high noise level. Just as the public identified Roosevelt with the appeal of boyhood, he and his friends identified him as an overgrown boy. "You must always remember," wrote one associate, "that the President is about six." When Roosevelt himself was asked why he had, in his fifties, gone on a dangerous expedition up the Amazon, he replied, "I had to go. It was my last chance to be a boy."[36]

An equally striking reversal was the growing tendency to label certain kinds of boys as "manly." In 1871, a teenage girl wrote for publication in a boys' newspaper an ode in praise of "our, noble manly boys." Twenty years later, an educator asserted that: "Boys among boys are ashamed to be unmanly." And Theodore Roosevelt, in an essay on American boys, prescribed that "the boy should be manly and able to hold his own."[37]

The erosion of cultural and social barriers between boyhood and manhood led ultimately to new relations between generations of males. Some fathers in the late nineteenth century breached formal authority and sought a new familiarity with their sons, following the urge, as one man put it, to "call our sons 'pals.'" At the same time, teacher-student relations at boarding schools were shifting. As the belief in the educative power of boyhood replaced the belief in boyhood depravity, the men at these institutions took a more egalitarian role. A boarding-school teacher became something of a manly older brother to his students—a model, a guide, a friend.[38]

With men seeking to preserve the boy inside them, with boys cultivating their manly qualities, and with the elders relating to youngsters as peers, the notions of boyhood and manhood were converging. The two stages of life had not entirely dissolved into one another, but they were now seen as different phases in the unfolding of the very same male essence.

This trend was reflected in the construction of a new set of developmental customs that provided a firm structure for the close new connection between boyhood and manhood. The habit of dressing young boys like young girls began to change at the turn of the century. Male children moved into trousers at age two or three, not six or seven. Now, a boy would have no clear memory of wearing anything other than pants.[39]

More dramatically, men at the start of the twentieth century were shaping the world of boyhood more closely than they had done one hun-

dred years before. The most sweeping changes came in the reordering
of education. Schooling in the northeastern states had been loose and
unsystematic through most of the nineteenth century, and there had
been no well-defined ladder of ascent to provide a sense of relation between boyhood and manhood.[40] In the last two decades of the century,
this system changed suddenly and drastically. Compulsory education
laws were passed, feeding children through systems that were tightly organized into age-graded ladders of ascent. The school year, traditionally
varied in length, fell into a nine-to-ten-month standard. Public high
schools proliferated. College education became more common as public
universities sprang up in every state, and the route to college lay directly
through public or private secondary schools. More middle-class jobs had
formal education requirements. Positions in the new worlds of engineering and corporate management sometimes required a college degree,
and the modern arrangement of professional schools emerged in law
and medicine.[41]

For a middle-class boy (or one who might aspire to middle-class status), there was now a ladder of ascent—with each rung carefully
marked—that led up through the primary and secondary grades, into
college, and on, if necessary, to postgraduate education. A schoolboy
could look up that ladder and know precisely when he would become a
man and what he had to do to reach that point. The rungs of that ladder
could tell him exactly where he was on his journey to manhood. Gone
were the eccentric routes of access, the vague age boundaries, and the
mysterious requirements. Gone, too, was the indulgence of idiosyncrasy
and of the slow, circuitous approach. To achieve manhood, one no longer
gathered experience—one met prerequisites.

At the same time that this system of ascent was developing, boyhood
was undergoing another change that set it in closer relation to manhood.
That change involved the shaping of boys' activities by men, a change
that was most evident in the development of modern sports. As we
know, baseball evolved out of a myriad of boys' ball games involving
some sort of home base. At first, male youth developed several variants
of baseball with nonstandardized rules. Eventually, employers formed
teams of young adults, and finally the very best players—without any
common affiliation—formed themselves into clubs on the basis of expertise. They smoothed out variations into one set of rules by the 1850s, and
the formal ball clubs provided popular entertainment which local boys
watched avidly. They, in turn, began to play the standardized version of
the game.

In a sense, boys had lent their game to adults and borrowed it back in a very different form. Once, they had played the game for fun and exercise and to establish the superiority of individual talents. Then adults took over the game and invested it with their own preoccupations. By the time boys relearned the game from their older athletic heroes, elaborate team competition had become the whole point of baseball. The common understanding of the game had changed so thoroughly that a man in the early twentieth century was shocked when he discovered a group of boys playing ball without caring who won or even keeping score.[42]

At the turn of the century, men seized control of another realm of boys' activity—the high school and college extracurriculum. We have seen that the extracurriculum had originally evolved to make up for the inadequacies of the college curriculum. The students themselves had founded literary societies and debating clubs in the early 1800s, and then formed athletic programs and student governments and newspapers later in the century. These teams and student organizations were funded and run by students with no assistance from the colleges until the 1880s and 1890s.[43]

At that point, the colleges moved to take control of the extracurriculum. Where they had once treated student societies and athletics as a noisy diversion from the serious academic purposes of the college, administrators by the late nineteenth century viewed them as a splendid tool for building manly character. For clubs and societies, the college provided money, space, legitimacy, and a faculty adviser who could offer continuity and set limits on behavior. For athletic teams, the administration hired coaches, bought equipment, provided facilities, arranged schedules, and tightened the rules of the game.[44]

During the 1890s, college life (primarily the extracurriculum) achieved a glamorous aura in the eyes of the public. This image, combined with the persuasive arguments of college administrators about the value of student activities, had a powerful impact on the public high schools that were springing up at the end of the nineteenth century. School superintendents and high school principals created an extracurricular realm at the new secondary schools that directly and consciously imitated that of the colleges. These high school clubs and teams bore even more of an adult imprint than those at the collegiate level. That was especially important, because it was in its high school form—as an adult-sponsored "learning experience"—that the extracurriculum affected the largest numbers of male youth. The extracurriculum as shaped by adults taught institutional loyalty, hard work, and competitive advancement—all in a spirit of "boyish" or "youthful" fun.[45]

Thus, grown men came to exercise greater control over boys' time and activity at the end of the nineteenth century. They established a clearer, more continuous link between boyhood and manhood, and they extended their sway over a larger portion of boyhood by extending the time and importance of schooling and by shaping boys' activities in accordance with their own concerns. In taking over boys' play, men's purpose was to foster habits they saw as crucial to manhood—group rivalry, competitive advancement, the rejection of luxury and ease, a spirit of vigorous ambition. They believed that these qualities came to boys more naturally than to men, and that it was therefore easier to nurture them and turn them into habits early in life. Men were seeking to cultivate the same "boyish" male essence in boys that they were trying to preserve or revive in their own adult selves.

Of course, boys continued to maintain their own sort of folk culture, with customs, rites, and values that one age group passed on to the next. As adults demanded more of boys' time and supervised it more closely, however, the culture of boyhood built itself increasingly around the team sports, the organized activities, and eventually the media images and symbols that grown men presented to boys. At the very time when the concepts of boyhood and manhood developed a closer, more organic relationship, the phases of life called boyhood and manhood were set more clearly in relationship to one another. No longer opposites, manhood and boyhood were established as different stages in the development of the same male nature.

Since manhood was no longer defined by its opposition to boyhood, its opposition to womanhood became that much more important, and even that relationship was in flux. While male and female remained contrary in definition, the place of women and of femininity in a man's life had become a delicate subject. That delicacy in itself would ultimately breed changes in the definition of manhood.

The Woman Within

In the 1880s and 1890s, there were some bourgeois men who found themselves with new habits and pursuits that were marked "feminine." Certain husbands were turning to their wives for intimacy and friendship. Fathers were engaging more often in the lives of their children. There is also evidence to suggest that turn-of-the-century men had become involved in such domestic details as home decoration. Historian Margaret Marsh has pointed out that there was even an advice literature in this era which prescribed "masculine domesticity."[46] Yet this phrase in itself suggests trouble for men. Within the governing metaphors of gender, *masculine domesticity* was a contradiction in terms. It presumed that men could—and should—carry out female tasks for which their male nature did not fit them. If a man was spending more time at home exercising the skills which supposedly belonged to women, what kind of a man was he?

Outside the domestic arena, other patterns of male experience were feeding men's self-doubt and confusion: the declining opportunity for manly autonomy in business and the professions; the rising tide of male neurasthenia in an era that viewed illness as a female weakness; and a new male preoccupation with rest and tranquility.[47]

Another symptom of femininity that crept into the lives of bourgeois males in the late nineteenth century was a growing fondness for leisure and ease. Henry Ward Beecher, the popular minister of the comfortable middle class, announced the value of leisured enjoyment as early as the 1850s. He told his Brooklyn congregation again and again: "You can afford, when you have done your best, to take things easy and enjoy yourself."[48]

The new belief in enjoyment often expressed itself in private correspondence. In 1885, long after he had achieved fame as a writer and minister, Edward Everett Hale vowed "to lead as leisure a life as is possible,—and, in short, be free of fancy to make myself a lazy gentleman of [fortune?], who has nothing to do but to have a good time." Charles Van Hise could not muster such self-indulgent language, but even he—a man of austere habits and ferocious energy—could admit the value of pleasure. He expressed this feeling in an 1897 letter to his wife, Alice: "A good time in the highest sense is not to be laughed at especially as one does not live more than once, in this world at least."[49] Van Hise's reflections on pleasure, like those of Hale and Beecher, were not a call to license or debauchery, but a justification of enjoyment once hard work had brought success. Still, however measured these calls for fun may have been, they represented a new language of self-indulgence that violated republican tenets of manhood.[50]

The specter of femininity seemed to emerge from more and more of a man's activities and impulses late in the nineteenth century. These male desires violated middle-class expectations of manliness and so raised questions about the present status and future direction of manhood.

Presumably men had possessed "feminine" tendencies throughout the nineteenth century, but something was encouraging their expression more strongly (or inhibiting their expression less effectively) as the century drew to a close. Different tendencies undoubtedly had roots in different sources. The quest for domestic pleasures, for instance, may have been a response to the changes of opportunity in the middle-class workplace, and the longing for repose may have reflected the accelerating pace of urban life. What brings these disparate tendencies together under one rubric is the issue of gender.

We know that the expectations for the sexes that developed at the start of the century were sharply contrasting, and that the symbolic spaces of the two spheres were clearly marked and highly distinct. Yet a boy lived in both of those spheres and was fully exposed to both sets of values. Indeed, at an early, impressionable age, he had closer, more extensive contact with women than with men, and part of a nineteenth-century mother's duty was to imprint her son with feminine values. To be sure, the boy later learned the values and patterns of behavior that his society labeled male, but they were laid over an earlier stratum of value and expectation that was considered female. For some boys, the male values became dominant; for others, the female held sway; most often, the two existed in competition for a boy's (and later a man's) loyalty. However he resolved the conflict, a middle-class male was always influenced by the feminine values that he learned in his most impressionable years.

If this analysis is correct, why did "feminine tendencies" of habit and thought emerge only in the late nineteenth century? After all, the constellation of gender values and child-rearing patterns that we have described here began to take shape around the start of the nineteenth century. The fact is that, where the effects of child-rearing are concerned, there will be a lag of decades between a change in childhood circumstances and the points in adulthood where various effects become visible. Moreover, the entire system of values and institutions that shaped gender in the nineteenth century did not snap into place as soon as the century started. They coalesced as a system over a decade or two. Then, year by year, they began to affect larger and larger numbers of people as more Americans were drawn into the matrix of middle-class life. Evidence suggests that, in the century's early decades, mother-son bonds were growing closer while fathers were moving further from the family orbit. Signs of many of the feminine trends described here—early cases of neurasthenia, yearnings for enjoyment and repose, occasional examples of marital intimacy—were appearing in the 1850s, especially among men raised in the 1810s and 1820s. About a generation later, the feminine tendencies arrived as a stronger, more visible cultural trend, with men born in the 1840s to 1860s notably affected. At the same time, external factors that elicited the tendencies—factors such as changes of opportunity in the middle-class workplace—emerged in the last quarter of the century.[51]

The feminine traits in question here were not intrinsically a problem. But in a society that elevated gender to such a high level of moral and political meaning, a man with feminine qualities was bound to face difficulties. The fear of womanly men became a significant cultural issue in the late nineteenth century, one discussed by men in a new, gendered language of manly scorn. Men in the late nineteenth century began to sort themselves out into hardy, masculine types and gentle, feminine types.

To be sure, this exercise in mutual sorting had been going on throughout the century. From the good boys and the bad boys of boy culture to the gender-coding of professions, the sifting process reflected the importance of gender as a social principle. The process was especially complex for men when virtue was tied so closely to the opposite sex. For example, Theodore Roosevelt, Sr., the father of the president, endured the teasing of his four older brothers about his purity and high-minded virtue. His brother Robert, an especially roguish fellow, disdained him as their mother's "darling innocent."[52] Since being manly and being good required such different behaviors, nineteenth-century men often sorted themselves (and each other) along a continuum between manliness and goodness.

In the final decades of the century, however, the terms of the sorting process began to change. First, virtue dropped out of the calculations. Autobiographies offer a clear measure of this shift in their treatment of "good" and "bad" boys. Memoirs written early in the century regarded boys just as their moral labels would suggest: a good boy was an exemplar of piety—and a rare occurrence; most boys were bad—brutish, sinful, and weak in the face of temptation. Then, in the autobiographies written in the last third of the century, the meanings of the labels changed. The bad boy was now the hero: the vigorous, assertive lad with spirit and spunk. The good boy had become a sort of wan villain, a dull, weak, submissive husk of a child. The bad boy was manly, the good boy was effeminate, and virtue simply did not matter.[53]

Goodness no longer distinguished one male from another in the late nineteenth century. Now, vigor and assertiveness separated true men from the rest. The separation of males into the tough and the tender—the manly and the unmanly—produced cultural types in the late nineteenth century that gained tremendous importance. Their resonance for

men of that era can be found in men's private writing. An 1889 letter
from Richard Cabot to his future wife, Ella Lyman, deals with these two
types at length. In the letter, Richard tried to explain the contrast between himself and Ella's friend George Morison by describing what they
did during the summer in the mountains:

> This life here in camp with its music and reading and writing and seeing
> people and sketching and paddling slowly round the edge of silent
> ponds.—imagine how he would hate it,—it suits me to a T. His long
> rough-camp excursions or tramps would be almost entirely tasteless and
> useless to me, the very salt of sane life gone—for him I see they are as
> good as camp is for me.

So far Richard's description was neutral: a vast gulf between two
types—contemplative, quiescent, aesthetic; robust, dynamic, aggressive.
But Richard went on to show which of them felt admirable and which
inferior. He reported with a sense of apology that "I have always fancied
[George] had to exercise charity not to look down on me. . . . I only tell
you all this, because it is a fair sample of one of my weak sides that I cannot easily know such men as him and other hearty and straight-forward
creatures."[54]

Richard Cabot faced a problem that Theodore Roosevelt, Sr., had not
confronted with his brothers. In the latter's era, the contrast between the
adventurous and the timid could be recast as that of the corrupt and the
virtuous. By the 1880s, however, the standard of virtue did less to support the manly worth of one who lacked dash and vigor. Whatever his
positive traits, Richard Cabot could not match up to "hearty, straightfor-
ward creatures."

A similar theme surfaced in an exchange of letters within the Eliot
family of Massachusetts. Young Charles Eliot, who was just about to
launch himself on a distinguished career as a landscape architect, was
seized by self-doubt during a trip to Europe. As he considered his professional future, he did not feel "so utterly incompetent" in "matters of
theory and taste"; rather, it was "in the more practical affairs of the profession, and particularly in dealing with men, that I am nowhere." He
was slow to reach "definite opinions," and that made him feel unsuited
for the masculine give-and-take of professional life: "I am most at a loss
when thrown with other men. I cannot think and at the same time talk
and give attention. I am never at my ease,—indeed, I am as far as possible from being so. . . . I know myself to be ill-made, or, as it were, an un-
baked loaf of the human bread-batch."[55]

The response from Charles's father, one of Harvard's most distinguished presidents, stressed their differences of character. The senior Eliot told his son: "I wish you were tough and strong like me." His advice recognized that his son was less "tough and strong" than the average man: "Where other men work eight hours a day, you must be content with five." Somewhat gratuitously, the father pointed out a few lines later: "I am strong and can work twelve hours a day." He did emphasize the young man's virtues, especially his "unusual capacity for enjoyment," but, in doing so, he pointed out that "you closely resemble your mother." In the father's mind, he and his son both had admirable traits, but his were robust and manly while his son's were sensitive and feminine.[56]

The Eliots, like Richard Cabot, were part of Boston's elite, but the contrast they presented between the strong and the sensitive man was common to less wealthy men as well. This is evident in the letters which James Cattell wrote to his father, Will. James often compared Will's energy and ambition to his own reticence and indecision. Will was an official of the Presbyterian Church—a minister and a former college president—while James was a graduate student who staunchly resisted his father's efforts to obtain him a university professorship. After receiving a letter in which the older man had criticized a relative with diffuse ambitions, the younger man replied, "I cannot help smiling sadly, Papa, whenever you describe Cousin Jo to me for I know that you are however unconsciously, talking and writing at me." James felt that he—reflective and uncertain—compared poorly with his forceful, decisive father: "You are a remarkable man, Papa, for you have a strong intellect and . . . character, and your affections are not wishy-washy, but a temperament like yours is apt—say in the second generation—to degenerate."[57]

Like other men of his time, Cattell leaned on powerful new cultural types. His generation in particular—men born from the 1840s to the 1860s—became preoccupied with the contrast between the strong, assertive man and the gentle contemplative one.[58] The preoccupation was rooted in personal experiences and reflections like those of Cabot, Eliot, and Cattell, but other men began to elaborate private types into public archetypes. By the twentieth century, the two cultural types had become a popular metaphor, a simple cluster of symbols that ordered and explained great matters of human life and society.

One thinker who seized on this metaphor was William James. James was a neurasthenic, a contemplative man averse to physical action, a man who stayed at home on grounds of health while his peers fought in the Civil War.[59] In other words, James came naturally to the theme of the assertive and the reflective. In developing the concepts of the "tender-minded" and the "tough-minded," James expanded this personal motif into a grand philosophical typology.

In 1906 and 1907, James delivered a series of lectures that became the keystone of pragmatism, America's most distinguished school of formal thought. He used the first lecture to describe two philosophical temperaments which, he said, were reconciled by pragmatism. One temperament preferred an empirical, materialist approach to problems, the other an abstract, idealist approach. James chose to call the former "tough-minded" and the latter "tender-minded." Living in a time when men were preoccupied with their own toughness and tenderness, James's choice of words was significant. He was speaking in a language that would resonate with other men's experience.[60]

Symbolically, James was integrating the male and female in philosophy and perhaps within himself as well. As he did this, he strove to be neutral—and he succeeded partially. His formal analysis recognized the values and problems of both the tough-minded and the tender, yet the structure of the first lecture betrayed a need to criticize the tender-minded more extensively. After treating briefly the shortcomings of tough-minded empiricism, James devoted nearly half of the lecture to his frustrations with the abstract idealism of the tender-minded.[61] If an observer intent on neutrality tilted toward the tough, it is not surprising that other men with more partiality than James praised the tough at the expense of the tender. In elaborating these cultural types into a metaphor with broad explanatory power, commentators turned male tenderness from a mixed blessing or a personal flaw into a social danger.

Theodore Roosevelt saw the tender, scrupulous man as a threat to the nation, and the tough, assertive one as a national savior. The basic formula of his "Strenuous Life" speech—a formula he repeated countless times in the early twentieth century—was to attack the man of gentle scruples as a symbol and cause of national decline, and then embody the country's greatest virtues in the man of bold assertiveness.[62] A typical version of Roosevelt's attack runs like this:

> The timid man, the lazy man, the man who distrusts his country, the overcivilized man, who has lost the great fighting, masterful virtues, the ignorant man, and the man of dull mind, whose soul is incapable of feeling the mighty lift that thrills "stern men with empires in their brains"— all these . . . shrink from seeing the nation undertake its new duties. . . . These are the men who fear the strenuous life, who fear the only national life which is really worth leading. They believe in that cloistered life which saps the hardy virtues in a nation, as it saps them in the individual.[63]

By contrast, Roosevelt insisted that the "highest form of success" would come "to the man who does not shrink from danger, from hardship, or from bitter toil, and who out of these wins the splendid ultimate triumph." To Roosevelt, that triumph was the achievement "of true national greatness," and in the context from which he spoke, such greatness meant a dominant role in world politics.[64] Men of tender minds and gentle spirits hesitated to take on that role.

Another sweeping use of the tough-and-tender contrast came from the thinking of psychologist G. Stanley Hall. He claimed, in a less direct fashion than Roosevelt, that the gentle, restrained male—and the array of symbolic forces that created him—were a threat to civilization, if not to the progress of evolution itself. In his groundbreaking work on personal development, Hall subscribed to the theory of recapitulation, the idea that the individual human developed in stages that repeated the evolution of the species. Significantly, Hall marked off separate tracks for male and female development. It was in tracing those two separate courses that he came to focus on the effeminate male and the manly male.

A highly developed differentiation of the sexes, in Hall's view, was both a sign of and a necessity for civilization. The period of life in which sex difference emerged was the period on which Hall focused his attention: adolescence. To Hall, adolescence was "a very critical period" when "modern man" built "a new and higher story . . . upon the basis of the older foundation of humanity." It was crucial, he believed, that the period of adolescence grew longer "as we proceed from barbaric to civilized man," because the richer complexity of true civilization took longer to mature. Hall also considered this a critical period because development in adolescence was more easily arrested than in earlier childhood, and an arrest in this period was harder to make up at another stage.[65]

Thus, the vital process of sex differentiation had to go forward smoothly at this stage if individual development and human evolution were to progress. Hall said of adolescent development, "Differentiation ought to be pushed to the very uttermost and everything should be welcomed that makes men more manly and women more womanly; while, on the other hand, all that makes for identity is degenerative."[66] Thus, by Hall's definition, feminine traits in a teenage boy (or masculine traits in a teenage girl) were threats to progress and marks of developmental failure. An adolescent boy with a feminine character was simply degenerate. In other words, a tender-minded boy with a gentle, reflective nature was an evolutionary mistake, clearly inferior to his tougher, more assertive peers. As Hall said, a teenage male who is "a perfect gentleman has something the matter with him."

The idea that human culture might in any way affect sex differentiation—or the way in which *manly* and *womanly* are defined—was anathema to Hall. He insisted that "natural segregation has pervaded every stage of history and every form of society from savagery up, and has an immense momentum of heredity behind it. It is not merely custom and tradition, as feminists are wont to assume, but the authoritative voice of nature herself."[67] By Hall's logic, feminists—and their male sympathizers—were blind to heredity, deaf to nature, and an impediment to civilization. According to Hall, the restrained youth and the assertive youth were more than neutral images—they were moral symbols in the progress of the human race.

Thus, the tender, reflective male and the tough, assertive one became cultural symbols as well as social types. The former not only bore the social stigma of male femininity in a society that elevated gender separation to the highest level of principle, but he also was a threat to his nation and even to the progress of human civilization. To have too much of "the woman within" was a personal problem for a man in the late nineteenth century. More than that, it made him a living symbol, a moral and social mistake.

The issue of the feminized male found a reflection in the changing language of manhood—and that language, in turn, provided an ongoing framework in which the issue was defined. The change is most visible in the language of politics. Because the political arena was by law a male club throughout the nineteenth century, politicians often used gendered imagery to mark the bounds of acceptable behavior—and to place their opponents outside those bounds. The history of those terms of scorn reveals crucial changes in the identification of men with women.

Male femininity as a part of American political language had its roots in republicanism. Luxury, idleness, and materialism were scorned by republicans as effeminate. By association, aristocratic pretensions were a mark of effeminacy. Thus, in the nation's early history, republican simplicity was manly, and the self-indulgence of the rich was womanly.[68] Charges of effeminacy became most extreme—and most effective—after the vote was extended to all white males, regardless of property.

In 1828, the Jacksonians used the issue of class resentment effectively against John Quincy Adams, when they charged him with bringing effeminate luxuries and amusements into the White House. The taint of aristocratic vice as a marker of unmanliness worked so well in smearing Adams that the Jacksonians came back to it again in their assault on the national bank. Martin Van Buren, for instance, produced a gem of gendered republican rhetoric. He charged that national banking tended:

> to produce throughout society a chain of dependence, to nourish in preference to the manly virtues that give dignity to human nature, a craving desire for luxurious enjoyment and sudden wealth, which renders those who seek them dependent on those who supply them; to substitute for republican simplicity and economical habits a sickly appetite for effeminate indulgence.[69]

As political historians have long noted, the opponents of Jackson then hung Van Buren with his own noose in the election of 1840. They labeled him successfully as an effeminate man with perfumed side-whiskers, golden spoons, and corsets to hide his ample girth.[70]

In the antebellum era, politicians also discovered that reformers from outside the political system made ripe targets for gender-laden contempt. Male abolitionists were accused of fighting "from behind the whale-bone and cotton padding of their female allies."[71] Even though reform causes shifted after the Civil War, the imagery of unmanliness continued to stick to reformers. George William Curtis, a leader of the Liberal Republicans who sought to cleanse the party of corruption, was, in 1877, the target of one of the most famous political attacks of that era. Roscoe Conkling, chieftain of the New York Republican Party, asked a party gathering: "Who are these men who are cracking their whips over Republicans and playing school-master to the Republican party and its conscience and convictions?" He answered his own question with devastating effect: "Some of them are the man-milliners, the dilettanti and carpet knights of politics. They forget that parties are not built by deportment, or by ladies' magazines or by gush."[72]

At the surface, Conkling was reminding Curtis and his reform allies that politics was a man's world, run by sterner principles than sentiment and good manners. Beneath that, he was using references to deportment, carpets, and ladies' magazines to associate reformers with the parlor society of women: they liked women and were like women. But in his use of the term *man-milliner* (the word for which the speech is most often remembered), Conkling was suggesting more than an association with women—for *milliner* alone would have done that. By using *man-milliner*, Conkling evoked the idea of a "man-woman."[73]

In the rhetoric of unmanliness, Conkling was participating in a significant change. The early nineteenth-century charges of effeminacy were

usually applied to abstractions ("effeminate virtue," "effeminate indulgence"), not to people.[74] But new forms of figurative language connecting men with femininity became popular in the late nineteenth century,
forms that unsexed a man, made him bisexual, or turned him into a
woman.

The most popular of these figures, which we might call the "third-sex"
metaphors, created a large gray area between man and woman where
male and female reformers existed. These freaks were sometimes portrayed as eunuchs, sometimes as hermaphrodites, and sometimes as a
monstrous new sex unto itself. An 1886 diatribe against reformers by
Senator John Ingalls of Kansas provides a vivid example. Male reformers
"sing falsetto," he said; they were "effeminate without being either masculine or feminine; unable to beget or bear; possessing neither fecundity
nor virility; endowed with the contempt of men and the derision of
women, and doomed to sterility, isolation, and extinction."[75]

Few charges of sexual ambiguity were so richly embellished as those
of Senator Ingalls, but he was by no means the creator of this invective
style. It was applied before the Civil War to women abolitionists ("unsexed females"), and after the war it was used frequently against members of either sex who favored women's suffrage or any other sort of
political reform. Reformers were "long-haired men and short-haired
women." If the dream of woman suffrage came true, women would "become taller and more brawny, and get bigger hands and feet, and a heavier weight of brain." Hand and foot size seemed a special concern of
those who followed the sexual transformation of reformers: a "mug-
wump" reformer was "a man who has small hands, small feet, a receding
chin and a culture much above his intellect." In sum, the men who
guarded the political arena imagined that acting on reform impulses unsexed a person.[76]

At the same time, a more direct and less mysterious transformation of
sexual language was taking place. Some unmanly men, instead of being
compared to women, were now *called* women. An early example of this
shift to metaphor came in an 1850 medical journal, where an article
spoke derisively of "the prudish Miss Nancies of Buffalo."[77] The men in
question here were not *like* Miss Nancy—they *were* "Miss Nancies."
This was a popular term of contempt in the late nineteenth and early
twentieth centuries, and received its most famous usage in 1916 when
Theodore Roosevelt, disgusted with Woodrow Wilson's refusal to enter
the Great War, referred to the president as a "white-handy Miss Nancy."
Similar terms, such as *old maid* and *Mary Jane*, became common during
the late nineteenth century. Moreover, sometimes women's names were

dropped in favor of simply calling a man a woman. For example, William Dean Howells noted that, in post–Civil War America, the professional writer was ridiculed as a "kind of mental and moral woman, to whom a real man, a businessman, could have nothing to say after the primary politenesses."[78]

A slightly less direct word became the most popular of all female terms for men—*sissy*. Originally a slang term for "little sister," it did not appear in the *Oxford English Dictionary* with reference to a male until the 1890s. Then, suddenly, four such usages appear and all of them come from the United States. Americans quickly seized on the word with an enthusiasm that suggests the fulfillment of a great need. At the turn of the century, a Massachusetts newspaper published an article on "sissyism" and struck such a responsive chord that several other newspapers and magazines printed their own speculations. When Rafford Pyke wrote an article for *Cosmopolitan* in 1902 on "What Men Like in Men," he made a digression about sissies that took up more than a third of the essay, well over a thousand words. In the minds of most people, said Pyke, a sissy was weak, slender, smooth-faced—like a woman; he was "polite and rather anxious to please"—like a woman; he was timid—like a woman; he was submissive—like a woman; and he especially liked the company of women. Given this description, it is little wonder that such a man was simply given a female label.[79]

As gendered terms of contempt switched in this fashion from simile to metaphor, the locus of a man's femininity shifted from external to internal, from likeness to identity. This was not historical accident. This shift happened in the late nineteenth century when men were discovering feminine habits and attitudes within themselves, encountering their own deep identification with female figures, contrasting tough and tender men to the detriment of the tender, and elaborating the tough-tender contrasts into grand metaphors in which feminine qualities in a man posed a threat to the nation and to human progress. At the historical moment when women seemed ready to break down the barriers between separate spheres, men were trying to redraw the lines of manly and womanly traits within the ranks of their own sex. To do this at a time when men seemed acutely aware of "the woman within" created painful problems.

In a society where gender distinctions seemed more important (and perhaps more sharply drawn) than ever, how could a man live comfortably with his own feminine side? The neurasthenic cycle could provide an outlet for men's inner division between the male and the female—with a vacation, rest, relaxation, perhaps a time of toughening, and then a return to work giving a man an excursion through women's proper pursuits and back into men's. In many cases, this meant ideas or patterns of work that focused on the conquest of feminine weakness. Certainly, the theories of former neurasthenics Theodore Roosevelt and G. Stanley Hall can be viewed in this light.

The cult of chivalry offered another approach to this gender dilemma. Already strong in the antebellum North, this phenomenon reached its peak at the end of the nineteenth century.[80] The chivalric fantasy encouraged men to pursue virtuous, feminine aims by manly, aggressive means. In the political arena, the progressives acted out this fantasy of the Christian Soldier—but, sensitive to the way in which previous generations of reformers had been mocked by charges of effeminacy, male progressives often adopted a rhetorical tone that was stridently masculine. Studies of individual progressive males show that they came from especially sheltered domestic environments where they were infused with values and habits their society denoted as feminine.[81] The tone and direction of the movement was affected from beginning to end by the struggles of men who sought to escape from "the woman within" even as they tried to appease her.

The progressive solution to this configuration of gender, politics, culture, and psychology seemed to run its course by 1920. This same generation, however, in its fevered attempts to deal with internalized feminine values, left a more lasting legacy to the definition of manhood, based on the manner in which men of the late nineteenth and early twentieth centuries responded to the homosexual communities then emerging in the nation's great cities.

The Soul of a Woman in the Body of a Man

The late nineteenth century marked a watershed in the history of homosexuality in the United States. The two major developments were: the growth of areas in major cities where those interested in sexual relations with members of their own sex could meet and develop a sense of community; and a distinct change in the way society viewed that sexual behavior and those people.

In the rapidly growing cities of the early nineteenth century, people with an abiding erotic interest in others of their own sex had begun to find each other. With so many humans gathered in one place, those with a same-sex orientation enjoyed an anonymity that would have been impossible in small towns. Besides, large cities, by their very size, were more likely to have a critical mass of residents who wanted to engage in forbidden forms of behavior. Also, acts of same-sex love, although they were illegal, were rarely prosecuted in major urban areas before the Civil War.[82]

Then, in the decades after the war, the situation changed. Whether from constant accretion of numbers or from growing internal cohesion, homosexual communities became more visible.[83] By the 1880s, prosecution became more frequent in large cities, and medical and social scientists developed a great interest in same-sex eroticism. These scholars began to shift the focus of attention from homosexual acts to the people who engaged in them. This shift from the act to the person coincided with an attempt to develop a more precise theory of what caused homosexual desire. At first, the dominant belief was that homosexuality was a degenerative disease, then, early in the new century, the consensus shifted to the idea that homosexuality was in-born.[84]

These theories had two important implications for the common view of homosexuals. The first was a change of understanding that shifted the roots of such desire from outside of nature—as late as 1866 it was called a "crime" that was "unnatural"—to a condition with natural causes.[85] The shift is indicated in a statement made in 1882 by a man struggling to deal with his love for other men, who believed that there are "those who are forced by nature to follow the inclinations of a diseased and perverted instinct."[86]

If homosexuality had natural, biological causes, it could no longer be seen as an episodic visitation from without. Now, it was a desire from within that formed a continuous part of a person's physical makeup. Instead of identifying the event ("unnatural act," "crime against nature," "sodomy") as the core of same-sex eroticism, the descriptive language turned its emphasis to the individual. In the last two decades of the nineteenth century, a whole new set of words came into being (*degenerate, pervert, invert, fairy, homosexual*) which labeled the person as the essence of the homoerotic. In less than a generation, the language for this phenomenon transformed itself into a language of personal identity.[87]

Most of these new words issued from the ideas of the scholars and physicians,[88] but the outside experts were not alone in building the perception of homosexuality as a social and personal identity. In these same years, men and women whose sexual desires focused on their own sex began to think of themselves as separate social groups. Those who lived in large cities formed communities within the whole, an experience that fostered a sense of "us" and "them." As John D'Emilio and Estelle

Freedman have written, such "women and men were self-consciously departing from the norm and creating a social milieu that nurtured their emergent sense of identity." This notion that a person's sexual nature determined the person's personal and social identity was part of a larger current of thought. Havelock Ellis, the eminent British sexologist, expressed the growing belief of his American counterparts that "sex penetrates the whole person; a man's sexual constitution is part of his general constitution. There is considerable truth in the dictum: 'A man is what his sex is.'"[89]

If one's sexuality defined one's identity and one's true inner self, then what was the true nature of male homosexuality?[90] How, that is, did observers and homosexuals themselves interpret the meaning of this newly defined identity? The answer is that both groups equated male homosexuality with womanhood. George Beard, the neurasthenia expert, summarized the view of many interested observers in 1884 when he wrote that those for whom "the sex [instinct] is perverted . . . hate the opposite sex and love their own; men become women and women men, in their tastes, conduct, character, feelings, and behavior."[91] The comments of Chicago vice investigators in 1911 typify the observations of those who described homosexual men. Such "inverts" "mostly affect the carriage, mannerisms, and speech of women [and] . . . are fond of many articles dear to the feminine heart."[92]

The statements of some male homosexuals themselves are actually quite close to those of the men who studied them.[93] They echoed the German lawyer who defended the morality of his fellow homosexuals, asserting that they had women's souls trapped in the bodies of men. An American man put the same idea in different words when he said that "my feelings are exactly those of a woman. . . . As near as I can explain it, I am a woman in every detail except external appearances." Other men expressed the same feelings in action. At drag balls and parties and at clubs where male prostitutes worked, men dressed as women, called each other by women's names, and sometimes spoke or sang in womanly falsetto.[94]

Thus, the observations of the late nineteenth-century men who studied male homosexuals coincided with the testimony and behavior of some of the men they studied on a fundamental point: male homosexuals were like men who became women. Even when observers misidentified a man's sexual orientation, their mistakes revealed the same bias. Some transvestites were heterosexual in their object choice, but because they dressed like women, they were mistaken for homosexuals; and men who assumed the "male" roles in same-sex relationships were often identified as "straight." In both cases of confused identification, the confusion grew out of the same assumption: that a male homosexual was a man who looked and acted like a woman, not a man who engaged in homosexual activity.[95]

This was a natural—and revealing—assumption in an era when men were preoccupied with the woman inside the man. Where homosexuality had been seen as an evil event, with its roots outside of human nature, now the act itself became an expression of a broader personal identity, a revelation of an inner essence. That essence was a statement about gender.

Homosexuality, like any other erotic urge or activity, takes on the trappings provided for it by the culture in which it appears. The trappings that middle-class culture provided in the late nineteenth century were outgrowths of its obsession with—and anxiety about—gender. The drag balls and parties of the homosexual community and the female impersonation in amateur theatricals at colleges and men's clubs can be seen as similar expressions of a fascination with "the woman within." We have seen that there were many outlets for men's feminine attitudes and impulses, ranging from the cycle of neurasthenic breakdowns to the "women's" reform role played by many progressives. The emergence of male homosexuality in its modern form was in two different ways an expression of the woman within. For men with powerful homoerotic urges and female identifications, the role of the effeminate homosexual served to express those identifications and urges. For men with strong female identifications and homoerotic urges that were controllable, weak, or only feared or suspected, the categorizing and conceptualization of the homosexual provided an outlet—a screen onto which men could project their unacceptable urges and identifications.

Indeed, there was a bond of sorts between those male homosexuals who were effeminate and their observers/labelers. Just as certain amateur theatricals were based on the link between the men who liked to play women and the spectators who were fascinated to see a woman played by a man, so the emerging definition of the homosexual as a male woman was based on a bond between some homosexual men who liked to project femininity and the scholar/spectator who needed to see a woman played by a man. It was no accident that the effeminate homosexual and his official observer both described him as a woman in the body of a man, for they were drawing on the same cultural obsession of the woman within. Nor was it an accident that the male homosexual who played the man's role was often excluded from the emerging public definition of *homosexual*. For this new definition was about more than homoeroticism—it was about a need to create a category of person who could represent men's unacceptable feminine impulses. It was also about the preoccupation of bourgeois culture with dividing all things (including the male sex) into male and female—and then applying its own set of gender roles to the division.

Thus, the male homosexuals who attracted public attention in the late nineteenth century provided a sort of mirror to the men who examined them. These particular homosexuals developed an identity for themselves that drew on the same fund of images and anxieties that their observers used. It was their observers, however, who defined homosexual identity in the eyes of the larger society. And that identity reflected above all else the gender preoccupations of the observers.

The image of the male homosexual played an especially important role in the redefinition of middle-class manhood that was taking place at the turn of the century. The effeminate homosexual provided a negative referent for the new masculinity, with its heavy emphasis on the physical marks of manliness. The emergent homosexual image soon acquired an awesome power to stigmatize. By the turn of the century, men were using the same terms of scorn for homosexual males that they used for artistic, tender-minded, or reformist men. For instance, the terms *Nancy* and *Miss Nancy*, which were already labels for heterosexual men who were insufficiently manly, were in use by 1899 as names for homosexual men.[96]

The homosexual male and the man who was insufficiently manly were understood in the same figures of speech. The latter was a sissy, an old maid—metaphorically, he was a woman. The former had the soul of a woman trapped in the body of a man; he and his kind were "men become women." The longer the association lasted between the homosexual and the unmanly man, the greater the power of the homosexual label to stigmatize any man.[97]

The stigma gained insidiousness from the modern notion that sexual "inversion" was not a beastly moral failure or an unnatural visitation, but a natural condition that might be lurking in anyone, regardless of the individual's purity or moral vigilance. This added urgency to a man's desire to distinguish himself from the homosexual. The more he feared he might be one of the stigmatized group, the more he needed to prove himself a man or—what was more difficult—come to terms with what was not manly about himself. Romantic friendship disappeared, as the sharp line was drawn between homosexual and heterosexual. Men with artistic sensitivities often cultivated a manly veneer; parents packed their sons off to boxing lessons or summer camps. Where the defining opposites of manhood had once been womanhood and boyhood, now they were womanhood and male homosexuality (the identity of the man who is a woman).

This change did not happen instantly. Men were still insulted by the epithet *boy*, and the slur of homosexuality did not develop all at once the devastating impact that it would possess by the late twentieth century. Still, though the stigma of homosexuality took time to reach its present status, it was a serious enough charge against someone's manhood even in the earliest years of the century. The creation of the homosexual image produced a deadly new weapon for maintaining the boundaries of manhood. Effeminacy had always been a troublesome accusation; now its force was becoming ruinous.

Individualism and Expressions of the Male Self

From the late eighteenth century to the early twentieth, the importance of the individual self grew constantly as the focus of American society and culture. But the history of the individual self during this period is really two distinct, if related, histories. One of these is the story of that autonomous social being, the "individual." The individual is a creature in relation to the state, the law, and the economy, a citizen and a public actor more than an inner being; its conceptual form in the nineteenth century owes most to the ideas of John Locke. Then there is a second and very different story, the history of the passionate or "romantic" self. Expressed in the work of Jean-Jacques Rousseau, the self is a spiritual and emotional concept, a secular version of the soul: the innermost core of the person, unique to each human being, the deepest substance that is left when all the layers of artifice and social convention are stripped away.[98] The contrasts are obvious: the individual is social, outward-facing; the personal self is inward-facing. Still, the two are related in fundamental ways. Historically, both moved dramatically out of the entanglement of custom and tradition during the late eighteenth century. Both can be seen as expressions of the American belief that the autonomous person is the basic unit of society and the ultimate source of cultural value.

Nevertheless, the two concepts are quite distinct and have very different histories in relation to gender. In the United States, individualism emerged as a governing idea in economics, politics, and law during the late eighteenth century. At the heart of individualism as Americans practiced it was the competitive pursuit of self-interest. Americans developed economic and political systems to harness competitive individualism for the creation of the greatest good. We have seen, however, that in practice this was a gender-specific idea. People feared the social side-effects of unrestrained individualism and constructed the metaphorical system of separate spheres to contain the damage wrought by the unchecked individual. Individualism was treated as a male phenomenon, while women were charged with control of the damage it might do to social relations and to personal well-being.

The public pursuit of self-interest was denied to women. The Seneca Falls Convention of 1848 used the language of one of individualism's sacred texts—the Declaration of Independence—to demand full individual rights for women.[99] Men, however, feared the destruction of social order and even sexual difference if they gave women those rights or allowed them full access to the learned professions and the business world. In the early twentieth century, even as women were achieving the right to vote, individualism was still a largely male prerogative.

The history of the passionate or romantic self is quite distinct from the history of individualism. The growing obsession with romantic love in the early nineteenth century did suggest that the cultural value of the passionate self was rising, but middle-class Americans of the 1800s often viewed the inner movings of the self with Calvinistic suspicion. As a result, the passionate self in the nineteenth century was not a source of expression so much as an object of manipulation. Words in common use during the nineteenth century—*self-made*, *self-control*, *self-interest*, *self-government*, *self-abuse*—reveal a strong and varied habit of manipulating the personal self to meet other ends.

The history of the passionate self in the nineteenth century was just as gendered a history as that of individualism. The male self was a particular object of suspicion, full of selfishness, tyranny, and lust. The inner woman—tender, kind, limited in carnal feeling, though given to ease and vanity—merited trust far more than the inner man. While men were expected to assert their bold, competitive nature, and women felt a demand for their tenderness and virtue, self-expression was thought dangerous unless it was carefully channeled. In this context, the intimacy expected in a nineteenth-century courtship made troublesome demands. It required deep self-revelation, which presented a struggle for men and sometimes even for women.[100]

As the nineteenth century drew to a close, middle-class attitudes toward self-expression changed dramatically. This change revealed itself in several realms of life. One was courtship. Self-expression had long been a prominent goal of couples, but the goal had always been described in terms of "candor" and "sincerity." At the end of the century, men and women in love began to speak the language of self-expression directly. Vernon Wright, a young architect, told his fiancée in 1899, "it is good to know and share our innermost consciousness and we need more than anything else to get acquainted—to really know our own and each other's true selves."

The drive for self-expression appeared in many other settings. As Henry Seidel Canby recalls it in his autobiography, he and his friends at the turn of the century "were typical of an American mood, of a new generation's resolve to get closer to real desires." After the turn of the century, self-expression became an imperative for parents and children alike. "Self-expression for youth is supposed to have brought about the great change in family life," writes Canby. "It was a cause, but an equally powerful one was self-expression for parents."[101]

As some middle-class Americans at the turn of the century began to press for assertion of the passionate self in the face of social custom, formal thinkers were taking a similar position. In 1905, William James avowed his "faith in personal freedom and its spontaneity" against the "herding and branding, licensing and degree-giving, authorizing and appointing" that was typical of "civilization." During this period, a new generation of Americans was avidly reading the work of such pioneering sexual theorists as Havelock Ellis. Historians John D'Emilio and Estelle Freedman have written that Ellis saw sexuality as "the wellspring of an individual's nature." In this context, sexual expression became the expression of a person's deepest self.[102]

Thus, the history of the personal self in the United States was taking a sharp swing at the turn of the century. Where middle-class culture had treated the passionate self as somewhat suspect and an object for manipulation, now it held this self in high esteem, and viewed it as a source of pride, pleasure, creativity, and personal worth.

Yet the new self-expression often meant different things for the two sexes. Men's call for greater passion, their rebellion against "feminized civilization," and their wish for access to the "animal" and the "primitive" inside of themselves can all be understood in terms of a desire to express more of the male "essence." Those rougher passions had been so harshly censured by official middle-class culture that, in the later years of the century, men lashed back. They wanted their "true self" to receive some honor, and they wanted greater freedom to play—at home, among friends, in the wilderness, or on the golf course. These men also wanted to create institutions to nurture what they felt was valuable but threatened in a boy's true character.

Men were largely successful in this drive for self-expression. Competition, boldness, ambition—passions that had violated the nineteenth century's official, republican code of manhood—became desirable qualities. Moreover, these men succeeded in creating institutional forms for their self-expressive impulses: country clubs, boys' organizations, huge sports stadia, and the beginnings of the "weekend" (a custom which started with shortened hours on Saturdays for some executives and professionals).[103] They managed to build social support for their own self-expression, even as they blocked outlets and acceptance for some of the same impulses in women.[104]

However, men were frustrated in their own attempts at certain forms of self-expression, those that were intimate and domestic. We have noted some changes in men's private lives at the end of the nineteenth century: more engaged relationships with children; fuller sharing of the male self in marriage. There were calls to masculine domesticity, and there were some stern warnings that fathers should play a larger family role if they wanted to save the manliness of their sons.[105] But the men who heeded these calls were hindered by the values of manhood, which expressed themselves in the expectations of peers and in the reluctance and anxiety that came from within. The part of a man's inner self that sought expression through intimacy was that part—tender, dependent, vulnerable, warm—which suited him poorly for success at his worldly tasks in a competitive marketplace. Since rough virtues like assertive drive and contentious ambition were more fully accepted as official standards of manhood, the softer, more feminine virtues became increasingly suspect. In the early twentieth century, as new forms of manhood took shape around older designs of worldly success, the urge to express warmth and dependence—which may well have been growing—was still being squeezed to the margins of men's lives.[106]

With the expansion of income and leisure time for the middle class, another means of self-expression rose in importance at the start of the twentieth century: consumption. Producers of goods and services did their best to encourage consumption as a form of self-expression. Indeed, they sought to make it an irresistible habit. A sign of their intent is the fact that advertising outlays increased from $50 million in 1867 to $500 million in 1900.[107]

To describe the full range of consumer tastes that men indulged during the early twentieth century would require a book in itself. A few of the possibilities may be suggested by looking at new modes of entertainment for men. The commercialization of sport had started before the turn of the century, but its modern institutional forms, including the first modern baseball stadia, the World Series, and the football bowl game have their origins in this period. Brief, intense fads like the dance-hall craze of the early teens came and went, while durable entertainment institutions like the motion picture captured the middle-class fancy by 1920. Then, too, the male love affair with the automobile blossomed in the early twentieth century.

Some of these modes of entertainment—for example, the motion picture—provided self-expression in vicarious form; but others, such as the automobile, provided self-expression not only in the choice of a product but in its use and care as well. Increasingly, men (and women) of the early twentieth century expressed their personal selves through their choice of goods and services and the style in which they used them. Certain uses of leisure time and certain consumer tastes became marks of manliness—whereas one hundred years before, any fondness for leisure or material goods would have been scorned as effeminate. Earlier standards, rooted in republican simplicity, were now replaced by those of a consumer economy.[108]

At the same time, the drive for self-expression and the transformation of middle-class work changed the definition of the traditional male virtue of independence. Formerly, this had meant autonomy in personal relations as well as freedom from reliance on political and social authority. At the start of the twentieth century, the anxiety about reliance on authority was fading. Above all, men now viewed independence as a freedom from external restraints on self-expression.

Manhood was not completely transformed at the turn of the century. People still admired courage, dominance, and a propensity for action as manly virtues. Independence and reason, though their definitions had shifted, were also still valued as male traits. A new physical, assertive emphasis had entered the definition of manhood, however, and, in the case of leisure, play, and consumption, what had once been considered effeminate was now accepted as masculine. Individualism remained central to manhood, but self-expression now colored manhood's meaning and changed its aspect.

MANHOOD IN THE
TWENTIETH CENTURY

FROM the late eighteenth century to the late twentieth, "manhood" has changed along with its environment. Two centuries ago, the town and the extended family formed the matrix of life in the Northern states. For some, the church congregation also provided a society in which a man (or woman) might develop an identity. Now, at the end of the 1900s, those institutions have faded in importance for most middle-class folk. Our primary community is the nuclear family, which is an isolated unit under the best of circumstances—and current circumstances are not the best, for a large proportion of nuclear families are riven by divorce. The large bureaucratic institutions where so many middle-class men work resemble eighteenth-century communities in certain ways: they are hierarchical, and they make elaborate demands on the individual. Unlike the more genuine communities of the colonial and revolutionary eras, however, the great corporate bodies of our time do not provide the individual with security, nor with any sense of organized connection to other people or to the flow of human history.

In the twentieth century, some of our most engaging experiences of community come from our participation in communities of consumption.[1] To be moved as part of a concert audience or to discover someone who shares one's tastes can be exciting experiences, but neither of them guarantees the sense of personal connection or support that a human community can provide.

As many social critics have recently noted, we lack even the rudiments of a language to discuss community and connection.[2] This point is starkly illustrated when a president of the United States, trying to praise the voluntary help that some people give to others, resorts again and again to the image of "a thousand points of light" to describe what he praises. Surely, a society that valued connectedness would be able to produce a more accurate image of human help and kindness than this vision of separation in a vast, cold darkness.

Of course, in losing a strong sense of community, we have gained something else vitally important. Once, men had their positions in society ascribed to them largely by birth; now, those positions are a matter of individual achievement. The weight of the community and the dead hand of the past rest more lightly upon the individual—especially the male individual—than they once did. Individual initiative, as a principle, has been applied far beyond matters of social status. Middle-class men of the last two centuries have had profoundly individualistic experiences; each one must earn approval, win love, attain power, make friendship, mold an identity.[3] Since the early 1800s, these have all become individual quests. They are (as we like to think of it) detached from social necessity in a way that was not possible two hundred or more years ago. Even where we have genuine communities in our own time (be it in the nuclear family, in friendship groups, or in small, informal organizations), they are created by individual effort. We cherish our belief in individual initiative, our sense that the fate of each person lies in that person's hands.

We also cherish our modern notion that the core of each individual is an inner essence, a unique combination of temperament, passion, and personal experience untouched by society. This idea of a deep, true passionate self has been with us for at least two centuries, but not until the turn of the twentieth century did middle-class men and women begin to rethink the relationship between the self and the molding efforts of the individual. For the American bourgeoisie, the nineteenth century was a time of self-making, both in the economic sense and in the sense of shaping the desires and talents of the inner self to fit the proper moral and social forms. The twentieth century, by contrast, has been increasingly a time of self-realization, when individuals have worked to let their impulses and personal potentials flourish. In little more than a hundred years, the balance of bourgeois values has tipped from self-discipline to self-expression, from self-denial to self-enjoyment.

The true male nature is thought to deserve the same thing that any other portion of the deepest self deserves—an outlet in the real world. Men are still perceived as more aggressive, more primitive, more lustful, more dominating, and more independent than women—but how can these manly passions fit into the organized civilization of the twentieth century? This is nearly the same question that men and women asked at the start of the nineteenth century, when men's aggressive ambitions were set loose from the restraints of hierarchy and communal opinion; but the context for asking the question is very different today.

Middle-class observers at the dawn of the nineteenth century treated "male" passions—assertive and competitive drives—with fearful condemnation. The cultural structure of separate spheres was erected to allow expression of those drives for the greater economic and political good in a way that would also isolate them from sanctuaries of civilization and provide their male carriers with a source of constant purification. In the twentieth century, the competitive, aggressive drives—though still defined as male—are seen with less fear and more reverence. We think of them as vital contents of a man's true self in an era when the true self is regarded as sacrosanct. Although impulses to dominance and assertion are still viewed with some suspicion, there is general agreement that they can be productive and that they deserve a social outlet without stigma. This, in turn, raises an important question for twentieth-century men: What are the best outlets for the "male" passions in the twentieth century?

Men have developed several ideals of manhood that have offered answers to this question. One ideal is the "team player." Based on an ethic of sublimation, this ideal takes competitive athletics as a model for fitting aggression and rivalry into the new bureaucratic work settings of the twentieth century.[4] While a man struggles to reach the top within his own organization through fierce competition with his teammates, he also cooperates with them in the contest between his organization and others. In this way, the old investment of aggressive, selfish passions in economic competition has gained new life in the modern world.

Another strategy for establishing a relationship between male passion and modern life is represented by the "existential hero." This ideal grows out of a belief that there is, in fact, no proper place for true masculine impulse within modern society. The hero who lives by this belief is suspicious of authority, wary of women, and disgusted with corrupt civilization. If he would be true to the purity of his male passions and principles, he must—and can only—live at the margins of society. This romantic ideal has been embodied in such popular figures as Humphrey Bogart, Ernest Hemingway, and John Wayne.[5] It has an economic counterpart in the cult of the entrepreneur who pursues his vision outside the contaminating influence of corporate institutions.

A third approach is signified by the ideal of the "pleasure seeker." This is a man who works hard at his job so that he can afford as much satisfaction of his passions after work as possible. Some men might find such outlets in exciting, dangerous sports like skydiving or rock climbing. They may seek adventure through risky drugs, risky driving, and risky games with money (speculation and other forms of high-stakes gambling). A pleasure-seeking middle-class man can become a consumer connoisseur, pursuing the finest clothes, the finest cars, the finest art and entertainment, or the finest women. One form of this ideal has found expression in *Playboy* magazine. Its pages make explicit what is only implied in other commercial media—that sex and beautiful women are consumer products, accoutrements to the good life. They are one outlet for the masculine passions of the pleasure seeker.[6]

In the late twentieth century, one more symbolic ideal of manhood has emerged, the "spiritual warrior." Conjured up in the teaching of Robert Bly and other leaders of the mythopoeic men's movement, this ideal was born of dissatisfaction with the other ideals and images of men that have recently dominated American culture. It grows from a direct, conscious focus on the passions that its advocates assume are naturally male.[7] The spiritual warrior believes he has lost touch with those passions and lost his ability to connect directly with other men. In the process, he has been prevented from fulfilling his deepest spiritual needs as well.[8]

This understanding of manhood appeals intensely to many men because of its focus on fatherhood. Bly and others lament the growing distance between fathers and sons in the modern world. The teachers of the spiritual warrior ideal see the disconnection of sons from their fathers repeating itself in the disconnection of men from passion, from the spirit, from their fellow men. Here begins a striking series of parallels with the movement toward primitive masculinity at the turn of the twentieth century. For the spokesmen of that movement voiced the same concerns about the absence of fathers that men are voicing today. They also expressed the same anxiety about the dangers of a boy learning his vision of manhood through the eyes of mothers and other women.[9]

Like their turn-of-the-century counterparts, the present critics urge men to restore their confused or missing sense of manliness through immersion in the mythology and rituals of premodern men. Indeed, the ancient tales to which a spiritual warrior now turns were first popularized in white, middle-class America by the fin-de-siècle generation of men who sought to recover the primitive sources of manhood, and the rituals a spiritual warrior undergoes during men's workshops today bear a vivid likeness to the rituals of the fraternal lodges that flourished in the late nineteenth century.[10] The spiritual warrior of today closely resembles his masculine-primitive ancestor of a century ago.

The resemblance between them goes beyond the imagery, the anxiety, and the prescriptions that they share. The social contexts in which the two movements emerged are notably similar. Both movements emerged during eras marked by material greed and self-seeking of an unusually intense sort. In gender terms, these phases of anxiety about manhood began while the male grip on power and privilege was under attack by women. Even more to the point, women at those two times were questioning familiar definitions of manhood and womanhood. The two movements arose at historical times when men were bound to feel confused and defensive about the meaning of manliness. A search for a deep, secure basis for male identity grew naturally out of these circumstances.

The uneasy gender environment that produced both movements also colored their content. The ideas of both groups turned away from women in an attempt to establish a firmer manhood. The late nineteenth-century advocates of primitive masculinity lived in an era when middle-class manhood was steeped in fraternal ritual, and they were themselves founders of boys' organizations rooted in the symbols of nature and premodern maleness. In the same vein, the late twentieth-century apostles of the spiritual warrior say that men must regain their manhood through common ritual that excludes women.

What appears as turning aside in some contexts emerges as misogyny in others. Many of the primitive masculinists and some publicists for the idea of the spiritual warrior have expressed hostility toward those women who pressed for change in gender arrangements. We have already observed the contemptuous language that late nineteenth-century men used against the advocates of equal rights for women; some of the same scorn has issued from certain quarters of the mythopoeic men's movement. The editor of the most popular men's newspaper, for instance, has announced that the women's movement is "largely driven by lesbians and that's why most women aren't feminists."[11] This statement is not only inaccurate, but it misinterprets feminist motivation and—in the prevailing climate of opinion about lesbianism—stigmatizes the women's movement.

To be fair, the opinions about women expressed in the most important text of the mythopoeic men's movement are quite different. The writing of Robert Bly explicitly rejects middle-class machismo and the disdain for all things feminine. Nor does Bly condemn feminism or feminists. However, Bly's anxiety about feminine influence on manly development has attracted men with attitudes resonant of those of a century ago.[12]

As much as those who pursue the ideal of the spiritual warrior differ among themselves in their response to women, their ideal is clearly different from the other ideals for expressing male passion in modern society. They seek outlets for passion that are free of consumerism and the competitive ethic. They want to be in touch with what they see as the spiritual core of maleness without having to live at the margins of society. Moreover, the ideal of the spiritual warrior defines male passions more broadly than the other ideals, to include spiritual yearnings and a longing for connection to others (primarily male others).

There is one important trait that all four ideals share, however: each of them signifies a turning away from women. The ideal of the spiritual warrior represents a ritual quest for manhood in an all-male setting. The ideal of the pleasure seeker may treat women as objects of pleasure or as accessory companions in his pursuit of enjoyment, but considers them largely irrelevant to the fulfillment of his yearnings. The ideal of the existential hero endorses separation from the confinement of civilization and the halter of permanent, personal commitment—and, given our cultural associations between women and the bonds of civilization, it is no surprise that adherents of this ideal view women's world with suspicion.

The world of the team player is less intrinsically exclusive of women than that of the other ideals. Pristine in its blindness to personal history, the great contest for success is technically open to anyone who can play and win according to its competitive rules. As we have seen historically, however, the middle-class male workplace was constructed by men according to shared male values and customs that are culturally alien to women. In recent years, women have made statistical inroads in the world of the team player, but as yet there is little change—culturally or statistically—at the level where most power is wielded.[13] In reality, the ideal of the team player posits a world where women have difficulty surviving even though they are not explicitly forbidden to enter.

To discuss access to power and the separation of men from women is to come face to face with the issue of sexism that underlies this book. In grappling with the issue, it helps to start with the word itself. *Sexism* has entered the language within the past quarter century.[14] It is commonly used in two different ways. The more frequent usage refers to prejudice based on sex. According to this meaning, both women and men can practice sexism or be the objects of it. Like any form of prejudice, this is an insidious human habit because it denies individual identity and promotes scorn for other groups. It can also be used to limit access and opportunity in ways that are patently unfair. Sexism in this sense is a serious and ongoing problem in our society, and men and women generally agree that the fight against this form of prejudice needs to be resolute and enduring.

There is a second form of sexism, a meaning of the word that circulates less broadly. This refers to the unequal distribution of power between the sexes. Sexism in this sense has existed in the United States throughout the nation's history. This book has examined the shifting sources of sexism, from the hierarchy and assigned social status of colonial society to the metaphor of separate spheres which once dominated—and still influences—thinking about women and men. The relationship of that metaphor to the idea of individualism is crucial for understanding the power relations between the sexes. The doctrine of the spheres enshrined individualism as a male privilege, making men's sphere the locus of individualism and women's sphere the place where a woman submerged her social identity in that of her husband. With the grant of the vote and the slow accumulation of other rights, women have made some progress toward power and the privileges of individualism in the twentieth century. They have opened new doors in the workplace, increased their awareness of themselves as a group with common interests, and thrust gender issues onto the nation's public agenda. Feminists have spread the idea that a woman can and should be a person with the same legal and political rights as a man, the same claim to self-definition, and even the same range of potential skills.[15]

In spite of these changes and hopeful portents, however, power is still unequally distributed. Most public officeholders in 1992 are men—and the higher the level of authority, the truer that statement becomes. Virtually all major positions of economic power are occupied by men. The same can be said of the great seats of cultural influence, whether they be editorships, executive posts, or directorships in film or television. Pessimists say that this situation is a sign of persistent sexism, while optimists say that women have just recently entered the pipelines of preferment and will make it to the top levels of power in a matter of years or a few decades. Whichever position one accepts, the point remains that women are still the victims of a sexist distribution of power.

I add the word *victim* to this discussion with some hesitation. It conjures up images of all women passively accepting their fate and all men inflicting that fate with conscious, malevolent intent—images that are unfair and distorted. Moreover, the word has different meanings in different settings; it strikes readers and listeners with widely varying effect. But it also has become a part of the public conversation about sex and gender, and a discussion of its uses can help to straighten out some common confusions. The preceding paragraph refers to a situation in which power is unequally distributed between two groups on a persisting basis; victims are members of a group consistently denied an equal share of power. In this case, women are the victims of sexism.

What, then, are we to make of the increasing number of men who claim they are the victims of gender arrangements in our society? How can men claim to be the victims when they hold a disproportionate share of power over women as a group? In the sense of group power, they can't truthfully say that they are victims. Even so, the claims of some men that they are victimized by gender arrangements should be taken seriously.

For the word *victim* also has a broader meaning that refers to anyone "who is harmed . . . by any act or circumstance."[16] A man might be such a victim in any number of ways. Some men who claim that they are harmed by women are really talking about having their feelings hurt in a relationship. This certainly can happen to men as well as women—indeed, it can happen in *any* relationship where a person's feelings are at risk.

Yet, the ways in which men are harmed by our current gender arrangements have much more to do with the system of ideas than with women. We have all learned a set of cultural types—the tough man and the tender, the real man and the sissy that have been accumulating cultural sanction for a century now. These types, or symbols, encourage males to value certain kinds of men and to scorn others. This process harms men who fit the wrong type. Less directly, it harms *all* men because they lose access to stigmatized parts of themselves—tenderness, nurturance, the desire for connection, the skills of cooperation—that are helpful in personal situations and needed for the social good.

In the end, men and women alike are harmed, because these symbols of right and wrong manhood have also become lodged in our political consciousness and in the decision-making culture of our great institutions. These symbols make certain choices automatically less acceptable, and in doing so they impoverish the process by which policy is made. We are biased in favor of options we consider the tough ones and against those we see as tender; we value toughness as an end in itself. We are disabled in choosing the wise risk from the unwise, and tend to value risk as its own form of good. In this manner, we are all hurt by the cultural configuration of manhood.[17]

The century-old association of homosexuality and unmanliness is another facet of our gender system that harms men. It hurts homosexual males most profoundly because it lays the basis for contempt, persecution, and discrimination against them. In ways that are less deeply damaging but equally real, men who are not homosexual are also wronged by the homosexual stigma. They lose the opportunity for the open intimacy of the romantic male friendships that were common in the nineteenth century; more broadly, the fear of homosexuality can block men's access to tender feelings and the skills that humans need in order to build connections with one another.

The homosexual stigma and the symbols of the real man and the wimp are not the only sources of trouble for men in our gender arrangements. Great harm is done to men by one of their most cherished possessions: the radical form of individualism that belongs to American males. Individualism—expressed in the form of the free agent, the independent citizen, the unfettered man on the make—is vital to a free society. Without it, the grand accomplishments of democratic ideals, republican institutions, personal liberties, and extraordinary prosperity might never have been achieved. In the absence of any countervailing notion of community or connection, however, individualism breeds its own ills—for the pure concept of individualism demands personal independence, not only from the demands of the state but also from the emotional bonds of intimacy, family, and community.

Such pure independence does not exist, even in a society as individualistic as ours. In the late twentieth century, however, we lack any great counterbalance such as an honored sense of social usefulness, of community, or even of domesticity in the nineteenth-century fashion. Instead, men, the beneficiaries of individualism, are also the bearers of a powerful, even fearful autonomy. In many cases, this male independence could best be called counterdependence, and it creates extreme harm to men's ability to connect with other people or groups.[18]

An increasing chorus of social criticism in recent years has called attention to men's personal isolation. Therapists and women's movement writers have observed men's difficulty in relationships with members of both sexes. To be sure, men form relationships with each other—often very fond ones—around shared activity, adventure, or competition ("male bonding," as some have called it), but it is not clear that this sort of relationship has provided the kind of nurturance and support that can help men through a personal emergency. The fact that women survive much longer than men after the death of a spouse is itself a tragic testimony to men's difficulty in creating personal networks that work effectively at times of emotional crisis.[19] Wives, children, and friends suffer as a result of this difficulty, but the greatest victims are the men themselves.

Observing the culture of individualism in the early nineteenth century, Alexis de Tocqueville observed that "it throws [a man] back forever upon himself alone and threatens in the end to confine him entirely within the solitude of his own heart."[20] De Tocqueville's words were prophetic. From then until now, men have claimed individualism for themselves and have held on to the power and privilege that come with it, but they have also felt the bitter side-effects of individualism: personal isolation and a withered sense of community. The key for men is not to abandon their individualism but to balance it with a renewed sense of connection; not to relinquish power to women but to share it in full and equal measure. We need new metaphors that take us beyond separate spheres and contending passions. How to make this change is a problem for men and women of our time to solve together. Whether we succeed will be a question for future historians to answer.

Appendix

THE PARAMETERS OF THE STUDY

As a new, sprawling topic, the history of manhood was too large for me to study whole. At the outset, I realized that I had to limit the scope of my project. I chose to narrow my focus to white, middle-class manhood in the northern United States, and I decided to concentrate on the nineteenth century. The reader may find it useful to know why and how I defined these choices.

When I began this project in 1978, the findings of gender historians and my own previous research and writing suggested that major changes in American manhood took place at the beginning and the end of the nineteenth century. Broad-based work on society and culture in the United States has identified the decades just before and after 1800 as a time of transformation. In particular, the work of women's historians has shown that the metaphors that still govern our beliefs about gender at the end of the twentieth century were born at the turn of the nineteenth. Meanwhile, students of men's roles have located significant change in the years surrounding 1900. Many current rituals and institutions of manhood date from this period. Thus, the years that bounded the nineteenth century were years of fundamental change in the history of gender.

The images and expectations that governed manhood in the late eighteenth century were very different from those of our own time. The rules and ideals of the early twentieth century closely resemble our own. Modern manhood, then, took shape in the nineteenth century. If we would understand this gender form in our own time, we must understand its origins in the 1800s.

In the nineteenth century, the society of the United States was already a diverse one. It was divided inwardly by class, region, race, and ethnicity. All those social divisions matter for a study of gender. Historians have long recognized that the different regions of the nation in the 1800s had distinct cultural identities, and historians of gender have recently found that those regional differences affected definitions of manhood and womanhood in significant ways. In limiting the scope of this study, I chose to screen out regional variance by examining manhood in the part of the country that proved dominant in politics, economics, and culture: the North. I have concentrated on that part of the North that might be called the Yankee diaspora. This area begins with New England and follows the main path of Yankee migration through New York and the Western Reserve and into the upper Midwest as far as the Mississippi. Men of Yankee roots were numerous, and they were also influential out of proportion to their numbers. Through their power in the pulpit, press, and publishing, and through their farflung economic ties, these men exercised a certain hegemony in nineteenth-century American culture. For that reason, their ideas about manhood and their broad notions of gender merit special attention.

I realize in retrospect that I have excluded non-Yankee Northerners more rigorously in the earlier eras of this study than in the later ones. My attempt to lay down a colonial basis for the subsequent history of manhood is derived exclusively from the New England experience, and the men who are the subjects of my study in the early nineteenth century are of Yankee origin, wholly or in part. Some of the men whose lives and words I have drawn on in the late nineteenth century, however, were men of Middle Atlantic stock, with Dutch, German, or Quaker roots. This mixing of cultural populations seemed to me acceptable, partly because, in places like New York, Philadelphia, and the Midwest, those groups were mingling by the late nineteenth century, and partly because men's ideas and experiences of gender late in the century no longer seemed differentiated by their Yankee or Middle Atlantic origins.

My intuitions on this matter have recently been borne out by David Hackett Fischer's momentous study of regional cultures in the history of the United States. Fischer has found that the gender folkways of New England and the Middle Atlantic were distinct from one another in the early 1700s, though they resembled each other more than they did the coastal and highland folkways of the Southern colonies. Then Fischer notes a general convergence between Yankee and Middle Atlantic cultures at the middle of the nineteenth century. As their folkways grew more and more alike, their differences from those of the South increased. This general convergence in Fischer's study supports my own sense that the gender attitudes of Yankee and Middle Atlantic men had grown indistinguishable by the late nineteenth century.[1]

My rationale for drawing lines of class where I did is much the same as my rationale for making regional distinctions. Middle-class values have been the dominant values in the United States for two centuries. Political and economic power rest to a great extent in the hands of the middle class. Education and publishing, the church and the media—all of these institutions are run by middle-class people. If, as social critics have often written, the United States is a bourgeois society, one good way to open up a new topic like the history of manhood is to study the bourgeoisie.

It is easy enough to talk about the middle class in sweeping terms; it is much harder to apply the concept to specific cases. This difficulty flows from several sources. First of all, scholars have used the term *middle class* in a variety of ways; some precision about its use is needed here. For the purpose of this study, the middle class includes men who earned a living in business, the professions, or the arts, and the wives and children of those men. As I applied this definition in my research, it netted a collection of men who were largely upper middle class—that is, they were more comfortable, more powerful, and generally better educated than someone like a shopkeeper who could also be counted as middle class.[2]

Another problem in using the term *middle class* is that it does not always fit the essential messiness of social reality. Some occupations straddled the boundaries between classes. Was a man who carved images on gravestones an artist or a skilled manual laborer? Did a farmer who dabbled as a self-trained physician count as middle class? To confuse matters further, many men passed in and out of the middle class as their occupations, their personal fortunes, and the health of the economy changed. What of a man like Cornelius Vanderbilt, who became one of the nation's richest men without abandoning his roots in the spiritual and medical folk culture of the rural North? To what class should we assign him? In addition, there is a particular ambiguity in making distinctions between upper-class and upper-middle-class men. Those who by wealth or birth could be called upper class commonly maintained a bourgeois outlook and values. Often, their business associates and their personal friends were upper middle class.

My policy for dealing with these many ambiguities was to be inclusive, to count a man as middle class where he was at least partially so. Within that context, I have tried to point out differences between classes and class subdivisions where they appeared. In addition, I have identified in the text the occupations and circumstances of the men who appear there, so that the reader can draw personal conclusions about a man's class status where it is ambiguous.

One common ambiguity deserves special mention. A great many middle-class men in the nineteenth century grew up on farms. In their cases, I have continued to follow an inclusive policy. I found it useful to do so, since most of these men came from prosperous rural families where the father combined farming with law, political leadership, real estate speculation, or other business ventures. In short, these fathers were prosperous leaders of rural communities, and their values closely resembled those of the urban middle class. Still, a few of the middle-class men who appear in this book had roots in less comfortable farming families. Where I have discussed their childhoods in the text, I have noted their background explicitly.

I have also limited the scope of this book by race. Given the facts of racism, slavery, and the distribution of the nonwhite population, only a handful of middle-class men in the nineteenth-century North were anything but white. This small number of black men came to their middle-class status by a route so painfully different from that of whites that they deserve separate treatment and should not be thrown into the mix of white, middle-class Yankees who populate this book.

NOTES

Archival sources throughout the notes have been abbreviated as follows:

AAS	American Antiquarian Society
CHS	Chicago Historical Society
CUL	Columbia University, Rare Book and Manuscript Library
EI	Essex Institute
HCL	Harvard College Library
HL	Huntington Library
HSWP	Historical Society of Western Pennsylvania, Library and Archives Division
LC	Manuscript Division, Library of Congress
MEHS	Maine Historical Society
MHGS	Massachusetts Historic Genealogical Society
MHS	Massachusetts Historical Society
MNHS	Minnesota Historical Society
NHHS	New Hampshire Historical Society, Manuscript Collections
NL	Newberry Library
NYHS	New York Historical Society
NYPL	New York Public Library (Astor, Lenox, and Tilden Foundations), Rare Books and Manuscripts Division
NYSLA	New York State Library Archives
SHSW	State Historical Society of Wisconsin, Archives
SL	Schlesinger Library, Radcliffe College
SSC	Sophia Smith Collection, Smith College
WRHS	Western Reserve Historical Society
YUL	Yale University Library, Manuscripts and Archives

Introduction: Toward a History of American Manhood

1. The approach to gender taken in this book falls under the rubric of "cultural construction." This mode of understanding gender derives most of all from the work of Michel Foucault (see esp. his *History of Sexuality,* 1 [New York, 1990] and *Archaeology of Knowledge* [New York, 1982]). Other approaches to the study of gender stress biological or evolutionary imperatives (see, for instance, Edward O. Wilson, *Sociobiology: The New Synthesis* [Cambridge, Mass., 1975]), or psychological archetypes of male and female (see, for instance, Robert Bly, *Iron John: A Book about Men* [Reading, Mass., 1990]).

2. On the distinction between sex and gender, see Janet Saltzman Chafetz, *Masculine Feminine or Human: An Overview of the Sociology of the Gender Roles,* 2nd ed. (Itsaca, Ill., 1978), 2–6. Some cultural constructionists even dismiss this distinction between sex and gender, viewing biological categories as themselves cultural constructions; see Suzanne J. Kessler and Wendy McKenna, *Gender: An Ethnomethodological Approach* (New York, 1978).

3. Historians in recent years have begun to realize that manhood has a history. Fundamental works include Peter Stearns, *Be A Man!: Males in Modern Society,* 2nd ed. (New York, 1990); Peter Filene, *Him/ Her/ Self: Sex Roles in Modern America,* 2nd ed. (Baltimore, 1986); Joe L. Dubbert, *A Man's Place: Masculinity in Transition* (Englewood Cliffs, N.J., 1979); Barbara Ehrenreich, *The Hearts of Men: American Dreams and the Flight from Commitment* (Garden City, N.Y., 1984); Ted Ownby, *Subduing Satan: Religion, Recreation, and Manhood in the Rural South, 1865–1920* (Chapel Hill, N.C., 1990); Mark C. Carnes, *Secret Ritual and Manhood in Victorian America* (New Haven, Conn., 1989). Two important collections of essays are Elizabeth H. Pleck and Joseph H. Pleck, eds., *The American Man* (Englewood Cliffs, N.J., 1980), and Mark C. Carnes and Clyde Griffen, eds., *Meanings for Manhood: Constructions of Masculinity in Victorian America* (Chicago, 1990).

4. Bly, *Iron John;* Sam Keen, *Fire in the Belly: On Being a Man* (New York, 1991).

5. As described in the preface, the Northern men discussed in this book are chiefly of Yankee stock, so the origins—and the relevant historical contrasts—in the colonial period involve manhood and society in New England.

6. William Bentley, *The Diary of William Bentley, D.D.* (Gloucester, Mass., 1962), vol. 3, 2–3; vol. 1, 244.

7. James R. McGovern, *Yankee Family* (New Orleans, 1975), 5–6, 8–9, 84, 99–100, 132. Quotations are on 99, 132.

8. McGovern, *Yankee Family,* 100, 89. On Mary Pierce Poor as a mother, see 72–75, 85–88.

9. McGovern, *Yankee Family*, 113–20. Quotation is on 114.

10. McGovern, *Yankee Family*, 113–20.

11. The most succinct statement of these criticisms is Joseph H. Pleck, "Men's Power with Women, Other Men, and Society," in Pleck and Pleck, *American Man*. For other representative statements, see Ehrenreich, *Hearts of Men;* Jack Nichols, *Men's Liberation: A New Definition of Masculinity* (New York, 1975); Perry Garfinkel, *In a Man's World: Father, Son, Brother, Friend and Other Roles Men Play* (New York, 1985); Marc Feigen Fasteau, *The Male Machine* (New York, 1975).

12. Sir Walter Scott, *Ivanhoe* (New York, 1941), 488.

13. On legal education, see Michael Grossberg, "Institutionalizing Masculinity: The Law as a Masculine Profession," in Carnes and Griffen, *Meanings for Manhood*, 143–44; quotation is on 144. The masculinity of the early federal government is a subject in James S. Young, *The Washington Community, 1800–1828* (New York, 1966). The emergence of male networks and the medical model is described in Regina Markell Morantz-Sanchez, *Sympathy and Science: Women Physicians in American Medicine* (New York, 1985), esp. chaps. 9–11.

Chapter 1: Community to Individual: The Transformation of Manhood at the Turn of the Nineteenth Century

1. Edmund S. Morgan, *The Puritan Family: Religion and Domestic Relations in Seventeenth-Century New England,* rev. ed. (New York, 1966), 19–20, 133, 136, 142–50.

2. *Genesis* 3:16.

3. Morgan, *Puritan Family,* 12–13.

4. Morgan, *Puritan Family,* 43–44; David Hackett Fischer, *Albion's Seed: Four British Folkways in America* (New York, 1989), 83; John Demos, *A Little Commonwealth: Family Life in Plymouth Colony* (New York, 1970), 83–84.

5. Philip Greven, Jr., *The Protestant Temperament: Patterns of Child-Rearing, Religious Experience, and Self in Early America* (New York, 1977), 211, 243–51; Phyllis Vine, "The Social Function of Eighteenth-Century Higher Education," *History of Education Quarterly,* 16 (1976), 412.

6. Steven Mintz and Susan Kellogg, *Domestic Revolutions: A Social History of American Life* (New York, 1988), 5–6.

7. Mintz and Kellogg, *Domestic Revolutions,* 6; Melvin Yazawa, *From Colonies to Commonwealth: Familial Ideology and the Beginnings of the American Republic* (Baltimore, 1985), 19–27.

8. Morgan, *Puritan Family,* 45–46, 115, 147–50; Laurel Thatcher Ulrich, *Good Wives: Image and Reality in the Lives of Women in Northern New England 1650–1750* (New York, 1982), 35–50.

9. See, for example, Samuel Gay to Martin Gay, Jan. 18 and Feb. 22, 1776, and Jotham Gay to Martin Gay, Apr. 21, 1760, Gay-Otis Manuscript Collection, CUL. On the importance of a man's performance of his duties, see also Benjamin Greene to Samuel and Stephen Salisbury, Sept. 9, 1781, Salisbury Family Papers, Box 4, AAS; William Bentley, *The Diary of William Bentley, D.D.* (Gloucester, Mass., 1962), vol. 1, 19; Joseph Jenkins to Rebekah Jenkins, n.d. [1803], Joseph Jenkins Letters, EI; Ernestus Plummer to Caroline Plummer, Mar. 9, 1808, Bowditch Family Papers, Box 12, EI.

10. Ulrich, *Good Wives,* 8.

11. "Good foundations" quoted in Greven, *Protestant Temperament,* 177; Theodore P. Greene, *America's Heroes: The Changing Models of Success in American Magazines* (New York, 1970), 45–46. Usefulness was a central theme of Timothy Pickering's letters to his son John, Nov. 15, 1786, Aug. 4, 1788, Oct. 14, 1793, Jan. 2 and Jan. 17, 1794, Apr. 28 and June 15, 1798, Pickering Family Papers, EI; William Bentley also stressed usefulness as a male virtue, see Bentley, *Diary,* vol. 1, 53; vol. 3, 223.

12. Alexander Anderson diary, June 18, 1795, NYHS; Benjamin Goodhue to Stephen Goodhue, Mar. 26, 1796, Goodhue Family Papers, EI. See also Benjamin Goodhue to Stephen Goodhue, Apr. 16, 1796; Nathan Mitchell diary, Sept. 27, 1786, MHGS; Joseph Jenkins to Rebekah Jenkins, n.d. [1803], Joseph Jenkins Letters, EI; Philip Schuyler to Angelica Church, July 17, 1804, Schuyler Family Papers, NYSLA; Bentley, *Diary,* vol. 4, 588; Ernestus Plummer to Caroline Plummer, Aug. 10, 1810, Bowditch Papers, Box 12, EI; Edmund Quincy to Samuel Salisbury, June 20, 1780, Salisbury Papers, Box 4, AAS; *The Literary Diary of Ezra Stiles,* ed. F. B. Dexter (New York, 1901), 418.

13. Timothy Pickering to George Williams, Mar. 21, 1786, Pickering Papers, EI; Bentley, *Diary,* vol. 1, 41, 199; John Pierce memoirs, vol. 1, July 2, 1806, Pierce Collection, MHS.

14. Philip Schuyler to Catherine Schuyler, Jan. 26, 1800, Schuyler Papers, NYSLA; Timothy Pickering to George Williams, Mar. 21, 1786, Pickering Papers, EI; James R. McGovern, *Yankee Family* (New Orleans, 1975), 271; Yazawa, *From Colonies,* 33–45.

15. Bentley quoted in Joseph Waters, "Biographical Sketch," in Bentley, *Diary,* vol. 1, xiv–xv; Alexander Anderson diary, Oct. 7, 1795, NYHS.

16. Darret Rutman, *Winthrop's Boston* (Chapel Hill, N.C., 1965); Bernard Bailyn, "The Apologia of Robert Keayne," *William and Mary Quarterly,* 3rd ser., 7 (1950); Bernard Bailyn, *The New England Merchants in the Seventeenth Century* (Cambridge, Mass., 1955).

17. Ulrich, *Good Wives,* esp. chaps. 2, 3, 9.

18. Danforth quoted in J. E. Crowley, *This Sheba, Self: The Conceptualization of Economic Life in Eighteenth-Century America* (Baltimore, 1974), xiv. See also John Demos, *Entertaining Satan: Witchcraft and the Culture of*

Early New England (New York, 1982), esp. 394–400; Kenneth Lockridge, *A New England Town: The First Hundred Years, Dedham, Massachusetts, 1636–1736* (New York, 1970), 91–164; Philip Greven, Jr., *Four Generations: Population, Land, and Family in Colonial Andover, Massachusetts* (Ithaca, N.Y., 1970); Richard L. Bushman, *From Puritan to Yankee: Character and Social Order in Connecticut, 1690–1765* (Cambridge, Mass., 1967); Jay Fliegelman, *Prodigals and Pilgrims: The American Revolution against Patriarchal Authority, 1750–1800* (Cambridge, Mass., 1982); Yazawa, *From Colonies*, 83–194.

19. Declaration of Independence, in Daniel Boorstin, ed., *An American Primer* (Chicago, 1966), 69; Royall Tyler, *The Contrast: A Comedy in Five Acts* (New York, 1970); Benjamin Goodhue to Stephen Goodhue, Mar. 24, 1798, Goodhue Papers, EI.

20. See Joseph Ellis, *After the Revolution: Profiles of Early American Culture* (New York, 1979), on the reluctance of the younger generation of revolutionaries to believe in individual economic enterprise as a social good.

21. On political individualism as a gendered issue, see Linda Kerber, *Women of the Republic: Intellect and Ideology in Revolutionary America* (Chapel Hill, N.C., 1980), 15–27, 284–85.

22. Jesse Appleton to Ebenezer Adams, Feb. 10, 1797, Jesse Appleton Letters, AAS; Fliegelman, *Prodigals and Pilgrims*, chaps. 2, 5, 6; Herman Lantz, Margaret Britten, Raymond Schmitt, and Eloise Snyder, "Pre-Industrial Patterns in the Colonial Family in America: A Content Analysis," *American Sociological Review*, 33 (June 1968), 413–26; Herman Lantz, Raymond Schmitt, and Richard Herman, "The Pre-Industrial Family in America: A Further Examination of Magazines," *American Journal of Sociology*, 79 (Nov. 1973), 577–78, 581; Ellen Rothman, *Hands and Hearts: A History of Courtship in America* (New York, 1984), 30–31, 35.

23. The following account of women's creation of a political role for themselves in the new republic is based especially on Kerber, *Women of the Republic*, and also on Mary Beth Norton, *Liberty's Daughters: The Revolutionary Experience of American Women, 1750–1800* (Boston, 1980), 228–99.

24. Through an apparent loophole in the New Jersey constitution, women in that state were able to vote from the 1780s until 1807. See Norton, *Liberty's Daughters*, 191–93.

25. New ideas about child-rearing that became popular in the late eighteenth century stressed the importance of affectionate nurture (see Fliegelman, *Prodigals and Pilgrims*). Since this quality had traditionally been—and still was—associated with women, it was natural that men should accept women's assertion that they were the sex fit to teach republican virtue.

26. Kerber, *Women of the Republic*, 285.

27. Kerber, *Women of the Republic*, 285.

28. Ruth Bloch, "The Gendered Meanings of Virtue in Revolutionary America," *Signs*, 13 (1987).

29. Daniel Webster to Habijah Fuller, Aug. 29, 1802, *The Writings and Speeches of Daniel Webster* (Boston, 1903), vol. 17.

30. The broad changes described here and in the paragraphs that follow are explored in David Hackett Fischer, "America: A Social History, Vol I, The Main Lines of the Subject, 1650–1975," unpub. MS, and *Growing Old in America*, expanded ed. (New York, 1978), 77–78, 99–112; in Richard Brown, *Modernization: The Transformation of American Life* (New York, 1976), and "Modernization and the Modern Personality in Early America, 1600–1865: A Sketch of a Synthesis," *Journal of Interdisciplinary History*, 2 (1972); and, in microcosm, in Daniel Scott Smith, "Population, Family, and Society in Hingham, Massachusetts" (Ph.D. diss., Univ. of California, Berkeley, 1973).

31. The best description of the new individualism and its implications is still Alexis de Tocqueville's *Democracy in America*. On the social and cultural conditions, see esp. vol. 2. The version used here is the Henry Reeve text, rev. Francis Bowen, ed. Phillips Bradley (New York, 1945).

32. Generations of historians have explored the attempts of early nineteenth-century Americans to answer these questions. A classic formulation is Marvin Meyers, *The Jacksonian Persuasion: Politics and Belief* (New York, 1957). A recent, compelling exploration is Paula Baker, "The Domestication of American Politics: Women and American Political Society, 1780–1920," *American Historical Review*, 89 (1984), 620–35.

33. James Fenimore Cooper, *The Last of the Mohicans* (New York, 1968 [1826]), 127, 324–35; Henry David Thoreau, *Walden*, ed. Sherman Paul (Boston, 1960), 70.

34. Not all debating clubs and literary societies were segregated by age. Some of them, especially in small towns, mixed adult men with male youths. But even in those settings, young men learned the purposeful channeling of energy incidentally—through competition and emulation—rather than through formal instruction. See, for instance, Samuel Howard to James C. Howard, Jan. 28, 1828, James C. Howard Papers, SHSW.

35. Linda Kerber has reviewed the historical literature on separate spheres insightfully in "Separate Spheres, Female Worlds, Women's Place: The Rhetoric of Women's History," *Journal of American History*, 75 (1988). The single most important interpretation is Nancy F. Cott, *The Bonds of Womanhood: "Woman's Sphere" in New England, 1780–1835* (New Haven, Conn., 1977).

36. Cott, *Bonds of Womanhood*, 63–74; Mary Ryan, *The Empire of the Mother: American Writing about Domesticity, 1830–1860* (New York, 1982).

37. L. E., "Home," *Ladies Magazine*, 3 (1830), 217–18.

38. Bloch, "Gendered Meanings," 37–58. On the evangelical roots of the doctrine of the spheres, see Cott, *Bonds of Womanhood*, 65.

39. On the creation of specialized commercial districts, see Stuart Blumin, *The Emergence of the Middle Class: Social Experience in the American City,*

1760–1900 (New York, 1989), 83–87; on women's increasing focus on domestic duties in prosperous households, see Cott, *Bonds of Womanhood,* 43–45, 57–62.

40. Cott, in *Bonds of Womanhood* (69–71), discusses the way in which the doctrine of the spheres proposed accommodations to the changes which it deplored.

41. Bloch, "Gendered Meanings," 53–58.

42. A large and rich historical literature that discusses the political implications of women's moral role has emerged in recent years. Important statements within this literature include Cott, *Bonds of Womanhood,* 197–206; Baker, "Domestication," 620–47; Mary Ryan, *The Cradle of the Middle Class: The Family in Oneida County, New York, 1790–1865* (New York, 1981), esp. chap. 5; Barbara Leslie Epstein, *The Politics of Domesticity: Women, Evangelism, and Temperance in Nineteenth-Century America* (Middletown, Conn., 1981); Carl N. Degler, *At Odds: Women and the Family in America from the Revolution to the Present* (New York, 1980), chap. 13.

43. Quoted in McGovern, *Yankee Family,* 85.

44. E. Anthony Rotundo, "American Fatherhood: A Historical Perspective," *American Behavioral Scientist,* 29 (1985), 9–10. This article appears in revised form as "Patriarchs and Participants: A Historical Perspective on Fatherhood," in Michael Kaufman, ed., *Beyond Patriarchy: Essays by Men on Pleasure, Power, and Change* (New York, 1987).

45. Fliegelman, *Prodigals and Pilgrims.*

46. Bloch, "Gendered Meanings."

47. The role of shaping a daughter's character already belonged in great measure to the woman. See Norton, *Liberty's Daughters,* 97.

48. To be sure, a woman had great—sometimes overwhelming—influence on family decisions. But by cultural agreement, the decisions were the man's to make. See chap. 7 on this point.

49. Fathers served as breadwinners, heads of household, and chief disciplinarians to daughters as well, but the focus here is on fathers and sons.

50. See E. Anthony Rotundo, "Fathers and Sons: Roles and Relationships," unpub. MS, 189–92.

51. On educational decisions, see Theodore Russell to Charles Russell, Dec. 18, 1831, and Nov. 6, 1832, Charles Russell Papers, MHS; Dean S. Howard to James Howard, Nov. 30, 1831, Howard Papers, SHSW; William H. Olmstead to Aaron Olmstead, June 7 and Nov. 8, 1838, Aaron Barlow Olmstead Papers, NYHS.

52. Often, the most useful thing a father could do was to offer a home and financial support to a young man through extended years of education and early career struggles. See Ryan, *Cradle,* 168–72; Ebenezer Gay to Arthur Gay, May 13, 1838, and May 9, 1839, Gay-Otis Collection, CUL.

53. Howard Doughty, *Francis Parkman* (Cambridge, Mass., 1983 [1962]), 87; Robert Abzug, *Passionate Liberator: Theodore Dwight Weld and the*

Dilemma of Reform (New York, 1980), 22–27; Char Miller, *Fathers and Sons: The Bingham Family and the American Mission* (Philadelphia, 1982), 73–77, 121–28.

54. Rotundo, "Fathers and Sons," 194–95; Rotundo, "American Fatherhood," 11–12.

55. For instance, Charles Russell to Theodore Russell, Sept. 27, 1834, Russell Papers, MHS; Othman Abbott, *Recollections of a Pioneer Lawyer* (Lincoln, Neb., 1929), 82. On changing expectations in this regard, see Kirk Jeffrey, "Family History: The Middle-Class Family in the Urban Context, 1830–1870" (Ph.D. diss., Stanford Univ., 1972), 207–8, and Rachel Deborah Cramer, "Images of the American Father, 1790–1860," unpub. MS, 51–52.

56. Rotundo, "Fathers and Sons," 271–72.

57. Sam Bass Warner, Jr., *Streetcar Suburbs: The Process of Growth in Boston, 1870–1900* (Cambridge, Mass., 1962); Kenneth Jackson, *The Crabgrass Frontier: The Suburbanization of the United States* (New York, 1985), 41–44; Blumin, 275–81.

58. Edward Everett Hale to Harriet Freeman, June 26 and Aug. 22, 1885, Papers of the Hale Family, Special Correspondence of Edward Everett Hale, LC; B. Franklin Kendall to Elizabeth Kendall, July 26, 1882, Kendall Papers, NYHS; Edward Wagenknecht, *The Seven Worlds of Theodore Roosevelt* (New York, 1958), 172–73.

59. Ulrich, *Good Wives,* 154–58; Norton, *Liberty's Daughters,* 85–94.

60. Ruth Bloch, "American Feminine Ideals in Transition: The Rise of the Moral Mother, 1785–1815," *Feminist Studies,* 4 (1978); Cott, *Bonds of Womanhood,* 84–87; James Barnard Blake diary, Aug. 3, 1851, AAS; William G. McLoughlin, *The Meaning of Henry Ward Beecher: An Essay on the Shifting Values of Mid-Victorian America, 1840–1870* (New York, 1970), 88.

61. Vine, "Social Function," 411–12; Greven, *Protestant Temperament,* 246–47; Ulrich, *Good Wives,* 154.

62. Norton, *Liberty's Daughters,* 92–94.

63. Jan Lewis, "Mother's Love: The Construction of an Emotion in Nineteenth-Century America," in Andrew E. Barnes and Peter N. Stearns, eds., *Social History and Issues in Human Consciousness: Some Interdisciplinary Connections* (New York, 1989). As represented in Lewis's article, the ideology of maternal nurture did not exist in its full-blown form until at least the 1820s. But as Cott has noted in (*Bonds of Womanhood,* 85–87), mothers and ministers were articulating some of its principles in the very earliest years of the century. For two examples of women who raised their children according to these precepts in the 1800s and 1810s, see the letters of Betsy Salisbury (Salisbury Papers, AAS) and Mary A. O. Gay (Gay-Otis Collection, CUL).

64. People were conscious of this connection, and the advantages of family

limitation for good mothering became an argument for birth control during the nineteenth century. See Degler, *At Odds*, 201.

65. Fischer, *Albion's Seed*, 101–2, on "sending out." On the late nineteenth
century, see Ryan, *Cradle*, 167–68.

66. Sarah Gilbert to Charles Russell, June 26, 1837, Russell Papers, MHS;
Poor quoted in McGovern, *Yankee Family*, 11. Not all mother-son relationships yielded affection or companionship, but such relations tended to
be hidden from view by the importance attached to that bond. For an example of a more distant mother-son relation, see Charles Milton Baldwin
diary, June 4, 1870, NYSLA.

67. McGovern, *Yankee Family*, 9; Abzug, *Passionate Liberator*, 16; Mary A. O.
Gay to W. Allan Gay, Feb. 15, Dec. 12, and Dec. 31, 1840, Sept. 2, 1847,
and Feb. 17, 1850, Gay-Otis Collection, CUL.

68. Henry Dwight Sedgwick, *Memoirs of an Epicurean* (New York, 1942), 21;
Betsy Salisbury to Stephen Salisbury, Jr., Sept. 16, 1809, Salisbury Papers,
AAS. See also letters of Apr. 11 and June 20, 1814.

69. John Kirk to his mother, Dec. 18, 1852, Kirk Letterbooks, vol. 1, CHS. See
also Sedgwick, *Memoirs*, 23; Lewis Wallace, *Lew Wallace: An Autobiography* (New York, 1906), 27; James Barnard Blake diary, Nov. 9, 1851, AAS.

70. See, for example, Betsy Salisbury to Stephen Salisbury, Jr., Sept. 16, 1809,
Salisbury Papers, AAS.

71. Betsy Salisbury to Stephen Salisbury, Jr., Apr. 11, June 20, July 5, and Aug.
9, 1814, Salisbury Papers, AAS; Polly Whittlesey to William Whittlesey,
Apr. 30, 1832, William W. Whittlesey Papers, WRHS. The simultaneous
training offered by mothers in ambition and pious morality is described
well in Ronald P. Byars, "The Making of the Self-made Man: The Development of Masculine Roles and Images in Ante-bellum America" (Ph.D.
diss., Michigan State Univ., 1979). Byars is perceptive generally about the
swirling crosscurrents of male-female relations before the Civil War.

Chapter 2: Boy Culture

1. Mrs. Manners, *At Home and Abroad; or How to Behave* (New York, 1853),
40–41.

2. The phrase is from Charles Dudley Warner, *Being a Boy* (Boston, 1897
[1877]), 66–67, but similar imagery appears throughout the source material: Lewis Wallace, *Lew Wallace: An Autobiography* (New York, 1906),
54–55; Daniel Carter Beard, *Hardly a Man Is Now Alive: The Autobiography of Dan Beard* (New York, 1939), 379; Ray Stannard Baker, *Native
American: The Book of My Youth* (New York, 1941), 30, 85, 208; Warner,
Being a Boy, 49, 87, 91, 150–51.

3. Henry Seidel Canby, *The Age of Confidence: Life in the Nineties* (New
York, 1934), 46.

4. John Demos, *A Little Commonwealth: Family Life in Plymouth Colony* (New York, 1970), 131–44; Ross Beales, "In Search of the Historical Child: Miniature Adulthood and Youth in Colonial America," *American Quarterly*, 27 (1975).

5. Edward Everett Hale, *A New England Boyhood* (Boston, 1964 [1893]), 22–23, 31.

6. E. Anthony Rotundo, "Manhood in America: The Northern Middle Class, 1770–1920" (Ph.D. diss., Brandeis Univ., 1982), 180–97, 347–56; Nancy F. Cott, *The Bonds of Womanhood: "Woman's Sphere" in New England, 1780–1835* (New Haven, Conn., 1977), 44–47, 57–60, 84–92; Mary Ryan, *The Cradle of the Middle Class: The Family in Oneida County, New York, 1790–1865* (New York, 1981), 157–65.

7. James R. McGovern, *Yankee Family* (New Orleans, 1975), 73; Ryan, *Cradle*, 162; Mrs. Manners, *At Home*, 40.

8. Beard, *Hardly a Man*, 76.

9. Philip Greven, Jr., *The Protestant Temperament: Patterns of Child-Rearing, Religious Experience, and Self in Early America* (New York, 1977), 45–46; Leonard Ellis, "Men among Men: An Exploration of All-Male Relationships in Victorian America" (Ph.D. diss., Columbia Univ., 1982), 395.

10. This approximate age is based on several pieces of evidence: Henry Dwight Sedgwick, *Memoirs of an Epicurean* (New York, 1942), 43; Beard, *Hardly a Man*, 79; Hale, *New England Boyhood*, 16–17; Kenneth S. Lynn, *William Dean Howells: An American Life* (New York, 1970), 43.

11. Gender segregation was not unique to middle-class Victorian children. Psychologists Eleanor Macoby and Carol Jacklin, in their research on group play among children ("Gender Segregation in Childhood," in Hayne W. Reese, ed., *Advances in Child Development and Behavior*, 20 [New York, 1987]), found that boys and girls nearly always segregated themselves when they could. Their findings held true across all cultural boundaries.
The virtual universality of gender-segregated play raises the possibility that this phenomenon has biological roots. However, anthropologist David Gilmore—noting the ubiquity of male self-segregation—has offered a complex explanation (*Manhood in the Making: Cultural Concepts of Masculinity* [New Haven, Conn., 1990]). At least one part of his explanation could account for gender segregation in children's play. Drawing on the theory of several ego psychologists, Gilmore notes that virtually all children are nurtured in infancy by their mothers. When they begin to separate themselves from the primal unity of that nurturing bond, all children face the task of establishing an identity as an independent human. That task is doubly difficult for boys. They must not only separate themselves from their mothers individually, they must also separate themselves as males from females, since virtually all known societies treat social maleness and femaleness as matters of importance. The desire felt by all children to return to primal unity with the mother is thus doubly threatening to boys

because it represents not just a surrender of one's independent social identity but a surrender of one's sex-appropriate gender identity as well (Gilmore, *Manhood*, 26–29). Theoretician Nancy Chodorow (*The Reproduction of Mothering: Psychoanalysis and the Sociology of Gender* [Berkeley, Calif., 1978]) has pointed out that one of the many consequences of this regressive threat to male identity is a devaluation of all things female in defense against earlier feminine attachment. This provides boys with a powerful stimulus to segregate themselves from girls. It also leaves the sexes with a tendency to different social needs and styles. As Chodorow notes, this tendency is exacerbated in modern societies by sharp sexual segregation of adults in daytime activity. All of this could account, theoretically, for the farflung custom of separate boys' and girls' play—without resort to biological explanation. Even if there are universal imperatives of psychology or physiology driving sex segregation in children's play, it is crucial to note the powerful role of culture in shaping that play into distinct patterns. In the case at hand, the force of custom suppressed tendencies toward separate play until about age six, then actively encouraged them—except at culturally determined times of the day and the week (for example, the evening, or the Sabbath) when mingling between brothers and sisters would be expected.

12. The "city states" quotation is from Canby, *Age of Confidence*, 35; see also 42–46; Wallace, *Autobiography*, 55; Sedgwick, *Memoirs*, 31; Lynn, *William Dean Howells*, 42; Howard Doughty, *Francis Parkman* (Cambridge, Mass., 1983 [1962]), 14–15.

13. For instance, Hale, *New England Boyhood*, 45, 53–54, 57–59.

14. Sedgwick, *Memoirs*, 31.

15. There is a danger of overstating the similarities between girls' and boys' lives before age six. They were given different toys to play with (McGovern, *Yankee Family*, 73), and mothers were kept keenly aware of the different worlds for which they were raising their toddlers (James Barnard Blake diary, Aug. 3, 1851, AAS; Kirk Jeffrey, "Family History: The Middle-Class American Family in the Urban Context, 1830–1870" [Ph.D. diss., Stanford Univ., 1972], 202–3), so that they must have treated their children differently according to sex. Still, the early domestic life of boys zealously discouraged basic "male" virtues like aggression and self-assertion in favor of "feminine" kindness and submission.

16. Beard, *Hardly a Man*, 76; Greven, *Protestant Temperament*, 45–46.

17. On girls' play and common culture, see Henrietta Dana Skinner, *An Echo from Parnassus: Being Girlhood Memories of Longfellow and His Friends* (New York, 1928), 87–111, 175–81; Mary Starbuck, *My House and I: A Chronicle of Nantucket* (Boston, 1929), esp. 212, 215; Lucy Larcom, *A New England Girlhood* (New York, 1961 [1889]), 17–117. On the interdependence of girls and women, see Carroll Smith-Rosenberg, "The Female World of Love and Ritual: Relations between Women in Nineteenth-Century America," *Signs*, 1 (1975), 14–19.

18. Alphonso David Rockwell, *Rambling Recollections: An Autobiography* (New York, 1920), 30–31, 56; Wallace, *Autobiography*, 55, 121; Beard, *Hardly a Man*, 203; Baker, *Native American*, 85; Hale, *New England Boyhood*, 40, 88, 151; Warner, *Being a Boy*, 49; Doughty, *Francis Parkman*, 14–15; Wheaton J. Lane, *Commodore Vanderbilt: An Epic of the Steam Age* (New York, 1942), 11, 13, 162.

19. Hale, *New England Boyhood*, 86.

20. Sedgwick, *Memoirs*, 20–21, 28–29; Hale, *New England Boyhood*, 22–23, 40.

21. Thomas Russell to John Brooks, Nov. 9, 1836, Charles Russell Papers, MHS; Wallace, *Autobiography*, 55; Beard, *Hardly a Man*, 78, 92; Lynn, *William Dean Howells*, 54–55; Ellis, "Men among Men," 251–53; Samuel McChord Crothers, "The Ignominy of Being Grown-Up," *Atlantic Monthly*, 98 (1906), 47. It is worth noting that much of the harshest violence seemed to take place in areas of the Midwest that were not many decades removed from frontier status and that were settled by Southern as well as Yankee stock.

22. John Mack Faragher, *Women and Men on the Overland Trail* (New Haven, Conn., 1979), 135–36.

23. Hale, *New England Boyhood*, 55, 151; Warner, *Being a Boy*, 127–28; Doughty, *Francis Parkman*, 14–15; Lynn, *William Dean Howells*, 45.

24. Beard, *Hardly a Man*, 92, 110; Hale, *New England Boyhood*, 23, 200–201; James Lovett, *Old Boston Boys and the Games They Played* (Boston, 1906); William Wells Newell, *Games and Songs of American Children* (New York, 1883).

25. Ellery H. Clark, *Reminiscences of an Athlete: Twenty Years on Track and Field* (Boston, 1911), 6; Beard, *Hardly a Man*, 102–3; Wallace, *Autobiography*, 22.

26. The boys' games of settlers and Indians were inspired not only by folklore but also by their reading. Cooper's *Leatherstocking Tales* was especially important in this regard (see Wallace, *Autobiography*, 54, and Canby, *Age of Confidence*, 192). Cowboys did not enter into these games until the final years of the century—the white men who fought Indians were called "the settlers" in the games of nineteenth-century boys.

27. Warner, *Being a Boy*, 89–91; Beard, *Hardly a Man*, 92; Clark, *Reminiscences*, 6.

28. Beard, *Hardly a Man*, 79; Hale, *New England Boyhood*, 82–83; Lynn, *William Dean Howells*, 45; Joseph Kett, *Rites of Passage: Adolescence in America, 1790 to the Present* (New York, 1977), 91–92.

29. Kett, *Rites of Passage*, 92; Bruce Laurie, *Working People of Philadelphia, 1800–1850* (New York, 1980); on privileged boys, see Hale, *New England Boyhood*, 136–37.

30. Charles Russell to Theodore Russell, Jan. 26, 1830, Russell Papers, MHS. Charles's instructions to Theodore are included in many letters to his wife,

Persis. See, for example, letters of Jan. 25 and May 31, 1830, Mar. 14, Dec. 8, and Dec. 16, 1831. See also Baker, *Native American,* 20.

31. Hale, *New England Boyhood,* 36–37.

32. Warner, *Being a Boy,* 50.

33. Rockwell, *Rambling Recollections,* 31.

34. Rockwell, *Rambling Recollections,* 31. Not all kin relationships were as amicable or as apparently lacking in ambivalence as the relationship between Alphonso Rockwell and his cousin. For a loyal but turbulent relationship between two brothers, Theodore and Thomas Russell, see Theodore to Persis Russell, Mar. 25 and Oct. 31, 183[4?], and Theodore Russell to Charles Russell, Sept. 21 and Dec. 14, 183[4?], Russell Papers, MHS.

35. Sedgwick, *Memoirs,* 32–33.

36. An interesting exception to this "nation-state" model of boyhood friendships is the passionate bond between Pierre and his cousin Glen Stanly in Herman Melville's novel *Pierre.* The open devotion and confiding intimacy of their relationship could be readily found in the ties between male youth in their late teens and twenties, but was extremely rare between nineteenth-century boys (Herman Melville, *Pierre, or the Ambiguities* [New York, 1971]).

37. On Roosevelt and his museum, see Kathleen Dalton, "The Early Life of Theodore Roosevelt" (Ph.D. diss., Johns Hopkins Univ., 1979), 171–72. The Indiana club is described in Wallace, *Autobiography,* 55.

38. Warner, *Being a Boy,* 50.

39. Lynn, *William Dean Howells,* 44; Beard, *Hardly a Man,* 78.

40. Lynn, *William Dean Howells,* 43; Sedgwick, *Memoirs,* 32–33; Canby, *Age of Confidence,* 42–45; W. S. Tryon, *Parnassus Corner: A Life of James T. Fields, Publisher to the Victorians* (Boston, 1963), 9. These antagonisms between towns and neighborhoods became the basis for the high school sports rivalries that blossomed late in the century.

41. Canby, *Age of Confidence,* 42–43 and more generally 40–45.

42. Sedgwick, *Memoirs,* 32–33. Sedgwick and his friends also understood their difference from boys further up the social scale: "Boys of Murray Hill, boys of what thirty years later was to be named the Four Hundred . . . would probably have thought us of very little significance."

43. Canby, *Age of Confidence,* 37; see also Stephen Salisbury, Jr., to Betsy Salisbury, Oct. 27, 1810, Salisbury Papers, Box 14, AAS; Beard, *Hardly a Man,* 110–11; Theodore Roosevelt, *The Strenuous Life: Essays and Addresses* (New York, 1902), 162–64.

44. Ellis, "Men among Men," 251–53.

45. Beard, *Hardly a Man,* 92, 103.

46. Canby, *Age of Confidence,* 40; Sedgwick, *Memoirs,* 33; Rockwell, *Rambling Recollections,* 31.

47. Male autobiographers who grew up in the nineteenth century sometimes talked about the democracy that existed among boys. What they meant in

modern terms is that their boy culture was a meritocracy in which a boy's demonstrated abilities, not his family's status, determined his standing among his peers. See Canby, *Age of Confidence*, 40, and Hale, *New England Boyhood*, 32–33.

48. See note 46.

49. Canby, *Age of Confidence*, 192.

50. Lynn, *William Dean Howells*, 45.

51. Rockwell, *Rambling Recollections*, 56; John William DeForest, *A Volunteer's Adventures: A Union Captain's Record of the Civil War* (New Haven, Conn., 1946), 57, 93; Beard, *Hardly a Man*, 96.

52. Beard, *Hardly a Man*, 47.

53. Wallace, *Autobiography*, 122. For further instances of boy culture demanding daring behavior, see John Doane Barnard journal, EI, 3–4; Rockwell, *Rambling Recollections*, 56; Canby, *Age of Confidence*, 44.

54. Ryan, *Cradle*, 161; Canby, *Age of Confidence*, 235 (see also 192–94).

55. Beard, *Hardly a Man*, 74–75; Rockwell, *Rambling Recollections*, 56.

56. For example, Canby, *Age of Confidence*, 45.

57. Wallace, *Autobiography*, 55.

58. See, for instance, Lynn, *William Dean Howells*, 44.

59. Crothers, "Ignominy," 47.

60. Lynn, *William Dean Howells*, 45; Wallace, *Autobiography*, 55; Canby even claimed that bullying, while it represented "primitive sadism," was laced with pleasure because it gave the victims "delicious terrors" (*Age of Confidence*, 37).

61. Hale, *New England Boyhood*, 37; Wallace, *Autobiography*, 55; Barnard, "Journal," EI, 3–4; Canby, *Age of Confidence*, 43–44.

62. Beard, *Hardly a Man*, 78.

63. Beard, *Hardly a Man*, 73–74.

64. Rockwell, *Rambling Recollections*, 35–36. Younger boys could—and sometimes did—use pranks for the same purposes against older boys (Beard, *Hardly a Man*, 76, 78–79).

65. Beard, *Hardly a Man*, 102.

66. Even in small towns where fathers worked close by, boys found it was their mothers who intervened in their daily activities with friends. See Wallace, *Autobiography*, 22, and Lynn, *William Dean Howells*, 42, 44.

67. Theodore to Charles Russell, Jan. 26, 1830, Russell Papers, MHS; Elisha Whittlesey to William Whittlesey, Dec. 13, 1830, and Elisha Whittlesey to Comfort Whittlesey, Jan. 20, 1840, William W. Whittlesey Papers, Container 1, WRHS; Baker, *Native American*, 20; Warner, *Being a Boy*, 41–43.

68. Wallace, *Autobiography*, 77–79; Barnard, "Journal," EI 3–4.

69. Beard, *Hardly a Man*, 102; Mark Twain, *The Adventures of Huckleberry Finn* (New York, 1968 [1884]), 346.

70. Sedgwick, *Memoirs*, 23; Warner, *Being a Boy*, 161; Mrs. Manners, *At Home and Abroad*, 42–43.

71. Beard, *Hardly a Man*, 111, 157–58; Lynn, *William Dean Howells*, 44.

72. Lynn, *William Dean Howells*, 44, 42; Beard, *Hardly a Man*, 157–58; Wallace, *Autobiography*, 22.

73. Hale, *New England Boyhood*, 55; Baker, *Native American*, 85.

74. Beard, *Hardly a Man*, 157–58.

75. Sedgwick, *Memoirs*, 20–21; Wallace, *Autobiography*, 27.

76. Beard, *Hardly a Man*, 111.

77. Mrs. Manners, *At Home and Abroad*, 43. See also Warner, *Being a Boy*, 73–74, and the comments in Mark Carnes, "The Making of the Self-made Man: The Emotional Experience of Boyhood in Victorian America," unpub. essay, 11.

78. Beard, *Hardly a Man*, 199.

79. The vituperation heaped on "goody-goodies" not only reflected boys' insecurity about their own tendencies to follow their mothers' advice and their desire to maintain the integrity of their subculture, it may also have represented a way for boys to deflect their own anger from their mothers (who, after all, were trying to frustrate them) onto more acceptable targets.

80. A useful discussion of the indefinite language of age in the early nineteenth century (and the indefinite phases of life which the language indicated) is Kett, *Rites of Passage*, 11–14.

81. Wallace, *Autobiography*, 80–82.

82. Rockwell, *Rambling Recollections*, 63.

83. The average age of puberty for boys in this era was about sixteen (Kett, *Rites of Passage*, 44).

84. Beard, *Hardly a Man*, 199.

85. A squabble between brothers over the use of a suit provides vivid evidence of clothing as a badge of "'civilized' manhood." See Theodore Russell to Persis Russell, Oct. 31, 183[4?], Russell Papers, MHS.

86. Rockwell, *Rambling Recollections*, 63.

87. Warner, *Being a Boy*, 1. See notes 28–31.

Chapter 3: Male Youth Culture

1. On semidependence, see Joseph Kett, *Rites of Passage: Adolescence in America, 1790 to the Present* (New York, 1977), 11–37. He writes usefully about the imprecision of the nineteenth-century language of age on 11–14.

2. The word *separation* and the phrase "leaving home" are used loosely here. That is, they refer to a process of separation rather than a particular moment of departure. In fact, young men usually returned to live at home one or more times after their first separation. What matters for our purposes, however, is the way males experienced the process of separation and faced the fact that—sooner or later—they would establish a perma-

nent life away from their childhood home. It was this set of experiences that young men found so trying.

3. The *Oxford English Dictionary* contains several British usages of *homesick* or *homesickness* from the last quarter of the eighteenth century (*The Compact Edition of the Oxford English Dictionary* [Oxford, 1971], vol. 1, 1323). No such word appears in the American materials from the late 1700s examined for this book. The earliest usage found here is in the June 28, 1806, entry in "Diary of Archelaus Putnam of New Mills," *The Historical Collections of the Danvers Historical Society,* 6 (1916), 20. Other mentions of homesickness include Stephen Salisbury, Jr., to Stephen Salisbury, Sr., July 9, 1812, Salisbury Family Papers, AAS; Reuben Hitchcock to Nabby Hitchcock, May 20, 1823, Hitchcock Papers, Container 9a, WRHS; Mark Dunning to Aaron Olmstead, May 19, 1837, Aaron Barlow Olmstead Papers, NYHS; Charles Russell to Persis Russell, Jan. 26, 1834, Charles Russell Papers, MHS; Elisha Whittlesey to William Whittlesey, Jan. 23, 1836, William W. Whittlesey Papers, Container 1, WRHS; Mary A. O. Gay to W. Allan Gay, Oct. 12, 1840, Gay-Otis Collection, CUL; John Kirk to "Brother Calvin," Mar. 26, 1853, Kirk Letterbooks, vol. 1, CHS; Walker Blaine to James G. Blaine, Apr. 6, 1869, Blaine Papers, LC.

4. Theodore Russell to Sarah Russell, May 25, 1835, Theodore Russell to Charles Russell, May 30, 1838, Russell Papers, MHS. Typically for his time, Theodore Russell used *man* ("Man is made for action") in a way that makes it difficult to separate the generic (*humankind*) from the sex-specific (*male*). A variety of contextual clues within the letter makes it clear that he meant the word here in the sex-specific sense.

5. On the symbolic meaning of home in the bourgeois culture of the time, see E. Anthony Rotundo, "American Manhood: The Northern Middle Class, 1770–1920" (Ph.D. diss., Brandeis Univ., 1982), 162–68; William Bridges, "Warm Hearth, Cold World: Social Perspectives on the Household Poets," *American Quarterly,* 21 (1969); Kirk Jeffrey, "The Family as Utopian Retreat from the City," *Soundings,* 55 (1972).

6. John Doane Barnard journal, EI, 33.

7. Daniel Webster to Thomas Merrill, Nov. 11, 1803, *The Writings and Speeches of Daniel Webster* (Boston, 1903), vol. 17.

8. *Diary and Letters of Rutherford Birchard Hayes, Nineteenth President of the United States,* ed. Charles Richard Williams (Columbus, Ohio, 1922), vol. 1, 107; Morton S. Bailey to James Cattell, Nov. 18, 1880, James Cattell Papers, Family Correspondence, LC.

9. Kett, *Rites of Passage,* 23–29, 31–36, 158–60; William R. Johnson, *Schooled Lawyers: A Study in the Clash of Professional Cultures* (New York, 1978).

10. See, for instance, Irving Bartlett, *Daniel Webster* (New York, 1978), 22; Aaron Olmstead to Lucy Olmstead, Feb. 16, 1839, Zalmon Olmstead to Aaron Olmstead, Mar. 13, 1839, Lucy Olmstead to Aaron Olmstead, Feb. 9, 1841, Olmstead Papers, NYHS.

11. Lucy Olmstead to Aaron Olmstead, Dec. 15, 1840, Olmstead Papers, NYHS. On another such odyssey, consult Barnard, "Journal," EI, 6–47.

12. Sergeant Kendall to Frank and Elizabeth Kendall, Jan. 16, 1888, Kendall Papers, NYHS. See also James Cattell to William and Elizabeth Cattell, Mar. 14, 1885, Cattell Papers, Family Correspondence, LC; Mark Barber to Martha Eaton, Apr. 6, 1890, Edward D. Eaton Papers, Box 8, SHSW; Isaac Holt, *In School from Three to Eighty* (Pittsfield, Mass., 1927), 83–85; Celia Parker Worley, *The Western Slope* (Evanston, Ill., 1903), 91–94; Bartlett, *Daniel Webster,* 33, 36–37. In a journal entry, Ralph Waldo Emerson indicated that this moral self-doubt was typical of young men (see Emerson quoted in Jonathan Katz, ed., *Gay American History: Lesbians and Gay Men in the U.S.A.* [New York, 1976], 460–61). Mothers, ministers, moral reform groups, and published advisers to young men were apprehensive about the moral future of young men left to their own devices in the antebellum cities. Their alarmed pronouncements fed young men's own uncertainties and established a symbolic cultural dilemma of enduring strength—the innocent young man exposed to the temptations of urban life. See Mary Ryan, *The Empire of the Mother: American Writing about Domesticity, 1830–1860* (New York, 1982), 59–70.

13. Char Miller, *Fathers and Sons: The Bingham Family and the American Mission* (Philadelphia, 1982), 66–67, 127.

14. Henry Dwight Sedgwick, *Memoirs of an Epicurean* (New York, 1942), 125. On the rejection of familial (and especially paternal) values, see Oliver Wendell Holmes, Jr., to parents, May 30, 1864, in Mark DeWolfe Howe, ed., *Touched with Fire: Civil War Letters and Diary of Oliver Wendell Holmes, Jr., 1861–64* (Cambridge, Mass., 1946); James Cattell to William and Elizabeth Cattell, Feb. 6, 1884, and Jan. 19, 1885, Cattell Papers, Family Correspondence, LC; Ray Stannard Baker, *Native American: The Book of My Youth* (New York, 1939), 323–36; Henry Seidel Canby, *The Age of Confidence: Life in the Nineties* (New York, 1934), 192–95; James R. McGovern, *Yankee Family* (New Orleans, 1975), 49–50.

15. Baker, *Native American,* 217.

16. Kett, *Rites of Passage,* 40; James McLachlan, "The *Choice of Hercules:* American Student Societies in the Early Nineteenth Century," in Lawrence Stone, ed., *The University in Society* (Princeton, N.J., 1974), 449–94.

17. Samuel Howard to James Howard, Jan. 28, 1828, James C. Howard Papers, SHSW; Charles Van Hise to Alice Ring, Nov. 24, 1878, Box 1, Charles Van Hise Papers, SHSW; Howard Doughty, *Francis Parkman* (Cambridge, Mass., 1983 [1962]), 25–26; W. S. Tryon, *Parnassus Corner: A Life of James T. Fields, Publisher to the Victorians* (Boston, 1963), 36–38; Ezekiel Webster to Daniel Webster, May 28, 1803, *Writings of Webster,* vol. 17; Kett, *Rites of Passage,* 38–40, 43, 56, 74–75; Mary Ryan, *The Cradle of the Middle Class: The Family in Oneida County, New York, 1790–1865* (New York, 1981), 128–31, 176–77; Helen Lefkowitz Horowitz,

Campus Life: Undergraduate Cultures from the Eighteenth Century to the Present (New York, 1987), 24, 26–29, 36–41; Stuart Blumin, *The Emergence of the Middle Class: Social Experience in the American City, 1760–1900* (New York, 1989), 211–16; John Mack Faragher, *Women and Men on the Overland Trail* (New Haven, Conn., 1979), 117.

18. Kett, *Rites of Passage*, 38–40, 43, 74–75; Ryan, *Cradle*, 134–35.

19. *Diary and Letters of Hayes*, vol. 1, 66, 74–75, 77; diaries, Papers of Frank Clarke, LC; Charles Flint, *Memories of an Active Life: Men, Ships, and Sealing Wax* (New York, 1923), 115, 118–28; Tryon, *Parnassus Corner*, 44–45; Horowitz, *Campus Life*, 36–41; Ryan, *Cradle*, 177. Fraternal lodges, being open to men of all ages, did not serve many of the functions that young men's associations usually did, but they did provide a familial sense of security for youthful members. See Mark C. Carnes, *Secret Ritual and Manhood in Victorian America* (New Haven, Conn., 1989); Mary Ann Clawson, *Constructing Brotherhood: Class, Gender, and Fraternalism* (Princeton, N.J., 1989).

20. Ryan, *Cradle*, 128–30, 176–77. See also Harris Merton Lyon, "The City of Lonesome Men," *Collier's*, 48 (1912).

21. Ryan, *Cradle*, 176, 129.

22. *Diary and Letters of Hayes*, vol. 1, 66; Sedgwick, *Memoirs*, 98; Tryon, *Parnassus Corner*, 30, 36; Doughty, *Francis Parkman*, 25. Drinking was a different popular form of shared nurture. See Sedgwick, *Memoirs*, 90–91, 98–99; Doughty, *Francis Parkman*, 25; Edward Everett Hale, *A New England Boyhood* (Boston, 1964), 191–93; Lyon, "Lonesome Men"; Horowitz, *Campus Life*, 2, 12–13, 42, 45.

23. Alphonso David Rockwell, *Rambling Recollections: An Autobiography* (New York, 1920), 92–93; *Diary and Letters of Hayes*, vol. 1, 66; Attic Nights described in Tryon, *Parnassus Corner*, 36, 44–46.

24. Flint, *Memories*, 115; Sedgwick, *Memoirs*, 90–91, 98–99; Doughty, *Francis Parkman*, 25–26; Daniel Carter Beard, *Hardly a Man Is Now Alive: The Autobiography of Dan Beard* (New York, 1939), 284–85; *Diary and Letters of Hayes*, vol. 1, 66; Hale, *New England Boyhood*, 126, 204; Tryon, *Parnassus Corner*, 37–44; Kett, *Rites of Passage*, 40, 56, 92–93; Charles Van Hise to Alice Ring, Dec. 7, 1878, Van Hise Papers, Box 1, SHSW.

25. Tryon, *Parnassus Corner*, 37.

26. Rockwell, *Rambling Recollections*, 92.

27. The Cataline quotation and the information about the Dartmouth incident come from Ezekiel Webster to Daniel Webster, May 28, 1803, *Writings of Webster*, vol. 17; on a similar conflict, see *Diary and Letters of Hayes*, vol. 1, 74–75, 77.

28. Kett, *Rites of Passage*, 58; Horowitz, *Campus Life*, 38, 42–44. See Leonard Ellis, "Men among Men: An Exploration of All-Male Relationships in Victorian America" (Ph.D. diss., Columbia Univ., 1982). This interclass scrim-

maging survived into the twentieth century on some campuses (Larry Hart, "Tales of Old Dorp," *Schenectady Gazette*, Nov. 25, 1986, 13).

29. Kett, *Rites of Passage*, 92–93; Flint, *Memories*, 25–26; Beard, *Hardly a Man*, 284–85.

30. Beard, *Hardly a Man*, 284.

31. Ryan, *Cradle*, 130; Tryon, *Parnassus Corner*, 29, 31–37; Kett, *Rites of Passage*, 42–43; Blumin, *Emergence*, 214–16.

32. "Substitute for college" from Tryon, *Parnassus Corner*, 37; Samuel Howard to James Howard, Jan. 28, 1828, James C. Howard Papers, Box 1, SHSW; Hale, *New England Boyhood*, 124–25; Ryan, *Cradle*, 177; Kett, *Rites of Passage*, 92–93.

33. Hale, *New England Boyhood*, 179; McLachlan, "The *Choice*," 449–94; Horowitz, *Campus Life*, 26–29, 31, 41; Kett, *Rites of Passage*, 56; L. Ellis, "Men among Men," 287–88; Charles Van Hise to Alice Ring, Nov. 24 and Dec. 7, 1878, Van Hise Papers, Box 1, SHSW; Doughty, *Francis Parkman*, 25–26; Rockwell, *Rambling Recollections*, 93–94, on the college curriculum and literary societies. The lyceum is discussed as a form of higher education in Hale, *New England Boyhood*, 124–27. On literary papers at fraternity meetings, see *Diary and Letters of Hayes*, vol. 1, 66, and Sedgwick, *Memoirs*, 90.

34. Ryan, *Cradle*, 130; Tryon, *Parnassus Corner*, 43–44.

35. See, for example, Rockwell, *Rambling Recollections*, 92.

36. Charles Van Hise to Alice Ring, Nov. 24, 1878, Van Hise Papers, Box 1, SHSW.

37. Charles Van Hise to Alice Ring, Dec. 7, 1878, Van Hise Papers, Box 1, SHSW.

38. Sedgwick, *Memoirs*, 33. See also, *Diary and Letters of Hayes*, vol. 1, 46–48, and Kenneth S. Lynn, *William Dean Howells: An American Life* (New York, 1970), 68–69.

39. *Diary and Letters of Hayes*, vol. 1, 66.

40. Tryon, *Parnassus Corner*, 36–44; Blumin, *Emergence*, 215–26; Don H. Doyle, "The Social Functions of Voluntary Associations in a Nineteenth-Century American Town," *Social Science History*, 1 (Spring 1977), 349–50.

41. The record of youthful male hedonism is described in Mary A. O. Gay to William Otis, Jan. 15, June 11 and 25, 1826, Gay-Otis Collection, CUL; Barnard, "Journal," EI, 56; Martin Van Buren to John Van Buren, June 25 and Sept. 3, 1830, Martin Van Buren Papers, LC; Sedgwick, *Memoirs*, 90–91, 96, 98–99; Hale, *New England Boyhood*, 191–93; Bartlett, *Daniel Webster*, 221; Doughty, *Francis Parkman*, 25; Kett, *Rites of Passage*, 40–41, 53–55; Horowitz, *Campus Life*, 23–55. On sexual temptation and indulgence, see Richard Sennett, *Families against the City: Middle-Class Homes in Industrial Chicago, 1872–1890* (New York, 1970), 112–13, and John D'Emilio and Estelle B. Freedman, *Intimate Matters: A History of Sexuality in America* (New York, 1988), 109–11, 180–83.

42. On town-gown violence, see David Allmendinger, Jr., "The Dangers of Antebellum Student Life," *Journal of Social History*, 7 (1973), 75–83. Fears about the threat of sexual desire to productive manliness are suggested in McGovern, 13; John G. Cawelti, *Apostles of the Self-made Man: Changing Concepts of Success in America* (Chicago, 1965), 49–50; Bartlett, 37; and esp. Smith-Rosenberg, "Sex as Symbol in Victorian Purity: An Ethnohistorical Analysis of Jacksonian America," in John Demos and Sarane Spence Boocock, eds., *Turning Points: Historical and Sociological Essays on the Family* (Chicago, 1978), 5241–42.

43. This distance was becoming less customary for young men from urban middle-class families in the late nineteenth century. See Ryan, *Cradle*, 169–73.

44. Kett, *Rites of Passage*, 40, 102, 199–201; David I. Macleod, *Building Character in the American Boy: The Boy Scouts, YMCA, and Their Forerunners, 1870–1920* (Madison, Wis., 1983). Thomas Wentworth Higginson hoped that the gymnasiums that opened in major cities during the 1850s would also serve as a distraction from—or an alternative to—vice (Higginson, *Out-Door Papers* [Boston, 1886 (1863)], 161–62).

45. Kett, *Rites of Passage*, 95, 103–7; Henry Ward Beecher, *Lectures to Young Men on Various Important Subjects* (Boston, 1856 [1844]); Joel Hawes, *Lectures Addressed to the Young Men of Hartford and New Haven* (Hartford, 1828); Sylvester Graham, *A Lecture to Young Men* (New York, 1974 [1834]).

46. What became of all the primal energy that was bridled or suppressed during the long years of male youth? It seems to have found three outlets in men's lives. Perhaps the most common was the search for excitement and adventure. Many men took bold chances in commerce or professional life. This helps to explain why dour, restrained Yankee businessmen so often proved to be such bold, imaginative risk-takers. Also, there was a men's world of pleasure and fantasy that provided a second outlet through gambling, drink, and prostitution. Lodges and men's clubs expressed male urges to fantasy and amusement that were not allowed in the worlds of work and home. Finally, the suppression of so much playful energy created a male market for a literature of fantasy and adventure. The novels of Sir Walter Scott and James Fenimore Cooper, the tales of Davy Crockett, the South Sea stories of Herman Melville, and (later) Western novels and the works of Mark Twain were all popular with grown men as well as boys. If this line of interpretation is correct, then these works of fiction appealed to men not as a full expression of male values and feelings but as a resonant echo of those impulses and emotions that men had forsaken in growing up. On the appeal of these authors, see the direct testimony of Baker, *Native American*, 42–44; Canby, *Age of Confidence*, 191–95; Wallace, *Autobiography*, 54; Sedgwick, *Memoirs*, 34, 72–75.

Chapter 4: Youth and Male Intimacy

1. Daniel Webster to J. Hervey Bingham, Feb. 11, 1800, *The Writings and Speeches of Daniel Webster* (Boston, 1903), vol. 17.

2. Webster to Thomas Merrill, May 1, 1804, in *Writings of Webster,* vol. 17.

3. Jonathan Katz, ed., *Gay American History: Lesbians and Gay Men in the U.S.A.* (New York, 1976), 451–56; John C. Miller, *Alexander Hamilton: A Portrait of Paradox* (New York, 1959), 21–24.

4. Carroll Smith-Rosenberg, "The Female World of Love and Ritual: Relations between Women in Nineteenth-Century America," *Signs,* 1 (1975), 1–29.

5. See, for example, Aaron Barlow Olmstead Papers, NYHS, and John Ward diaries and notebooks, NYHS.

6. Alphonso David Rockwell, *Rambling Recollections: An Autobiography* (New York, 1920), 31.

7. Gerald N. Grob, *Edward Jarvis and the Medical World of Nineteenth-Century America* (Knoxville, Tenn., 1978), 19–21.

8. Charles Milton Baldwin diary, NYSLA; see Grob, *Edward Jarvis,* 20, 27.

9. Morton S. Bailey to James Cattell, Sept. 5, 1881, and Oct. 15, 1882, James Cattell Papers, Family Correspondence, LC. For other examples of emotional support between close friends, see James Barnard Blake diary, Jan. 15, 1851, AAS; Ward diary, Jan. 18, 1864, NYHS; Sergeant Kendall to B. Franklin and Elizabeth Kendall, Mar. 14, 1889, Kendall Papers, NYHS; Howard Doughty, *Francis Parkman* (Cambridge, Mass., 1983 [1962]), 145–46; Rockwell, *Rambling Recollections,* 134–35.

10. Morton S. Bailey to James Cattell, Sept. 5, 1881, Cattell Papers, Family Correspondence, LC.

11. Daniel Webster to J. Hervey Bingham, Feb. 11, 1800, Sept. 22, 1801, Oct. 26, 1801, and Oct. 6, 1803, *Writings of Webster,* vol. 17.

12. Daniel Webster to J. Hervey Bingham, Dec. 28, 1800, Sept. 10, 1801, Oct. 26, 1801, May 18, 1802, July 22, 1802, *Writings of Webster,* vol. 17. Such words of affection were common to the correspondence of many young male intimates in the nineteenth century. See Katz, *Gay American History,* 651, n. 75, and Peter Gay, *The Tender Passion* (New York, 1986), 207–10.

13. Daniel Webster to J. Hervey Bingham, Feb. 11, 1800 and Oct. 26, 1801, *Writings of Webster,* vol. 17; on the sharing of feelings in other young men's friendships, see Rockwell, *Rambling Recollections,* 134–35; Robert Abzug, *Passionate Liberator: Theodore Dwight Weld and the Dilemma of Reform* (New York, 1980), 186, 233; Gay, *Tender Passion,* 210; John Lambert to Sergeant Kendall, n.d. [1891] and June 9, 1891, Kendall Papers, NYHS; Donald Yacovone, "Abolitionists and the Language of Fraternal Love," in Mark C. Carnes and Clyde Griffen, eds., *Meanings for Manhood: Constructions of Masculinity in Victorian America* (Chicago, 1990).

14. For the same phenomenon, see John Doane Barnard journal, EI, 10; Blake diary, July 13, 1851, AAS; Gary L. Williams, "The Psychosexual Fears of Joshua Speed and Abraham Lincoln, 1839–1842," paper presented at the meetings of the Organization of American Historians, Apr. 1980; Abzug, *Passionate Liberator,* 193.

15. Daniel Webster to J. Hervey Bingham, Jan. 2, 1805, *Writings of Webster,* vol. 17.

16. Such promises of enduring commitment were not uncommon between intimate male friends in youth. See Blake diary, Jan. 5, 1851; Abzug, *Passionate Liberator,* 233; Charles B. Strozier, *Lincoln's Quest for Union: Public and Private Meanings* (New York, 1982), 42.

17. Daniel Webster to J. Hervey Bingham, Apr. 3, 1804, *Writings of Webster,* vol. 17.

18. Daniel Webster to Thomas Merrill, Nov. 11, 1803, *Writings of Webster,* vol. 17.

19. Daniel Webster to J. Hervey Bingham, Feb. 22, 1803, *Writings of Webster,* vol. 17. Other young men possessed the same sense that their intimate friendships resembled marriage, perhaps even setting a standard of love by which marriage could be measured: John Lambert to Sergeant Kendall, n.d. [1891], Kendall Papers, NYHS; Abzug, *Passionate Liberator,* 190–91.

20. Blake diary, Jan. 5 and Dec. 31, 1851, AAS.

21. Blake diary, Dec. 31, 1851, AAS. Blake's intense bond with Mary added a curious dimension to his friendship with Vanderhoef. Perhaps the strangest moment of their triangular relationship was the one which happened after Blake and Vanderhoef went to bed together one night: "Ere we closed our eyes in slumber, we embraced each other, and with tears blending as they coursed down our cheeks we uttered from the fullness of our hearts, God bless dear Mary" (Blake diary, July 13, 1851, AAS). The meaning of this three-way intimacy is not clear. Was the physical affection between Blake and Vanderhoef a substitute for contact they both wished to have with Mary? Was their mutual love for Mary a safety valve for some of the love they felt for each other? Was this simply a displaced instance of Oedipal rivalry? And what was the significance of this triangle for Mary? Even though the answers to those questions are not evident, we can say with certainty that this three-way bond was not unique. Henry David Thoreau and his beloved brother, John, courted the same woman (Richard Lebeaux, *Young Man Thoreau* [Amherst, Mass., 1977], 116–22), and Charles Stuart—intimate friend and "spiritual lover" to abolitionist Theodore Weld—proposed marriage to Theodore's sister Cornelia, who was the woman closest to Theodore when he was a bachelor (Abzug, *Passionate Liberator,* 166).

22. Blake diary, Dec. 27, 1851, AAS.

23. Blake diary, July 10, 1851; see also Blake's entry for July 13, 1851.

24. More casual, public touching was also acceptable between young men and

could have great emotional significance. See Ward diary, Apr. 15, 1864, NYHS.

25. Gay, *Tender Passion*, 207–9.

26. Gay, *Tender Passion*, 206–11.

27. Gay, *Tender Passion*, 210.

28. Smith-Rosenberg, "The Female World," 8.

29. In writing about "manly intimacy" among upper-class Britons, Jeffrey Richards ("'Passing the Love of Women': Manly Love and Victorian Society," in J. A. Mangan and James Walvin, eds., *Manliness and Morality: Middle-Class Masculinity in Britain and America, 1800–1940* [New York, 1987], 92–102), has provided us with a clear summary of the historical precedents that Victorian men used to justify their intimate attachments, but two other authors (Katz, *Gay American History*, 451–52, and Gay, *Tender Passion*, 237–49) are helpful on the classical roots of these relationships. It is striking—though hardly surprising—that all of the classical models were male friendships, even though same-sex intimacy was common to both sexes in the nineteenth century. While it is not clear whether women took these male relationships as their own models, it is clear that men dominated the public discourse on this issue and presented members of their own sex as the standard by which same-sex intimacy could be justified.

30. See Yacovone, "Abolitionists," 86, as well as Richards, "Passing the Love."

31. The foregoing interpretation of middle-class attitudes toward homosexuality draws on evidence presented in Katz, *Gay American History*, 26–53, on Katz's own interpretation, 448–49, on Michael Lynch, "The Age of Adhesiveness: Male-Male Intimacy in New York City, 1830–1880," paper presented at the meetings of the American Historical Association, Dec. 1985, 6–11, and on Gay, *Tender Passion*, 201–19.

32. Lewis Wallace, *Lew Wallace: An Autobiography* (New York, 1906), 19; Rockwell, *Rambling Recollections*, 181–82; Lebeaux, *Young Man Thoreau*, 59; Claude M. Fuess, *Daniel Webster* (Boston, 1930), vol. 1, 25; Yacovone, "Abolitionists," 94.

33. Elisha Whittlesey to William Whittlesey, Nov. 25, 1838, William Wallace Whittlesey Papers, Container 1, WRHS.

34. Strozier, *Lincoln's Quest*, 41–42.

35. Smith-Rosenberg, "Female World"; Lillian Faderman discussed women's romantic friendships in these same lifelong terms in *Surpassing the Love of Men: Romantic Friendships and Love between Women from the Renaissance to the Present* (New York, 1981).

36. On father-son overtones, see Robert Abzug's interpretation of the relationship between Theodore Weld and Charles Stuart (*Passionate Liberator*, 33–34).

37. Daniel Webster to J. Hervey Bingham, Dec. 28, 1800, *Writings of Webster*, vol. 17.

38. *Diary and Letters of Rutherford Birchard Hayes, Nineteenth President of the United States,* ed. Charles Richard Williams (Columbus, Ohio, 1922), vol. 1, Aug. 1, 1831.

39. Morton S. Bailey to James Cattell, Oct. 15, 1882, Cattell Papers, Family Correspondence, LC.

40. Strozier, *Lincoln's Quest,* 41–49.

41. Gay, *Tender Passion,* 210.

42. Erik Erikson, *Childhood and Society,* 2nd ed. (New York, 1963), 61–63; Erik Erikson, *Identity: Youth and Crisis* (New York, 1968), 19–35.

43. Irving Bartlett, *Daniel Webster* (New York, 1978), 45.

44. Smith-Rosenberg, "Female World," 60.

45. Smith-Rosenberg, "Female World," 60–71.

46. It seems that nineteenth-century voluntary associations offered middle-class people a kind of sanction to set aside certain gender expectations. Just as female voluntary associations gave women an opportunity for "manly" self-assertion without undermining their female identity, so, too, men's organizations provided men with an outlet for "feminine" relational needs without corroding the integrity of their male identity.

Chapter 5: The Development of Men's Attitudes toward Women

1. J. A. Webber to Henry Giles, Dec. 26, 1815, Giles Family Papers, no. 20, NYHS; Adriel G. Ely to Aaron Olmstead, Aug. 8, 1836, Aaron Barlow Olmstead Papers, NYHS.

2. Theodore Russell to Sarah Russell, May 25, 1835, and Theodore Russell to Charles Russell, May 30, 1838, Charles Russell Papers, MHS.

3. Robert Abzug, *Passionate Liberator: Theodore Dwight Weld and the Dilemma of Reform* (New York, 1980), 13–14, 166–67; Lu Burlingame to Will Adkinson, Dec. 19, 1869, Florence Burlingame Adkinson Papers, SL. On the uses of the brother-sister model in advice literature, see Carroll Smith-Rosenberg, "Sex as Symbol in Victorian Purity: An Ethnohistorical Analysis of Jacksonian America," in John Demos and Sarane Spence Boocock, eds., *Turning Points: Historical and Sociological Essays on the Family* (Chicago, 1978), 5241–42. For a forceful interpretation of nine-teenth-century brother-sister relationships (somewhat overdrawn in the American case), see Stephen Mintz, *A Prison of Expectations: The Family in Victorian Culture* (New York, 1983), 147–87.

4. Henry Seidel Canby, *The Age of Confidence: Life in the Nineties* (New York, 1934), 36; Edward Everett Hale, *A New England Boyhood* (Boston, 1964 [1893]), 49.

5. On brotherly protection, see Hale, *New England Boyhood,* 129; Charles Milton Baldwin diary, Feb. 15 and 16, 1868, NYSLA; Frank P. Fetherston diary, Mar. 16 and May 4, 1888, NYHS. Sedgwick is quoted in Rachel Deb-

orah Cramer, "Images of the American Father, 1790–1860," unpub. MS, 68. Sedgwick's service to her own brothers is described in Mintz, *Prison,* 160–64, 169–70, and Carl N. Degler, *At Odds: Women and the Family in America from the Revolution to the Present* (New York, 1980), 158–59.

6. Howard Doughty, *Francis Parkman* (Cambridge, Mass., 1983 [1962]), 7, 285, 287; Richard Lebeaux, *Young Man Thoreau* (Amherst, Mass., 1977), 45; Abzug, *Passionate Liberator,* 13–14, 166–67.

7. Seargent Prentiss to Anna Prentiss, n.d., in George Prentiss, *Bright Side of Life* (New York, 1901), 317.

8. At this point in history, a woman's active choice of "single blessedness" was just becoming a viable option, but it was still not the expected choice. See Lee V. Chambers-Schiller, *Liberty, a Better Husband: Single Women in America; the Generations of 1780–1840* (New Haven, Conn., 1990); Degler, *At Odds,* 151–65.

9. Aaron Olmstead to Lucy Olmstead, Feb. 16, 1839, Lucy Olmstead to Aaron Olmstead, June 20, 1839, and Sept. 15, 1838, Olmstead Papers, NYHS.

10. Lucy Olmstead to Aaron Olmstead, Sept. 15, 1838, Dec. 15, 1840, and Feb. 9, 1841, Olmstead Papers, NYHS.

11. Canby, *Age of Confidence,* 36; Ellen Rothman, *Hands and Hearts: A History of Courtship in America* (New York, 1984), 23.

12. Charles Dudley Warner, *Being a Boy* (Boston, 1897 [1877]), 52–53, 98–99; Mrs. Manners, *At Home and Abroad; or How to Behave* (New York, 1853), 40–41; Daniel Carter Beard, *Hardly a Man Is Now Alive: The Autobiography of Dan Beard* (New York, 1939), 203; Thomas Wentworth Higginson, *Out-Door Papers* (Boston, 1886 [1863]), 96, 99, 217.

13. Doughty, *Francis Parkman,* 16; Canby, *Age of Confidence,* 38; Mary Ryan, *The Cradle of the Middle Class: The Family in Oneida County, New York, 1790–1865* (New York, 1981), 164.

14. Canby, *Age of Confidence,* 36–38; Beard, *Hardly a Man,* 97–98; Warner, *Being a Boy,* 98–99, 153–54, 159.

15. Kenneth S. Lynn, *William Dean Howells: An American Life* (New York, 1970), 47; Beard, *Hardly a Man,* 74, 97, 102; Warner, *Being a Boy,* 52–53, 98.

16. Warner, *Being a Boy,* 52, 99.

17. George Dillinat to Thomas Russell, May 28, 1838, Russell Papers, MHS.

18. Beard, *Hardly a Man,* 199, 202–3.

19. George Dillinat to Thomas Russell, May 28, 1838, Russell Papers, MHS.

20. Daniel Webster to James Merrill, June 7, 1802, and to Habijah Fuller, July 2, 1803, *The Writings and Speeches of Daniel Webster* (Boston, 1903), vol. 17; Aaron Olmstead to Adriel Ely, Aug. 31, 1836, Olmstead Papers, NYHS; John Ward diary, Dec. 29, 1860, NYHS; Irving Bartlett, *Daniel Webster* (New York, 1978), 31; Canby, *Age of Confidence,* 159; Alphonso David Rockwell, *Rambling Recollections: An Autobiography* (New York, 1920), 181; Hale, *New England Boyhood,* 126; Rothman, *Hands and*

Hearts, 23; Joseph Kett, *Rites of Passage: Adolescence in America, 1790 to the Present* (New York, 1977), 40–42.

21. Ward diary, Jan. 1, 1861, NYHS; Henry Dwight Sedgwick, *Memoirs of an Epicurean* (New York, 1942), 140–41; Warner, *Being a Boy,* 63; Rockwell, *Rambling Recollections,* 109; Rothman, *Hands and Hearts,* 23–24.

22. Warner, *Being a Boy,* 108.

23. Warner, *Being a Boy,* 102.

24. Levi Lockling to Aaron Olmstead, Sept. 28, 1838, Olmstead Papers, NYHS. For evidence of the shared obsession with young women, see Daniel Webster to James Hervey Bingham, Feb. 25, 1802, and Jan. 5, 1805, to Habijah Fuller, Feb. 26, 1802, to Mr. Cook, Jan. 14, 1803, and to Thomas Merrill, June 7, 1802, *Writings of Webster,* vol. 17; Levi Lockling to Aaron Olmstead, Feb. 12, 1838, Olmstead Papers, NYHS; Horace Leete to Ralph Leete, Ralph Leete Papers, Container 1, WRHS; Bartlett, *Daniel Webster,* 30–33.

25. John Doane Barnard journal, EI, 24; Daniel Webster to Habijah Fuller, Dec. 21, 1802, *Writings of Webster,* vol. 17; George Dillinat to Thomas Russell, May 28, 1838, Russell Papers, MHS. Also, J. A. Webber to Henry Giles, Dec. 26, 1815, Giles Papers, NYHS; Levi Lockling to Aaron Olmstead, Feb. 12 and Sept. 28, 1838, Olmstead Papers, NYHS; Henry Lawrence to Peter Hitchcock, Jr., Nov. 16, 1840, Peter Hitchcock Family Papers, Container 11, WRHS.

26. James Hervey Bingham to Daniel Webster, Apr. 8, 1803, *Writings of Webster,* vol. 17; William Rice to David Damon, Apr. 21, 1808, David Damon Papers, MHS.

27. Daniel Webster to Habijah Fuller, Dec. 21, 1802, *Writings of Webster,* vol. 17.

28. Daniel Webster to Habijah Fuller, July 2, 1803, *Writings of Webster,* vol. 17. Also Aaron Olmstead to Adriel Ely, Aug. 31, 1836, Olmstead Papers, NYHS.

29. Daniel Webster to Habijah Fuller, May 3, 1802, *Writings of Webster,* vol. 17.

30. Levi Lockling to Aaron Olmstead, Feb. 12, 1838, Olmstead Papers, NYHS; Daniel Webster to Thomas Merrill, June 7, 1802, *Writings of Webster,* vol. 17.

31. See note 30. Also "Diary of Archelaus Putnam of New Mills," *The Historical Collections of the Danvers Historical Society,* 6 (1918), 17; J. A. Webber to Henry Giles, Dec. 26, 1815, Giles Papers, NYHS; George Dillinat to Thomas Russell, May 28, 1838, Russell Papers, MHS.

32. Aaron Olmstead to Adriel Ely, Aug. 31, 1836, Olmstead Papers, NYHS.

33. Lewis Wallace, *Lew Wallace: An Autobiography* (New York, 1906), 211. Also Daniel Webster to Thomas Merrill, Nov. 11, 1803, *Writings of Webster,* vol. 17; and Edward Polk to Henry Giles, Mar. 19, 1818, Giles Papers, NYHS.

34. For sacred or beautiful associations, see, for instance, Daniel Webster to Thomas Merrill, Nov. 11, 1803, *Writings of Webster*, vol. 17, and Aaron Olmstead to Adriel Ely, Aug. 31, 1836, Olmstead Papers, NYHS. For wicked or tempting associations, see Daniel Webster to Habijah Fuller, May 3, 1802, *Writings of Webster*, vol. 17, and Adriel Ely to Aaron Olmstead, Aug. 8, 1836, Olmstead Papers, NYHS. For both in the same letter see J. A. Webber to Henry Giles, Dec. 26, 1815, Giles Papers, NYHS.

35. Horace Leete to Ralph Leete, Apr. 14, 1845, Leete Papers, WRHS; and Warner, *Being a Boy*, 99. See also Lucien Boynton diary, in *American Antiquarian Society Proceedings*, 43 (1933), 343, and Rothman, *Hands and Hearts*, 41–42.

36. *The Journal of Henry David Thoreau*, eds. Bradford Torrey and Francis H. Allen (New York, 1962), vol. 1, 253; Daniel Webster to Thomas Merrill, May 28, 1804, *Writings of Webster*, vol. 17.

37. "Snaring" quotations: Daniel Webster to James Hervey Bingham, July 23, 1802, *Writings of Webster*, vol. 17; "Diary of George Younglove Cutler," in Emily Vanderpoel, *Chronicles of a Pioneer School* (Cambridge, Mass., 1903), 197–98; empathy with fish: Barnard "Journal," 24; see also Daniel Webster to Habijah Fuller, May 3, 1802, *Writings of Webster*, vol. 17.

38. Daniel Webster to Thomas Merrill, June 7, 1802, *Writings of Webster*, vol. 17; Adriel Ely to Aaron Olmstead, Aug. 8, 1836, Olmstead Papers, NYHS; Sedgwick, *Memoirs*, 161–62.

39. Charles R. Flint, *Memories of an Active Life: Men, and Ships, and Sealing Wax* (New York, 1923), 138–39.

40. Rafford S. Pyke, "What Men Like in Women," *Cosmopolitan*, 31 (1901), 609–13.

41. Horace Leete to Ralph Leete, Apr. 25, 1846, Leete Papers, WRHS; Pyke, "What Men Like," 610–12. Also, Sedgwick, *Memoirs*, 125.

42. James Barnard Blake diary, Apr. 27, 1851, AAS; Tennyson quoted in Sergeant Kendall to B. Franklin and Elizabeth Kendall, Jan. 20, 1889, Kendall Papers, NYHS.

43. Grant quoted in Rothman, *Hands and Hearts*, 92. William Lloyd Garrison II to Ellen Wright, Sept. 3, 1864, Garrison Collection, SSC. See also Richard Cabot to Ella Lyman, n.d. [1888], Ella Lyman Cabot Papers, SL, and Rothman, *Hands and Hearts*, 184–89.

Chapter 6: Love, Sex, and Courtship

1. Historians have differed widely on the relative importance of love and the necessities of religion and economics in Puritan courtship and marriage. David Hackett Fischer has leaned strongly in the direction of love in *Albion's Seed: Four British Folkways in America* (New York, 1989), 78–79, with Edmund Morgan leaning heavily the other way in *The Puritan Fam-*

ily: Religion and Domestic Relations in Seventeenth-Century New England, rev. ed. (New York, 1966), 26–64. Somewhere in between is Laurel Thatcher Ulrich in *Good Wives: Image and Reality in the Lives of Women in Northern New England, 1650–1750* (New York, 1982), 108–24.

2. This understanding of the romantic self is largely derived from Karen Lystra, *Searching the Heart: Women, Men, and Romantic Love in Nineteenth-Century America* (New York, 1989), esp. 30.

3. James W. White to Mary E. Thorn, May 10, 1850, James W. White Papers, HSWP. Also Herman Lantz, Raymond Schmitt, and Richard Herman, "The Pre-Industrial Family in America: A Further Examination of Magazines," *American Journal of Sociology*, 79 (Nov. 1973), 577–78, and Herman R. Lantz, Jane Keyes, and Martin Schultz, "The American Family in the Preindustrial Period: From Base Lines in History to Change," *American Sociological Review*, 40 (1975), 28–29. But remnants of suspicion about romance carried over from earlier times. See Ellen Rothman, *Hands and Hearts: A History of Courtship in America* (New York, 1984), 39–40.

4. Champion Chase to Mary Butterfield, Mar. 22, 1848, Champion Spalding Chase Papers, YUL; "contrive together" quoted in Rothman, *Hands and Hearts*, 108; author unknown to Miss S. Dawes, May 1825, Thomas Dawes Papers, MHS. Also, Charles Van Hise to Alice Ring, Apr. 29, 1879, Charles Van Hise Papers, Box 1, SHSW.

5. Kingman quoted in Rothman, *Hands and Hearts*, 108; Jarvis quoted in Gerald N. Grob, *Edward Jarvis and the Medical World of Nineteenth-Century America* (Knoxville, Tenn., 1978), 20. For two different interpretations of courting couples' obsession with candor, see Lystra, 31–37, and Rothman, *Hands and Hearts*, 43–44, 108–14.

6. Young men and women were so accustomed to their contrasting approaches to life that the contrast governed the way they regarded even the most intimate emotional matters. Ellen Rothman has noted that women "were expected to receive offers of marriage. . . . They tended to look at falling in love as something that would or would not happen to them, while men conveyed a sense that they could, or should, make it happen" (*Hands and Hearts*, 105).

7. Lucien Boynton diary in *American Antiquarian Society Proceedings*, 43 (1933), 340, 343.

8. Eliza Southgate to Moses Porter, n.d. [1800], in *A Girl's Life Eighty Years Ago: Selected Letters of Eliza Southgate Bowde*, ed. Clarence Cook (New York, 1884), 41.

9. Rothman, *Hands and Hearts*, 188.

10. "Diary of George Younglove Cutler," Aug. 31, 1820, in Emily Vanderpoel, *Chronicles of a Pioneer School* (Cambridge, Mass., 1903), 196–97.

11. See Daniel Webster to Thomas Merrill, Nov. 11, 1803, *The Writing and Speeches of Daniel Webster* (Boston, 1903), vol. 17.

12. John Doane Barnard journal, EI, 9. See also Barnard, "Journal," 16, 24;

Alexander Hamilton Rice to Augusta E. McKim, Mar. 2, 1844, Alexander Hamilton Rice Papers, MHS; Winan Allen to Annie Cox, Nov. 19, 1863, Cox-Allen Papers, NL.

13. Champion Chase to Mary Butterfield, Sept. 25, 1846, Chase Papers, YUL; George Moore diary, Aug. 7, 1838, AAS.

14. "Circumstances of comfort" quoted in Mary Ryan, *The Cradle of the Middle Class: The Family in Oneida County, New York, 1790–1865* (New York, 1981), 179; Charles Van Hise to Alice Ring, Mar. 8, 1879, Van Hise Papers, SHSW. Also, Alphonso David Rockwell, *Rambling Recollections: An Autobiography* (New York, 1920), 109.

15. Ephraim Abbott to Mary Pearson, Dec. 30, 1808, Ephraim Abbott Papers, AAS; Ray Stannard Baker, *Native American: The Book of My Youth* (New York, 1941), 217. Sometimes the barriers to a marriage were increased by a young man insisting on enough money to support an elaborate lifestyle (Sylvester Lusk to Mary Lusk, June 4, 1829, Sylvester Lusk Miscellaneous Manuscripts, NYHS) or by a young woman expecting the same of her fiancé (Horace Leete to Ralph Leete, Apr. 14, 1845, Ralph Leete Papers, WRHS).

16. John March to Alice Hale, Apr. 2, 1832, March Correspondence, EI; Annie Wilson to James Wilson, Jr., Nov. 18, 1858, James Wilson, Jr., Papers, NHHS.

17. What of the young men who were still at home? They grew steadily in number during the second half of the century (see Ryan, *Cradle*, 167–68). They, too, had good reason to be eager to marry—to have a home of their own, run according to their own needs, under their own authority, with wives of their own.

18. Levi Lockling to Aaron Olmstead, Sept. 28, 1838, Aaron Barlow Olmstead Papers, NYHS; Stephen Tuckerman to Betsy Salisbury, May 27, 1829, Salisbury Family Papers, Box 23, AAS. See also Horace Leete to Ralph Leete, Apr. 25, 1846, Leete Papers, WRHS.

19. Rothman, *Hands and Hearts*, 22–23; Ryan, *Cradle*, 179.

20. Morgan, *Puritan Family*, 30–33; Rothman, *Hands and Hearts*, 161–62.

21. Ryan, *Cradle*, 180; Rothman, *Hands and Hearts*, 166–67.

22. Quotations from Rothman, *Hands and Hearts*, 108.

23. Grob, *Edward Jarvis*, 20–27.

24. Ephraim Abbott to Mary Pearson, Oct. 27, 1813, Abbott Papers, AAS; Rothman, *Hands and Hearts*, 17–22.

25. M. H. Prentiss to Arabella Carter, Oct. 13, 1828, Timothy Carter Papers, MEHS; Alexis de Tocqueville, *Democracy in America*, trans. Henry Reeve (New York, 1945), vol. 2, 213; Nancy F. Cott, *The Bonds of Womanhood: "Woman's Sphere" in New England, 1780–1835* (New Haven, Conn., 1977), 80.

26. See note 16.

27. Carroll Smith-Rosenberg, *Disorderly Conduct: Visions of Gender in Victo-*

rian America (New York, 1985), 115–17; Kate Gannett Wells, "Why More Girls Do Not Marry," *North American Review,* 152 (1891), 176–77; Maud Rittenhouse diary, June 1882 and Aug. 28, 1892, in Isabelle Rittenhouse Mayne, *Maud,* ed. Richard Lee Strout (New York, 1939), 108, 554. On female sexuality as it was constructed by the nineteenth-century middle class, see Nancy Cott's classic essay, "Passionlessness: An Interpretation of Victorian Sexual Ideology, 1790–1850," *Signs,* 4 (1978), 219–36. For evidence that this ideology held limited power over the behavior of mid- and late-century women, see Carl N. Degler, *At Odds: Women and the Family in America from the Revolution to the Present* (New York, 1980), 265–69.

28. Charles Rosenberg, "Sexuality, Class and Role in Nineteenth-Century America," *American Quarterly,* 35 (1973), 145–46. Ben Barker-Benfield, "The Spermatic Economy: A Nineteenth-Century View of Sexuality," in Michael Gordon, ed., *The American Family in Social-Historical Perspective* (New York, 1973), 338–72; John S. Haller, Jr., and Robin M. Haller, *The Physician and Sexuality in Victorian America* (New York, 1974), 191–234; Leonard Ellis, "Men among Men: An Exploration of All-Male Relationships in Victorian America" (Ph.D. diss., Columbia Univ., 1982), 203–5; Joseph Kett, *Rites of Passage: Adolescence in America, 1790 to the Present* (New York, 1977), 208.

29. Haller and Haller, *Physician and Sexuality,* 215.

30. Sylvester Graham, *A Lecture to Young Men* (New York, 1974 [1834]), 25; Rosenberg, "Sexuality, Class and Role," 139.

31. Rosenberg, "Sexuality, Class and Role," 137–41, 153; Peter T. Cominos, "Late Victorian Sexual Responsibility and the Social System," *International Review of Social History,* 8 (1963), 18–48, 216–50.

32. Daniel Scott Smith, "The Dating of the American Sexual Revolution: Evidence and Interpretation," in Gordon, *American Family,* 323.

33. Rosenberg, "Sexuality, Class and Role," 140.

34. Physician quoted in Rosenberg, "Sexuality, Class and Role," 140–41; Rittenhouse diary, Aug. 28, 1892, in Mayne, *Maud,* 554.

35. Rosenberg, "Sexuality, Class and Role," 150.

36. Suggestive on this point are Rosenberg, "Sexuality, Class and Role," 135 (n. 8), and Ruth Bloch, "American Feminine Ideals in Transition: The Rise of the Moral Mother, 1785–1815," *Feminist Studies,* 4 (1978), 103–13.

37. The sexual conflicts that were already building before puberty are suggested by an episode in the boyhood of William Dean Howells. A woman from nearby Dayton, Ohio, who had been seduced and abandoned by a leading citizen there, came to live with the Howells family. Will (a preteen at this point) reacted to her presence in his house with phobic avoidance (Kenneth S. Lynn, *William Dean Howell: An American Life* [New York, 1970], 57–58).

38. Henry Seidel Canby, *Age of Confidence: Life in the Nineties* (New York, 1941), 165; Ryan, *Cradle,* 122; Rosenberg, "Sexuality, Class and Role,"

150; Webster quoted in Irving Bartlett, *Daniel Webster* (New York, 1978), 37.

39. Charles Van Hise to Alice Ring, Jan. 12, 1879, Van Hise Papers, SHSW.

40. Lewis quoted in Degler, *At Odds,* 271; Canby, *Age of Confidence,* 159.

41. Canby, *Age of Confidence,* 165, 157–59.

42. Canby, *Age of Confidence,* 162.

43. Canby, *Age of Confidence,* 162–63. For another account of the pursuit of sex beyond one's own social world, see Henry Dwight Sedgwick, *Memoirs of an Epicurean* (New York, 1942), 88–89.

44. The best overall source of information on prostitution actually deals with the early twentieth century: Ruth Rosen, *The Lost Sisterhood: Prostitution in America, 1900–1915* (Baltimore, 1982). A useful sifting of evidence to show that middle-class males must have been frequent brothel customers at the turn of the century is in John D'Emilio and Estelle B. Freedman, *Intimate Matters: A History of Sexuality in America* (New York, 1988), 182 (and see in general 181–83).

45. Rothman, *Hands and Hearts,* 55.

46. Lawrence Chamberlain to Fannie Adams, n.d. [1852], Chamberlain Papers, SL; Frank Lillie to Frances Crane, Sept. 24, 1894, Crane Papers, CHS; Elias Nason to Mira Bigelow, June 19, 1833, Elias Nason Papers, AAS.

47. See, for example, Rothman, *Hands and Hearts,* 126–33.

48. Rothman, *Hands and Hearts,* 54.

49. Canby, *Age of Confidence,* 162.

Chapter 7: Marriage

1. Ellen Rothman, *Hands and Hearts: A History of Courtship in America* (New York, 1984), 78–80.

2. Rothman, *Hands and Hearts,* 169–72; George W. Hervey, *The Principles of Courtesy* (New York, 1852), 145–48; *Beadle's Dime Book of Practical Etiquette for Ladies and Gentlemen* (New York, 1859), 50–53; Florence Hartley, *The Ladies Book of Etiquette and Manual of Politeness* (Boston, 1873), 259–63; W. R. Andrews, *The American Code of Manners* (New York, 1880), 121–29; *The Correct Thing in Good Society* (Boston, 1888), 145–59; [Mrs. Abby Buchanan Longstreet], *Social Etiquette of New York* (New York, 1882), 126–52; Mrs. John Sherwood, *Manners and Social Usages* (New York, 1887), 82–132.

3. Stanton quoted in Carl N. Degler, *At Odds: Women and the Family in America from the Revolution to the Present* (New York, 1980), 175; Richard Cabot to Ella Lyman, n.d. [1888], Ella Lyman Cabot Papers, SL.

4. Daniel Wise, *The Young Lady's Counsellor* (New York, 1852), 234–35.

5. George Tuckerman to Betsy Salisbury, July 21, 1809, Salisbury Papers, AAS.

6. Charles Van Hise to Alice Ring, Jan. 12, 1879, Charles Van Hise Papers, SHSW.

7. Champion Chase to Mary Butterfield, July 11, 1845, Champion Spalding Chase Papers, YUL; John Patch to Margaret Poor, Apr. 26, 1846, John Patch Papers, EI; Parkman quoted in Howard Doughty, *Francis Parkman* (Cambridge, Mass., 1983 [1962]), 210.

8. Augusta Anna Elliott to James Alvin Bell, Nov. 18, 1860, James Alvin Bell Papers, HL; Mary Poor to Henry Poor, Apr. 24, 1867, Apr. 2, 1868, and June 30, 1869, Poor Papers, SL. For sentiments like Mary Poor's, see Martha Eaton to Edward Eaton, Nov. 20, 1891, and n.d. [1891], Edward D. Eaton Papers, SHSW.

9. *The Love Life of Byron Caldwell Smith* (New York, 1930), 63. On the complementarity of the sexes and their proper roles, see also George Moore diary, Jan. 26, 1837, AAS.

10. Alexander Hamilton Rice to Augusta McKim, Mar. 2, 1844, Alexander Hamilton Rice Papers, MHS; Mary Ryan, *The Cradle of the Middle Class: The Family in Oneida County, New York, 1790–1865* (New York, 1981), 179. On comfort as a standard of good breadwinning, see the divorce testimony in Elaine Tyler May, *Great Expectations: Marriage and Divorce in Post-Victorian America* (Chicago, 1980), esp. 137–42, and Robert Griswold, *Family and Divorce in California, 1850–1890: Victorian Illusions and Everyday Realities* (Albany, N.Y., 1982), 98–99.

11. Rachel Deborah Cramer, "Images of the American Father, 1790–1860," unpub. MS, 47.

12. John Kirk to "Cousin Sally," Apr. 1, 1853, John Kirk Letterbooks, vol. 1, CHS. For a similar use of a different Pauline text on marriage, see Edward Eaton to Martha Eaton, July 17, 1881, Eaton Papers, SHSW.

13. James R. McGovern, *Yankee Family* (New Orleans, 1975), 64.

14. "Diary of George Younglove Cutler," Aug. 31, 1820, in Emily Vanderpoel, *Chronicles of a Pioneer School* (Cambridge, Mass., 1903), 196–97. Cutler was not aware of the ways in which married women maintained and expanded their networks of sociability or support (on these networks, see for instance Carroll Smith-Rosenberg, "The Female World of Love and Ritual: Relations between Women in Nineteenth-Century America," *Signs*, 1 [1975], and Nancy F. Cott, *The Bonds of Womanhood: "Woman's Sphere" in New England, 1780–1835* [New Haven, Conn., 1977], 160–96). Still, Cutler correctly perceived the *formal structure* of social relationships in marriages. The duties of a middle-class woman tended to keep her at home for a good portion of her time, while those of her husband usually forced him into a world of social contact. Thus, middle-class women were not confined to their social relationships with their husbands to the extent that Cutler suggests, but they had to make more of an effort than men to maintain daily social contact with peers beyond the household.

15. Hill's sentiments summarized in Joseph Taylor to Elizabeth Hill, May 19, 1866, Joseph D. Taylor Papers, SHSW.

16. Alexander Hamilton Rice to Augusta McKim, Mar. 2, 1844, Rice Papers, MHS.

17. Charles Van Hise to Alice Van Hise, Oct. 21, 1891, Van Hise Papers, SHSW. See also Rothman, *Hands and Hearts*, 146; John Mack Faragher, *Women and Men on the Overland Trail* (New Haven, Conn., 1979), 163–68.

18. Mary Poor to Lucy Hedge, Nov. 11, 1855, Poor Papers, SL; McGovern, *Yankee Family*, 100.

19. William Cattell to James Cattell, Apr. 19, 1885, James Cattell Papers, Family Correspondence, LC.

20. Elizabeth Cattell to William Cattell, Aug. 24, 1880, Cattell Papers, LC; see also Elizabeth Cattell to James Cattell, May 5, 15, 20, and 25, 1883, and Nov. 19, 1885, Cattell Papers, LC.

21. Theodore Russell to Charles Russell, July 19, 1848, Charles Russell Papers, MHS.

22. William Dall to Caroline Dall, June 27, 1887, Caroline Dall Papers, MHS. For a fuller sense of the spectrum of possible arrangements within conventional limits, see the couples' decisions related in John Kirk to Gent, Milligan, and Birt, Dec. 18, 1852, Kirk Letterbooks, CHS; McGovern, *Yankee Family*, 91–99; Degler, *At Odds*, 42–43.

23. On finances, see Ebenezer Gay to W. Allan Gay, May 13, 1838, Feb. 26 and May 9, 1839; on place of residence, Mary A. O. Gay to William Otis, Jan. 9, 1832; and on dealing with son Charles, Mary A. O. Gay to William Otis, June 10, 1827, Gay-Otis Collection, CUL.

24. See Henry Dwight Sedgwick, *Memoirs of an Epicurean* (New York, 1942), 121–23, and more briefly, Edward Eaton to Martha Eaton, Mar. 17, 1890, Eaton Papers, SHSW.

25. John Doane Barnard journal, EI, 35; Arial Bragg, *Memoirs of Col. Arial Bragg* (Milford, Mass., 1846), 40.

26. Griswold, *Family and Divorce*, 105; Carroll Smith-Rosenberg, *Disorderly Conduct: Visions of Gender in Victorian America* (New York, 1985), 124–25.

27. Michael Grossberg, *Governing the Hearth: Law and the Family in Nineteenth-Century America* (Chapel Hill, N.C., 1985), 27.

28. On divorce in the nineteenth century, a useful brief introduction is Degler, *At Odds*, 165–76. Other important and more detailed works are May, *Great Expectations*; Griswold, *Family and Divorce*; and William O'Neill, *Divorce in the Progressive Era* (New Haven, Conn., 1967). A poignant case of virtual abandonment is that of Charles and Harriet Strong described in Karen Lystra, *Searching the Heart: Women, Men, and Romantic Love in Nineteenth-Century America* (New York, 1989), 219–25. Charles's work as a mine superintendent kept him living separately from Harriet, but the physical distance expressed a large emotional gap, too. On the abandonment sometimes involved in moving west, see Griswold, *Family and Divorce*, 85–87.

29. Mary Gay was born into the Otis family of political fame in Massachusetts

(see John J. Waters, Jr., *The Otis Family in Provincial and Revolutionary Massachusetts* [Chapel Hill, N.C., 1968]), and Ebenezer Gay came from a family which produced a famous minister and many successful merchants.

30. Mary A. O. Gay to William Otis, Dec. 21, 1800, Gay-Otis Collection, CUL.

31. For instance, Mary A. O. Gay to William Otis, Jan. 9, 1832; Ebenezer Gay to W. Allan Gay, Feb. 26, 1839; Mary A. O. Gay to W. Allan Gay, Dec. 13 and 31, 1840, Gay-Otis Collection, CUL.

32. Mary A. O. Gay to W. Allan Gay, Apr. 5, 1841; see also letter of Dec. 31, 1840, Gay-Otis Collection, CUL.

33. Mary A. O. Gay to W. Allan Gay, Oct. 29, 1839, Gay-Otis Collection, CUL.

34. In her study of romantic love, Karen Lystra examines five marriages in which love and romance died out. In four of those cases, Lystra bases her account wholly or primarily on the wife's viewpoint (*Searching*, 206–19). See also the letters of Lucy Gray to Joshua Gray, Gray Correspondence, Hooker Collection, SL; the letters of Pamela to George Paul, George H. Paul Papers, Box 3, SHSW; and Mary Ryan's account of Lavinia Johnson's marriage (*Cradle*, 196–97)—all accounts of estranged relationships, with the wife's testimony and the husband's silence.

35. Mark C. Carnes, *Secret Ritual and Manhood in Victorian America* (New Haven, Conn., 1989), 1, and more generally 1–9, is useful on the breadth of fraternal membership among middle-class men. Leonard Ellis, "Men among Men: An Exploration of All-Male Relationships in Victorian America" (Ph.D. diss., Columbia Univ., 1982), 331–80, is a lively, opinionated introduction to the history and culture of men's clubs.

36. Mary Ann Clawson, *Constructing Brotherhood: Class, Gender, and Fraternalism* (Princeton, N.J., 1989), 175; Carnes, *Secret Ritual*, 79–82, 120–27.

37. An Old New Yorker, "Clubs—Club Life—Some New York Clubs," *Galaxy*, 22 (1876), 227, 228.

38. Junius Henri Brown, *The Great Metropolis: A Mirror* (Hartford, Conn., 1869), 453.

39. Henry Seidel Canby, *The Age of Confidence: Life in the Nineties* (New York, 1934), 173–74; also, Ellis, "Men among Men," 368–69.

40. Pender quoted in Degler, *At Odds*, 31; Stowe also quoted in Degler, *At Odds*, 32. See as well Gerald F. Linderman, *Embattled Courage: The Experience of Combat in the American Civil War* (New York, 1987), 95.

41. C. A. Bristed, "Club Life," *Nation 1* (1865), 12.

42. New Yorker, "Clubs," 238.

43. McGovern, *Yankee Family*, 56–70.

44. Mary Poor to John and Lucy Pierce, July 23, 1842, and Nov. 28, 1847; Mary Poor to Feroline Fox, Feb. 25, 1849, Poor Papers, SL.

45. Quoted in Degler, *At Odds*, 35. Even when the Poor family took summer vacations on the farm in Maine where Henry grew up, he could not pull himself away from work to join the others (McGovern, *Yankee Family*, 84).

46. Mary Poor to Henry Poor, Aug. 8, 1867; see also Henry Poor to Mary Poor, Sept. 13, 1860, and Aug. 6, 1867, Poor Papers, SL.

47. Mary Poor to Constance Poor, July 23, 1884; see also Mary Poor to Henry Poor, Aug. 4, 1885, Poor Papers, SL; and McGovern, *Yankee Family*, 128–36.

48. Henry Poor to Mary Poor, July 19, 1845, and July 25, 1858, Poor Papers, SL. Henry Poor was an affectionate husband in spite of his absence, but some husbands who were frequently away did not possess the same deep fondness for the women they married. John Kirk, salesman and evangelical abolitionist, was kind and respectful toward his wife but he showed no signs of affectionate yearning during their long separations. In fact, he wished for even more time on the road. (John Kirk to Gent, Milligan, and Birt, Dec. 18, 1852; to his mother, Mar. 13, 1853; to Susan Kirk, Apr. 3, 1853, Kirk Letterbooks, CHS.)

49. Quoted in McGovern, *Yankee Family*, 131.

50. "On the go": Henry Poor to Mary Poor, Apr. 12, 1870; "without blushing": Henry Poor to Mary Poor, July 12, 1846; see also Henry Poor to Mary Poor, Mar. 22, 1849, Oct. 26, 1867, June 5, 1868, and July 15, 1868; Mary Poor to Feroline Fox, June 12, 1853, Poor Papers, SL.

51. Henry Poor to Mary Pierce, Aug. 2, 1840, Poor Papers, SL.

52. Henry Poor to Mary Poor, June 27, 1847, Poor Papers, SL.

53. McGovern, *Yankee Family*, 77.

54. Kirk Jeffrey, "Family History: The Middle-Class American Family in the Urban Context, 1830–1870" (Ph.D. diss., Stanford Univ., 1972), 168.

55. For another clear example of this sort of relationship, see the patterns in the marriage of Theodore and Sarah Russell (Russell Papers, MHS). In particular note C. Theodore Russell to Charles Russell, May 30, 1838, Feb. 12, 1845, and Aug. 31, 1847; Lizzy Russell to Charles Russell, Dec. 18, 1843; and Sarah Russell to Thomas Russell, Jan. 16, 1845.

56. Irving Bartlett, *Daniel Webster* (New York, 1978), 90–95 (quotation on 93).

57. *The Compact Edition of the Oxford English Dictionary* (Oxford, 1971), vol. 1, 427.

58. Lystra, *Searching*, chap. 2.

59. Quotation is from Charles Russell to Persis Russell, Jan. 25, 1830; on homesickness, see Charles Russell to Persis Russell, Jan. 26, 1834, Feb. 28, 1836, and Feb. 27, 1837; for a sampling of Charles's state-of-the-body reports, see his letters to Persis of Jan. 25, 1830, Mar. 14, Nov. 23, and Dec. 12, 1831, and Jan. 26, 1834, Russell Papers, MHS.

60. Charles Russell to Thomas Russell, Oct. 22, 1845, Russell Papers, MHS.

61. Some of these orders are contained in Charles Russell to Persis Russell, Jan. 25 and May 31, 1830, Mar. 14, 1831, and Jan. 26, 1834, Russell Papers, MHS.

62. Charles Russell to Persis Russell, Feb. 28, 1836, Russell Papers, MHS.

63. Charles Russell to Persis Russell, Feb. 28, 1836, Russell Papers, MHS.

64. Lystra, *Searching*, 42.

65. An intimate late-century marriage typical of its time was that of Edward

and Martha Eaton. Both Midwesterners, they lived most of their adult life together in Beloit, Wisconsin, where Edward served as president of Beloit College. See Eaton Papers, SHSW.

66. B. Franklin Kendall to Elizabeth Kendall, July 23, 1882, Kendall Papers, NYHS; Alice Van Hise to Charles Van Hise, Aug. 16, 1891, Van Hise Papers, SHSW; Elizabeth Cattell to William Cattell, Aug. 24, 1880, Cattell Papers, LC.

67. B. Franklin Kendall to Elizabeth Kendall, July 23, 1882, Kendall Papers, NYHS; Elizabeth Cattell to William Cattell, Aug. 24, 1880, Cattell Papers, LC. See also Elizabeth Cattell to James Cattell, May 25, 1885, Cattell Papers, LC.

68. Charles Van Hise to Alice Ring, Apr. 29, 1879, Van Hise Papers, SHSW.

69. Charles Van Hise to Alice Van Hise, Feb. 1, 1889, Van Hise Papers, SHSW.

70. Alice Van Hise to Charles Van Hise, Aug. 16, 1891, Van Hise Papers, SHSW.

71. For a small taste of this different environment, see Robert M. Crunden, *Ministers of Reform: The Progressives' Achievement in American Civilization 1889–1920* (New York, 1982), 13–15, 73–76, on the University of Wisconsin in this era.

72. For more hints of the Van Hises' own ambivalence about issues of gender, see Charles Van Hise's letters to Alice Ring, Jan. 12, 1879, and to Alice Van Hise, July 22, 1890, Mar. 30 and Oct. 20, 1891, Van Hise Papers, SHSW.

73. This is the broad theme of John D'Emilio and Estelle Freedman's pioneering history of sexuality, *Intimate Matters: A History of Sexuality in America* (New York, 1988).

74. Quoted in Degler, *At Odds,* 259.

75. Wise, *Young Lady's Counsellor,* 234.

76. Helpful on Mosher and her study is Rosalind Rosenberg, *Beyond Separate Spheres: Intellectual Roots of Modern Feminism* (New Haven, Conn., 1982), 180–87.

77. Clelia Duel Mosher, *The Mosher Survey: Sexual Attitudes of Forty-five Victorian Women,* eds. James MaHood and Kristine Wenberg (New York, 1980), 24, 175–76.

78. Lystra, *Searching,* 77–78.

79. See D'Emilio and Freedman, *Intimate Matters,* 110, 179.

80. Degler, *At Odds,* 211–15.

81. Degler, *At Odds,* 225.

82. Twenty-three of the forty-six women surveyed in the Mosher study cited pleasure as a purpose of intercourse.

83. It was Carl Degler who noticed this common thread running through such diverse writings. The quotations here are from *At Odds,* 274–76, but other statements cited by Degler in other contexts fit the same pattern (see 205, 266).

84. Mosher, *Survey,* 302, 304, 408.

85. Mosher, *Survey,* 328, 254, 25.

86. Edward Eaton to Martha Eaton, Nov. 24, 1892, Eaton Papers, SHSW.

87. Edward Eaton to Martha Eaton, July 10, 1881, Eaton Papers, SHSW.

88. Charles Van Hise to Alice Van Hise, Jan. 31, 1889, Van Hise Papers, SHSW. In the same sensual, affectionate vein, see B. Franklin Kendall to Elizabeth Kendall, July 23 and 26, 1882, Kendall Papers, NYHS, and Peter Gay, *The Tender Passion* (New York, 1986), 88–89.

89. Although both Peter Gay and Karen Lystra downplay change over time in their discovery of erotic marriages in the nineteenth century, their own most vivid examples come from the last quarter of the century. See Gay, *Tender Passion,* 80–89, and Lystra, *Searching,* 91–100.

90. No such expressions occurred at all in the primary research for this book. But see scattered instances in Lystra, *Searching,* 60–87.

91. But Mosher's population was statistically representative of the larger population of wives of professional men at the turn of the century, so the small size of the sample may not be a barrier to its statistical usefulness. See Degler, *At Odds,* 222.

92. See Lystra, *Searching,* 59.

93. Mosher, *Survey,* 43–44. It is no accident that middle-class women and men in the nineteenth century used the same term, *union,* for love, marriage, and sex. Ideally, the three existed in the same ethereal realm of oneness. See Jeffrey, "Family History," 181–82; Degler, *At Odds,* 277; and Lystra, *Searching,* 71.

94. Robert Griswold and Carl Degler are leading advocates of the position, though Degler qualifies his position carefully in *At Odds,* 50.

95. Margaret Marsh has taken this position in "Suburban Men and Masculine Domesticity, 1870–1915," in Mark C. Carnes and Clyde Griffen, eds., *Meanings for Manhood: Constructions of Masculinity in Victorian America* (Chicago, 1990), 245, n. 6; as has Suzanne Lebsock, *The Free Women of Petersburg: Status and Culture in a Southern Town* (New York, 1984), 30–33.

96. Definitive statements about nineteenth-century trends in marital closeness are further complicated by the fact that closeness is a qualitative matter that does not easily allow for subtle quantitative comparisons over time.

97. Charles Russell to Persis Russell, Feb. 27, 1837, Russell Papers, MHS.

Chapter 8: Work and Identity

1. Arthur H. Cole, "The Tempo of Mercantile Life in Colonial America," *Business History Review,* 33 (1959).

2. Cole, "Tempo," 293.

3. Theodore Russell to Charles Russell, May 30, 1838, Charles Russell Papers, MHS. In a similar vein, James Barnard Blake wrote in his diary that "it is not man's nature to be idle, to do nothing at all" (Blake diary, Apr. 13,

1851, AAS), and Adriel Ely compared himself to a woman (and a sinful one at that) during a period of unemployment: "A want of business [left me] like a woman of loose virtue, open to be assailed by every class of bad habits" (Adriel Ely to Aaron Olmstead, Oct. 16, 1836, Aaron Barlow Olmstead Papers, NYHS). A man without work, simply, was not a man.

4. Mary Clarke to Willie Franklin, Sept. 10, 1868, Mary Clarke Letters in Harold Frederic Papers, NYPL; Alexander Hamilton Rice to Augusta McKim, Mar. 2, 1844, Alexander Hamilton Rice Papers, MHS; Lucien Boynton diary, June 29, 1839, in *American Antiquarian Society Proceedings*, 43 (1933). Further connections between manliness and work are made in Mary A. O. Gay to William Otis, Feb. 5, 1829, Gay-Otis Collection, CUL; Blake diary, Mar. 4, 1851, AAS; M. S. Bailey to James Cattell, Nov. 15, 1880, James Cattell Papers, Family Correspondence, LC; Robert Griswold, *Family and Divorce in California, 1850—1890: Victorian Illusions and Everyday Realities* (Albany, N.Y., 1982), 92–95.

5. W. Allan Gay to Ebenezer Gay, Feb. 13, 1839, Gay-Otis Collection, CUL; John Kirk to Brother Calvin, Mar. 9, 1853, Kirk Letterbooks, vol. 1, CHS; Charles Flint, *Memories of an Active Life: Men, Ships, and Sealing Wax* (New York, 1923), 280; Alexander Hamilton Rice to Augusta McKim, Mar. 2, 1844, Rice Papers, MHS. See similar phrases in Theodore Russell to Charles Russell, May 30, 1838, Russell Papers, MHS; Lester Ward, *Young Ward's Diary*, ed. Bernhard Stern (New York, 1935), Apr. 2, 1861; George Laflin to Louis Laflin, Oct. 3, 1895, Laflin Papers, CHS.

6. Alexander Hamilton Rice to Augusta McKim, Mar. 2, 1844, Rice Papers, MHS. A similar phrase expresses a similar idea in Theodore Russell to Charles Russell, May 30, 1838, Russell Papers, MHS.

7. *Diary and Letters of Rutherford Birchard Hayes, Nineteenth President of the United States*, ed. Charles Richard Williams (Columbus, Ohio, 1922), vol. 1, 107; Ray Stannard Baker, *Native American: The Book of My Youth* (New York, 1941), 217. See also Daniel Webster to Thomas Merrill, Mar. 10, 1805, *The Writings and Speeches of Daniel Webster* (Boston, 1903), vol. 17; Horace Leete to Ralph Leete, Jan. 6, 1844, Ralph Leete Papers, WRHS.

8. John Doane Barnard journal, EI, 10; Baker, *Native American*, 217; Joseph Kett, *Rites of Passage: Adolescence in America, 1790 to the Present* (New York, 1977), 30–33; Char Miller, *Fathers and Sons: The Bingham Family and the American Mission* (Philadelphia, 1982), 75–76.

9. On Howells and the arts-politics split, see Kenneth S. Lynn, *William Dean Howells: An American Life* (New York, 1970), 84–85, 238. Teachers and college presidents are gender-typed in Henry Ward Beecher's novel *Norwood*, which is quoted in William G. McLoughlin, *The Meaning of Henry Ward Beecher: An Essay on the Shifting Values of Mid-Victorian America, 1840–1870* (New York, 1970), 165.

10. D. Samuel Howard, a young engineer, reported that his debating society in Fulton, New York, tackled the following question: "Which opens the great-

est field for eloquence the pulpit or the barr." This debate topic suggests a similarity between the two professions even as it follows the nineteenth-century habit of setting the two in opposition (D. Samuel Howard to James Howard, Jan. 28, 1828, James C. Howard Papers, SHSW).

11. Reuben Hitchcock to Sarah Hitchcock, Dec. 16, 1848, Peter Hitchcock Papers, WRHS.

12. Quotations from James R. McGovern, *Yankee Family* (New Orleans, 1975), 65.

13. For two other negative assessments of the traits nurtured by the practice of law, see these letters by two future lawyers: Daniel Webster to J. Hervey Bingham, May 18, 1802, *Writings of Webster,* vol. 17, 111; *Diary and Letters of Hayes,* vol. 1, 83.

14. The Higginson essay is found in Thomas Wentworth Higginson, *Out-Door Papers* (Boston, 1886 [1863]), 7, 6. The descriptions of Channing and Thacher are quoted in Ann Douglas, *The Feminization of American Culture* (New York, 1977), 107.

15. Alexis de Toqueville, *Democracy in America,* trans. Henry Reeve (New York, 1945), vol. 1, 288.

16. Elizur Wright, Sr., to Elizur Wright, Jr., May 26, 1826, Elizur Wright, Jr., Letters, WRHS.

17. John Kirk to the Young Converts, Mar. 20, 1853, Kirk Letterbooks, vol. 1, CHS; Richard Cabot to Ella Lyman, n.d. [1888], Ella Lyman Cabot Papers, SL; Robert M. Crunden, *Ministers of Reform: The Progressives' Achievement in American Civilization 1889–1920* (New York, 1982), 3–38.

18. Tracy quoted in Robert Abzug, *Passionate Liberator: Theodore Dwight Weld and the Dilemma of Reform* (New York, 1980), 74; Beecher quoted by Harriet Beecher Stowe in Annie Fields, *Life and Letters of Harriet Beecher Stowe* (Boston, 1897), 95.

19. Of course, women, too, were instrumental in the course of those movements. (See, for instance, Mary Ryan, *The Cradle of the Middle Class: The Family in Oneida County, New York, 1790–1865* [New York, 1981].) 105–44; Blanche Glassman Hersh, *The Slavery of Sex: Feminist Abolitionists in America* [Urbana, Ill., 1978]; Barbara Berg, *The Remembered Gate—Origins of American Feminism: Women and the City, 1800–1860* [New York, 1978]; Jean Fagan Yellin, *Women and Sisters: The Antislavery Feminists in American Culture* [New Haven, Conn., 1989]). In fact, movements such as abolitionism and Progressivism were shaped by the interaction of values and cultural styles marked *male* and *female*. It is worth noting that the metaphorical language of Christian warfare probably had the same effect on women that it did on ministers, liberating aggressions that cultural sanctions otherwise held in check.

20. Daniel Webster to Thomas Merrill, Mar. 10, 1805, *Writings of Webster,* vol. 17; Alexander Hamilton Rice to Augusta McKim, Mar. 2, 1844, Rice Papers, MHS.

21. See Mary A. O. Gay to William Otis, Nov. 22, 1832, Gay-Otis Papers, CUL; George Laflin to Louis Laflin, Oct. 3, 1895, Laflin Papers, CHS; Gerald N. Grob, *Edward Jarvis and the Medical World of Nineteenth-Century America* (Knoxville, Tenn., 1978), 33.

22. M. S. Bailey to James Cattell, Nov. 18, 1880, Cattell Papers, LC; Daniel Webster to Thomas Merrill, Mar. 10, 1805, *Writings of Webster*, vol. 17; also see Charles W. Eliot, *Charles Eliot, Landscape Architect* (Cambridge, Mass., 1924), 91.

23. W. Allan Gay to Ebenezer Gay, Feb. 13, 1839, Gay-Otis Papers, CUL; Baker, *Native American*, 274. Also, *Diary and Letters of Hayes*, vol. 1, 82–83, 107.

24. Mary Butterfield to Champion Chase, July 28, 1846, Champion S. Chase Papers, YUL.

25. "Diary of George Younglove Cutler," Aug. 31, 1820, in Emily Vanderpoel, *Chronicles of a Pioneer School* (Cambridge, Mass., 1903), 196–97; Artemis B. Muzzey, *The Young Man's Friend* (Boston, 1836), 102; Anna B. Rogers, "Some Faults of American Men," *Atlantic Monthly*, 103 (1909), 736.

26. Richard Cabot to Ella Lyman, n.d. [1888], Cabot Papers, SL. Statements like this are hard to avoid in doing research on middle-class men in the nineteenth century. See, for instance, Mark Barber to Martha Eaton, Apr. 6, 1890, Edward D. Eaton Papers, SHSW; Polly Whittlesey to William Whittlesey, May 4, 1841, William Wallace Whittlesey Papers, 1830–1869, WRHS; Sylvester G. Lusk to Sylvester Lusk, Jan. 11, 1840, Sylvester Lusk Miscellaneous Manuscripts, NYHS; Thomas Russell to Charles Russell, Aug. 3, 1846, Russell Papers, MHS; Elizabeth Cattell to James Cattell, Jan. 22 and 26, 1885, Cattell Papers, LC; Ellen Rothman, *Hands and Hearts: A History of Courtship in America* (New York, 1984), 95–96; McGovern, *Yankee Family*, 84, 99–100, 131–32.

27. The cultural background to men's work obsession is described in Daniel T. Rodgers, *The Work Ethic in Industrial America, 1850–1920* (Chicago, 1978).

28. The chief example is Christopher Lasch, *Haven in a Heartless World: The Family Besieged* (New York, 1979).

29. Serena Ames to George Wright, Feb. 6, 1869, George B. Wright and Family Papers, SHSW.

30. James Cattell to William and Elizabeth Cattell, Nov. 22, 1885, Cattell Papers, LC.

31. John Kirk to "Brother Calvin," Mar. 26, 1853, Kirk Letterbooks, vol. 1, CHS; William Dall to Caroline Dall, July 6, 1885, Caroline Dall Papers, MHS; Richard Cabot to Ella Lyman, Sept. 12, 1889, Cabot Papers, SL; Lynn, *William Dean Howells*, 64–65; Irving Bartlett, *Daniel Webster* (New York, 1978), 66–67.

32. Charles Van Hise to Alice Van Hise, July 19, 1911, Charles Van Hise Papers, SHSW; also see letters of June 18, July 23, and July 26, 1911.

33. Even for men, work did not always succeed as an antidote to grief. See Bartlett, *Daniel Webster,* 95; W. S. Tryon, *Parnassus Corner: A Life of James T. Fields, Publisher to the Victorians* (Boston, 1963), 139.

34. Charles Van Hise to Alice Van Hise, July 19, 1911, Van Hise Papers, SHSW.

35. Sylvester G. Lusk to Sylvester Lusk, Jan. 23 and Sept. 18, 1836, Lusk Manuscripts, NYHS; George Dryer to Horatio Dryer, spring 1874, Dryer Papers, NYHS. Also see Elizabeth Cattell to James Cattell, Jan. 26, 1885, Cattell Papers, LC.

36. Griswold, *Family and Divorce,* 93, 95.

37. Samuel G. Stevenson to Charles Russell, Feb. 14, 1830, and June 3, 1831, Russell Papers, MHS.

38. Letter from naval officers is quoted in Mary A. O. Gay to William Otis, Oct. 20, 1829, Gay-Otis Collection, CUL. See also John William DeForest to Harriet DeForest in John William DeForest, *A Volunteer's Adventures: A Union Captain's Record of the Civil War* (New Haven, Conn., 1946), 46.

39. Quoted in Griswold, *Family and Divorce,* 95.

40. John Pierce memoirs, vol. 1, Oct. 20, 1807, Pierce Collection, MHS.

41. Bartlett, *Daniel Webster,* 219; Grob, *Edward Jarvis,* 32.

42. McGovern, *Yankee Family,* 114, 115.

43. *Best Quotations for All Occasions,* rev. ed., ed. Lewis C. Henry (New York, 1962), 55.

44. Charles Van Hise to Alice Ring, July 22, 1878, Van Hise Papers, SHSW.

45. Barnard journal, EI, 47.

46. Barnard journal, EI, 47.

47. Barnard journal, EI, 16, 24.

48. Benjamin Ward to Linda Raymond, July 14, 1822, Gertrude Foster Brown Papers, SL; George P. Rudd to Edward Rudd, Oct. 7, 1858, Huntting-Rudd Papers, SL.

49. William Cattell to James Cattell, Dec. 14, 1884, Cattell Papers, LC.

50. Quotations from Elizabeth Cattell to James Cattell, Nov. 19, 1885, and Harry Cattell to James Cattell, June 8, 1885; also, William Cattell to James Cattell, Jan. 1, 1885, and Elizabeth Cattell to James Cattell, May 5 and 25, 1885, Cattell Papers, LC.

51. Neurasthenia was not only a disease of men from the comfortable classes. It afflicted upper-middle-class women and men of other classes as much as it affected upper-middle-class men. Those other social groups understood the disease differently, however, probably because it was interpreted differently for them by medical professionals. The class dimensions of neurasthenia have been explored by historian F. G. Gosling. By examining case studies of 307 individual neurasthenics, Gosling found that 36 percent of all patients for whom an occupation was listed were professionals. Since two of Gosling's categories—"housewives" and "other" (students, retirees, for example)—were of indeterminate social class, professionals accounted

for just over half of those whose class could be determined. This is significant because doctors diagnosed professional men differently from men of
other classes. While the former were usually understood as victims of overwork, the latter were seen more often as suffering from enlarged appetites
for sex, alcohol, or drugs. This finding becomes even more striking when
one considers that Gosling reports no difference between the symptoms
presented by professional men and men of other classes (F. G. Gosling,
*Before Freud: Neurasthenia and the American Medical Community,
1870–1910* [Urbana, Ill., 1987], 31–32, 54–55).

In addition to Gosling, there are many important works on neurasthenia. Especially helpful are Barbara Sicherman, "Uses of a Diagnosis: Doctors, Patients, and Neurasthenia," *Journal of the History of Medicine,* 32
(1977), and Howard Feinstein, "The Use and Abuse of Illness in the James
Family Circle," in Robert Brugger, ed., *Our Selves/ Our Past: Psychological Approaches to American History* (Baltimore, 1981). Also, consult Tom
Lutz, *American Nervousness, 1903: An Anecdotal History* (Ithaca, N.Y.,
1991). Basic texts from the nineteenth century are two books by George
Beard, *American Nervousness: Its Causes and Consequences* (New York,
1881), and *A Practical Treatise in Nervous Exhaustion, Neurasthenia, Its
Symptoms, Nature, Sequences, Treatment* (New York, 1880); and S. Weir
Mitchell, *Wear and Tear, or Hints for the Overworked* (Philadelphia,
1887).

52. Sergeant Kendall to B. Franklin and Elizabeth Kendall, Apr. 19 and May
    1, 1886, Jan. 10, 1887, and Mar. 14 and 21, 1889, Kendall Papers, NYHS;
    Edward Everett Hale to Harriet Freeman, Aug. 18, 1885, Papers of the
    Hale Family, Special Correspondence of Edward Everett Hale, LC; James
    Cattell to William and Elizabeth Cattell, Aug. 13, 1884, and May 21 and
    June 27, 1885, Cattell Papers, LC; Howard Doughty, *Francis Parkman*
    (Cambridge, Mass., 1983 [1962]), 222; Tryon, *Parnassus Corner,* 358;
    Abzug, *Passionate Liberator,* 61, 158. This list of symptoms is consistent
    with a list compiled by a doctor in 1899 of the most prominent neuras-
    thenic symptoms presented by 333 patients at a New York clinic. The only
    symptom on that list not mentioned by the men studied here was noctur-
    nal emissions (Gosling, *Before Freud,* 34).

53. Gosling, *Before Freud,* 34.

54. Doughty, *Francis Parkman,* 222–23; Howard Feinstein, *Becoming William
    James* (Ithaca, N.Y., 1984), 68–75, 241–50; Abzug, *Passionate Liberator,*
    59–62; Thomas Russell to Charles Russell, Aug. 3, 1846, and Theodore
    Russell to Charles Russell, Dec. 18, 1848, Russell Papers, MHS.

55. J. H. Blake to Caroline Dall, June 29, 1884, Dall Papers, MHS; James Cat-
    tell to William Cattell, Aug. 13, 1884, Cattell Papers, LC; Howells quoted
    in Lynn, *William Dean Howells,* 254; Gosling, *Before Freud,* 92–93.

56. The metaphor of draining a closed system of energy is presented in John S.
    Haller and Robin M. Haller, *The Physician and Sexuality in Victorian*

America (New York, 1974), 9–15, described less formally in James Cattell to William and Elizabeth Cattell, June 21, 1885 (Cattell Papers, LC), and explored in countless variations in Lutz, *American Nervousness.*

57. The popular phrase "used up," for a man who overstrained his energy system, appears in John Ward diary, Jan. 8, 1864, NYHS; and J. H. Blake to Caroline Dall, June 29, 1884, Dall Papers, MHS.

58. James Cattell to William and Elizabeth Cattell, June 21, 1885, Cattell Papers, LC. On doctor's treatment of hysteria, see Carroll Smith-Rosenberg, "The Hysterical Woman: Sex Roles and Role Conflict in Nineteenth-Century America," *Journal of Interdisciplinary History,* 4 (1973); Ann Douglas Wood, "'The Fashionable Diseases': Women's Complaints and Their Treatment in Nineteenth-Century America," and Regina Morantz, "The Lady and Her Physician," in Mary Hartman and Lois Banner, eds., *Clio's Consciousness Raised* (New York, 1974).

59. James Cattell to William and Elizabeth Cattell, Aug. 13, 1884, Cattell Papers, LC. On exercise as a cure, see also Thomas Russell to Charles Russell, July 21, 1847, Russell Papers, MHS; Dr. Rufus Thurston to Martha Eaton, Oct. 29, 1891, Eaton Papers, SHSW; Abzug, *Passionate Liberator,* 61; and esp. Gosling, *Before Freud,* 120–22.

60. There were some cures, though, which emphasized a lot of strenuous exercise. See Lutz, *American Nervousness,* 32.

61. Charlotte Perkins Gilman, *The Yellow Wallpaper* (New York, 1973); Wood, "Fashionable Diseases," 5–13; Morantz, "Lady," 41–43; Gosling, *Before Freud,* 110–15.

62. Dr. Rufus Thurston to Martha Eaton, Oct. 29, 1891, Eaton Papers, SHSW; Gosling, *Before Freud,* 115–16.

63. Dr. Rufus Thurston to Martha Eaton, Oct. 29, 1891; L. E. Holden to Edward Eaton, July 30, 1892; Allen Eaton to Edward Eaton, May 2, 1900, Eaton Papers, SHSW.

64. Gosling, *Before Freud,* 108–10, 116–20, 122–37.

65. Gosling, *Before Freud,* 55.

66. On the common medical view of the demands made upon women by their bodies, see Carroll Smith-Rosenberg and Charles Rosenberg, "The Female Animal: Medical and Biological Views of Woman and Her Role in Nineteenth-Century America," *Journal of American History,* 60 (1973).

67. This view was first advanced for both sexes by Barbara Sicherman, "Uses of a Diagnosis."

68. Feinstein, *William James,* 154–222; Doughty, *Francis Parkman,* 87; Abzug, *Passionate Liberator,* 24–25, 153. See also Miller, *Fathers and Sons,* 73–76.

69. Edward Eaton to C. D. Eaton, Nov. 8, 1891, Eaton Papers, SHSW.

70. Feinstein, *William James,* 195.

71. Feinstein, *William James,* 205.

72. Gosling, *Before Freud,* 31.

73. See chap. 9.

74. In this regard, it is revealing that ten of the fifteen neurasthenic men studied here were either ministers or the sons of clergy. Being a minister or being raised by one is surely no guarantee of abstention from worldly pleasures, but in the nineteenth century it did seem to increase the chances of abstemiousness.

Chapter 9: The Male Culture of the Workplace

1. Arthur H. Cole, "The Tempo of Mercantile Life in Colonial America," *Business History Review*, 33 (1959); Stuart Blumin, *The Emergence of the Middle Class: Social Experience in the American City, 1760–1900* (New York, 1989), 21–22.

2. L. E., "Home," *Ladies Magazine*, 3 (1830), 217–18; Abigail Dodge to James Alvin Dodge, Jan. 4, 1848, in H. Augusta Dodge, ed., *Gail Hamilton's Life in Letters* (Boston, 1901), 20. See also, Charles Van Hise to Alice Ring, Oct. 6, 1878 and Sept. 11, 1881, Charles Van Hise Papers, SHSW; Kirk Jeffrey, "Family History: The Middle-Class American Family in the Urban Context, 1830–1870" (Ph.D. diss., Stanford Univ., 1972), 96–97.

3. W. S. Tryon, *Parnassus Corner: A Life of James T. Fields, Publisher to the Victorians* (Boston, 1963), 49–54, 72–76.

4. Tryon, *Parnassus Corner*, 76.

5. Personal communication with Barbara Rotundo. See also Barbara Rotundo, "Mrs. James T. Fields: Hostess and Biographer" (Ph.D. diss., Syracuse Univ., 1968).

6. Quotations from William R. Johnson, *Schooled Lawyers: A Study in the Clash of Professional Cultures* (New York, 1978), 28, 31; more generally, see 28–31.

7. Johnson, *Schooled Lawyers*, 30–31; Robert Wiebe, "Lincoln's Fraternal Democracy," in John L. Thomas, ed., *Abraham Lincoln and the American Political Tradition* (Amherst, Mass., 1986), 25.

8. Michael Grossberg, "Institutionalizing Masculinity: The Law as a Masculine Profession," in Mark C. Carnes and Clyde Griffen, eds., *Meanings for Manhood: Contructions of Masculinity in Victorian America* (Chicago, 1990), 136–37. My interpretation of the culture of the nineteenth-century legal profession follows the one outlined by Grossberg in this essay.

9. Lewis Wallace, *Lew Wallace: An Autobiography* (New York, 1906), 216–17.

10. Usher Linder, quoted in Wiebe, "Lincoln's Democracy," 26.

11. Wiebe, "Lincoln's Democracy," 27.

12. Flint, *Memories of an Active Life: Men, Ships, and Sealing Wax* (New York, 1923), 27, 263, 302–5.

13. Flint, *Memories*, 106.

14. Flint, *Memories*, 27, 262–66, 304, 318.

15. See, for example, Flint, *Memories*, 32, 44–45.

16. On gambling, see Wheaton J. Lane, *Commodore Vanderbilt: An Epic of the Steam Age* (New York, 1942), 303, 308; Henry Watterston, *The History of the Manhattan Club: A Narrative of the Activities of a Half a Century* (New York, 1916), xxxii, xxxvi; and, more generally, Ann Fabian, *Card Sharps, Dream Books, and Bucket Shops: Gambling in Nineteenth-Century America* (Ithaca, N.Y., 1990). On amateur drama, Daniel Carter Beard, *Hardly a Man Is Now Alive: The Autobiography of Dan Beard* (New York, 1939), 284–85; Flint, *Memories*, 25–26; Jerome A. Hart, *In Our Second Century: From an Editor's Notebook* (San Francisco, 1931), 330–31; Mark A. DeWolfe Howe, *A Partial History of the Tavern Club* (Cambridge, Mass., 1934), 78–81; The Century Association, *The Century, 1847–1946* (New York, 1947), 38. On debates, see John Pierce memoirs, vol. 1, Apr. 29 and Aug. 20, 1806, and Oct. 20, 1807, Pierce Collection, MHS, and D. Samuel Howard to James Howard, Jan. 28, 1828, James C. Howard Papers, SHSW.

17. Leonard Ellis, "Men among Men: An Exploration of All-Male Relationships in Victorian America" (Ph.D. diss., Columbia Univ., 1982), 544.

18. John D'Emilio and Estelle B. Freedman, *Intimate Matters: A History of Sexuality in America* (New York, 1988), 130–38; Michael Lynch, "The Age of Adhesiveness: Male-Male Intimacy in New York City, 1830–1880," paper presented at American Historical Association, Dec. 1985.

19. For a variety of suggestive approaches to the history of alcohol use, see Susanna Barrows and Robin Room, eds., *Drinking: Behavior and Belief in Modern History* (Berkeley, Calif., 1991), 29–143, 376–98; Thomas Brennan, *Public Drinking and Popular Culture in Eighteenth-Century Paris* (Princeton, N.J., 1987); on drinking habits in all-male settings in the early nineteenth-century United States, see W. J. Rohrabaugh, *The Alcoholic Republic: An American Tradition* (New York, 1979), 14–16.

20. An Old New Yorker, "Clubs—Club Life—Some New York Clubs," *Galaxy* 22 (1876), 231; Ellis, "Men among Men," 365–69.

21. Ellis, "Men among Men," 332–55, 364–65; Wiebe, "Lincoln's Democracy," 27; New Yorker, "Clubs," 238; Flint, *Memories*, 138–39.

22. Mark C. Carnes, *Secret Ritual and Manhood in Victorian America* (New Haven, Conn., 1989), 110–25.

23. See notes 3, 4, 6, 7; also, Herman Melville, "Bartleby the Scrivener," and "Jimmy Rose," in *Herman Melville: Selected Tales and Poems,* ed., Richard Chase (New York, 1950), 92–143.

24. Ellis, "Men among Men," 366–67; New Yorker, "Clubs," 231.

25. Tryon, *Parnassus Corner,* 176; Joseph Kett, *Rites of Passage: Adolescence in America, 1790 to the Present* (New York, 1977), 102; Alphonso David Rockwell, *Rambling Recollections: An Autobiography* (New York, 1920), 182.

26. See note 7 and Henry Dwight Sedgwick, *Memoirs of an Epicurean* (New York, 1942), 33.

27. See, for example, Wiebe, "Lincoln's Democracy," 24–25.

28. Joseph Tuckerman to Betsy Salisbury, Jan. 7, 1821, Salisbury Papers, AAS. When Edward Eaton, a college president with ministerial training, found himself tempted by the offer of a church in Milford, Massachusetts, he explained its attraction in words that echo those of Tuckerman. At the Milford church, Eaton believed he would "have a happy, quiet, useful life." In the end, Eaton opted for the turmoil of his presidency (Edward Eaton to Martha Eaton, May 18, 1901, Edward D. Eaton Papers, SHSW).

29. Ann Douglas, *The Feminization of American Culture* (New York, 1977), 114–23.

30. The primary interpretations of the clergy's status problems in addition to Douglas, *Feminization*, 17–49, 94–139, are Daniel Calhoun, *Professional Lives in America: Structure and Aspiration, 1750–1850* (Cambridge, Mass., 1965), 88–177, and Donald Scott, *From Office to Profession: The New England Ministry, 1750–1850* (Philadelphia, 1978).

31. Sectarian rivalry is a subtheme of Sydney Ahlstrom, *A Religious History of the American People* (New York, 1975), vol. 1, 471–592.

32. Calhoun, *Professional Lives,* 88–177.

33. Rockwell, *Rambling Recollections,* 207.

34. Rockwell, *Rambling Recollections,* 35.

35. Judith Walzer Leavitt, *Brought to Bed: Childbearing in America, 1750 to 1950* (New York, 1986), 37–63.

36. Gerald N. Grob, *Edward Jarvis and the Medical World of Nineteenth-Century America* (Knoxville, Tenn., 1978), 19, 32, 54; Rockwell, *Rambling Recollections,* 35.

37. Calhoun, *Professional Lives,* 6–7; Edward Jarvis quoted in Grob, *Edward Jarvis,* 32.

38. Johnson, *Schooled Lawyers,* 24–33.

39. For all of the gender similarity in their status problems, the ministry and medicine were headed in different directions as far as prestige was concerned. Over the course of the nineteenth century, the status of the clergy was in decline, while the prestige of the medical profession rose in later years.

40. Faye Dudden has suggested that the shift from men as family consumers to women took place for middle-class households during the 1850s (*Serving Women: Household Service in Nineteenth-Century America* [Middletown, Conn., 1983], 136–37). But advertising assuming a female consumer force and articles addressing the woman as shopper were common by the 1840s (Mary Ryan, *The Cradle of the Middle Class: The Family in Oneida County, New York, 1790–1865* [New York, 1981], 199–201; Blumin, *Emergence,* 185–86).

41. Of course, men bargained constantly with women at home. As we saw in chap. 7, wives worked hard to influence their husbands, and husbands tried to persuade their wives to run the house in a way that they—the husbands—saw fit. Much of this bargaining may have been hidden from con-

scious view by the elaborate mythologies that surrounded domestic roles, and some of it was forgiven in the name of love. Still, dealing with women who wanted to "wear the pants" was one of the most disconcerting aspects of home life for many bourgeois men. They did not like bargaining with women in any setting.

42. Sedgwick, *Memoirs*, 122.

43. Tryon, *Parnassus Corner*, 73–74.

44. Sheila Rothman, *Woman's Proper Place: A History of Changing Ideals and Practices, 1870 to the Present* (New York, 1978), 18–21.

45. Rothman, *Woman's Place*, 52–56.

46. The nature of a nineteenth-century male doctor's professional interactions with women—by contrast with a lawyer's—were problematic to him. For most of the century, physicians met women clients in the women's homes more often than in professional medical spaces. The most important interactions were not highly structured in the way that courtroom procedure was. Also, the doctor's professional dealings with women fell into two distinctly different categories—the female patient and the mother or wife of a patient. In the latter case, the woman gained some power in the relationship by her superior knowledge of the patient and the symptomatic details of the illness. In the former case, it is clear that doctors had the upper hand, but how much they used it and in what manner is a matter of debate among historians. See Carroll Smith-Rosenberg, "The Hysterical Woman: Sex Roles and Role Conflict in Nineteenth-Century America," *Journal of Interdisciplinary History*, 4 (1973); Ann Douglas Wood, "'The Fashionable Diseases': Women's Complaints and Their Treatments in Nineteenth-Century America," in Mary Hartman and Lois Banner, eds., *Clio's Consciousness Raised* (New York, 1974); G. J. Barker-Benfield, *Horrors of the Half-Known Life: Male Attitudes toward Women and Sexuality in Nineteenth-Century America* (New York, 1976), 61–132, and, most convincingly, Regina Morantz, "The Lady and Her Physician," in Hartman and Banner, eds., *Clio's Consciousness Raised*.

47. Quoted in Grossberg, "Masculinity," 142–43.

48. See Grossberg, "Masculinity," 139–43, especially on "the mystique of the robe" and judicial patriarchy. Grossberg describes women as "supplicants" in the courtroom.

49. Grossberg, "Masculinity," 145. The foregoing account follows Grossberg's interpretation (145–50) and that of D. Kelly Weisberg, "Barred from the Bar: Women and Legal Education in the United States, 1870–1890," *Journal of Legal Education*, 28 (1977).

50. *In re Lockwood*, 154 U.S. 116 (1893); Weisberg, "Barred from the Bar," 486–87.

51. Grossberg, "Masculinity," 147–48.

52. Grossberg, "Masculinity," 148–50.

53. Cynthia Fuchs Epstein, *Women in Law* (New York, 1981), 4.

54. Regina Markell Morantz-Sanchez, *Sympathy and Science: Women Physicians in American Medicine* (New York, 1985), 144.

55. Morantz-Sanchez, *Sympathy and Science*, 150–53.

56. Charles Rosenberg, *The Care of Strangers: The Rise of America's Hospital System* (New York, 1987), 151–211; Morris J. Vogel and Charles Rosenberg, eds., *The Therapeutic Revolution: Essays in the Social History of American Medicine* (Philadelphia, 1980); Paul Starr, *The Social Transformation of American Medicine* (New York, 1982); Morris J. Vogel, *The Invention of the Modern Hospital: Boston, 1870–1930* (Chicago, 1980).

57. Mendenhall's account is quoted at length in Morantz-Sanchez, *Sympathy and Science*, 116–17. For accounts of similar medical-school incidents, see 115–16, 118–19.

58. Morantz-Sanchez, *Sympathy and Science*, 53, 145.

59. Mary Roth Walsh, *"Doctors Wanted, No Women Need Apply": Sexual Barriers in the Medical Profession, 1835–1875* (New Haven, Conn., 1976), 107–8; Morantz-Sanchez, *Sympathy and Science*, 266–311.

60. On women's entry (and male resistance) in other professions, see Barbara Harris, *Beyond Her Sphere: Women and the Professions in American History* (Westport, Conn., 1978); Rosalind Rosenberg, *Beyond Separate Spheres: Intellectual Roots of Modern Feminism* (New Haven, Conn., 1982); Margaret Rossiter, *Women Scientists in America* (Baltimore, 1982).

61. Francis Parkman, "The Woman Question," *North American Review,* 129 (1879), 316; Aileen Kraditor, *The Ideas of the Woman Suffrage Movement 1890–1920* (New York, 1965), 14–15; quotation is from Carl N. Degler, *At Odds: Women and the Family in America from the Revolution to the Present* (New York, 1980), 351.

62. Parkman, "Woman Question," 321; Kraditor, *Ideas,* 19–20.

63. Kraditor, *Ideas,* 17–18; Parkman, "Woman Question," 312.

64. Paula Baker, "The Domestication of American Politics: Women and American Political Society, 1780–1920," *American Historical Review,* 89 (1984), 626–28, 630–31.

65. Baker, "Domestication," 628–29.

66. Baker, "Domestication," 630–31.

67. The literature on this world of female political action is abundant. See the works cited in chap. 8, n. 19, and Carroll Smith-Rosenberg, *Disorderly Conduct: Visions of Gender in Victorian America* (New York, 1985), 109–28; Ruth Bordin, *Women and Temperance: The Quest for Power and Liberty, 1873–1900* (Philadelphia, 1981); Keith Melder, *Beginnings of Sisterhood: The American Women's Rights Movement, 1800–1850* (New York, 1977); Degler, *At Odds,* 279–361; Baker, "Domestication," 632–38.

68. Grover Cleveland, "Would Woman Suffrage Be Unwise?" in Aileen Kraditor, ed., *Up from the Pedestal: Selected Writings in the History of American Feminism* (Chicago, 1968), 201.

69. Baker, "Domestication," 634; Kraditor, *Ideas*, 15, 18–19.

70. Parkman, "Woman Question," 312; Kraditor, *Ideas*, 17–18; Degler, *At Odds*, 348–49.

71. Quoted in Ellen Carol DuBois, *Feminism and Suffrage: The Emergence of an Independent Women's Movement in America, 1848–1869* (Ithaca, N.Y., 1978), 47.

Chapter 10: Passionate Manhood: A Changing Standard of Masculinity

1. Eddy quoted in Joseph Kett, *Rites of Passage: Adolescence in America, 1790 to Present* (New York, 1977), 162–63; Thomas Wentworth Higginson, *Out-Door Papers* (Boston, 1886 [1863]), 19; Edward Everett Hale, *A New England Boyhood* (Boston, 1964 [1893]), 177, 179.

2. James R. McGovern, *Yankee Family* (New Orleans, 1975), 123; Leonard Ellis, "Men among Men: An Exploration of All-Male Relationships in Victorian America" (Ph.D. diss., Columbia Univ., 1982), 249; Charles Flint, *Memories of an Active Life: Men, Ships, and Sealing Wax* (New York, 1923), 24; Higginson, *Out-Door Papers*, 27–28.

3. Henry Dwight Sedgwick, *Memoirs of an Epicurean* (New York, 1942), 51. See also McGovern, *Yankee Family*, 117, and Lois Banner, *American Beauty* (New York, 1983), 242.

4. Theodore P. Greene, *America's Heroes: The Changing Models of Success in American Magazines* (New York, 1970), 127–31, 258–62.

5. James Cattell to William and Elizabeth Cattell, Dec. 1, 1884, James Cattell Papers, Family Correspondence, LC. Other instances of young men preoccupied with body image and physical measurements include Sarah Swan Weld Blake, ed. *Diaries and Letters of Francis Minot Weld, M.D.* (Boston, 1925), 32; George Dryer to Rev. Horatio Dryer, Aug. 31, 1870, Dryer Papers, NYHS; Sergeant Kendall to B. Franklin and Elizabeth Kendall, Sept. 5, 1882, Kendall Papers, NYHS; Oliver Wendell Holmes, Jr., to Amelia Holmes, Sept. 23, 1861, and to Amelia and Oliver Wendell Holmes, Sr., Apr. 23, 1862, in Mark DeWolf Howe, ed., *Touched with Fire: Civil War Letters and Diary of Oliver Wendell Holmes, Jr., 1861–1864* (Cambridge, Mass., 1946), 11, 44–45; Higginson, *Out-Door Papers*, 24, 155; Kenneth S. Lynn, *William Dean Howells: An American Life* (New York, 1970), 194.

6. Kett, *Rites of Passage*, 224; Raymond Brown to Gertrude Foster, Feb. 1, 1892, Gertrude Foster Brown Papers, SL; Bingham quoted in Char Miller, *Fathers and Sons: The Bingham Family and the American Mission* (Philadelphia, 1982), 149; see also Howard Doughty, *Francis Parkman* (Cambridge, Mass., 1983 [1962]), 319. The equation of character and body shape appeared in its negative form, too. In his analysis of magazine arti-

cles, Theodore Greene found that—in the years 1904 to 1913—only villains had unimpressive physiques (Greene, *America's Heroes,* 258–62).

7. Quoted in Greene, *America's Heroes,* 78.

8. Quoted in Susan Curtis, "The Son of Man and God the Father: The Social Gospel and Victorian Masculinity," in Mark C. Carnes and Clyde Griffen, eds., *Meanings for Manhood: Constructions of Masculinity in Victorian America* (Chicago, 1990), 72.

9. Ellis, "Men among Men," 267. See also Flint, *Memories,* 104–6.

10. Marion Foster Washburne, "Studies in Domestic Relations," *Harper's Bazaar,* 38 (1904), 242. This same revised concept of male reason appears in Rafford Pyke, "What Men Like in Men," *Cosmopolitan,* 33 (1902); Pyke asserts that man's aversion to self-analysis leaves him "free to smash his way through life as a mastodon would smash his way through a prehistoric jungle" (402–3).

11. Charles Van Hise to Alice Van Hise, Dec. 22, 1917, Charles Van Hise Papers, SHSW; *The Heart of John Burroughs' Journal,* ed. Clara Barrus (Boston, 1928), 87. See also Ellen Rothman, *Hands and Hearts: A History of Courtship in America* (New York, 1984), 199, and Kenneth Lynn's analysis of the same issue as it appeared in William Dean Howells's *The Landlord of Lion's Head* (Lynn, *William Dean Howells,* 309).

12. Sergeant Kendall to B. Franklin and Elizabeth Kendall, Jan. 10, 1887, Kendall Papers, NYHS. See as well Charles Van Hise to Alice Ring, Dec. 11, 1876, Van Hise Papers, SHSW.

13. Seymour Hudgens, *Exeter, Schooldays, and Other Poems* (Cambridge, Mass., 1882), 44.

14. From speech to Iowa State Teacher's Association, Nov. 4, 1910, *Theodore Roosevelt Cyclopedia* (New York, 1941), 587.

15. Quoted in Mark A. DeWolf Howe, *A Partial History of the Tavern Club* (Cambridge, Mass., 1934), 74–76.

16. Quoted in Everett Carter, *Howells and the Age of Realism* (Philadelphia, 1954), 12.

17. John William DeForest, *A Volunteer's Adventures: A Union Captain's Record of the Civil War* (New Haven, Conn., 1946), 130–31, 200; Christine Terhune Herrick, "Man, the Victim," *Munsey's Magazine,* 27 (1902), 889. On the provision of "manly" spaces with "primitive" decor in late nineteenth-century homes, see Eileen Boris, *Art and Labor: Ruskin, Morris, and the Craftsman Ideal in America* (Philadelphia, 1986), 64, 76–77.

18. Higginson, *Out-Door Papers,* 138; Joseph Henry Harper, *I Remember* (New York, 1934), 65. For other hunters, see McGovern, *Yankee Family,* 117; Flint, *Memories,* 25, 26; George Dryer to Rev. Horatio Dryer, n.d. [1874], Dryer Papers, NYHS.

19. T. Jackson Lears, *No Place of Grace: Antimodernism and the Transformation of American Culture* (New York, 1981), 52; Daniel Carter Beard,

Hardly a Man Is Now Alive: The Autobiography of Dan Beard (New York, 1939), 10–11.

20. For instance, Flint, *Memories,* 25; Howe, *Tavern Club,* 62–63; Beard, *Hardly a Man,* 284–85.

21. Quoted in Mark C. Carnes, *Secret Ritual and Manhood in Victorian America* (New Haven, Conn., 1989), 104.

22. On the popularity and influence of these books, see Doughty, *Francis Parkman,* 138; Henry Seidel Canby, *The Age of Confidence: Life in the Nineties* (New York, 1934), 189; Richard Lebeaux, *Young Man Thoreau* (Amherst, Mass., 1977), 68–69; Carroll Smith-Rosenberg, *Disorderly Conduct: Visions of Gender in Victorian America* (New York, 1985), 92–108; John Cawelti, *Apostles of the Self-made Man: Changing Concepts of Success in America* (Chicago, 1965), 68–73.

23. Doughty, *Francis Parkman,* 23.

24. Hamlin Garland, "Do You Fear the Wind?" in Hamlin Garland, *The Trail of the Goldseekers: A Record of Travel in Prose and Verse* (New York, 1899), 95. Daniel Carter Beard, a friend of Garland, quoted the poem in *Hardly a Man,* 360. Edward Everett Hale also equates animals and savages in Hale, *New England Boyhood,* 48. Animals and "primitive peoples" were together on the minds of late nineteenth-century men when they gave names to athletic teams, from the Dartmouth Indians and the Princeton Tigers to the Boston Braves and the Chicago Cubs.

25. *Burroughs' Journal,* 98.

26. John William DeForest to Harriet DeForest, Apr. 6, 1862, in DeForest, *Volunteer's Adventures,* 7–8; Theodore Roosevelt's "wolf" statement is quoted in Kathleen Dalton, "Theodore Roosevelt and the Idea of War," *The Theodore Roosevelt Association Journal,* 7 (1981), 7; Jack London, *Call of the Wild* (New York, 1903). Also, Herrick, "Man, the Victim," 889; Pyke, "What Men Like," 402.

27. Higginson, *Out-Door Papers,* 138–39.

28. See Carroll Smith-Rosenberg and Charles Rosenberg, "The Female Animal: Medical and Biological Views of Woman and Her Role in Nineteenth-Century America," *Journal of American History,* 60 (1973).

29. Kate Gannett Wells, "Why More Girls Do Not Marry," *North American Review,* 152 (1891), 176; Maud Rittenhouse diary, June 1882, in Isabelle Rittenhouse Mayne, *Maud,* ed. Richard Lee Strout (New York, 1939), 108; Eleanor Abbot, *Being Little in Cambridge When Everyone Else Was Big* (New York, 1936), 104; "abnormal idea" quoted in John D'Emilio and Estelle B. Freedman, *Intimate Matters: A History of Sexuality in America* (New York, 1988), 177.

30. Rothman, *Hands and Hearts,* 237.

31. Wells, "Why More Girls," 176.

32. Theodore Roosevelt, *The Strenuous Life: Essays and Addresses* (New York, 1902), 268; Smith quotation, 275–76.

33. James Cattell to William and Elizabeth Cattell, May 28, 1885, Cattell Papers, LC; Katherine Dummer to Walter Fisher, Dec. 1, 1914, Ethel Sturges Dummer Papers, SL. See Richard Cabot to Ella Lyman, Nov. 16, 1889, Ella Lyman Cabot Papers, SL.

34. Rev. William Whitmarsh of the Knights of Pythias is quoted in Mark Carnes, "A Pilgrimage for Light: Fraternal Ritualism in America" (Ph.D. diss., Columbia Univ., 1982), 140; evangelical speaker quoted in Joseph Kett, *Rites of Passage: Adolescence in America, 1790 to the Present* (New York, 1977), 196–97; *Herald* quoted in Wheaton J. Lane, *Commodore Vanderbilt: An Epic of the Steam Age* (New York, 1942), 321. See further, Carnes, "Pilgrimage," 137–42; Kett, *Rites of Passage*, 196, 197; Lears, *Antimodernism*, 75; Ray Stannard Baker, *Native American: The Book of My Youth* (New York, 1941), 71.

35. Holmes quoted in Gerald F. Linderman, *Embattled Courage: The Experience of Combat in the American Civil War* (New York, 1987), 282; Walker quoted in George Fredrickson, *The Inner Civil War: Northern Intellectuals and the Crisis of Union* (New York, 1965), 223. The time lag between the Civil War and its glorification is described in Linderman, 266–97. The war also provided the leading spokesman for the next generation, Theodore Roosevelt, with a lens through which to view the world. See Dalton, "Idea of War."

36. William James, "The Moral Equivalent of War," in *Essays on Faith and Morals* (New York, 1943), 323; Roosevelt, *Strenuous Life*, 257. See also Stephen Crane's view of the war's "divine message" and manhood in *The Red Badge of Courage*, in *Great Short Works of Stephen Crane* [New York, 1968], 125).

37. Quoted in Linderman, *Embattled Courage*, 289–90. See Fredrickson, *Inner War*, 225–78.

38. James, "Moral Equivalent," 325.

39. Linderman, *Embattled Courage*, 275–94.

40. Sarah Grand quoted from the *North American Review* in Lears, *Antimodernism*, 112; Roosevelt in Richard Hofstadter, *The American Political Tradition and The Men Who Made It* (New York, 1948), 213; Sandburg in Linderman, *Embattled Courage*, 294. See also Canby, *Age of Confidence*, 205.

41. Robert L. Beisner, in *Twelve against Empire* (New York, 1968), was the first to point out this generational split.

42. Roosevelt, *Strenuous Life*, 20–21.

43. Ernest Howard Crosby, "The Military Idea of Manliness," *The Independent*, 53 (1901), 873–75.

44. Crosby, "Military Idea," 874.

45. Oliver Wendell Holmes, Jr., "The Soldier's Faith," in *Speeches* (Boston, 1913), 59.

46. Kett, *Rites of Passage*, 174; see also 172, 198, 203, 233–34; Jeffrey Hantover, "The Boy Scouts and the Validation of Masculinity," in Elizabeth H.

Pleck and Joseph H. Pleck, eds., *The American Man* (Englewood Cliffs, N.J., 1980), 293–99; David I. Macleod, *Building Character in the American Boy: The Boy Scouts, YMCA, and Their Forerunners, 1870–1920* (Madison, Wis., 1983).

47. Roosevelt, *Strenuous Life*, 258; Miller, *Fathers and Sons*, 163.

48. Greene, *America's Heroes*, 127–31, 137, 161–63.

49. Greene, *America's Heroes*, 239–40, 258–62. These years produced one public figure who remained a consistent hero in the mold of the strong leader—Theodore Roosevelt. Greene describes him as the "only major political hero" from the "idols-of-power" period (1894–1903) and the autobiographies of his contemporaries treat him with a God-like reverence (see Beard, *Hardly a Man*, 10–11; Baker, *Native American*, 308–9; Flint, *Memories*, 103–6; William Allen White, *Autobiography* [New York, 1946], 298). For a complex and convincing analysis of the Roosevelt cult, see Kathleen Dalton, "Why America Loved Teddy Roosevelt, or, Charisma Is in the Eyes of the Beholders," in Robert Brugger, ed., *Ourselves/ Our Past: Psychological Approaches to American History* (Baltimore, 1981), 269–91.

50. Greene, *America's Heroes*, 45–53.

51. Nancy Struna, "Puritans and Sport," *Journal of Sports History*, 2 (1977); David Hackett Fischer, *Albion's Seed: Four British Folkways in America* (New York, 1989), 146–51.

52. Melvin L. Adelman, *A Sporting Time: New York City and the Rise of Modern Athletics, 1820–1870* (Chicago, 1986); Ellis, "Men among Men," 581–85; Stuart Blumin, *The Emergence of the Middle Class: Social Experience in the American City, 1760–1900* (New York, 1989), 213–14.

53. James D'Wolf Lovett, *Old Boston Boys and the Games They Played* (Boston, 1906), 55–63; Doughty, *Francis Parkman*, 26; Blumin, *Emergence*, 208.

54. W. S. Tryon, *Parnassus Corner: A Life of James T. Fields, Publisher to the Victorians* (Boston, 1963), 31; Doughty, *Francis Parkman*, 26.

55. Higginson, *Out-Door Papers*, 70, 138–39; Clyde Griffen, "Reconstructing Masculinity from the Evangelical Revival to the Waning of Progressivism: A Speculative Synthesis," in Carnes and Griffen, *Meanings for Manhood*, 189.

56. "Life at Phillips Exeter," *Bulletin of the Phillips Exeter Academy*, 14 (1918), 33; Miller, *Fathers and Sons*, 114

57. John R. Betts, *America's Sporting Heritage, 1850–1950* (Reading, Mass., 1974); Benjamin G. Rader, *American Sports: From the Age of Folk Games to the Age of Television*, 2nd ed. (Englewood Cliffs, N.J., 1990); Donald Mrozek, *Sport and American Mentality, 1880–1910* (Knoxville, Tenn., 1983); Ellis, "Men among Men," 488–90; Ellery H. Clark, *Reminiscences of an Athlete; Twenty Years on Track and Field* (Boston, 1911), 16–47; McGovern, *Yankee Family*, 123.

58. Walker quoted in Fredrickson, *Inner War*, 223; Walter Camp and Loren Deland, *Football* (Boston, 1896), 78; Linderman, *Embattled Courage*, 294.

On the larger issue of the cultural meaning of athletics at the end of the century, see Joe L. Dubbert, *A Man's Place: Masculinity in Transition* (Englewood Cliffs, N.J., 1979), 163–90.

59. Kett, *Rites of Passage,* 176; Johann F. Herbart, *Outlines of Educational Doctrine* (New York, 1901), 189.

60. Henry Sheldon, *Student Life and Customs* (New York, 1969 [1901]), 250; Clark, *Reminiscences,* 9. See also Roosevelt, *Strenuous Life,* 155–58; Ellis, "Men among Men," 207–8; Fredrickson, *Inner War,* 223.

61. Cunningham LaPlace, "The Reflections of a Sub-Freshman's Father," *The Outlook,* 80 (1905), 574; Gulick quoted in Kett, *Rites of Passage,* 203. Fredrickson, *Inner War,* 224; Ellis, "Men among Men," 541.

62. Sheldon, *Student Life,* 250. Also, Roosevelt, *Strenuous Life,* 155–58.

63. Ellis, "Men among Men," 207; Sedgwick, *Memoirs,* 52. Also "Charlie" to Edward and Martha Eaton, Dec. 28, 1881, Edward D. Eaton Papers, SHSW.

64. Roosevelt, *Strenuous Life,* 160; Clark, *Reminiscences,* 32. See Sheldon, *Student Life,* 250.

65. Flint, *Memories,* 32; Pyke, "What Men Like in Men," 405; Roosevelt, *Strenuous Life,* 164; Sheldon, *Student Life,* 250–51. And see Lovett, *Boston Boys,* 201.

66. LaPlace, "Reflections," 574; Sheldon, *Student Life,* 250. Lovett, *Boston Boys,* 196, 214; Hale, *New England Boyhood,* 29; Ellis, "Men among Men," 208, 249.

67. Steven A. Riess, *Touching Base: Professional Baseball and American Culture in the Progressive Era* (Westport, Conn., 1980); Ronald A. Smith, *Sports and Freedom: The Rise of Big-Time College Athletics* (New York, 1990); Elliott J. Gorn, *The Manly Art: Bare-Knuckle Prize Fighting in America* (Ithaca, N.Y., 1986), 194–206, 216–25, 250–54.

68. Ellis, "Men among Men," 540–42, 582–88. It is worth noting that the "home" enjoyed by baseball players was populated by an all-male family. As with so much of the organized play of men in the second half of the century (in lodges or men's clubs, for example), men entertained themselves by creating male households to belong to. For other interpretations of baseball's cultural appeal at the end of the century, see Riess, *Touching Base;* Steven Gelber, "Working at Playing: The Culture of the Workplace and the Rise of Baseball," *Journal of Social History,* 16 (June 1983); Melvin Adelman, "Baseball, Business and the Workplace: Gelber's Thesis Reexamined," *Journal of Social History,* 23 (winter 1989): 283–302.

69. M. S. Bailey to James Cattell, Nov. 18, 1880, Cattell Papers, LC; Ellis, "Men among Men," 279. Also, see Michael Grossberg, "Institutionalizing Masculinity: The Law as a Masculine Profession," in Carnes and Griffen, eds., *Meanings for Manhood,* 143–44.

70. Beard, *Hardly a Man,* 199; Sergeant Kendall to B. Franklin and Elizabeth Kendall, Jan. 6, 1888, Mar. 21 and 29, 1889, B. Franklin Kendall to

Sergeant Kendall, Apr. 6, 1890, Kendall Papers, NYHS; Frank P. Fetherston diary, Apr. 6, 1888, NYHS; H. C. Mabley, "The Woodville Contest," *Amateur Press* (Akron, Ohio), 1 (1884), AAS.

71. George Dryer to Rev. Horatio Dryer, Sept. 23, 1870, Dryer Papers, NYHS. See Holmes in Howe, *Touched with Fire*, 75.

72. *The Compact Edition of the Oxford English Dictionary* (Oxford, 1971), vol. 1, 490.

Chapter 11: Roots of Change: The Women Without and the Woman Within

1. Ray Stannard Baker, *Native American: The Book of My Youth* (New York, 1941), 308–9. The irony is that Baker later became a staunch Wilsonian and critic of Roosevelt (Kathleen M. Dalton, "The Manly Reformer: Theodore Roosevelt and American Culture," MS draft).

2. On the changes in the economy, see Glen Porter, *The Rise of Big Business, 1860–1910* (New York, 1973), and Alfred D. Chandler, Jr., *The Visible Hand: The Managerial Revolution in American Business* (Cambridge, Mass., 1977). Chandler is also helpful on the emerging structure and culture of corporate bureaucracy, a subject that is illuminated by Olivier Zunz, *Making America Corporate, 1870–1920* (Chicago, 1990). The figures on the white-collar work force are from Peter Filene, *Him/ Her/ Self: Sex Roles in Modern America,* 2nd ed. (Baltimore, 1986), 73. Filene's analysis of the relationship between the changing nature of middle-class work and changes in bourgeois manhood (72–74) has strongly influenced my own understanding. I have also been influenced by a similar interpretation in Jeffrey Hantover, "The Boy Scouts and the Validation of Masculinity," in Elizabeth H. Pleck and Joseph H. Pleck, eds., *The American Man* (Englewood Cliffs, N.J., 1980).

3. Zunz, *Making America Corporate,* 108, 118–19, 144; Stuart Blumin, *The Emergence of the Middle Class: Social Experience in the American City, 1760–1900* (New York, 1989), 291–92.

4. Harris Merton Lyon, "The City of Lonesome Men," *Collier's,* 48 (1912), 25.

5. Sedgwick, *Memoirs,* 185.

6. Michael Grossberg, "Institutionalizing Masculinity: The Law as a Masculine Profession," in Mark C. Carnes and Clyde Griffen, eds., *Meanings for Manhood: Constructions of Masculinity in Victorian America* (Chicago, 1990), 143.

7. See James R. McGovern, "David Graham Phillips and the Virility Impulse of the Progressives," *New England Quarterly,* 39 (1966); Hantover, "Boy Scouts," 187–88.

8. Women had become established in the federal bureaucracy much earlier,

making significant inroads by 1870. See Cindy Sondik Aron, *Ladies and Gentlemen of the Civil Service: Middle-Class Workers in Victorian America* (New York, 1987).

9. Aron, *Civil Service*, 162–65, 181–83; Blumin, *Emergence*, 263–65; Zunz, *Making America Corporate*, 117–19.

10. George Fredrickson, *The Inner Civil War: Northern Intellectuals and the Crisis of Union* (New York, 1965), 222; Henry Sheldon, *Student Life and Customs* (New York, 1969 [1901]), 250. On the word *overcivilized*, see *The Compact Edition of the Oxford English Dictionary* (Oxford, 1971), vol. 1, 2033. See also Daniel Carter Beard, *Hardly a Man Is Now Alive: The Autobiography of Dan Beard* (New York, 1939), 361; Theodore Roosevelt, *The Strenuous Life: Essays and Addresses* (New York, 1902), 7–8, 255, 268–69.

11. *Oxford English Dictionary*, compact ed., vol. 1, 422.

12. Henry James, *The Bostonians* (Baltimore, 1966), 290. See also Junius H. Browne quoted in Joe L. Dubbert, *A Man's Place: Masculinity in Transition* (Englewood Cliffs, N.J., 1979), 100.

13. Quoted in Michael S. Kimmel, "Introduction," in Michael S. Kimmel and Thomas Mosmiller, eds., *Against the Tide: Pro-Feminist Men in the United States—A Documentary History* (Boston, 1992), 13.

14. G. Stanley Hall, "Feminization in Schools and Home: The Undue Influence of Women Teachers—The Need of Different Training for the Sexes," *World's Work* 16 (1908), 10238.

15. On woman-dominated child-rearing and its implications for boys, see Joseph Kett, *Rites of Passage: Adolescence in America, 1790 to the Present* (New York, 1977), 43–44, 47, 224; Edward S. Martin, "The Use of Fathers," *Harper's New Monthly Magazine*, 117 (1908), 763; Hall, "Feminization," 10238–39; Ellis, "Men among Men," 220; Jeffrey Hantover, "Sex Role, Sexuality, and Social Status: The Early Years of the Boy Scouts of America" (Ph.D. diss., Univ. of Chicago, 1976), 184, 187–91. On women's cultural role, see Ann Douglas, *The Feminization of American Culture* (New York, 1978), 93, 143–309; Nancy F. Cott, *The Bonds of Womanhood: "Woman's Sphere" in New England, 1780–1835* (New Haven, Conn. 1977), 126–58; Barbara Welter, "The Feminization of American Religion, 1800–1860," in Mary Hartman and Lois Banner, eds., *Clio's Consciousness Raised* (New York, 1974); Blumin, *Emergence*, 183–85; T. Jackson Lears, *No Place of Grace: Antimodernism and the Transformation of American Culture* (New York, 1981), 17, 23–26.

16. Ruth Bordin, *Women and Temperance: The Quest for Power and Liberty, 1873–1900* (Philadelphia, 1981); David J. Pivar, *Purity Crusade: Sexual Morality, and Social Control 1868–1900* (Westport, Conn., 1972); Mark C. Carnes, *Secret Ritual and Manhood in Victorian America* (New Haven, Conn., 1989), 79–80.

17. Duffield Osborne, "A Defense of Pugilism," *North American Review*, 146 (1888), 434–35.

18. In a complex, restrained mode, see a similar statement in "Certain Dangerous Tendencies in American Life," *The Atlantic Monthly*, 42 (1878), 398. This was, in a sense, the unconscious project of fraternal ritual in the late nineteenth century. Mark Carnes describes convincingly the rejection of genteel, liberal Protestantism ("female") and the infusion of darkness, death, and the Old Testament wrath ("male") into the rites of fraternal organizations in the mid to late nineteenth century (Carnes, *Secret Ritual*, 39–150). See also Tom Lutz, *American Nervousness, 1903: An Anecdotal History* (Ithaca, N.Y., 1991), 36–37, where a similar point is made, though in different language.

19. Regina Markell Morantz-Sanchez, *Sympathy and Science: Women Physicians in American Medicine* (New York, 1985), 52; Grossberg, "Masculinity," 145–46; Cleveland in Aileen Kraditor, ed., *Up from the Pedestal: Selected Writing in the History of American Feminism* (Chicago, 1968), 199–203.

20. On Social Darwinism, Richard Hofstadter, *Social Darwinism in American Thought, 1860–1915* (Boston, 1944).

21. Lears, *Antimodernism*, 145–46.

22. See Charles Rosenberg, "Sexuality, Class and Role in Nineteenth-Century America," *American Quarterly*, 35 (1973), 140, on tickling. For toys, see James R. McGovern, *Yankee Family* (New Orleans, 1975), 73.

23. Arthur S. Pier, *St. Paul's School, 1855–1934* (New York, 1934), 33; Henry A. Kittredge, "Andover, Past and Present . . . " *New England Magazine*, 39 (1909), 584.

24. Thomas Wentworth Higginson, *Out-Door Papers* (Boston, 1886 [1863]), 22; Mary Ryan, *The Cradle of the Middle Class: The Family in Oneida County, New York, 1790–1865* (New York, 1981), 113–64. See also John William DeForest, *A Volunteer's Adventures: A Union Captain's Record of the Civil War* (New Haven, Conn., 1946), 62–63, 101, 129, 145; Mrs. Manners, *At Home and Abroad; or How to Behave* (New York, 1853), 40–41.

25. *Letters and Journals of Thomas Wentworth Higginson, 1846–1906*, ed. Mary Thacher Higginson (Boston, 1921), 261; Mary Paul to George H. Paul, July 12, 1858, George H. Paul Papers, SHSW. Also, unsigned letter to Caroline Dall, June 20, 1884, Caroline Dall Papers, MHS.

26. Hall, "Feminization," 10240.

27. On the cultural glorification of boyhood and its virtues in etiquette books, at men's club dinners, and on the athletic field, respectively, see Mrs. John Sherwood, *Manners and Social Usages* (New York, 1887), 17; Mark A. DeWolfe Howe, *A Partial History of the Tavern Club* (Cambridge, Mass., 1934), 75; and Sedgwick, *Memoirs*, 263.

28. Beard, *Hardly a Man*, 205; Higginson, *Out-Door Papers*, 101. See also Beard, *Hardly a Man*, 57, 63; Lewis Wallace, *Lew Wallace: An Autobiography* (New York, 1906).

29. Beard, *Hardly a Man*, 205; James D'Wolf Lovett, *Old Boston Boys and the*

Games They Played (Boston, 1906), 77; Higginson, *Out-Door Papers*, 162, 14 (also 22, 30, 70); Samuel Eaton to Edward and Martha Eaton, Aug. 1, 1892, Edward D. Eaton Papers, SHSW ("keen youthful zest").

30. Francis J. Biddle, *A Casual Past* (Garden City, N. Y., 1961), 186.

31. It is worth noting that late-century men (who only saw their sons at home) found them tame and feminized, while women (who had more contact with the boy-world outside the home) found them rough and unruly. Of course, the gap between what fathers and mothers saw in their sons was also a product of the different standards by which they measured the boys.

32. Hantover, "Boy Scouts;" David I. Macleod, *Building Character in the American Boy: The Boy Scouts, YMCA, and Their Forerunners, 1870–1920* (Madison, Wis., 1983), esp. 3–59; Kett, *Rites of Passage*, 199–204, 222–28.

33. References to men as boys were not unknown in the first two-thirds of the nineteenth century (Margaret Cursins journal, vol. 5, May 2, 1813, HCL; Irving Bartlett, *Daniel Webster* [New York, 1978], 21), but they were unusual and often required an apology ("it gives me confidence in your continuing the same good boy—excuse the epithet" [Mary A. O. Gay to W. Allan Gay, Feb. 15, 1840, Gay-Otis Collection, CUL]). The one exception was that men often referred to large, all male groups (a company of soldiers, a wagonload of "forty-niners," for example) as boys. Significantly, these were groups whose behavior was far from civilized—"boyish" by the standard nineteenth-century definition. Such references are scattered, for instance, through Gerald F. Linderman, *Embattled Courage: The Experience of Combat in the Civil War* (New York, 1987), and through J. S. Holliday, *The World Rushed In: The California Gold Rush Experience* (New York, 1981).

34. On mothers, see Elizabeth Cattell to James Cattell, Dec. 25, 1885, James Cattell Papers, LC; Adelbert Ames to Blanche Butler, June 9, 1870, in Blanche Butler Ames, ed., *Chronicles from the Nineteenth-Century: Family Letters of Blanche Butler and Adelbert Ames* (priv. printing, 1957), 159; George B. Wright to Serena Ames, Aug. 21, 1859, George B. Wright and Family Papers, MNHS. For courting couples, see Ellen Rothman, *Hands and Hearts: A History of Courtship in America* (New York, 1984), 206. Among married couples, see Marion Foster Washburne, "Studies in Domestic Relations," *Harper's Bazaar*, 38 (1904), 243; Edward Eaton to Martha Eaton, Nov. 24, 1892, Eaton Papers, SHSW; David G. Pugh, "Virility's Virtue: The Making of the Masculinity Cult in American Life, 1828–1890," (Ph.D. diss., Washington State Univ., 1978), 130; and Linderman, *Embattled Courage*, 95.

35. *Burroughs' Journal*, 86; Edward Bok, "Editorial," *Ladies' Home Journal*, June 1892, 12. Also, The Century Association, *The Century Association, 1847–1946* (New York, 1947), 40; Higginson, *Out-Door Papers*, 162.

36. Macleod, *Building Character*, 55; Roosevelt is quoted in William Davison Johnston, *TR Champion of the Strenuous Life: A Photographic Biography*

of Theodore Roosevelt (New York, 1958), 127. Roosevelt's good friend Owen Wister wrote the first modern cowboy novel, *The Virginian*, in 1902—and dedicated it to Roosevelt. Lois Banner has made the same point about the figure of the cowboy and about the boyish qualities of turn-of-the-century heroes like Roosevelt. Her brief but telling comments on Richard Harding Davis as a boy/man/hero are especially worth consulting (Lois Banner, *American Beauty* [New York, 1983], 247).

37. May Morrill, "Our Boys," *Our Boys* (Chicago), 2 (1871), AAS; Henry Siglar, *Where to Begin* (Newburgh, N. Y., 1891), 6; Roosevelt, *Strenuous Life*, 162. Joseph Kett has aptly commented that earlier generations would have found "a reference to the 'manly boy' as a contradiction," yet the phrase had profound developmental meaning in the late nineteenth century (Kett, *Rites of Passage*, 203).

38. Henry Seidel Canby, *The Age of Confidence: Life in the Nineties* (New York, 1934), 72; Ellis, "Men among Men," 229.

39. Photographic evidence makes it clear that by 1920, boys younger than six years old were wearing breeches, not gowns.

40. On nineteenth-century schooling, see Lawrence Cremin, *American Education: The Metropolitan Experience, 1870–1980* (New York, 1988), 545–46.

41. Kett, *Rites of Passage*, 152–62.

42. On early baseball, see Melvin L. Adelman, *A Sporting Time: New York City and the Rise of Modern Athletics* (Chicago, 1986). The boys who were not keeping score are described in Kett, *Rites of Passage*, 226.

43. James McLachlan, "The *Choice of Hercules*: American Student Societies in the Early Nineteenth Century," in Lawrence Stone, ed., *The University in Society* (Princeton, N.J., 1974); Helen Lefkowitz Horowitz, *Campus Life: Undergraduate Cultures from Eighteenth Century to the Present* (New York, 1987), 12–15; Kett, *Rites of Passage*, 56.

44. Kett, *Rites of Passage*, 174–78, 181–83.

45. Kett, *Rites of Passage*, 183–89.

46. Margaret Marsh, "Suburban Men and Masculine Domesticity, 1870–1915," in Mark Carnes and Clyde Griffen, eds., *Meanings for Manhood: Reconstructions of Masculinity in Victorian America* (Chicago, 1990), esp. 122–23.

47. On the preoccupation in some circles with rest and tranquility, see John Ward diary, Dec. 26, 1860 and Jan. 1, 1861, NYHS; Edward Everett Hale to Harriet Freeman, n.d. [1885], The Papers of the Hale Family, Special Correspondence of Edward Everett Hale, LC; Richard Cabot to Ella Lyman, Aug. 29, 1889, Ella Lyman Cabot Papers, SL; Lears, *Antimodernism*, 225–40.

48. William G. McLoughlin, *The Meaning of Henry Ward Beecher: An Essay on the Shifting Values of Mid-Victorian America, 1840–1870* (New York, 1970), 94–98, 109–11 (Beecher quotation is on 111). The issue of repose as a cultural ideal is explored with insight in Daniel T. Rodgers, *The Work*

Ethic in Industrial America, 1850–1920 (Chicago, 1978), 94–124, esp. 97–98, 109–14.

49. Edward Everett Hale to Harriet Freeman, July 7, 1885, Hale Papers, LC; Charles Van Hise to Alice Van Hise, July 1, 1897 (also Charles to Alice, Aug. 15, 1897), Van Hise Papers, SHSW. See John Kirk to "Cousin Henry," Feb. 14, 1853, Kirk Letterbooks, vol. 1, CHS.

50. In this, the language of manly play paralleled the language of the play movement for children. See Dominick Cavallo, *Muscles and Morals: Organized Playgrounds and Urban Reform, 1880–1920* (Philadelphia, 1981).

51. A similar line of argument is used by Carnes (*Secret Ritual,* 113–16) to explain the appeal of a distinctive set of fraternal rituals in the late nineteenth century.

52. Robert B. Roosevelt to Theodore Roosevelt, Sr., Feb. 2, 1852, Roosevelt Papers, LC.

53. Early autobiographies: see, for example, Henry Clarke Wright, *Human Life: Illustrated in My Individual Experience as a Child, a Youth, and a Man* (Boston, 1849); Ray Parker, *Memoirs of the Life and Religious Experience of Ray Parker* (Providence, 1829); Horace Lane, *The Wandering Boy, Careless Sailor, and Result of Inconsideration: A True Narrative* (Skaneat-eles, N.Y., 1839); James Pearse, *A Narrative of the Life of James Pearse* (Rutland, Vt., 1825). Later autobiographies include those of Wallace, Beard, Sedgwick, Baker, Canby, Rockwell, and Hale.

54. Richard Cabot to Ella Lyman, n.d. [1889], Cabot Papers, SL.

55. Charles Eliot, *Landscape Architect,* ed. Charles W. Eliot (Cambridge, Mass., 1924), 91.

56. Eliot, *Landscape Architect,* 91–92.

57. James Cattell to William and Elizabeth Cattell, Nov. 28, 1884, Cattell Papers, LC. This focus on the contrast of the strong, assertive man and the gentle, contemplative one was also a recurring theme in the novels of the late nineteenth and early twentieth centuries. For discussions of the theme in the work of William Dean Howells and David Graham Phillips, see Kenneth S. Lynn, *William Dean Howells: An American Life* (New York, 1970), 308–9, and McGovern, "Virility Impulse," 346–47.

58. As with so many of the manly preoccupations of the late nineteenth century, this contrast was an obsession of Francis Parkman half a century earlier. See Howard Doughty, *Francis Parkman* (Cambridge, Mass., 1983 [1962]), 69–70.

59. Howard M. Feinstein, *Becoming William James* (Ithaca, N.Y., 1984), 207, 212–13; Fredrickson, *Inner War,* 158–61, 229–31.

60. William James, *Pragmatism and Four Essays from The Meaning of the Truth,* ed. Ralph Barton Perry (New York, 1955), 22.

61. James, *Pragmatism,* 17–37.

62. On the contradiction between this tough view and his admiration for his father who mixed the qualities of a man and a woman, see Kathleen Dal-

ton, "Theodore Roosevelt and the Idea of War," *The Theodore Roosevelt Association Journal*, 7 (1981), 8–9. Dalton argues that Roosevelt's warrior ethic served the function, among others, of redeeming his beloved father, who had bought a substitute instead of fighting in the Civil War.

63. Roosevelt, *Strenuous Life*, 7–8.

64. Roosevelt, *Strenuous Life*, 21.

65. Hall, "Feminization," 10240; on Hall's use of recapitulation theory, see Dorothy Ross, *G. Stanley Hall: The Psychologist as Prophet* (Chicago, 1972), 162–66.

66. Hall, "Feminization," 10241.

67. Hall, "Feminization," 10240. The rhetorical device used here by Hall has interesting gender implications. The feminists whom he derided may have been wrong in his view, but they still had the moral authority of women. So, rather than take them on directly, Hall feminizes nature and gives "her" an "authoritative voice" through which he projects his opinions. By attributing his opinions to Mother Nature, Hall creates a device that gives him both the scientific and the moral high ground for attacking the feminist viewpoint.

68. See, for example, Philip Greven, Jr., *The Protestant Temperament: Patterns of Child-Rearing, Religious Experience, and Self in Early America* (New York, 1977), 243, 246, 336, 351.

69. Marvin Meyers, *The Jacksonian Persuasion: Politics and Belief* (New York, 1960), 161.

70. Pugh, "Virility's Virtue," 46–47.

71. "Whale-bone" quoted in Bertram Wyatt-Brown, "The Abolitionist Controversy: Men of Blood, Men of God," in Howard H. Quint and Milton Cantor, eds., *Men, Women, and Issues in American History* (Homewood, Ill., 1975), vol. 1, 222.

72. Richard Hofstadter, *Anti-Intellectualism in American Life* (New York, 1963), 188–89; also see 188, n. 2, and 189, n. 4.

73. On the implications of the term, see Hofstadter, *Anti-Intellectualism*, 189 and Banner, *American Beauty*, 227. The same term may have been used earlier, in the notorious 1840 campaign against Van Buren (Banner, *American Beauty*, 230).

74. For an application of this term to a *class* of people, see Jonathan Katz, ed., *Gay American History: Lesbians and Gay Men in the U.S.A.* (New York, 1972), 655 n. 133.

75. Hofstadter, *Anti-Intellectualism*, 188. On "mannish lesbians" as an "intermediate sex," see Carroll Smith-Rosenberg, *Disorderly Conduct: Visions of Gender in Victorian America* (New York, 1985), 265, 285–87.

76. Wyatt-Brown, "Controversy," 222; Hofstadter, *Anti-Intellectualism*, 190; Baker, *Native American*, 308.

77. Quoted in Virginia G. Drachman, "The Loomis Trial: Social Mores and Obstetrics in the Mid-Nineteenth Century," in Judith Walzer Leavitt, ed.,

Women and Health in America: Historical Readings (Madison, Wis., 1984), 172. The medical journal in which the phrase appeared was published in Louisville, Kentucky. Combined with an apparent use of the phrase by Andrew Jackson (Bruce Curtis, "The Wimp Factor," *American Heritage* [1989], 42), it seems that "Miss Nancy" may have been a label with Southern origins.

78. Karen Lystra, *Searching the Heart: Women, Men, and Romantic Love in Nineteenth-Century America* (New York, 1989), 48; Sedgwick, *Memoirs,* 110; Lynn, *William Dean Howells,* 283.

79. *Oxford English Dictionary,* compact ed., vol. 2, 4064; Rafford Pyke, "What Men Like in Men," *Cosmopolitan,* 33 (1902), 404–5.

80. John Fraser, *America and the Patterns of Chivalry* (New York, 1982). See also Mark DeWolfe Howe, ed., *Touched with Fire: Civil War Letters and Diary of Oliver Wendell Homes, Jr., 1861–1864* (Cambridge, Mass., 1946), 122, n. 1; Sergeant Kendall to B. Franklin and Elizabeth Kendall, Jan. 20, 1889, Kendall Papers, NYHS; Celia Parker Worley, *The Western Slope* (Evanston, Ill., 1903), 92; David Kennedy, *Over Here: The First World War and American Society* (New York, 1980), 212–16.

81. For individual studies, see Kathleen M. Dalton, "Theodore Roosevelt: Manliness and Morality in the Progressive Era," unpub. MS; Joe L. Dubbert, "Progressivism and the Masculinity Crisis," in Pleck and Pleck, *American Man;* McGovern, "Virility Impulse." Hofstadter, *Anti-Intellectualism,* 191–96, provides historical context on the problems of reformers' manliness and the stridently masculine Progressive response.

82. Michael Lynch, "The Age of Adhesiveness: Male-Male Intimacy in New York City, 1830–1880," American Historical Association, Dec. 1985; John D'Emilio and Estelle B. Freedman, *Intimate Matters: A History of Sexuality in America* (New York, 1988), 123.

83. D'Emilio and Freedman, *Intimate Matters,* 226–28.

84. D'Emilio and Freedman, *Intimate Matters,* 226; Smith-Rosenberg, *Disorderly Conduct,* 265–72; Katz, 40–42.

85. Katz, *Gay American History,* 33, 41; Smith-Rosenberg, *Disorderly Conduct,* 268–69.

86. Katz, *Gay American History,* 38.

87. Katz, *Gay American History,* 41, 44–49, 52; *Oxford English Dictionary,* compact ed., vol. 2, 3942, 3961, 3990, 3999, 4036.

88. Katz, *Gay American History,* 4; Smith-Rosenberg, *Disorderly Conduct,* 286–87.

89. D'Emilio and Freedman, *Intimate Matters,* 227, 225–26.

90. Carroll Smith-Rosenberg asks the same question about female homosexuality during this period in *Disorderly Conduct,* 270–96.

91. Quoted in D'Emilio and Freedman, *Intimate Matters,* 227.

92. Quoted in D'Emilio and Freeman, *Intimate Matters,* 227–28. See a similar

description in Katz, *Gay American History,* 52. Also see Smith-Rosenberg, *Disorderly Conduct,* 270–72.

93. Indeed, George Chauncey, Jr. ("Christian Brotherhood or Sexual Perversion? Homosexual Identities and the Construction of Sexual Boundaries in the World War I Era," in Martin Duberman, Martha Vicinus, and George Chauncey, Jr., eds., *Hidden from History: Reclaiming the Gay and Lesbian Past* [New York, 1989]), has argued that the medical language and scientific theory of the era simply reflected accurate observation of language and behavior in the emerging homosexual communities. Chauncey's article not only describes the death of romantic friendship as an acceptable form of male behavior, but helps in sorting out recent theories on the historical construction of sexual identities (see esp. 312–17).

94. Quotation is from D'Emilio and Freedman, *Intimate Matters,* 226. Smith-Rosenberg, *Disorderly Conduct,* 267; Katz, *Gay American History,* 40, 44, 47.

95. Chauncey, "Brotherhood or Perversion?" 315–16.

96. Katz, *Gay American History,* 44.

97. Chauncey ("Brotherhood or Perversion?" 294–317) describes a striking symbolic moment in the development of the ruinous power attached to the accusation of homosexuality among men.

98. Lystra, *Searching,* 28–30.

99. "The Seneca Falls Declaration of Sentiments and Resolutions," in Daniel Boorstin, ed., *An American Primer* (Chicago, 1966), 359–64.

100. Rothman, *Hands and Hearts,* 110–13, 227–30.

101. Vernon Wright to Grace Clark, Feb. 25, 1899, George B. Wright and Family Papers, MNHS; Canby quotations from 183 and 71, but see also 72–73, 78.

102. James quoted in Fredrickson, *Inner War,* 237; Ellis quoted in D'Emilio and Freedman, *Intimate Matters,* 226, but see generally 223–26.

103. Joe L. Dubbert, *A Man's Place,* 177; Macleod, *Building Character;* Ross Goodner, "America Gets the Bug," in Gordon Menzies, ed., *The World of Golf* (London, 1982), 65–73.

104. Smith-Rosenberg, *Disorderly Conduct,* 279–83, describes men's largely successful efforts to thwart new women's institutions—reform movements, colleges, settlement houses—that were developing at the start of the century.

105. Marsh, "Men and Domesticity," 122–23; Rotundo, "Fathers and Sons: Roles and Relationships," unpub. MS, 291–97.

106. Filene, *Him/ Her/ Self,* 79.

107. Daniel J. Boorstin, *The Americans: The Democratic Experience* (New York, 1973), 89–166, esp. 146.

108. *World Almanac and Book of Facts 1990* (New York, 1989), 892, 953; Lewis Erenberg, *Steppin' Out: New York Nightlife and the Transformation of*

American Culture (Westport, Conn., 1981); Robert Sklar, *Movie-Made America: A Cultural History of the Movies* (New York, 1975), 44–45.

Epilogue: Manhood in the Twentieth Century

1. The term "communities of consumption" is Daniel Boorstin's. See Boorstin, *The Americans: The Democratic Experience* (New York, 1973), 89–164.

2. The central text here is Robert N. Bellah et al., *Habits of the Heart: Individualism and Commitment in American Life* (New York, 1985). For an earlier statement of this theme, see Philip Slater, *The Pursuit of Loneliness: American Culture at the Breaking Point* (Boston, 1970).

3. Alexis de Tocqueville in *Democracy in America* (trans. Henry Reeve [New York, 1945]) described much of this and anticipated its consequences. Most poignantly, see vol. 2, 144–47.

4. In his study of male heroes in magazines, Theodore P. Greene (*America's Heroes: The Changing Models of Success in American Magazines* [New York, 1970]) notes the rise of "Idols of Organization" in the mid-1910s. Greene describes these men as hard-working, efficient organizers who brought nineteenth-century persistence and industry into a bureaucratic work setting. The new hero was a team player who believed deeply in efficient organization and cooperation. As Greene depicts him, "the new 'Idol of Organization' was neither the creator nor the owner of the enterprise which he ran. The new demand was for men who could take over existing organizations and run them with a minimum of human friction and a maximum of practical results" (Greene, *America's Heroes*, 333–34).

5. On Hemingway as a model of manhood, see Leonard Kriegel, *On Men and Masculinity* (New York, 1979), 89–112. The existential hero—and variations on the ideal—in American movies are treated in Donald Spoto, *Camerado: Hollywood and the American Man* (New York, 1978). See also an essay on Clint Eastwood as a late twentieth-century hero: Robert Mazzocco, "The Supply-Side Star," *New York Review of Books*, Apr. 1, 1982.

6. The very term *playboy* shows how old standards of manhood have been turned on their heads. The idea that a man should aspire to be a boy would have been sufficiently shocking to an eighteenth-century Yankee. The idea that this boy-man's goal in life was to play would have seemed downright effeminate. For an analysis of *Playboy* that stresses rebellion against domesticity rather than regression, see Barbara Ehrenreich, *The Hearts of Men: The American Dream and the Flight from Commitment* (New York, 1984), 42–51. See also her analysis of the Beat movement of the 1950s as another reaction to twentieth-century middle-class concepts of home and family (52–67). Harvey Cox, looking at the surface of the magazine more

than its underlying philosophy, has described *Playboy* as a guide to a style of manhood (based largely on consumption) that emphasizes the pursuit of pleasure. See Harvey Cox, *The Secular City: Secularization and Urbanization in Theological Perspective* (New York, 1966), 172–78.

7. The mythopoeic men's movement differs with this book in its basic assumptions about gender. Its stance is "essentialism": manhood begins with a timeless, unchanging core of qualities that all men ultimately possess. The stance of this book is one of "cultural construction": manhood is a mental category created and recreated by cultures as they, and their social and physical environments, change.

8. For a useful summary of what the men's movement is about, see Jack Thomas, "The New Man: Finding Another Way to Be Male," *Boston Globe*, Aug. 21, 1991, 43, 46–47; "Following the Beat of a Different Drum," Aug. 21, 1991, 43, 46; and "The Bible of the Men's Movement," Aug. 21, 1991, 43, 47.

9. These concerns are summarized in Edward S. Martin, "The Use of Fathers," *Harper's New Monthly Magazine*, 117 (1908); G. Stanley Hall, "Feminization in Schools and Home: The Undue Influence of Women Teachers—The Need of Different Training for the Sexes," *World's Work*, 16 (1908); and C. P. Seldon, "Rule of Mother," *North American Review* (1895). Joe L. Dubbert explores the turn-of-the-century literature on absent fathers in *A Man's Place: Masculinity in Transition* (Englewood Cliffs, N.J., 1979), 140–44.

10. Mark Carnes's views on nineteenth-century fraternal ritual as they related to father-son ties are condensed in his "Middle-Class Men and the Solace of Fraternal Ritual," in Mark C. Carnes and Clyde Griffen, *Meanings for Manhood: Constructions of Masculinity in Victorian America* (Chicago, 1990), 37–52.

11. Chris Harding quoted in Thomas, "New Man," 46.

12. Robert Bly, *Iron John: A Book about Men* (Reading, Mass., 1990), esp. 25.

13. Some of the changes and the roadblocks are summarized in Lisa Belkin, "Bars to Equality of Sexes Seen as Eroding, Slowly," *New York Times*, Aug. 20, 1989, 1, 26; Alison Leigh Cowan, "Women's Gains on the Job: Not without a Heavy Toll," *New York Times*, Aug. 21, 1989, 1, 14.

14. Compare, for instance, *Webster's Seventh New Collegiate Dictionary* (Springfield, Mass., 1963) with the New College Edition of *The American Heritage Dictionary of the English Language* (Boston, 1976) thirteen years later.

15. Sheila Rothman, *Woman's Proper Place: A History of Changing Ideals and Practices, 1870 to the Present* (New York, 1978), 231–42.

16. *American Heritage Dictionary*, 1428.

17. A powerful example of this skewed policy-making can be found in Marc Fasteau, "Vietnam and the Cult of Toughness in American Foreign Pol-

icy," in Elizabeth H. Pleck and Joseph H. Pleck, eds., *The American Man* (Englewood Cliffs, N.J., 1980), 379–415.

18. This radical individualism has an impact on the family as well; see Ruth Sidel, *Women and Children Last: The Plight of Poor Women in Affluent America* (New York, 1986), and Andrew Hacker, *Two Nations: Black and White, Separate, Hostile, Unequal* (New York, 1992).

19. "Not So Merry Widowers," *Time*, Aug. 10, 1981, 45.

20. De Tocqueville, *Democracy in America*, vol. 2, 106.

Appendix: The Parameters of the Study

1. David Hackett Fischer, *Albion's Seed: Four British Folkways in America* (New York, 1989), 813, 854–59.

2. For other uses of "middle class" in the study of nineteenth-century America, see Burton Bledstein, *The Culture of Professionalism: The Middle Class and the Development of Higher Education in America* (New York, 1976); Mary Ryan, *Cradle of the Middle Class: The Family in Oneida County, New York, 1790–1865* (New York, 1981); Stuart Blumin, *The Emergence of the Middle Class: Social Experience in the American City, 1760–1900* (New York, 1989).

INDEX